The Clinician's Practical Guide to Attention-Deficit/Hyperactivity Disorder

by

Marianne Mercugliano, M.D.

Thomas J. Power, Ph.D.

and

Nathan J. Blum, M.D.

The Children's Seashore House
of The Children's Hospital of Philadelphia
Pennsylvania

with invited contributors

·P A U L·H·
BROOKES
PUBLISHING CO

Baltimore • London • Toronto • Sydney

Paul H. Brookes Publishing Co.
Post Office Box 10624
Baltimore, Maryland 21285-0624

www.pbrookes.com

Typeset by Brushwood Graphics, Inc., Baltimore, Maryland.
Manufactured in the United States of America by
Hamilton Printing Company, Rensselaer, New York.

Most of the case studies that are described in this book are completely fictional. Selected case studies are composites that are based on the authors' experiences. These case studies do not represent the lives or experiences of specific individuals; any similarity to actual individuals or circumstances is coincidental, and no implications should be inferred.

Any information about medical treatments is in no way meant to substitute for a physician's advice or expert opinion; readers should consult a medical practitioner if they are interested in more information.

Library of Congress Cataloging-in-Publication Data

Mercugliano, Marianne.
    The clinician's practical guide to attention-deficit/hyperactivity disorder   /   by Marianne Mercugliano, Thomas J. Power, and Nathan J. Blum ; with invited contributors.
      p.   cm.
    Includes bibliographical references and index.
    ISBN 1-55766-358-0
    1. Attention-deficit hyperactivity disorder.   I. Power, Thomas J.   II. Blum, Nathan J.
III. Title.
    [DNLM: 1. Attention Deficit Disorder with Hyperactivity—diagnosis.   2. Attention Deficit Disorder with Hyperactivity—therapy.   WS 350.8.A8M556c 1999]
RJ506.H9M47   1999
616.85'89—dc21
DNLM/DLC
for Library of Congress   98-35194
                                                             CIP

British Library Cataloguing in Publication data are available from the British Library.

Contents

About the Authors

Marianne Mercugliano, M.D., Co-director, ADHD/School Problems Evaluation and Treatment Program, and Attending Physician, The Children's Seashore House of The Children's Hospital of Philadelphia; Assistant Professor of Pediatrics, Division of Child Development and Rehabilitation, University of Pennsylvania School of Medicine. Dr. Mercugliano received her medical degree from the University of Pennsylvania School of Medicine. Her postgraduate training included a residency in pediatrics at The Children's Hospital of Philadelphia, a postdoctoral fellowship in developmental disabilities at the Kennedy Institute of The Johns Hopkins University, and a postdoctoral research fellowship in neuropsychopharmacology in the Departments of Pharmacology and Psychiatry at the University of Pennsylvania. Dr. Mercugliano has been the principal investigator of laboratory research grants to study the development of neurotransmitter systems, behavior, and medication effects and has published in both clinical and basic science journals. Her academic interests include neurochemistry, nutrition, medical issues associated with ADHD, and psychopharmacology. She is the medical consultant to the Community Schools Project at The Children's Seashore House and is a member of the American Academy of Pediatrics and the American Academy of Cerebral Palsy and Developmental Medicine.

Thomas J. Power, Ph.D., Co-director, ADHD/School Problems Evaluation and Treatment Program, The Children's Seashore House of The Children's Hospital of Philadelphia; Assistant Professor, School Psychology in Pediatrics, Division of Child Development, University of Pennsylvania School of Medicine. Dr. Power received his doctoral degree in school psychology from the University of Pennsylvania. His academic interests include school-based assessment and treatment of attention and learning problems, preventive intervention for children at risk, and collaboration with medical professionals. He has published extensively in pediatric, psychological, and psychiatric journals. He is Director of the Community Schools Program at The Children's Seashore House, which is designed to provide preventive assistance to school-age children who are at risk for behavior, social, and academic problems. Dr. Power is a principal investigator on federally sponsored and foundation-sponsored grants to establish and evaluate early intervention programs for students in urban schools and to train students of psychology to integrate health and education services for children and adolescents.

Nathan J. Blum, M.D., Co-director, Behavioral Pediatrics Clinic, Medical Director, Center for Complex Medical Management, and Attending Physician, The Children's Seashore House of The Children's Hospital of Philadelphia; Assistant Professor, Pediatrics, Division of Child Development, University of Pennsylvania School of Medicine. Dr. Blum received his medical degree from The Johns Hopkins University School of Medicine and completed a residency in pediatrics at The Children's Hospital of Philadelphia. He completed a postdoctoral fellowship in developmental-behavioral pediatrics at The Children's Seashore House of The Children's Hospital of Philadelphia. He is Co-director of the Behavioral Pediatrics Clinic for management of common behavior problems in children at Children's Hospital. In addition to publishing in peer-reviewed journals, Dr. Blum is a co-editor of a textbook of pediatric primary care and is one of the authors of the "Ask the Experts" feature in *Contemporary Pediatrics*. His academic interests encompass common behavior problems in children, self-injurious behavior in children with developmental disabilities, and the coordinated management of behavioral, medical, and psychological problems in children with chronic illnesses.

About the Contributors

Mark C. Clayton, M.D., Fellow, Child Development and Rehabilitation, The Children's Seashore House of The Children's Hospital of Philadelphia. Dr. Clayton received his medical degree from Tulane University School of Medicine and completed his pediatrics residency at St. Louis Children's Hospital. Dr. Clayton provides medical consultation in the ADHD/School Problems Evaluation and Treatment Program and the Community Schools Program. His interests include development and behavior in school-age children, psychopharmacology, and bioethics.

Tracy E. Costigan, M.A., Pediatric Psychology Intern, The Children's Seashore House of The Children's Hospital of Philadelphia and University of Pennsylvania School of Medicine. Ms. Costigan is completing her doctoral degree in the Department of Clinical and Health Psychology at Allegheny University of the Health Sciences in Philadelphia. Her research focuses on peer social interaction and social cognition in children with behavior difficulties and preventing aggression in elementary school lunch and recess programs.

Ricardo B. Eiraldi, Ph.D., Pediatric Psychologist, The Children's Seashore House of The Children's Hospital of Philadelphia. Dr. Eiraldi received his doctoral degree in clinical psychology from Hahneman University. Dr. Eiraldi is the Assistant Director of the ADHD/School Problems Evaluation and Treatment Program and a clinical associate in pediatrics at the University of Pennsylvania School of Medicine. His clinical and research work focuses on the evaluation and treatment of children and adolescents with attention-deficit/hyperactivity disorder (ADHD), school-based interventions for children with behavior and academic difficulties, and bilingual parent–teacher consultation models for inner-city Hispanic children and adolescents.

James L. Karustis, Ph.D., Clinical Associate in Pediatrics, The Children's Seashore House of The Children's Hospital of Philadelphia and University of Pennsylvania School of Medicine. Dr. Karustis is Coordinator for Satellite Programs for the ADHD/School Problems Evaluation and Treatment Program. He received his doctoral degree in clinical developmental psychology from Bryn Mawr College and is a certified school psychologist. His research interests include the assessment and treatment of internalizing and academic problems.

Stephen S. Leff, Ph.D., Clinical Associate, University of Pennsylvania School of Medicine; Child Clinical Psychologist, The Children's Seashore House of The Children's Hospital of Philadelphia. Dr. Leff received his doctoral degree in clinical child psychology at the University of North Carolina at Chapel Hill. Dr. Leff is Director of the PLAYS Program (Playground, Lunchroom, and Youth Survival), which is part of the Community Schools Program. Dr. Leff's main research and clinical interests are in the areas of violence prevention, promoting children's social skills and peer relationships, and ADHD.

Winifred Lloyds Lender, Ph.D., Psychologist, Santa Barbara, California; former post-doctoral fellow in pediatric psychology at The Children's Seashore House of The Children's Hospital of Pennsylvania and the University of Pennsylvania School of Medicine. Dr. Lender received her doctoral degree in school psychology from the University of Pennsylvania and is a certified school psychologist. Her interests include the assessment and treatment of behavior difficulties and ADHD in preschool-age children.

Edward Moss, Ph.D., Director, Outpatient Neuropsychology Services, The Children's Seashore House of The Children's Hospital of Philadelphia; Clinical Associate in Pediatrics, University of Pennsylvania School of Medicine. Dr. Moss received his doctoral degree in experimental cognition from City University of New York. His clinical work at The Children's Seashore House focuses on the neuropsychological assessment of children and adolescents with learning disabilities and ADHD. Dr. Moss also collaborates with clinical researchers at The Children's Hospital of Philadelphia and the University of Pennsylvania School of Medicine in the areas of adult ADHD, the genetics of learning disabilities, and the assessment and surgical treatment of children with intractable epilepsy.

Foreword

Attention-deficit/hyperactivity disorder (ADHD) is the most common behavioral disorder in children.[1] Despite the extensive amount of research that has been undertaken over a number of years to clarify its diagnosis and treatment, it remains controversial in both its diagnosis and its treatment. Interest and concerns about this condition and its treatment seem to wax and wane. One treatment, the use of stimulant medication, has clearly been affected by changes in public attitude. Methylphenidate hydrochloride use has increased each year since Safer and Krager began monitoring it in 1971,[2] with the exception of the years between 1987 and 1990, when there was an active campaign to discredit stimulant medication in the treatment of children.[3] Since 1993, there has been a marked increase in stimulant use from between 2½-fold[4] and 6-fold,[5] prompting concern that the use of stimulant medication may be excessive.[6]

Part of the difficulty and challenge of ADHD is that its diagnosis and treatment require input from so many different disciplines. The severe cases, particularly those with significant comorbidity, require child psychiatric management. Comorbid neurological conditions sometimes indicate the need for child neurology input. Comorbid motor coordination sometimes requires occupational and, in some instances, physical therapy input, and language disorders require speech-language therapy input. Parent training and behavior management often require psychology input. Because many of the manifestations occur at school and frequently co-occur with learning disabilities, educational personnel play a significant part. For most of the cases, however, because of the high frequency of this condition, primary care clinicians are often the first professionals whom parents approach and usually play a major role in both the diagnosis and the management of this condition. This role is increasing, especially as managed care increasingly limits access to mental health services.

Despite the prominent role of the primary care clinicians, most of the literature published about ADHD is not written from the perspective of the primary care clinician. The literature is sometimes confusing, overwhelming, and not practical for the needs of primary care clinicians. They need a source that is, on the one hand, comprehensive to provide them with the total picture and, on the other hand, realistic and oriented toward the role that they play as primary care clinicians.

The Clinician's Practical Guide to Attention-Deficit/Hyperactivity Disorder was designed to meet those needs, which is evidenced, in part, by its being written by developmental and behavioral pediatricians and a pediatric school psychologist who are able to understand the role of the primary care clinician. It is comprehensive and well researched and covers the diagnostic issues, providing suggestions and resources that the clinician can use in developing a realistic approach to the diagnosis and management of children with ADHD, as well as to the identification of significant comorbid conditions. This book informs the clinician about the therapies that are or that should be available to them, provides the clinician with practical suggestions regarding the management of children with this condition, and provides practical advice about how clinicians can communicate with their patients and their patients' families.

The authors provide detailed references to allow the reader to obtain more specific information in a particular area or to seek out the basis for recommendations. A good example of the primary care perspective is the incorporation of the *Diagnostic and Statistical Manual for Primary Care (DSM-PC) Child and Adolescent Version.*[7]

The diagnosis and the treatment of ADHD require the input and, particularly, the research perspectives of a number of different professional disciplines. Some aspects of the diagnosis and treatment of ADHD are likely to remain controversial. The information in this book enables primary care clinicians to be as up to date as possible about this condition.

Mark L. Wolraich, M.D.
Department of Pediatrics
Vanderbilt University
Child Development Center
Nashville, Tennessee

ENDNOTES

1. Shaywitz & Shaywitz (1988).
2. Safer & Krager (1988).
3. Safer & Krager (1992).
4. Safer, Zito, & Fine (1996).
5. Drug Enforcement Administration (1995).
6. Angier (1994), Diller (1996), McGinnis (1997).
7. American Academy of Pediatrics (1994).

REFERENCES

American Academy of Pediatrics. (1994). *Diagnostic and statistical manual for primary care (DSM-PC) child and adolescent version.* Elk Grove, IL: Author.

Angier, N. (1994, July 24). The debilitating malady called boyhood. *New York Times*, Section 4, pp. 1–4.

Diller, L.H. (1996). The run on Ritalin: Attention deficit disorder and stimulant treatment in the 1990's. *Hastings Center Report, 26*, 12–18.

Drug Enforcement Administration. (1995). *Yearly aggregate production quotas.* Washington, DC: Drug Enforcement Administration, Office of Public Affairs.

McGinnis, J. (1997, September 18). Attention deficit disaster. *The Wall Street Journal*, p. A-14.

Safer, D.J., & Krager, J.M. (1988). A survey of medication treatment for hyperactive/inattentive students. *JAMA, 260*, 2256–2258.

Safer, D.J., & Krager, J.M. (1992). Effect of a media blitz and a threatened lawsuit on stimulant treatment. *JAMA, 268*, 1004–1007.

Safer, D.J., Zito, J.M., & Fine, E.M. (1996). Increased methylphenidate usage for attention deficit disorder in the 1990's. *Pediatrics, 98*, 1084–1088.

Shaywitz, B.A., & Shaywitz, S.E. (1988). Attention deficit disorder: Current perspectives. In J.F. Kavanagh & T.J. Truss (Eds.), *Learning disabilities: Proceedings of the National Conference* (pp. 369–523). Parkton, MD: York Press.

Preface

A substantial number of visits to providers of children's health care are for behavioral and developmental issues. Concerns about difficulties with discipline, mood lability, aggression, and hyperactivity in the preschool years are common. During the school years, a short attention span, difficulties with following rules and directions, and poor school performance also are common. Many, though not all, children who present with these symptoms ultimately will be diagnosed with attention-deficit/hyperactivity disorder (ADHD). ADHD is the most common neurodevelopmental disability in childhood with a prevalence of 3%–5% in the school-age population. Clinicians, therefore, need to understand how to explore the initial chief concerns described above, how to make and exclude diagnoses of ADHD and related disorders, how to appropriately involve and use the services of various types of professionals in diagnosis and treatment, when to recommend and how to use both pharmacological and nonpharmacological management strategies, and how to approach the specific issues related to ADHD in adolescents and in parents.

In spite of the frequency with which these issues are encountered in the clinical care of children, they are rarely addressed in an organized and comprehensive way during clinical training. Thus, many clinicians have had to learn about ADHD on the job and through reading and continuing education programs. Because of the complexity of the symptoms of ADHD and their impact on many aspects of a child's functioning, sorting through diagnostic and treatment issues is difficult, especially in the primary care setting when many issues must be addressed in a short time. Children have often been referred to specialists in child development, neurology, and psychiatry for diagnosis and management of ADHD. Although specialists may have more experience with patients with ADHD, they often are geographically distant and have less experience with the child's family, school, and community. As more patients and their primary care physicians participate in managed care organizations, there is likely to be increasing demand that common pediatric concerns, such as ADHD, be managed to a greater degree in the primary care setting. In addition, the limited availability of specialists and managed care organizations in some regions means that specialists in neurology, psychiatry, and psychology with training primarily in adult disorders increasingly will be asked to consult on and manage childhood ADHD. Finally, physician extenders, such as nurse practitioners and physician assistants, will play a greater role in the care of children with chronic and complex disorders. *The Clinician's Practical Guide to Attention-Deficit/Hyperactivity Disorder* was written specifically to address the needs of these clinicians as well as clinical psychologists, all of whom must grapple with a multitude of issues as they attempt to provide the best care possible for their patients with ADHD.

This book is organized as a "road map" from initial presentation through the steps of diagnosis and treatment. Each chapter, which is meant to be read in a single sitting, briefly reviews research-based knowledge on a particular topic and then provides practical guidelines for navigating a particular aspect of care. We have included reproducible forms for the clinician's use to expedite the acquisition and communication of information. References and resources for parents and professionals are provided at the end of each chapter. Chapters related to counseling include more assessment and treatment strategies than we expect a medical professional to accomplish in the primary care setting. These chapters are meant to serve as a thorough introduction for readers who will be serving as therapists, as well as a guide for medical professionals about the components of psychoeducational assessment and nonpharmacological therapy. The primary goal is to provide in one place everything that the primary care clinician needs. Topics covered include presentation; diagnosis; nonpharmacological treatment; pharmacological treatment; long-term management; ADHD in preschool-age children, adolescents, and adults; and special issues, such as alternative treatments and educational and legal advocacy. This book provides meaningful, easily accessible assistance to clinicians and, ideally, improved care for children with ADHD in their own communities.

Acknowledgments

To Mark L. Batshaw, M.D., who was the Physician-in-Chief at The Children's Seashore House during the inception and writing of this book, for his leadership and support. To Anthony L. Rostain, M.D., for his expertise, ideas, and vision. To Bill Culbertson, Ph.D., Lisa Harvatine, C.R.N.P., M. Bidi McSorley, M.D., and Susan K. Miller, M.D., for their helpful reviews of the manuscript. To Eileen Graber, Renee Trusty-Dunlap, and Rondabay Liggins for their conscientious technical assistance. To Scott Beeler, Christa Horan, and Lisa Benson, Paul H. Brookes Publishing Co., Inc., for their professional expertise and camaraderie.

To our spouses, children, parents,
and the families who entrust their care to us
for giving us
the motivation to do what we do,
the desire to strive to do it better,
and the support that allows ideas to become realities

Introduction

What Is Attention-Deficit/ Hyperactivity Disorder?

Children who appear inattentive, hyperactive, and impulsive are a diagnostic and therapeutic challenge for clinicians. Inattention, hyperactivity, and impulsivity are behavioral characteristics that are found to varying degrees in many children. The criteria for determining when these symptoms are causing a disorder and even the underlying conceptualization of the disorder have changed many times. Research that is summarized in this chapter provides strong evidence that neurobiological and genetic factors account for some of the differences in these characteristics among children; however, this book examines a variety of other child, family, school, and community factors that influence these behavioral characteristics (see Table 1). The challenge for clinicians who are evaluating a child for attention-deficit/hyperactivity disorder (ADHD) is not only to determine whether the child's level of inattention and/or hyperactivity and impulsivity are significantly out of proportion to what is expected for children of a similar age (or developmental level) but also to identify other child, family, school, and/or community factors that may be influencing these symptoms. The more thoroughly a clinician understands the role of these factors for an individual child, the better the clinician can confidently diagnose and recommend interventions for children who are inattentive and/or hyperactive and impulsive.

HISTORY

Medical interest in hyperactive and inattentive behaviors has grown dramatically since the early 1900s. In the early 1900s, it was observed that a variety of disorders that affect the brain, such as tumors, infections, and trauma, could lead to abnormalities in behavior and learning. In 1908, Tredgold stated that in cases of mild brain injury during birth,

1

Table 1. Factors that may influence an individual's attention span

Child factors
  Attention-deficit/hyperactivity disorder
  Learning disabilities
  Intelligence
  Sensory impairments
  Temperament
  Chronic illness
  Medications
  Developmental disorders
  Behavioral and emotional disorders
Family factors
  Family stressors
  • Illnesses and deaths
  • Relationships
  • Finances
  Family environment
  Parental emotional illness
  Child abuse or neglect
School/community factors
  Quality of education program
  • Teaching style
  • Appropriateness of instructional materials
  • Class size and classroom environment
  Safety
  Toxin exposure (e.g., lead)

the initial symptoms may go away rapidly and it is only when the child begins school-ing that the deficiency is noted.[1] Although Tredgold's statement was largely ignored for the next 40 years, interest in the effect of brain injury on behavior continued to grow. The encephalitis epidemic of 1917–1918 affected a large number of children and drew attention to the postencephalitic behavior problems that were exhibited by many of the children. These children's behavior disorders were characterized by irritability, impulsivity, hyperactivity, emotional lability, and antisocial behaviors. Further study of individuals who incurred traumatic brain injuries or had other organic brain disorders supported the idea that these behaviors, as well as a variety of learning problems, are characteristic of individuals who incur brain injuries. In the 1940s, Strauss, who was studying individuals with brain injuries, renewed interest in Tredgold's theory when he hypothesized that all individuals who exhibit these behaviors or learning problems must have incurred brain injuries. These children were referred to as having "minimal brain damage."[2]

In the 1960s, "minimal brain damage" was changed to "minimal brain dysfunc-tion" (MBD) as it was recognized that many individuals who had the previously de-scribed problems did not have brain injuries. MBD was defined as a heterogeneous dis-order that included children with learning difficulties as well as those with a short attention span, hyperactivity, and impulsivity. Attempts to divide MBD into subgroups with more homogeneous features led to the distinction of those with learning disabili-ties and those with problems with attention, hyperactivity, and impulsivity. One of the first attempts to define this latter group occurred in the *Diagnostic and Statistical Manual of Mental Disorders, Second Edition* (DSM-II).[3] In this manual, children who were overactive, restless, and distractible and had a short attention span were described as having the "hyperkinetic reaction of childhood."

Since 1968, the name and the diagnostic criteria for this disorder have been revised a number of times. The DSM-III[4] emphasized inattention and impulsivity as the primary symptoms. Children with these symptoms were diagnosed with attention-deficit disorder (ADD), and children with these symptoms and hyperactivity were diagnosed with attention-deficit disorder with hyperactivity (ADD-H). At the time, critics of the DSM-III definition argued that there was not sufficient evidence to support the existence of these two separate disorders. In the revised version of the DSM-III (DSM-III-R[5]), a single disorder, attention-deficit hyperactivity disorder, characterized by inattention, hyperactivity, and impulsivity, was described; however, subsequent research seems to support the idea that there is a group of children whose primary problem is inattention[6] and that, especially in younger children, there may be a group whose primary problem is hyperactivity and impulsivity.[7] Thus, the DSM-IV[8] has split ADHD into three subtypes:

1. ADHD, predominantly inattentive type
2. ADHD, predominantly hyperactive-impulsive type
3. ADHD, combined type (for children with significant inattention, hyperactivity, and impulsivity)

Although the DSM-IV conceptualization of ADHD is the most widely accepted and, thus, is the one that is used in this book, there continues to be some controversy about whether ADHD should be considered one disorder, multiple disorders, or not a disorder at all.

DSM-IV DIAGNOSTIC CRITERIA

ADHD is diagnosed based on criteria set forth in the DSM-IV. This manual provides guidelines for the diagnosis of ADHD and other developmental, behavior, or emotional disorders by providing a list of symptoms that may be indicative of the disorder and criteria for determining whether an individual has a disorder. These criteria include

- The number of symptoms that are present
- The age at which the symptoms occur
- The duration of the symptoms
- The degree of impairment caused by the symptoms
- Consideration of potential alternative explanations for the symptoms

Behaviors that are indicative of ADHD are divided into a list of nine symptoms of inattention and nine symptoms of hyperactivity and impulsivity (see Table 2). To make the diagnosis of ADHD, six of the nine criteria on either or both lists must be present. In addition, an individual can be diagnosed with ADHD only when the symptoms have been present for at least 6 months and cause some impairment in two or more settings (home, social, and school or work).

Table 2. DSM-IV diagnostic criteria for attention-deficit/hyperactivity disorder

A. Either (1) or (2):
  (1) six (or more) of the following symptoms of **inattention** have persisted for at least 6 months to a degree that is maladaptive and inconsistent with developmental level:
  Inattention
    (a) often fails to give close attention to details or makes careless mistakes in schoolwork, work, or other activities
    (b) often has difficulty sustaining attention in tasks or play activities
    (c) often does not seem to listen when spoken to directly
    (d) often does not follow through on instructions and fails to finish schoolwork, chores, or duties in the workplace (not due to oppositional behavior or failure to understand instructions)
    (e) often has difficulty organizing tasks and activities
    (f) often avoids, dislikes, or is reluctant to engage in tasks that require sustained mental effort (such as schoolwork or homework)
    (g) often loses things necessary for tasks or activities (e.g., toys, school assignments, pencils, books, or tools)
    (h) is often easily distracted by extraneous stimuli
    (i) is often forgetful in daily activities
  (2) six (or more) of the following symptoms of **hyperactivity-impulsivity** have persisted for at least 6 months to a degree that is maladaptive and inconsistent with developmental level:
  Hyperactivity
    (a) often fidgets with hands or feet or squirms in seat
    (b) often leaves seat in classroom or in other situations in which remaining seated is expected
    (c) often runs about or climbs excessively in situations in which it is inappropriate (in adolescents or adults, may be limited to subjective feelings of restlessness)
    (d) often has difficulty playing or engaging in leisure activities quietly
    (e) is often "on the go" or acts as if "driven by a motor"
    (f) often talks excessively
  Impulsivity
    (g) often blurts out answers before questions have been completed
    (h) often has difficulty awaiting turn
    (i) often interrupts or intrudes on others (e.g., butts into conversations or games)
B. Some hyperactive-impulsive or inattentive symptoms that caused impairment were present before age 7 years.
C. Some impairment from symptoms is present in two or more settings (e.g., at school [or work] and at home).
D. There must be clear evidence of clinically significant impairment in social, academic, or occupational functioning.
E. The symptoms do not occur exclusively during the course of a Pervasive Developmental Disorder, Schizophrenia, or other Psychotic Disorder and are not better accounted for by another mental disorder (e.g., Mood Disorder, Anxiety Disorder, Dissociative Disorder, or a Personality Disorder).

Reprinted with permission from the *Diagnostic and Statistical Manual of Mental Disorders, Fourth Edition*, pp. 83–85. Copyright © 1994 American Psychiatric Association.

The degree of impairment is likely to vary across settings and even within a setting, depending on the demands for sustained attention, the novelty of the situation, and the structure or supervision provided; however, the impairment must be severe enough to cause clinically significant disruption in social, academic, or occupational functioning. Furthermore, children with developmental delays can be diagnosed with

ADHD, but the clinician must consider whether the symptoms are inconsistent with the individual's developmental level rather than with his or her chronological age. ADHD is thought always to begin in childhood; thus, although the diagnosis can be made in individuals who are older than 7 years, the clinician should be able to confirm that some of the symptoms that are causing impairment were present before 7 years of age.

The DSM-IV also recognizes that symptoms of inattention, hyperactivity, and impulsivity are nonspecific and may occur during the course of other neurodevelopmental or psychiatric disorders. A clinician should not make the diagnosis of ADHD when the symptoms occur exclusively as part of a **pervasive developmental disorder** (e.g., autism) or schizophrenia or other psychotic disorders. In addition, although many children with ADHD also have mood or anxiety disorders (discussed later in this introduction), a clinician should not make the diagnosis of ADHD when a mood disorder, anxiety disorder, or other psychiatric disorder is thought to be the primary cause of the symptoms of inattention or hyperactivity and impulsivity.

If an individual meets the criteria for ADHD, then he or she can have one of three subtypes based on the number of symptoms present from the list of inattention symptoms and the number present from the list of hyperactivity-impulsivity symptoms. If the individual has at least six of nine symptoms on both lists, then he or she is diagnosed with ADHD, combined type; individuals who have at least six of nine symptoms on only the list of inattention symptoms are diagnosed with ADHD, predominantly inattentive type; and those who have at least six of the nine symptoms on only the list of hyperactivity-impulsivity symptoms are diagnosed with ADHD, predominantly hyperactive-impulsive type.

PREVALENCE OF ADHD

ADHD is estimated to affect 3%–5% of school-age children in the United States.[9] It affects boys approximately 4 times more frequently than girls, although boys often outnumber girls by an even greater margin in referral settings. The more frequent referral of boys for treatment is likely to be related to the more frequent co-occurrence of disruptive behavior disorders (**oppositional defiant disorder** [ODD] and **conduct disorder** [CD]) and ADHD in this population.

The prevalence rate in adolescents and adults is not well defined; however, because ADHD is thought always to have its onset in childhood, studies of the natural history of ADHD provide evidence for the likely prevalence in these populations. It is estimated that 50%–70% of children with ADHD continue to meet diagnostic criteria for ADHD as adolescents and that 8%–33% continue to have ADHD as adults.[10] An even higher percentage may continue to have some symptoms of ADHD as adults.[11] This would suggest a prevalence of 1.5%–4% in adolescents and 1%–2% in adults.

Studies using the DSM-III-R criteria found that from 2% to more than 5% of preschool-age children met the diagnostic criteria for ADHD.[12] The addition in the DSM-IV of the hyperactive-impulsive type of ADHD is likely to increase the number of preschool-age children who meet the diagnostic criteria for ADHD.

ASSOCIATED FEATURES OF ADHD

Children with ADHD have difficulties with modulating and organizing their behavior in response to the changing demands of their environment; thus, they have difficulties with developing and implementing plans to carry out goal-directed behaviors (e.g., getting dressed before school, completing homework). Furthermore, when they have learned a plan or a strategy in one situation, they have trouble with learning to use the plan or the strategy in other, similar situations. They appear to have difficulties with recognizing the consequences of a behavior and with learning from past mistakes. They have a low tolerance for difficult or frustrating activities and tend to have trouble in situations that require delayed gratification (e.g., waiting one's turn); thus, they often appear to lack motivation for all but the most stimulating, interesting, or rewarding activities. These characteristics are so common in children with ADHD that some researchers have hypothesized that a delay in the development of the ability to inhibit responses, not inattention, may be the core deficit in ADHD.[13]

Children with ADHD are known to be at high risk for other behavior, emotional, social, and academic difficulties. In both primary care and psychiatric settings, nearly 67% of children with ADHD are reported to have significant problems with negativistic, defiant, and hostile behaviors toward parents or other authority figures.[14] These children, who may be diagnosed with ODD, frequently lose their temper, disobey rules, become angered or annoyed easily by others, and tend to blame others for their mistakes. A smaller but significant percentage (20%–30%) of children with ADHD demonstrate behaviors that violate the basic rights of others (e.g., frequent aggression, use of weapons, cruelty to animals) or violate major age-appropriate social norms (e.g., theft, property destruction). These children, who may be diagnosed with CD, are important to recognize because they appear to be at highest risk for developing delinquency in adolescence and antisocial or criminal behavior in adulthood.[15]

The symptoms of the disruptive behavior disorders (sometimes referred to as **externalizing** behavior disorders) usually are recognized easily in children with ADHD. **Internalizing,** or emotional, disorders, such as anxiety or depression, more often are overlooked. Screening for anxiety and depression (see Chapter 3) is an important component in the evaluation of ADHD for two reasons. First, many children with ADHD also have a mood or an anxiety disorder. Researchers estimate that 20%–30% of individuals with ADHD also have an anxiety disorder.[16] Estimates for mood disorders vary more, ranging from 10% to more than 40% of individuals with ADHD.[17] In these cases, treatment of both the ADHD and the anxiety or mood disorder may be needed to improve the outcome. Second, children with anxiety and/or depression may appear inattentive, unmotivated, or distracted primarily as a result of these conditions, not of ADHD. This consideration is especially important when adolescents or adults describe the new onset of difficulties with completing tasks or following instructions; depression and anxiety disorders are likely to begin in this age group, whereas ADHD is not. Determining whether depression or an anxiety disorder is present in addition to ADHD or is the cause of the symptoms of inattention, impulsivity, or hyperactivity can be a difficult clinical decision. Such decisions are discussed further in Chapter 2.

Learning disabilities can cause ADHD-like symptoms but also can be present in addition to ADHD. Children with learning disabilities who do not fully understand their class work may appear inattentive, or they may become unmotivated because they repeatedly experience failure. They may respond to this situation by bothering other children, making frequent jokes, or giving wise-crack answers in class as a way of avoiding work. For these children, it may be better to be viewed by their peers as the "class clown" than as "stupid." It is estimated that 25% or more of children with ADHD also have a learning disability.[18] Once again, the clinician is in the difficult position of having to distinguish whether symptoms that resemble ADHD are due to the learning disability or to ADHD in addition to a learning disability (see Chapter 3 for further discussion).

The impact of ADHD on a child's peer relationships may be one of the most disabling aspects of the disorder. Some children with ADHD fail to perceive social cues that are expressed verbally through speech and language or nonverbally through facial expressions and body movements. These children appear socially awkward. For other children, the high level of activity and accompanying noise may disrupt social situations, and the inattention may lead to poor performance during structured games or activities. The impulsivity may lead them to interrupt conversations or to barge in on games and may make them more likely to exhibit aggressive behaviors or to lose control of their temper when conflicts or frustrating situations arise. All of these factors contribute to the peer rejection that children with ADHD frequently experience.

ADHD: A BEHAVIORAL DIAGNOSIS

ADHD is a behavioral diagnosis. Although a medical exam and psychological tests are necessary to evaluate the possibility of alternative or coexisting diagnoses, there are no medical tests, physical examination findings, office-based psychological tests, or neuropsychological tests that are both sensitive and specific for ADHD (see Chapters 1–3). Diagnosing ADHD requires clinicians to make judgments about whether behaviors that are thought to be indicative of inattention, hyperactivity, or impulsivity are occurring often and to a degree that is inconsistent with the child's developmental level. Because many children with ADHD do not exhibit symptoms in the clinician's office (especially when the visits are brief), the clinician usually must rely on others' reports of the child's behavior in making these decisions. It is best to obtain reports from more than one source as any given source may be biased by inappropriate demands or expectations of the child and/or limited sampling of the child's behavior across different settings.

Interviews and/or behavior rating scales usually are used to collect this behavior information. Interviews allow the clinician to obtain descriptions of the nature, frequency, severity, and duration of specific behaviors and determine whether these descriptions are inconsistent with the child's developmental level; however, interviewing multiple informants can be very time consuming. Rating scales often are used as an efficient mechanism for obtaining information from multiple informants. They also may be helpful in judging the severity of the child's symptoms because the scores can be compared with population norms. When interpreting the results of a single rating scale that has been completed about a specific child, however, the clinician must recognize that the scores represent only the informant's quantified opinions about that child's behavior and, thus, potentially are subject to all of the biases described previously. (For further discussion, see Chapter 2.)

LIMITATIONS OF THE DSM-IV

Clinicians who use the DSM-IV to guide them in diagnosing ADHD will find a number of limitations of the diagnostic system. The number of symptoms that are needed to make the diagnosis of ADHD does not vary with the severity of the individual symptoms or with the age of the individual who is being assessed; thus, an older individual with a few severe symptoms may not meet the diagnostic criteria for ADHD, whereas a younger child with many less-severe symptoms might meet the criteria, even though the former might experience more functional impairment. For the individual with a few severe symptoms, the diagnosis of ADHD not otherwise specified that is included in the DSM-IV might be utilized, but the manual provides no criteria for when to make this diagnosis. Nonetheless, individuals with a few severe symptoms or milder symptoms that still are causing impairment may be brought to primary care physicians or other mental health providers for assistance.

The requirements that symptoms occur in at least two settings and be present before age 7 years can be problematic. The multisetting criterion is beneficial in that it ensures that the clinician will consider the role that variability in environmental factors across settings may play in the expression of a child's symptoms; however, it is problematic in that it does not allow the clinician to diagnose ADHD for children who may have significant difficulties with the attention demands of school but do not have problems at home.[19]

Similarly, the criterion that symptoms be present before age 7 years is useful in highlighting that ADHD rarely is the correct diagnosis when inattention, hyperactivity, or impulsivity is occurring for the first time in adolescence or in adulthood (see Chapters 13 and 14); however, there is not good evidence that age 7 years is a valid cutoff,[20] and it may be problematic in excluding children whose limited attention spans begin to create difficulties as academic demands for sustained attention, organization, and work productivity increase, for instance, during the junior high school years.[21]

In response to these issues regarding the ADHD diagnosis and similar issues regarding other DSM-IV diagnoses, the American Academy of Pediatrics and the American Psychiatric Association have collaborated to publish *The Classification of Child and Adolescent Mental Diagnoses in Primary Care: Diagnostic and Statistical Manual for Primary Care (DSM-PC) Child and Adolescent Version*.[22] The DSM-PC divides clusters of symptoms into three categories: 1) developmental variations, 2) problems, and 3) disorders. For the symptoms of inattention, hyperactivity, and impulsivity, this classification system recognizes that a parent or a teacher may complain about these symptoms when the child's level of inattention and/or hyperactivity and impulsivity are within the normal range but the interaction between environmental or caregiver stressors (which also are summarized in the DSM-PC) and these child characteristics is what creates the concern. In other cases, children may have problems with inattention and/or hyperactivity and impulsivity that for one of the reasons discussed previously would not meet DSM-IV criteria for ADHD but still requires treatment. These children are described as having a "problem" with inattention or hyperactivity and impulsivity. Children whose symptoms meet DSM-IV criteria for ADHD are described as having a "disorder." The DSM-PC provides guidelines that vary with the age of the child to help clinicians distinguish developmental variations from problems or disorders (see Tables 3 and 4).

ETIOLOGY OF ADHD

This introduction has highlighted some of the difficulties and controversies that are related to making the diagnosis of ADHD. Perhaps the greatest controversy regarding ADHD is whether it should be regarded as a disorder at all.[23] Although there are many points of view, most incorporate one or some combination of the following three hypotheses. First, ADHD represents a specific or limited number of biologically based disorders of brain function. This hypothesis has strong roots in the historical view of ADHD symptoms as indicative of MBD, and it continues to stimulate research into the genetics and neurobiology of ADHD. Second, the symptoms of ADHD represent the final common pathway of many different types of brain dysfunction, and clinicians should focus on identifying the underlying dysfunction and not be satisfied with the ADHD diagnosis.[24] Individuals who support this hypothesis liken the symptoms of

Table 3. DSM-PC guidelines for the classification of hyperactive-impulsive behaviors

	Common developmental presentations		
	Early childhood	**Middle childhood**	**Adolescence**
Variation	The child runs in circles, doesn't stop to rest, may bang into objects or people, and asks questions constantly.	The child plays active games for long periods. The child may occasionally do things impulsively, particularly when excited.	The adolescent engages in active social activities (e.g., dancing) for long periods, may engage in risky behaviors with peers.
Behavior Problem	The child frequently runs into people or knocks things down during play, gets injured frequently, and does not want to sit for stories or games.	The child may butt into other children's games, interrupts frequently, and has trouble completing chores.	The adolescent engages in "fooling around" that begins to annoy others and fidgets in class or while watching television.
Disorder	The child runs through the house, jumps and climbs excessively on furniture, will not sit still to eat or be read to, and is often into things.	The child is often talking and interrupting, cannot sit still at mealtimes, is often fidgeting when watching television, makes noise that is disruptive, and grabs from others.	The adolescent is restless and fidgety while doing any and all quiet activities, interrupts and "bugs" other people, and gets into trouble frequently. Hyperactive symptoms decrease and are replaced with a sense of restlessness.

Used with permission of the American Academy of Pediatrics. *The Classification of Child and Adolescent Mental Diagnoses in Primary Care: Diagnostic and Statistical Manual for Primary Care (DSM-PC) Child and Adolescent Version,* 1996.

ADHD to the symptoms of inflammation and point out that acceptance of inflammation as a diagnosis would limit the understanding of the many disorders that cause inflammation. Third, ADHD is primarily a dimensional and not a categorical diagnosis. Individuals who support this hypothesis point out that attention span, activity level, and the ability to control impulses are characteristics of an individual's temperament that are normally distributed in the population (e.g., height, intelligence). From this viewpoint, many children who have been diagnosed with ADHD would be better described as having what the DSM-PC calls normal "developmental variations" or "problems" with their attention, activity, and impulsivity. Individuals who support this hypothesis reject the idea that most individuals who have been diagnosed with ADHD have a disorder of brain function. They point out that the distinction between typical individuals and individuals with ADHD often is arbitrary or statistical (individuals who score a certain number of standard deviations above the mean) and believe that, in most cases, it is a poor match between the individual's temperament and environmental demands that is the primary cause of the problem.[25]

There can be no debate that individuals who incur brain injuries often manifest symptoms of ADHD. In addition, many disorders that are known to affect brain development have been shown to predispose individuals to developing ADHD. These include prenatal lead or alcohol exposure[26]; prematurity[27]; encephalitis; meningitis; inborn errors of metabolism[28]; and many genetic syndromes, including neurofibromatosis, Klinefelter syndrome, Turner syndrome, and Williams syndrome. Nonetheless, most

Table 4. DSM-PC guidelines for the classification of inattentive behaviors

	Common developmental presentations		
	Early childhood	**Middle childhood**	**Adolescence**
Variation	The preschooler has difficulty attending, except briefly, to a story book or quiet task such as coloring or drawing.	The child may not persist very long with a task the child does not want to do such as read an assigned book, homework, or a task that requires concentration such as cleaning something.	The adolescent is easily distracted from tasks he or she does not want to perform.
Behavior Problem	The child is sometimes unable to complete games or activities without being distracted, is unable to complete a game with another child of comparable age, and only attends to any activity for a very short period of time before shifting attention to another object or activity.	At times the child or adolescent misses some instructions and explanations in school, begins a number of activities without completing them, has some difficulty completing games with other children or grown-ups, becomes distracted, tends to give up easily, may not complete or succeed at new activities, has some social deficiency, and does not pick up on subtle social cues from others.	
Disorder	The child is unable to function and play appropriately, and may appear immature, does not engage in any activity long enough, is easily distracted, is unable to complete activities, has a much shorter attention span than other children the same age, often misses important aspects of an object or situation (e.g., rules of games or sequences) and does not persist in various self-care tasks (dressing or washing) to the same extent as other children of a comparable age.	The child or adolescent has significant school and social problems, often shifts activities, does not complete tasks, is messy and careless about school work, starts tasks prematurely and without appropriate review of the instructions, appears as if his or her mind is elsewhere and as if he or she were not listening, has difficulty organizing tasks, dislikes activities that require close concentration, is easily distracted, and is often forgetful.	

Used with permission of the American Academy of Pediatrics. *The Classification of Child and Adolescent Mental Diagnoses in Primary Care: Diagnostic and Statistical Manual for Primary Care (DSM-PC) Child and Adolescent Version,* 1996.

children who are diagnosed with ADHD have not sustained a brain injury or a disorder that is known to affect brain development.

The search for etiological factors that are responsible for ADHD in individuals without one of these disorders has focused on four areas: 1) studies of neurotransmitter systems, 2) neuropsychological studies, 3) structural or functional neuroimaging studies, and 4) genetic studies. Studies in animals implicate the catecholamine neurotransmitters—dopamine and norepinephrine—in a variety of behaviors that are related to attention span and impulsivity. In addition, most of the medications that are effective for ADHD (stimulants, tricyclic antidepressants, and monoamine oxidase inhibitors) increase dopamine and norepinephrine transmission in the brain. Despite these facts, studies that measure the level of catecholamine neurotransmitters or their metabolites in blood, urine, or cerebrospinal fluid (CSF) have not been able consistently to find differences between individuals with and without ADHD.[29] Complicating the interpretation of these findings is that measures of catecholamines in blood, urine, or CSF may not reflect what is occurring at synapses in the brain. For example, research has found that neurons in certain brain regions have inhibitory autoreceptors for dopamine but that neurons in other regions do not. When dopamine binds to these inhibitory autoreceptors, further release of dopamine from the neuron is inhibited. This has led some researchers to hypothesize that although stimulants would increase dopamine release in regions of the brain without inhibitory autoreceptors, the primary therapeutic effect of stimulants in ADHD may be to inhibit dopamine release in the brain regions where inhibitory autoreceptors are present.[30] It is not clear whether there are differences in the levels of **catecholamine** neurotransmitters in the brains of individuals with and without ADHD, and it is likely that a hypothesis that they are increased or decreased may be overly simplistic in that it does not account for variations in how neurotransmitters function within the brain.

Neuropsychological studies of animals and humans with lesions in specific brain regions have demonstrated that those with frontal lobe lesions (especially in the prefrontal cortex) seem to have impairments in executive functions, such as organizing, planning, prioritizing, and self-monitoring as well as in maintaining vigilance and inhibiting responding. The similarities between these problems and those of individuals with ADHD have led to the hypothesis that ADHD represents a form of frontal lobe dysfunction.[31] Studies using neuropsychological tests that assess the frontal lobe function of behavioral inhibition have found that individuals with ADHD perform more poorly than individuals without ADHD.[32] These tests require individuals to respond to one stimulus but not respond (i.e., inhibit one's response) to similar or competing stimuli. For instance, individuals with ADHD usually have difficulties with the Stroop Color-Word Test,[33] which requires them to rapidly name the color of the ink (red, green, or blue) in which a color name is printed when the color name is different from the color of the ink; however, neuropsychological tests that assess other frontal lobe functions, such as planning and organizing information, do not consistently find deficits in individuals with ADHD[34] despite the clinical observation that these tasks often are difficult for these individuals. Whether this indicates that the tests lack sensitivity to subtle abnormalities in ADHD or that problems with planning and organizing are related to comorbid conditions or factors other than frontal lobe function is not clear.

Neuropsychological tests also highlight that there are different components of attention that are mediated by different brain regions. For example, the decision about whether an event is worth attending to seems to be a parietal lobe function, whereas frontal lobes are more involved in developing the plan on how to respond to the event.[35] These types of studies also differentiate the ability to continue to work on long, repetitive tasks (sustained attention) from the ability to concentrate intensely on a task (focused attention). This has been a particular area of interest in the study of ADHD because of the suggestion that individuals with ADHD, combined type, have a primary deficit in sustained attention, whereas individuals with ADHD, predominantly inattentive type, may have a primary deficit in focused attention.[36]

Brain imaging is another method that has been used to investigate areas of the brain that may be affected by ADHD. Standard magnetic resonance imaging (MRI) scans of the brain do not reveal structural abnormalities in individuals with ADHD; however, experimental studies that use MRI to quantitate the volume of specific brain regions have found subtle differences between the brains of individuals with and without ADHD. For example, they have found that the usual asymmetry between the anterior left and right hemispheres and left and right caudate nucleus is not present in individuals with ADHD[37]; however, it is not clear whether these findings are specific to ADHD as similar findings have been reported in those with dyslexia. Similarly, differences in the size of the corpus callosum, suggesting a possible alteration in communication between the two cerebral hemispheres, have been reported but are not consistent among studies.

Functional imaging technology that utilizes MRI or positron emission tomography (PET) scanning to investigate metabolic activity in the brain has been applied to the search for an etiology for ADHD. These studies generally have found that individuals with ADHD have decreased glucose metabolism in the frontal and parietal or temporal cortex as well as subcortical structures such as the basal ganglia and the thalamus.[38] Although these studies provide some of the strongest evidence of differences in the function of specific brain regions in individuals with ADHD, significant differences in the findings among studies remain. Together, there is some convergence of neuropsychological and functional brain imaging studies that suggest that parts of the frontal and possibly parietal lobes are important in ADHD; however, these studies also demonstrate the complexity of such brain functions as paying attention and the difficulties with trying to identify particular brain regions that are affected in individuals with ADHD.

Another approach to attempting to understand the etiology of ADHD is to study the genetics of the disorder. Studies of twins, siblings, and families, as well as adoption studies, all provide evidence for the importance of genetic factors in ADHD. Concordance for the diagnosis of ADHD has been found in 59%–81% of monozygotic (single egg) twins as compared with only about one third of same-sex, dizygotic (two eggs) twins.[39] Similar to the results in dizygotic twins, studies of first-degree relatives (siblings and parents) of individuals with ADHD have found that about 25% of these relatives will be diagnosed with ADHD as compared with only 4%–8% of the relatives of individuals who do not have ADHD.[40] Adopted relatives of individuals with ADHD are less likely to have ADHD than the biological relatives of those individuals.[41] Combined, these studies provide convincing evidence of an important genetic component to ADHD; however, the specific gene or (more likely) genes that are involved in ADHD have not been identified. Attempts to identify such genes are ongoing (see Section III).

CONCLUSION

The debate and the investigation into the etiologies of ADHD continue to stimulate research that will lead to increased understanding of the interaction among genetics, neuroscience, and human behavior. Although these investigations still are in their infancy, they have revealed that a variety of brain injuries and some unknown genetic factors can cause ADHD symptoms. It also is clinically apparent that some individuals who have been diagnosed with ADHD may be better viewed as having what the

DSM-PC has labeled a developmental variation or a problem that may not be indicative of brain dysfunction. Furthermore, attention is a more complicated construct than what the current conceptualization of ADHD is able to account for, and the primary area of dysfunction may not be a short attention span for some children with ADHD. Although it is hoped that the increasing understanding of ADHD will lead to a diagnostic system that more clearly reflects etiological factors and informs treatment, the diagnosis of ADHD, a specific ADHD type, or even a "problem" with inattention or hyperactivity and impulsivity does not imply the need for any specific treatment; rather, the diagnostic process should lead the clinician to understand the relative strengths and weaknesses of a child, his or her family, and the environment. This understanding will enable the clinician to guide the family to appropriate behavioral; educational; and, when needed, medical interventions.

ENDNOTES

1. Strother (1973).
2. Strauss & Kephart (1955).
3. American Psychiatric Association (1968).
4. American Psychiatric Association (1980).
5. American Psychiatric Association (1987).
6. Morgan, Hynd, Riccio, & Hall (1996).
7. Lahey et al. (1994).
8. American Psychiatric Association (1994).
9. Ibid.
10. Klein & Mannuzza (1991), Shaffer (1994).
11. Weiss, Hechtman, Milroy, & Perlman (1985).
12. Keenan, Shaw, Walsh, Delliquadri, & Giovannelli (1997), Lavigne et al. (1996).
13. Barkley (1997).
14. Biederman et al. (1992).
15. Fischer, Barkley, Fletcher, & Smallish (1993).
16. Biederman et al. (1992), Eiraldi, Power, & Nezu (1997).
17. Ibid.
18. Barkley (1998).
19. Power & DuPaul (1996).
20. Barkley & Biederman (1997).
21. Applegate et al. (1997).
22. American Academy of Pediatrics (1996).
23. Weinberg & Brumback (1992).
24. Levine (1992).
25. Carey & McDevitt (1995).
26. Bellinger & Needleman (1983), Brown et al. (1991).
27. Szatmari, Saigal, Rosenbaum, Campbell, & King (1990).
28. Shaywitz & Shaywitz (1988).
29. Mercugliano (1995), Zametkin & Rapoport (1987).
30. Castellanos (1997).
31. Benson (1991).
32. Barkley, Grodzinsky, & DuPaul (1992).
33. Stroop (1935).
34. Barkley et al. (1992).
35. Mesulam (1990).
36. Barkley et al. (1992).
37. Castellanos (1997).
38. Mercugliano (1995).
39. Hechtman (1996).
40. Biederman et al. (1992).
41. Hechtman (1996).

REFERENCES

American Academy of Pediatrics. (1996). *The classification of child and adolescent mental diagnoses in primary care: Diagnostic and statistical manual for primary care (DSM-PC) child and adolescent version.* Elk Grove Village, IL: Author.

American Psychiatric Association. (1968). *Diagnostic and statistical manual of mental disorders* (2nd ed.). Washington, DC: Author.

American Psychiatric Association. (1980). *Diagnostic and statistical manual of mental disorders* (3rd ed.). Washington, DC: Author.

American Psychiatric Association. (1987). *Diagnostic and statistical manual of mental disorders* (3rd ed., rev.). Washington, DC: Author.

American Psychiatric Association. (1994). *Diagnostic and statistical manual of mental disorders* (4th ed.). Washington, DC: Author.

Applegate, B., Lahey, B.B., Hart, E.L., Biederman, J., Hynd, G.W., Barkley, R.A., Ollendick, T., Frick, P.J., Greenhill, L., McBurnett, K., Newcorn, J.H., Kerdyk, L., Garfinkel, B., Waldman, I., & Shaffer, D. (1997). Validity of the age-of-onset criterion for ADHD: A report from the DSM-IV field trials. *Journal of the American Academy of Child and Adolescent Psychiatry, 36,* 1211–1221.

Barkley, R.A. (1997). Behavioral inhibition, sustained attention, and executive functions: Constructing a unifying theory of ADHD. *Psychological Bulletin, 121,* 65–94.

Barkley, R.A. (1998). *Attention-deficit hyperactivity disorder: A handbook for diagnosis and treatment* (2nd ed.). New York: Guilford Press.

Barkley, R.A., & Biederman, J. (1997). Toward a broader definition of the age-of-onset criterion for attention-deficit hyperactivity disorder. *Journal of the American Academy of Child and Adolescent Psychiatry, 36,* 1204–1210.

Barkley, R.A., Grodzinsky, G., & DuPaul, G.J. (1992). Frontal lobe functions in attention deficit disorder with and without hyperactivity: A review and research report. *Journal of Abnormal Child Psychology, 20,* 163–188.

Bellinger, D.C., & Needleman, H.L. (1983). Lead and the relationship between maternal and child intelligence. *Journal of Pediatrics, 102,* 523–527.

Benson, F.D. (1991). The role of frontal dysfunction in attention deficit hyperactivity disorder. *Journal of Child Neurology, 6,* S9–S12.

Biederman, J., Faraone, S.V., Keenan, K., Benjamin, J., Krifcher, B., Moore, C., Sprich-Buckminster, S., Ugaglia, K., Jellinek, M.S., Steingard, R., Spencer, T., Norman, D., Kolodny, R., Kraus, I., Perrin, J., Keller, M.B., & Tsuang, M.T. (1992). Further evidence for family genetic risk factors in attention deficit hyperactivity disorder: Patterns of comorbidity in probands and relatives in psychiatrically and pediatrically referred samples. *Archives of General Psychiatry, 49,* 728–738.

Brown, R.T., Coles, C.D., Smith, I.E., Platzman, K.A., Silverstein, J., Erickson, S., & Falek, A. (1991). Effects of prenatal alcohol exposure at school age: II. Attention and behavior. *Neurotoxicology and Teratology, 13,* 369–376.

Carey, W.B., & McDevitt, S.C. (1995). *Coping with children's temperament: A guide for professionals.* New York: Basic Books.

Castellanos, F.X. (1997). Toward a pathophysiology of attention-deficit/hyperactivity disorder. *Clinical Pediatrics, 36,* 381–393.

Eiraldi, R.B., Power, T.J., & Nezu, C.M. (1997). Patterns of comorbidity associated with subtypes of attention-deficit/hyperactivity disorder among 6- to 12-year-old children. *Journal of the American Academy of Child and Adolescent Psychiatry, 36,* 503–514.

Fischer, M., Barkley, R.A., Fletcher, K.E., & Smallish, L. (1993). The adolescent outcome of hyperactive children: Predictors of psychiatric, academic, social, and emotional adjustment. *Journal of the American Academy of Child and Adolescent Psychiatry, 32,* 324–332.

Hechtman, L. (1996). Families of children with attention deficit hyperactivity disorder: A review. *Canadian Journal of Psychiatry, 41,* 350–360.

Keenan, K., Shaw, D.S., Walsh, B., Delliquadri, E., & Giovannelli, J. (1997). DSM-III-R disorders in preschool children from low-income families. *Journal of the American Academy of Child and Adolescent Psychiatry, 36,* 620–627.

Klein, R.G., & Mannuzza, S. (1991). Long-term outcome of hyperactive children: A review. *Journal of the American Academy of Child Psychiatry, 30,* 383–387.

Lahey, B.B., Applegate, B., McBurnett, K., Biederman, J., Greenhill, L., Hynd, G.W., Barkley, R.A., Newcorn, J., Jensen, P., Richters, J., Garfinkel, B., Kerdyk, L., Frick, P.J., Ollendick, T., Perez, D.,

Hart, E.L., Waldman, I., & Shaffer, D. (1994). DSM-IV field trials for attention deficit hyperactivity disorder in children and adolescents. *American Journal of Psychiatry, 151,* 1673–1685.

Lavigne, J.V., Gibbons, R.D., Christoffel, K.K., Arend, R., Rosenbaum, D., Binns, H., Dawson, N., Sobel, H., & Isaacs, C. (1996). Prevalence rates and correlates of psychiatric disorders among preschool children. *Journal of the American Academy of Child and Adolescent Psychiatry, 35,* 204–214.

Levine, M.D. (1992). Commentary: Attentional disorders. Elusive entities and their mistaken identities. *Journal of Child Neurology, 7,* 449–453.

Mercugliano, M. (1995). Neurotransmitter alterations in attention-deficit/hyperactivity disorder. *Mental Retardation and Developmental Disabilities Research Reviews, 1,* 220–226.

Mesulam, M.M. (1990). Large-scale neurocognitive networks and distributed processing for attention, language, and memory. *Annals of Neurology, 28,* 597–613.

Morgan, A.E., Hynd, G.W., Riccio, C.A., & Hall, J. (1996). Validity of DSM-IV ADHD predominately inattentive type and combined types: Relationship to previous DSM diagnoses/subtype differences. *Journal of the American Academy of Child and Adolescent Psychiatry, 35,* 325–333.

Power, T.J., & DuPaul, G.J. (1996). Attention-deficit hyperactivity disorder: The reemergence of subtypes. *School Psychology Review, 25,* 284–296.

Shaffer, D. (1994). Attention deficit hyperactivity disorder in adults. *American Journal of Psychiatry, 151,* 633–638.

Shaywitz, S.E., & Shaywitz, B.A. (1988). Attention deficit disorder: Current perspective. In J.F. Kavanagh & T.J. Truss, Jr. (Eds.), *Learning disability: Proceedings of the National Conference* (pp. 369–523). Baltimore: York Press.

Strauss, A.A., & Kephart, N.C. (1955). *Psychopathology and education of the brain-injured child* (Vol. 2). New York: Grune & Stratton.

Stroop, J.R. (1935). Studies of interference in serial verbal reactions. *Journal of Experimental Psychology, 18,* 643–662.

Strother, C.R. (1973). Minimal cerebral dysfunction: A historical overview. *Annals of the New York Academy of Sciences, 205,* 6–17.

Szatmari, P., Saigal, S., Rosenbaum, P., Campbell, D., & King, S. (1990). Psychiatric disorders at five years among children with birth weights, <1000 g: A regional perspective. *Developmental Medicine and Child Neurology, 32,* 954–962.

Weinberg, W.A., & Brumback, R.A. (1992). The myth of attention deficit-hyperactivity disorder: Symptoms resulting from multiple causes. *Journal of Child Neurology, 7,* 431–461.

Weiss, G., Hechtman, L., Milroy, T., & Perlman, T. (1985). Psychiatric status of hyperactives as adults: A controlled prospective 15 year follow-up of 63 hyperactive children. *Journal of the American Academy of Child Psychiatry, 24,* 211–220.

Zametkin, A.J., & Rapoport, J.L. (1987). Neurobiology of attention deficit disorder with hyperactivity: Where have we come in 50 years? *Journal of the American Academy of Child Psychiatry, 26,* 676–686.

Assessment for Attention-Deficit/ Hyperactivity Disorder

The assessment for attention-deficit/hyperactivity disorder (ADHD) is best conceptualized as a comprehensive evaluation of a child's difficulties with learning and behavior. The specific concerns likely will depend on the age of the child. Preschool-age children are most likely to present with concerns about overactivity, noncompliance ("does not listen," "does not sit in circle time"), and/or aggression. School-age children are most likely to present with multiple concerns, including

- Short attention span
- Failure to complete school work
- Trouble with following directions
- Noncompliance with rules
- Moodiness
- Rejection by peers
- Academic underachievement
- Low self-esteem

The initial presentation of ADHD in adolescence and young adulthood is less common but may occur in mild cases, in especially bright students who have been able to keep up academically in the earlier grades, in females who are less often disruptive, and in those who have the predominantly inattentive type of ADHD.

To perform a comprehensive evaluation of ADHD, the clinician must accomplish three broad objectives:

1. "Rule in" the diagnostic features of ADHD.
2. "Rule out" the diagnostic features of another disorder that may masquerade as ADHD.
3. Determine the presence of coexisting diagnoses or problems that are contributing to the overall clinical picture and that require treatment.

The diagnostic features of ADHD generally are "ruled in" when the parent interview confirms the criteria that are outlined in the *Diagnostic and Statistic Manual of Mental Disorders, Fourth Edition* (DSM-IV)[1] and parent and teacher reports on rating scales are supportive. The specific diagnostic criteria for ADHD may be obtained by informal direct questioning of the parents or through the use of a structured interview. Some interview formats come in parent and child versions (see Chapter 2). Most of the behavior rating scales in common use do not correspond directly to the DSM-IV criteria, although a group of ADHD researchers and clinicians have collaborated to norm the ADHD Rating Scale-IV[2] for parents and teachers, which does correspond to DSM-IV criteria (see Chapter 2).

The "ruling out" portion of the evaluation refers to making sure that the child does not have another disorder that is causing ADHD-like symptoms. These include medical/neurological conditions, other developmental/learning disorders, or untreated psychiatric disorders (see Chapter 1). In many instances, the symptoms of another disorder exist in addition to, rather than instead of, ADHD.

For medical disorders, it is wise to defer a diagnosis of ADHD when an underlying condition is identified for which treatment has not yet been instituted (e.g., **thyrotoxicosis**) or when behavioral symptoms are part of a neurodegenerative condition (e.g., **adrenoleukodystrophy**). It is not useful to defer the diagnosis when a medical or a neurological condition that has been identified does not have its own treatment (e.g., a history of lead intoxication, a diagnosis of **fetal alcohol, fragile X,** or **Tourette syndrome**), even when it is the possible cause of the ADHD, or when it has been optimally treated (hearing or visual impairment, seizure disorder). The clinician may want to defer a diagnosis of ADHD when a learning disability or psychiatric diagnosis also is present but has not been addressed. Persistent ADHD symptoms, despite adequate treatment of a learning disability or a psychiatric disorder, indicate that it is appropriate to consider both diagnoses.

Clinicians may be reluctant to make a diagnosis of ADHD when the psychosocial environment is chaotic or otherwise suboptimum. Although such an environment can have a negative impact on the functioning of any child, having a child with ADHD can also have a negative impact on the stability of the family. Addressing the problems is more important than making a diagnosis at a specific point in time. Clinicians who are involved in complex cases find that assessment often is an ongoing process that is intertwined with treatment rather than a time-limited event that uniformly precedes any intervention.

An assessment generally includes a comprehensive history (medical, behavioral, developmental, educational, social, and genetic), a physical examination (general and neurological), collection of behavioral data from multiple sources using interviews and rating scales, and a direct assessment of the child's behavior and learning. The decision about which professional will conduct specific parts of the evaluation must be made on an individual basis, but the primary clinician necessarily retains a central role.

The individual whom parents seek for an evaluation—most often their primary medical clinician or perhaps a nonmedical professional who has helped their child with related problems—becomes the coordinator of the evaluation by conducting the portion of the evaluation that is within his or her realm of expertise and seeking additional information from others. A common scenario is that the primary medical clinician will do the history and examination, and a school psychologist or a private psychologist will perform the psychoeducational evaluation; either or both may include rating scales and other screening measures for coexisting internalizing and externalizing disorders. A treating therapist can provide ongoing insight related to the presence of any coexisting disorders as well. Medical specialists, such as child psychiatrists, neurologists, or developmental/behavioral pediatricians, or teams in multidisciplinary programs may be called upon to perform some or all of the evaluation when the coordinator identifies special complexities. The following chapters provide organized and concise guidelines for the parts of the evaluation that the coordinating clinician chooses to conduct, and they define the specific types of evaluations that the clinician will seek from others. Outlines and forms are included to assist clinicians with collecting and summarizing information.

ENDNOTES

1. American Psychiatric Association (1994).
2. DuPaul, G.J., Power, T.J., Anastopoulos, A.D., & Reid, R. (1999).

REFERENCES

American Psychiatric Association. (1994). *Diagnostic and statistical manual of mental disorders* (4th ed.). Washington, DC: Author.
DuPaul, G.J., Power, T.J., Anastopoulos, A.D., & Reid, R. (1999). *ADHD Rating Scale-IV.* New York: Guilford Press.

History and Examination 1

A thorough history of the child who may have attention-deficit/hyperactivity disorder (ADHD) comprises the core of the clinician's evaluation. It can provide seminal evidence for or against the existence of ADHD and other disorders and can identify issues that require further investigation and/or treatment. It includes elaboration of the main concern(s) and their historical development; a complete medical history covering the pre- and perinatal periods, infancy, and development; behavior history; educational history; review of systems; family history; and social history. Much of this information can be obtained from a questionnaire that the parent(s) complete before the initial visit (see Appendix A). The necessary information that does not lend itself to a checklist format (e.g., elaboration of the main concern, family/social history, current school issues, previous treatment), as well as additional information about positive responses on the checklist, can be obtained in about 10 minutes (see Appendix B).

Elaborating the main concern means dissecting from a general statement ("He is a behavior problem," "She is immature," "He is in danger of being retained") the specific problems ("He talks out of turn and does not follow directions in class," "She cannot keep friends," "He has never caught on well to reading and is falling further and further behind"). The importance of specificity lies in developing a clear understanding of the problems, choosing treatments, and assessing their effectiveness. Usually there are several specific problems spanning behavior, academics, and social interactions. It is useful to determine when concerns first were raised and the order in which they developed. For example, the child whose parents first were concerned because of hyperactivity when the child was 3 years old is different from the child whose parents first were concerned because of little expressive language when the child was 2 years old, and both are different from the 10-year-old child with declining grades and declining self-esteem. All (or none) of these children may have ADHD, but their coexisting diagnoses and specific treatments are likely to differ.

The results of any prior evaluations and interventions and their effectiveness should be reviewed. If previous treatments such as counseling, medication, or educational interventions were reported to be ineffective, then sufficient detail is needed to allow a judgment as to why this was so. A common reason for "ineffective" counseling is that the counselor used cognitive strategies or play therapy with the child rather than practical, behavior management strategies that involve parent training. Common reasons for medication "ineffectiveness" include suboptimum dosage or schedule and a lack of concomitant nonpharmacological interventions. Medication sometimes is discontinued or presumed ineffective because "problems still exist" when it *is* effective for core symptoms but is unrealistically expected to solve all of the problems that the child and the family are experiencing. Also, failure to coordinate the resources of home and school can contribute to the apparent failure of psychological and medical approaches.

PRENATAL HISTORY

The prenatal history is used to determine whether risk factors are present for abnormal brain development or brain injury. Although there is consensus among experts in the field that most children with ADHD have not sustained a brain injury or brain damage and that ADHD often is familial (see Introduction and the overview of Section III), a number of prenatal, perinatal, and environmental factors that have been associated with ADHD may have etiological significance, especially in apparently nonfamilial cases. Birth asphyxia does not appear to be a common cause of ADHD,[1] although certain adverse prenatal and perinatal events show a modest association with subsequent referral for "hyperactivity."[2] Children who have ADHD but no family history of ADHD are more likely to have had prenatal, perinatal, or infancy complications, but those with a family history of ADHD are no more likely to have had these complications than are children without ADHD.[3] Following is a list of possible nongenetic etiological factors:

- Prenatal infections
- Prenatal exposure to alcohol,[4] cocaine,[5] and other drugs
- Elevated lead level/lead intoxication[6]
- Treated phenylketonuria[7]
- Prenatal exposure to maternal cigarette smoking[8]
- Acquired brain injury (hypoxia/ischemia, trauma, infection)[9]
- Syndromes (fetal alcohol, fragile X,[10] Tourette, Turner,[11] Williams, XYY)
- Neurological disease (neurofibromatosis I,[12] Sydenham's chorea, tuberous sclerosis)
- Prematurity[13]
- Intrauterine growth retardation/malnutrition[14]
- Atopy/otitis media[15]

Some etiologies, such as fetal alcohol exposure, cocaine exposure, elevated lead levels, and prematurity, appear to be related to ADHD in the majority—although not all—of the studies. In addition, a specific association with ADHD (or one or more of its symptoms), as opposed to developmental disorders in general, has not been proved conclusively for any factor. Syndromes, toxin exposures, and perinatal conditions that include ADHD symptoms as part of the profile also typically include cognitive and psychiatric disorders (e.g., fetal alcohol syndrome, Williams syndrome). In addition, the specific ways in which attention is affected may differ among different etiologies, even though the observable behaviors on which the diagnosis of ADHD is based may be similar. For example, Coles et al. (1997) found that deficits on neuropsychological measures of attention differ between children with ADHD and those with characteristic facial features of fetal alcohol syndrome and a history of fetal alcohol exposure.

Some findings are reported to be more prevalent among children with ADHD than among the general population in some studies, but their role as causative or contributing factors has not been established. These include early otitis media, allergies, and maternal cigarette smoking. Other factors, such as early malnutrition and prenatal congenital infection, are presumed to have a potential causative relationship because of their known potential for detrimental effects on the developing nervous system. Although outcome studies of asymptomatic congenital infection and early malnutrition exist, they do not specifically address the presence or absence of ADHD. Obviously, the type of study that is required to delineate clearly the nature of the association between early factors and the subsequent development of ADHD is difficult to perform because it requires long-term follow-up and careful controls for genetic and environmental factors. In summary, there are many neurobiological factors that may contribute to ADHD symptoms. There is little evidence to suggest that insults to the developing nervous system cause isolated ADHD in the absence of other neurodevelopmental sequelae, and there has been a paucity of research addressing this specific and difficult question.

DEVELOPMENTAL AND EDUCATIONAL HISTORY

The developmental history is used to identify early developmental delays and to determine the chronicity, stability, and specificity of the parents' concerns. Although specific early milestones are unlikely to be recalled accurately by the time the child is in school, a history of concerns about the development of language, fine motor skills (e.g., using utensils, buttoning, tying), gross motor skills (e.g., running, jumping, riding a bike), or independence skills (e.g., dressing, toileting) may be revealing. Fine motor skill deficits are common in children with ADHD and may contribute to difficulties with writing. When these are noted on examination, a diagnosis of **developmental coordination disorder** may be appropriate and an occupational therapy consultation may be helpful when functional impairment is present (e.g., laborious or difficult-to-read handwriting; impaired self-help skills). **Kinesthetic abilities** also may be deficient in some children with ADHD and may contribute to motor/motor planning difficulties.[16]

The endorsement of delays in language development may be suggestive of the presence of a **developmental language disorder** or a **pervasive developmental disorder** (PDD). If PDD is present, then there will be other evidence of this in the history and child assessment. This evidence characteristically includes a history of stereotypical behaviors and/or restricted interests, unusual patterns of language use (with or without language delay), and impaired social interaction. In contrast, a developmental language disorder in the preschool years may appear to have resolved by school age but often will manifest then as difficulties with reading, reading comprehension, spelling, listening, or memory. Thus, a more thorough assessment of language and academic skills may be required; if deficits are found, then a formal psychoeducational evaluation is indicated to determine eligibility for and type of specialized educational interventions.

Global developmental delays may signal **mental retardation** or (rarely) a neurodegenerative disorder and also require a formal assessment and a special educational program. In addition to uncovering developmental concerns, the clinician should ask the parents about concerns about the loss of previously acquired milestones. Academic and behavioral symptoms may be the first signs of rare neurodegenerative disorders, although they usually are not the only symptoms. Often, parents will endorse a loss of milestones because the child's ability to get along socially or to pay attention are more problematic than they used to be. It may be that falling further behind what is expected for age makes the child seem "worse" than he or she was previously, when, in fact, this does not constitute the loss of a skill. More specific questioning regarding the loss of words, self-help skills, memory, and fine motor skills will, in most cases, reassure the clinician that the child has not actually lost skills. Following is a list of neurodegenerative and other neurological disorders that present in school-age children and typically show academic and behavioral deterioration early in their course[17]:

- Adrenoleukodystrophy: increased pigmentation of extremities, adrenal insufficiency, spasticity
- Juvenile Huntington's chorea: chorea, psychiatric disturbances, rigidity, ataxia, seizures
- Mucopolysaccharidoses: facial and skeletal changes, joint contractures
- Neurofibromatosis I: café-au-lait spots, optic glioma, hemihypertrophy, neuromas
- Sanfilippo syndrome: skeletal changes, short stature, hepatosplenomegaly
- Subacute sclerosing panencephalitis: seizures, tics, myoclonus, blindness, deafness
- Tuberous sclerosis: seizures, adenoma sebaceum, depigmented nevi, shagreen spots
- Wilson's disease: hepatic necrosis, jaundice, choreoathetosis, Kayser-Fleischer rings

Understanding the development and chronicity of symptoms in the home and educational environments will help rule out a neurodegenerative disorder and will provide clues as to the etiology of associated academic problems. For example, hyperactivity that first was noted at the age of 3 in combination with no loss of milestones in an otherwise healthy 8-year-old almost certainly rules out a degenerative process. Hyperactivity that first was noted at age 3 in an 8-year-old who also may be exhibiting a **learning disability** may suggest that both disorders are present rather than that inattentive and disruptive behavior in the classroom is purely secondary to learning difficulty or poor **instructional match**. Likewise, if the initial concern was poor development of reading skills or if this concern was present from the first year in school in conjunction with concerns about attention span, then the clinician should suspect the presence of a learning disability (with or without ADHD). Attention problems do not tend to affect skill acquisition selectively (e.g., just in reading or math) and do not commonly lead to academic delays as early as kindergarten or first grade in children of average or above-average intelligence. Although instructional mismatch can impair attention,[18] it is uncommon for reading disability to be a "cause" of classroom behavior problems.[19] Some learning disorders that may present instead of or in addition to ADHD include the following:

- Mental retardation
- PDD (PDD not otherwise specified, Asperger's syndrome) (*Note:* ADHD usually is not diagnosed in the presence of a PDD; see the *Diagnostic and Statistical Manual of Mental Disorders, Fourth Edition* [DSM-IV][20] for the diagnostic criteria for PDDs.)

- Developmental language disorder
- Nonverbal learning disorder
- Disorders of reading, mathematics, spelling, and/or writing

(For further discussion of learning disabilities and learning problems that are associated with ADHD and that do not meet strict criteria for a learning disability, see Chapters 3, 6, and 8 and the reviews by Beitchman & Young, 1997, and Church, Lewis, & Batshaw, 1997.)

The primary care provider may need to request information from the school to have a full picture of the child's learning history and status. Examples of letters requesting information about school performance and educational intervention for school-based ADHD-related difficulties (for elementary school students and for secondary school students) can be found in Appendix C. An academic performance questionnaire for teachers can be used in conjunction with this cover letter (see Appendix A of Chapter 3).

MEDICAL HISTORY

The medical history is helpful for ruling out the presence of medical conditions that may contribute to concentration difficulties (see Table 1) and may highlight areas for special consideration if pharmacological treatment is considered. It includes questions about allergies, other reactions to foods or medications, rashes, recurrent or unusual illnesses, hospitalizations, trauma, sleep, and eating and elimination habits and a review of systems covering the neurological, cardiovascular, gastrointestinal, and other systems. The behavior history should include questions about social skills; fears; anxiety level; depressive symptoms; suicidal ideation; grandiosity and manic symptoms; self-esteem; anger control; aggression; antisocial behaviors; repetitive behaviors such as motor or vocal **tics,** nervous habits; **compulsions** and rituals; and evidence for unusual thinking such as **obsessions, hallucinations,** and **delusions.** Much of this information can be obtained from rating scales if one of the wide-range scales is used (see Chapter 2). Some authors, in attempts to further categorize subgroups of children who exhibit ADHD symptoms, have used the label Primary Disorder of Vigilance for children (who otherwise probably would be diagnosed with ADHD, predominantly inattentive type) who are sleepy, inattentive, and easily bored and who are restless or fidgety in an effort to stay awake.[21] Further research is needed to determine the validity of subtyping within the nonhyperactive group.

Table 1. Medical conditions that may cause ADHD-like symptoms

Thyroid dysfunction (hyperthyroidism, hypothyroidism, peripheral resistance to thyroid hormone [Foley, 1992; Hauser et al., 1993])

Iron deficiency (with or without anemia)

Sleep disorders (narcolepsy, obstructive sleep apnea)

Visual impairment

Hearing impairment

Seizure disorders (absence, partial complex)

Mass lesions of the brain, hydrocephalus

Complex migraines or other cerebrovascular disease

Behavior-altering medications (stimulants, decongestants, beta-agonists, methylxanthines, steroids, recreational drugs)

Chronic medical disease with widespread effects (cardiac, pulmonary, renal)

SOCIAL AND FAMILY HISTORY

The social history is important in assessing the family's impact on the child's behavior and vice versa as well as peer relationships. Social adversity has been shown to have an impact on the functioning and coexisting diagnoses in children with ADHD.[22] Important initial information includes the family members and other caregivers. The status of the marital relationship and the level of agreement between parents in regard to the child's symptoms and their management is important to both diagnosis and treatment. Extreme marital or family conflict can lead to difficulties with self-regulation and school performance, and the clinician might withhold a diagnosis of ADHD pending family intervention. Alternatively, marital conflict and divorce are more common in the families of children with ADHD, and conflict often is caused by differences in perception of the degree or nature of the child's symptoms. In many cases, the parent who spends more time managing day-to-day issues, such as getting ready for school, completing homework, and social situations (usually the mother), feels the problems more acutely. It also is common that children follow directions better from their fathers than from their mothers.[23] Whether there is any relationship between these two observations remains to be determined, but the result often is that the mother feels responsible, ineffective, and unsupported.

It is helpful for the clinician to understand the particular styles that parents use in their interactions with their child. Certain parenting styles are problematic for children with ADHD. A lax parenting style provides insufficient supervision, rules, and consequences for rule breaking. An overreactive parenting style is overly punitive in a sporadic fashion, depending more on the state of the parent than on the behavior of the child. How the child is disciplined and the degree to which positive strategies for good behavior versus punishment for negative behavior are used may illuminate the need for parent training in behavior management strategies. Many parents of children with ADHD do not routinely use positive reinforcement of good behavior but rather use punishment as the primary discipline strategy. Because children with ADHD characteristically do not learn well from mistakes or punishment, such families are at risk of using increasingly severe punishment strategies, including corporal punishment. A parent may say, "I don't know what else to take away from him!" It has been hypothesized that this situation increases the risk of depression and conduct problems in the child. When corporal punishment occurs repeatedly and when the parent delivers punishment in a state of extreme anger, it may be abusive and should be considered as such. Treatment of the underlying issues that lead to family violence still must be primary, but the involvement of child protective services may serve as a catalyst for the initiation of parent training in more acceptable behavior management strategies and as an avenue to obtaining additional supportive services.

In contrast to the parenting styles that can have a negative impact on the behavior of children with ADHD, a high degree of family cohesion and parent–child involvement can be beneficial to a child with ADHD. A level of parent–child involvement that might appear to be excessive in another family can be beneficial to the child with ADHD and his or her family in terms of supervision, organization, and mutual support.[24] The assessment of parenting skills and behavior management interventions for children with ADHD are discussed in greater depth in Chapter 5.

Understanding how the child interacts with siblings and peers is important in making treatment recommendations. Several characteristics have an impact on sibling and peer functioning, which are described further in Chapters 5 and 6. Chapter 6 also includes a set of additional interview questions to further delineate social skills deficits with peers. Chapter 12 includes another set of interview questions to analyze parents' discipline and behavior management strategies.

The family history can be diagnostically supportive for both ADHD and coexisting diagnoses and may be useful in medication considerations. Approximately 25% of first-degree relatives of a **proband** with ADHD will have ADHD, a rate that is higher than that in both families with and without a history of psychiatric disorders.[25] The relatives of probands with ADHD and coexisting diagnoses (depressive and conduct disorders) have similar coexisting diagnoses.[26] Familial-genetic factors also have been shown to be important in epidemiological rather than referred samples,[27] and several types of studies indicate that the familial clustering of ADHD largely is genetic rather than psychosocial in origin (see the overview of Section III for further discussion about the genetics of ADHD). Although the diagnosis of ADHD was made less frequently in previous generations, asking about similar personality traits in other relatives; early difficulties with learning or behavior at school; and the presence of overactivity, restlessness, and difficulties with finishing or persisting with tasks in adulthood often is revealing. It also is important to ask about a family history of related problems, such as reading problems, tics, obsessions, compulsions, substance abuse, antisocial behaviors, mental health diagnoses, hospitalizations, and medication treatment. A strong family history of a certain type of mental health disorder should heighten the clinician's suspicion about the presence of the disorder or its precursors in the child who is being evaluated. This knowledge can be helpful if the symptoms of the coexisting disorder are considered borderline and a decision needs to be made about intervention, if the child does not respond as expected to treatment for ADHD, or if additional symptoms of the coexisting disorder begin to emerge over time.

In addition to identifying possible familial coexisting diagnoses, a careful family history can be helpful in making decisions about second-line or additional pharmacological strategies. A medication that was effective for a first-degree relative may be useful as a second-line drug in a child with a limited response or who experiences side effects to a stimulant (e.g., one might be more willing to try an antidepressant next rather than a different stimulant). Likewise, if a mother reports that she became highly agitated while she was taking a particular medication, then the clinician might be more inclined not to prescribe it for her son or to discontinue it when he shows increased aggression, rather than attribute it to something else. It is important to ask parents to consider specific relatives one at a time as they ponder the list of relevant characteristics and diagnoses to increase the likelihood that they will recall information that they may not have had previous reason to consider or to consider related to their child. Table 2 shows a list of the most frequent mental health disorders that may present instead of or in addition to ADHD.

EXAMINATION

The physical examination focuses on signs of etiology, coexisting diagnoses, and findings that may have implications for medication use. A thorough general physical and neurological examination is required (see Appendix D). For assessing etiology, most important are growth parameters (including head circumference if not previously measured), **dysmorphic features** of the face and body, and **neurocutaneous signs.** For assessing underlying medical illness or findings that may have an impact on medication

Table 2. Mental health disorders that may present instead of or in addition to ADHD

Anxiety disorders (Bernstein, Borchardt, & Perwein, 1997)
- Generalized anxiety disorder
- Separation anxiety disorder
- Phobia
- Panic disorder (panic attacks)
- Obsessive compulsive disorder

Disruptive behavior disorders
- Oppositional defiant disorder
- Conduct disorder

Mood disorders (Birmaher, Ryan, Williamson, Brent, & Kaufman, 1996; Birmaher, Ryan, Williamson, Brent, Kaufman, Dahl, et al., 1996)
- Dysthymia
- Major depression
- Bipolar disorder (Geller & Luby, 1997)
- Mood disorder (not otherwise specified)
- Post-traumatic stress disorder (Glod & Teicher, 1996)
- Adjustment reaction

Personality disorders
- Borderline personality disorder
- Antisocial personality disorder

Note: See the DSM-IV for diagnostic criteria for these disorders.

Note: ADHD usually is not diagnosed in the presence of psychotic features, though children with ADHD may evolve to later warrant a diagnosis that includes psychotic features.

use, most important are vital signs; vision, hearing, and lung and cardiovascular exams; evidence of adenopathy, organomegaly, and thyromegaly; and allergic signs.

An individual interview may provide a sense of the child's level of interaction, expressive language skills, and range of affect. Reports of tics, obsessions, and compulsions often are not obtained until sufficient rapport is established; the individual interview, especially with the preadolescent and adolescent, will help to establish this. Poor eye contact, repetitive behaviors or perseverative thinking, inability to answer open-ended questions, use of few words, pressured speech, tangentiality, a **phonological (articulation) disorder,** and depressed or overly anxious mood can be identified during a brief individual interview, which will suggest the presence of language, mood, or other coexisting diagnoses. Unfortunately, there is no specific behavior that is diagnostic, but the clinician's observations can be useful as supportive evidence when they are consistent with other types of evidence, or they can suggest the need for a more in-depth assessment in certain areas.

A neurological exam is performed to rule out focal neurological signs and to assess fine motor skills and neurological soft signs. Fine motor skills may be assessed by the ability to pick up tiny objects with a pincer grasp, accurate finger-to-nose movements on cerebellar exam, rapid and accurate pegboard completion, isolated finger movements, and sequential finger opposition. Neurological soft signs are findings that would not be abnormal in a child of a younger age, such as incoordination, nonpurposeful movements, poor cortical sensory skills, and poor directionality (see Table 3 for a list of neurological soft signs).

Neurological soft signs are common in children with ADHD and learning disabilities. Although most clinicians would agree that these signs are nonspecific and not diagnostic, they can be useful in two ways. First, when soft signs are excessive, they may

Table 3. Neurological soft signs

Incoordination
- Difficulties with accuracy on finger-to-nose testing (not caused by dysmetria)
- Tremulousness
- Difficulties with balancing on one foot
- Rapid, poorly graded movements

Nonpurposeful movements
- Excess movements of the shoulder or elbow during finger-to-nose testing
- Distal choreiform movements of the mouth or the hands during the **Romberg test**
- Difficulties with sustaining eye gaze or motor persistence during strength testing
- Mirror movements of the opposite fingers when performing fine motor skills with one hand
- Posturing of the upper extremities when walking on toes, heels, or the inside or outside of the feet

Poor cortical sensory skills
- Inability to identify objects that are placed in the hands after age 5 years (stereognosis)
- Inability to identify numbers written in the hands after age 8 years (graphesthesia)
- Extinction of distal points when two points are touched simultaneously on the body with the eyes closed

Poor directionality
- Inability to identify right and left (by 7–8 years)

signal the presence of fine motor problems that contribute to difficulties with writing or with gross motor problems resulting in "clumsiness" (and its attendant difficulties such as frequent injuries or peer rejection related to poor athletic ability). Second, when multiple soft signs are present more prominently than expected or on the opposite side of the body than expected (during the school years, soft signs are more prominent on the nondominant side), they may be considered a focal finding that might lead the clinician to consider further neurological investigation, especially when other historical features, signs, or symptoms that are suggestive of focal neurological dysfunction are present. Becoming familiar with the normal developmental maturation of coordination and disappearance of soft signs requires that the clinician choose several to be examined consistently in children of different ages, with and without learning and attention problems.[28] For example, it is common for school-age children to have decerebrate-like posturing (arms externally rotated, hands pronated) of the arms when they walk on the insides of their feet and decorticate-like posturing (arms internally rotated, hands supinated) when they walk on the outsides of their feet (the Fog test[29]). Preschool-age children often are unable to imitate this type of gait and may show posturing while attempting to get into the proper position or when concentrating on walking on their heels or on their toes. During the early school years, children generally can perform the Fog test and will show posturing of both arms. During the second half of the elementary years, posturing often will disappear in the dominant arm and the nondominant arm will show persistent or more prominent posturing. Posturing tends to disappear altogether by 10–12 years but may persist longer in children with learning or attention problems. Those with persistent inability to imitate the gait, severe bilateral posturing, or posturing on the dominant side may be showing signs of more pervasive motor problems.

Mirror movements (also called *synkinesias*), an example of nonpurposeful movements, also show a typical developmental pattern. A common way to elicit them is with sequential finger opposition whereby the child sequentially touches his or her thumb to each finger on the same hand. The other hand, when resting palm up in the lap, "mirrors" the sequential finger opposition. Preschool-age children often cannot imitate sequential finger opposition but will show mirror movements when asked to perform an easier task: repeatedly touching the thumb to the first finger (rapid finger opposition). Young elementary school–age children generally can perform sequential finger opposition. They do so with better coordination and less extraneous movement in the dominant hand, and they show mirror movements of either hand. Older elementary school–age children tend to be able to perform mirror movements in their nondominant hand only. By 10–12 years, most children can perform sequential finger opposition similarly with their dominant and nondominant hands and will not show mirror movements, but, again, the persistence of less skill and mirror movements on the nondominant side is common in children with neurodevelopmental diagnoses. Highly prominent mirror movements have been shown to correlate with mid-line defects of the motor pathways and or neurophysiological abnormalities in some cases.[30] The child who is right-handed but who postures more on the right, has poorer finger-to-nose coordination on the right, and has a developmental language disorder may be showing several signs of inefficiency in left brain function. Likewise, the child with a **nonverbal learning disorder** may have more prominent left-sided soft signs than would be expected among children of the same age. Whether brain imaging studies, which are not routinely recommended in the course of an ADHD evaluation, should be pursued in such children depends on the presence of additional features such as craniofacial dysmorphic features; growth or head circumference abnormalities; genetic counseling issues; or any question as to the congenital, static nature of the presenting problem.

CONCLUSION

Following completion of a comprehensive history and examination, the clinician should have a substantial amount of information pertaining to symptoms of ADHD, the resulting degree of functional impairment, the presence of coexisting diagnoses in the child and his or her family, the child's medical status, family function, and educational status. This information will allow the clinician to determine the need for review of other existing information, further specific assessments, and immediate interventions. A tentative summary and initial treatment recommendations may be helpful for the family at this time, with the understanding that treatment response and ongoing assessment are important in further refining the diagnostic summary and treatment plans.

ENDNOTES

1. Handley-Derry et al. (1997).
2. Chandola, Robling, Peters, Melville-Thomas, & McGuffin (1992).
3. Sprich-Buckminster, Biederman, Milberger, Faraone, & Lehman (1993).
4. Brown et al. (1991), Coles, Russell, & Scheutze (1997), Steinhausen, Willms, & Spohr (1993).
5. Delaney-Black et al. (1996), Griffith, Azuma, & Chasnoff (1994), Landry & Whitney (1996).
6. Kahn, Kelly, & Walker (1995), Tuthill (1996).
7. Burgard, Rey, Rupp, Abadi, & Rey (1997), Pietz et al. (1997).
8. Milberger, Biederman, Faraone, Chen, & Jones (1996).
9. Kaufman, Fletcher, Levin, Miner, & Ewing-Cobbs (1993).
10. Doran (1997).
11. Commings (1990).
12. Dilts et al. (1996).
13. Buehler, Als, Duffy, McAnulty, & Liederman (1995), Klebanov, Brooks-Gunn, & McCormick (1994), Schothorst & Van Engeland (1996).

14. Galler & Ramsey (1989).
15. Daly et al. (1997), Roberts et al. (1989), Roth, Beyreiss, Sclenzka, & Beyer (1991).
16. Parush, Sohmer, Steinberg, & Kaitz (1997), Whitmont & Clark (1996).
17. Swaiman (1994).
18. Gickling & Armstrong (1978).
19. Smart, Sanson, & Prior (1996).
20. American Psychiatric Association (1994).
21. Reviewed in Weinberg & Emslie (1991).
22. Biederman et al. (1995).
23. Reviewed in Barkley (1998).
24. Rostain, Power, & Atkins (1993).
25. Biederman, Faraone, Keenan, Knee, & Tsuang (1990).
26. Biederman et al. (1992).
27. Gross-Tsur, Shalev, & Amir (1991).
28. Pine et al. (1996).
29. Fog & Fog (1963).
30. Britton, Meyer, & Benecke (1991).

REFERENCES

Barkley, R.A. (1998). *Attention-deficit hyperactivity disorder: A handbook for diagnosis and treatment* (2nd ed.). New York: Guilford Press.

Beitchman, J.H., & Young, A.R. (1997). Learning disorders: A review of the past 10 years. *Journal of the American Academy of Child and Adolescent Psychiatry, 36,* 1020–1032.

Bernstein, G.A., Borchardt, C.M., & Perwein, A.R. (1997). Anxiety disorders in children and adolescents: A review of the past 10 years. Part I. *Journal of the American Academy of Child and Adolescent Psychiatry, 35,* 1110–1119.

Biederman, J., Faraone, S.V., Keenan, K., Benjamin, J., Krifcher, B., Moore, C., Sprich-Buckminster, S., Ugaglia, K., Jellinek, M.S., Steingard, R., Spencer, T., Norman, D., Kolodny, R., Kraus, I., Perrin, J., Keller, M.B., & Tsuang, M.T. (1992). Further evidence for family-genetic risk factors in attention deficit hyperactivity disorder. *Archives of General Psychiatry, 49,* 728–738.

Biederman, J., Faraone, S.V., Keenan, K., Knee, D., & Tsuang, M.T. (1990). Family-genetic and psychosocial risk factors in DSM-III attention deficit disorder. *Journal of the American Academy of Child and Adolescent Psychiatry, 29,* 526–533.

Biederman, J., Faraone, S.V., Mick, E., Spencer, T., Wilens, T., Kiely, K., Guite, J., Ablon, J.S., Reed, E., & Warburton, R. (1995). High risk for attention deficit hyperactivity disorder among children of parents with childhood onset of the disorder: A pilot study. *American Journal of Psychiatry, 152,* 431–435.

Birmaher, B., Ryan, N.D., Williamson, D.E., Brent, D.A., & Kauffman, J. (1996). Childhood and adolescent depression: A review of the past 10 years. Part II. *Journal of the American Academy of Child and Adolescent Psychiatry, 35,* 1575–1583.

Birmaher, B., Ryan, N.D., Williamson, D.E., Brent, D.A., Kauffman, J., Dahl, R.E., Perel, J., & Nelson, B. (1996). Childhood and adolescent depression: A review of the past 10 years. Part I. *Journal of the American Academy of Child and Adolescent Psychiatry, 35,* 1427–1439.

Britton, T.C., Meyer, B.-U., & Benecke, R. (1991). Central motor pathways in patients with mirror movements. *Journal of Neurology, Neurosurgery, and Psychiatry, 54,* 505–510.

Brown, R.T., Coles, C.D., Smith, I.E., Platzman, K.A., Silverstein, J., Erickson, S., & Falek, A. (1991). Effects of prenatal alcohol exposure at school age: II. Attention and behavior. *Neurotoxicology and Teratology, 13,* 1–8.

Buehler, D.M., Als, H., Duffy, F.H., McAnulty, G.B., & Liederman, J. (1995). Effectiveness of individualized developmental care for low-risk preterm infants: Behavioral and electrophysiological evidence. *Pediatrics, 96,* 923–932.

Burgard, P., Rey, F., Rupp, A., Abadi, V., & Rey, J. (1997). Neuropsychologic functions of early treated patients with phenylketonuria, on and off diet: Results of a cross-national and cross-sectional study. *Pediatric Research, 41,* 368–374.

Chandola, C.A., Robling, M.R., Peters, T.J., Melville-Thomas, G., & McGuffin, P. (1992). Pre- and perinatal factors and the risk of subsequent referral for hyperactivity. *Journal of Child Psychology and Psychiatry, 33,* 1077–1090.

Church, R.P., Lewis, M.E.B., & Batshaw, M.L. (1997). Learning disabilities. In M.L. Batshaw (Ed.), *Children with disabilities* (4th ed., pp. 471–497). Baltimore: Paul H. Brookes Publishing Co.

Coles, C.D., Platzman, K.A., Raskind-Hood, C.L., Brown, R.T., Falek, A., & Smith, I.E. (1997). A comparison of children affected by prenatal alcohol exposure and attention deficit, hyperactivity disorder. *Alcoholism, Clinical & Experimental Research, 21,* 150–161.

Coles, C.D., Russell, C.L., & Schuetze, P. (1997). Maternal substance use: Epidemiology, treatment outcome, and developmental effects: An annotated bibliography. *Substance Use & Misuse, 32,* 149–168.

Commings, D.E. (1990). ADHD in Tourette syndrome. In *Tourette syndrome and human behavior* (pp. 99–104). Duarte, CA: Hope Press.

Daly, J.M., Biederman, J., Bostic, J.Q., Maraganore, A.M., Lelon, E., Jellinek, M., & Lapey, A. (1997). The relationship between childhood asthma and attention deficit hyperactivity disorder: A review of the literature. *Journal of Attention Disorders, 1,* 31–40.

Delaney-Black, V., Covington, C., Ostrea, E., Jr., Romero, A., Baker, D., Tagle, M.-T., Nordstrom-Klee, B., Sylvestre, M.A., Angelilli, M.-L., Hack, C., & Long, J. (1996). Prenatal cocaine and neonatal outcome: Evaluation of dose-response relationship. *Pediatrics, 98,* 735–740.

Dilts, C.V., Carey, J.C., Kircher, J.C., Hoffman, R.O., Creel, D., Ward, K., Clark, E., & Leonard, C.O. (1996). Children and adolescents with neurofibromatosis 1: A behavioral phenotype. *Developmental and Behavioral Pediatrics, 17,* 229–239.

Doran, S. (1997). Fragile X syndrome and attention deficit hyperactive disorder. *ADHD Report, 5,* 8–11.

Fog, E., & Fog, M. (1963). Cerebral inhibition examined by associated movements. In M. Bax & R. MacKeith (Eds.), *Minimal cerebral dysfunction* (pp. 52–57). London: Spastic International Medical Publications.

Foley, T.P. (1992). Thyrotoxicosis in childhood. *Pediatric Annals, 21,* 43–49.

Galler, J.R., & Ramsey, F. (1989). A follow-up study of the influence of early malnutrition on development: Behavior at home and school. *Journal of the American Academy of Child and Adolescent Psychiatry, 28,* 254–261.

Geller, B., & Luby, J. (1997). Child and adolescent bipolar disorder: A review of the last 10 years. *Journal of the American Academy of Child and Adolescent Psychiatry, 36,* 1168–1176.

Gickling, E.E., & Armstrong, D.L. (1978). Levels of instructional difficulty as related to on-task behavior, task completion, and comprehension. *Journal of Learning Disabilities, 11,* 32–39.

Glod, C.A., & Teicher, M.H. (1996). Relationship between early abuse, posttraumatic stress disorder, and activity levels in prepubertal children. *Journal of the American Academy of Child and Adolescent Psychiatry, 34,* 1384–1393.

Griffith, D.R., Azuma, S.D., & Chasnoff, I.J. (1994). Three-year outcome of children exposed prenatally to drugs. *Journal of the American Academy of Child and Adolescent Psychiatry, 33,* 20–27.

Gross-Tsur, V., Shalev, R.S., & Amir, N. (1991). Attention deficit disorder: Association with familial-genetic factors. *Pediatric Neurology, 7,* 258–261.

Handley-Derry, M., Low, J.A., Burke, S.O., Waurick, M., Killen, H., & Derrick, E.J. (1997). Intrapartum fetal asphyxia and the occurrence of minor deficits in 4- to 8-year-old children. *Developmental Medicine and Child Neurology, 39,* 508–514.

Hauser, P., Zametkin, A., Martinez, P., Vitello, B, Matochik, J.A., Mixson, A.J., & Weintraub, B.D. (1993). Attention-deficit hyperactivity disorder in people with generalized resistance to thyroid hormone. *New England Journal of Medicine, 328,* 997–1001.

Kahn, C.A., Kelly, P.C., & Walker, W.O., Jr. (1995). Lead screening in children with attention deficit hyperactivity disorder and developmental delay. *Clinical Pediatrics, 34,* 498–501.

Kaufman, P.M., Fletcher, J.M., Levin, H.S., Miner, M.E., & Ewing-Cobbs, L. (1993). Attentional disturbance after pediatric closed head injury. *Journal of Child Neurology, 8,* 348–353.

Klebanov, P.K., Brooks-Gunn, J., & McCormick, M.C. (1994). Classroom behavior of very low birth weight elementary school children. *Pediatrics, 94,* 700–708.

Landry, S.H., & Whitney, J.A. (1996). The impact of prenatal cocaine exposure: Studies of the developing infant. *Seminars in Perinatology, 20,* 99–106.

Milberger, S., Biederman, J., Faraone, S.V., Chen, L., & Jones, J. (1996). Is maternal smoking during pregnancy a risk factor for attention deficit hyperactivity disorder in children? *American Journal of Psychiatry, 153,* 1138–1142.

Parush, S., Sohmer, H., Steinberg, A., & Kaitz, M. (1997). Somatosensory functioning in children with attention deficit hyperactivity disorder. *Developmental Medicine and Child Neurology, 39,* 464–468.

Pietz, J., Fatkenheuer, B., Burgard, P., Armbruster, M., Esser, G., & Schmidt, H. (1997). Psychiatric disorders in adult patients with early-treated phenylketonuria. *Pediatrics, 99,* 345–350.

Pine, D.S., Scott, M.R., Busner, C., Davies, M., Fried, J.A., Parides, M., & Shaffer, D. (1996). Psychometrics of neurological soft signs. *Journal of the American Academy of Child and Adolescent Psychiatry, 35,* 509–515.

Roberts, J.E., Burchinal, M.R., Collier, A.M., Ramey, C.T., Koch, M.A., & Henderson, F.W. (1989). Otitis media in early childhood and cognitive, academic, and classroom performance of the school-aged child. *Pediatrics, 83,* 477–485.

Rostain, A.L., Power, T.J., & Atkins, M.S. (1993). Assessing parents' willingness to pursue treatment for children with attention-deficit hyperactivity disorder. *Journal of the American Academy of Child and Adolescent Psychiatry, 32,* 175–181.

Roth, N., Beyreiss, J., Schlenzka, K., & Beyer, H. (1991). Coincidence of attention deficit disorder and atopic disorders in children: Empirical findings and hypothetical background. *Journal of Abnormal Child Psychology, 19,* 1–13.

Schothorst, P.F., & Van Engeland, H. (1996). Long-term behavioral sequelae of prematurity. *Journal of the American Academy of Child and Adolescent Psychiatry, 35,* 175–183.

Smart, D., Sanson, A., & Prior, M. (1996). Connections between reading disability and behavior problems: Testing temporal and causal hypotheses. *Journal of Abnormal Child Psychology, 24,* 363–383.

Sprich-Buckminster, S., Biederman, J., Milberger, S., Faraone, S.V., & Lehman, B.K. (1993). Are perinatal complications relevant to the manifestation of ADD? Issues of comorbidity and familiality. *Journal of the American Academy of Child and Adolescent Psychiatry, 32,* 1032–1037.

Steinhausen, H.-C., Willms, J., & Spohr, H.-L. (1993). Long-term psychopathological and cognitive outcome of children with fetal alcohol syndrome. *Journal of the American Academy of Child and Adolescent Psychiatry, 32,* 990–994.

Swaiman, K.F. (1994). Intellectual and motor deterioration. In K.F. Swaiman (Ed.), *Pediatric neurology: Principles and practice* (2nd ed., pp. 147–157). Philadelphia: Mosby.

Tuthill, R.W. (1996). Hair lead levels related to children's classroom attention-deficit behavior. *Archives of Environmental Health, 51,* 214–220.

Weinberg, W.A., & Emslie, G.J. (1991). Attention deficit hyperactivity disorder: The differential diagnosis. *Journal of Child Neurology, 6S,* S23–S36.

Whitmont, S., & Clark, C. (1996). Kinaesthetic acuity and fine motor skills in children with attention deficit hyperactivity disorder: A preliminary report. *Developmental Medicine and Child Neurology, 38,* 1091–1098.

RESOURCES FOR CLINICIANS

Accardo, P.J., Blondis, T.A., Whitman, B.Y., & Stein, M. (Eds.). (in press). *Attention deficit disorders and hyperactivity in children and adults.* New York: Marcel Dekker.

American Academy of Pediatrics. (1996). *The classification of child and adolescent mental health diagnoses in primary care: Diagnostic and statistical manual for primary care (DSM-PC) child and adolescent version.* Elk Grove Village, IL: Author.

Barkley, R.A. (1998). *Attention-deficit hyperactivity disorder: A handbook for diagnosis and treatment* (2nd ed.). New York: Guilford Press.

Beitchman, J.H., & Young, A.R. (1997). Learning disorders: A review of the past 10 years. *Journal of the American Academy of Child and Adolescent Psychiatry, 36,* 1020–1032.

Brown, F.R., III, Voigt, R.G., & Elksnin, N. (1996). AD/HD: A neurodevelopmental perspective. *Contemporary Pediatrics, 13,* 25–44.

Capin, D.M. (1996). Developmental learning disorders: Clues to their diagnosis and management. *Pediatrics in Review, 17,* 284–290.

Church, R.P., Lewis, M.E.B., & Batshaw, M.L. (1997). Learning disabilities. In M.L. Batshaw (Ed.), *Children with disabilities* (4th ed., pp. 471–497). Baltimore: Paul H. Brookes Publishing Co.

Goldstein, S., & Goldstein, M. (1990). *Managing attention disorders in children.* New York: John Wiley & Sons.

Hinshaw, S.P., March, J.S., Abikoff, H., Arnold, L.E., Cantwell, D.P., Conners, C.K., Elliott, G.R., Halperin, J., Greenhill, L.L., Hechtman, L.T., Hoza, B., Jensen, P.S., Newcorn, J.H., McBurnett, K., Pelham, W.E., Richters, J.E., Severe, J.B., Schiller, E., Swanson, J., Vereen, D., Wells, K., & Wigal, T. (1997). Comprehensive assessment of childhood attention-deficit hyperactivity disorder in the context of a multisite, multimodal clinical trial. *Journal of Attention Disorders, 1,* 217–234.

Kandt, R.S. (1984). Neurologic examination of children with learning disorders. *Pediatric Clinics of North America, 31,* 297–315.

Shaywitz, B.A., & Shaywitz, S.E. (1994). Learning disabilities and attention disorders. In K.F. Swaiman (Ed.), *Pediatric neurology: Principles and practice* (2nd ed., pp. 1119–1151). Philadelphia: C.V. Mosby.

Silver, L.B. (1992). *Attention-deficit hyperactivity disorder: A clinical guide to diagnosis and treatment.* Washington, DC: American Psychiatric Press.

Swaiman, K.F. (Ed.). (1994). *Pediatric neurology: Principles and practice* (2nd ed.). Philadelphia: C.V. Mosby.

Weinberg, W.A., & Emslie, G.J. (1991). Attention deficit hyperactivity disorder: The differential diagnosis. *Journal of Child Neurology, 6S,* S23–S36.

Wolraich, M.L., & Baumgaertel, A. (1997). The practical aspects of diagnosing and managing children with attention deficit hyperactivity disorder. *Clinical Pediatrics, 36,* 497–504.

Parent Questionnaire for
School-Age Child Development Evaluations

PARENT QUESTIONNAIRE FOR SCHOOL-AGE CHILD DEVELOPMENT EVALUATIONS

Child's name _____ Date of birth _____

Name(s) of parent(s)_____ Telephone _____

Name(s)/age(s) of sibling(s)_____ Address _____

_____ _____

Is your child adopted?   N   Y   If yes, then answer what you know about the birth and family history and leave what you don't know blank.

Before Birth	No	Yes	If yes, then please explain.
Mother had fever or infection	___	___	_____
Mother had a medical condition	___	___	_____
Mother required medication	___	___	_____
Mother used alcohol or street drugs	___	___	_____
Mother smoked cigarettes	___	___	_____
Concerns about baby's growth or health?	___	___	_____

At Birth	No	Yes	If yes, then please explain.
Was baby born early or late?	___	___	_____
Forceps, vacuum, or C-section required?	___	___	_____
Baby's birth weight	___	___	_____
Baby had trouble in delivery room/nursery	___	___	_____
Baby required intensive care nursery	___	___	_____
Baby needed to stay longer than mother	___	___	_____

Infants and Toddlers	No	Yes	If yes, then please explain.
Baby had trouble sleeping	___	___	_____
Baby had trouble with feeding/formula	___	___	_____
Baby grew poorly	___	___	_____
Baby had trouble with keeping a schedule	___	___	_____
Baby had an unusual or recurrent illness	___	___	_____
Baby was slow to sit, crawl, or walk	___	___	_____
Baby was slow to gesture/communicate	___	___	_____
Baby was slow to use hands, fingers	___	___	_____
Concern about baby's health/development	___	___	_____
Baby's doctor had concerns	___	___	_____
A friend or relative had concerns	___	___	_____

The Clinician's Practical Guide to Attention-Deficit/Hyperactivity Disorder
by Marianne Mercugliano, Thomas J. Power, and Nathan J. Blum   ©1999 by Paul H. Brookes Publishing Co.

Development

Record the age when your child first:

Used two-word phrases _____

Spoke in sentences _____

Rode tricycle _____

Rode two-wheeler _____

Tied shoes _____

Toilet-trained—days _____

Toilet-trained—nights _____

Could identify all letters in the alphabet _____

Wrote first name _____

When did you first have concerns about your child? _____

What were they? _____

School History

	No	Yes
Did your child attend day care/nursery school before kindergarten?	____	____
If yes, any difficulties there?_____		
Has your child ever received special help or special education?	____	____
Has your child had an evaluation at school for current difficulties?	____	____
Has your child had an evaluation by another professional?	____	____
(If yes, then please obtain and attach copies of the reports.)		

Medical History

Has your child had:	No	Yes	If yes, then please explain.
Hospitalization?	____	____	_____
Unusual illness?	____	____	_____
Recurrent medical problem?	____	____	_____
Seizure?	____	____	_____
Episode of loss of consciousness?	____	____	_____
Hearing test? when? results?	____	____	_____
Vision test? when? results?	____	____	_____
Low iron or anemia or high lead level?	____	____	_____
Allergies? (if yes, to what?)	____	____	_____
Other reactions to food/medicine?	____	____	_____
Any other abnormal blood test?	____	____	_____
When was last blood test?	____	____	_____
Child on medications regularly/frequently?	____	____	_____

The Clinician's Practical Guide to Attention-Deficit/Hyperactivity Disorder
by Marianne Mercugliano, Thomas J. Power, and Nathan J. Blum   ©1999 by Paul H. Brookes Publishing Co.

Review of Symptoms	No	Yes, in past	Yes, currently
(Check)			
Frequent ear infections	_____	_____	_____
Frequent skin infections	_____	_____	_____
Respiratory/sinus infections	_____	_____	_____
Recurrent allergic symptoms	_____	_____	_____
Rashes	_____	_____	_____
Neurological problems	_____	_____	_____
Stomach or intestinal problems	_____	_____	_____
Kidney or bladder problems	_____	_____	_____
Bone, muscle, or joint problems	_____	_____	_____
Trouble with falling asleep	_____	_____	_____
Trouble with staying asleep	_____	_____	_____
Trouble with getting up in the morning	_____	_____	_____
Daytime sleepiness/napping	_____	_____	_____
Poor or picky appetite	_____	_____	_____
Staring spells	_____	_____	_____
Frequent headaches or stomachaches	_____	_____	_____
Tics/nervous habits	_____	_____	_____
Obsessions/compulsions	_____	_____	_____
Repetitive or unusual behaviors	_____	_____	_____
Refusal to comply with requests	_____	_____	_____
Forgets while trying to comply	_____	_____	_____
Sees or hears things that are not there	_____	_____	_____
Aggressive toward others	_____	_____	_____
Trouble with making/keeping friends	_____	_____	_____
Trouble with getting along with siblings	_____	_____	_____
Explosive temper	_____	_____	_____
Seems angry more than he/she should be	_____	_____	_____
Seems depressed	_____	_____	_____
Low self-esteem	_____	_____	_____
Has mentioned dying/suicide	_____	_____	_____
Anxious about school	_____	_____	_____
Anxious about family members	_____	_____	_____
Anxious about safety	_____	_____	_____
Anxious about many things	_____	_____	_____
Has specific fears or phobias	_____	_____	_____
Lacks remorse	_____	_____	_____
Cruel to animals/smaller children	_____	_____	_____
Sets fires/interested in fires	_____	_____	_____

The Clinician's Practical Guide to Attention-Deficit/Hyperactivity Disorder
by Marianne Mercugliano, Thomas J. Power, and Nathan J. Blum   ©1999 by Paul H. Brookes Publishing Co.

Think about each of your child's relatives in the categories below, and check whether any have experienced the items listed on the left.

Family History	Mother	Father	Brother(s)	Sister(s)
Attention deficit disorder	_____	_____	_____	_____
School problems—behavior	_____	_____	_____	_____
School problems—learning	_____	_____	_____	_____
Special education	_____	_____	_____	_____
Delinquency	_____	_____	_____	_____
Substance abuse	_____	_____	_____	_____
Depression	_____	_____	_____	_____
Bipolar disorder	_____	_____	_____	_____
Suicide	_____	_____	_____	_____
Anxiety disorder	_____	_____	_____	_____
Tics/repetitive habits	_____	_____	_____	_____
Obsession/compulsion	_____	_____	_____	_____
Schizophrenia	_____	_____	_____	_____
Thyroid problems	_____	_____	_____	_____
On medication for a mental health reason	_____	_____	_____	_____

Family History	Maternal grandparents	Paternal grandparents	Great aunts/uncles
Attention deficit disorder	_____	_____	_____
School problems—behavior	_____	_____	_____
School problems—learning	_____	_____	_____
Special education	_____	_____	_____
Delinquency	_____	_____	_____
Substance abuse	_____	_____	_____
Depression	_____	_____	_____
Bipolar disorder	_____	_____	_____
Suicide	_____	_____	_____
Anxiety disorder	_____	_____	_____
Tics/repetitive habits	_____	_____	_____
Obsession/compulsion	_____	_____	_____
Schizophrenia	_____	_____	_____
Thyroid problems	_____	_____	_____
On medication for a mental health reason	_____	_____	_____

The Clinician's Practical Guide to Attention-Deficit/Hyperactivity Disorder
by Marianne Mercugliano, Thomas J. Power, and Nathan J. Blum   ©1999 by Paul H. Brookes Publishing Co.

Family History	Maternal aunts/uncles	Paternal aunts/uncles	Maternal cousins	Paternal cousins
Attention deficit disorder	_____	_____	_____	_____
School problems—behavior	_____	_____	_____	_____
School problems—learning	_____	_____	_____	_____
Special education	_____	_____	_____	_____
Delinquency	_____	_____	_____	_____
Substance abuse	_____	_____	_____	_____
Depression	_____	_____	_____	_____
Bipolar disorder	_____	_____	_____	_____
Suicide	_____	_____	_____	_____
Anxiety disorder	_____	_____	_____	_____
Tics/repetitive habits	_____	_____	_____	_____
Obsession/compulsion	_____	_____	_____	_____
Schizophrenia	_____	_____	_____	_____
Thyroid problems	_____	_____	_____	_____
On medication for a mental health reason	_____	_____	_____	_____

The Clinician's Practical Guide to Attention-Deficit/Hyperactivity Disorder
by Marianne Mercugliano, Thomas J. Power, and Nathan J. Blum   ©1999 by Paul H. Brookes Publishing Co.

B

Assessment Summary

ASSESSMENT SUMMARY

Chief concerns _____

_____

_____

Current School Issues

School name/location _____
Grade/teacher/type of class _____
Academic concerns _____
Behavior concerns _____
Social concerns _____
Any special interventions currently? _____

_____

_____

Family Issues

Family members _____

_____

Marital discord _____
Parents' views of child's problems _____

_____

For what is child disciplined? _____
How? _____
By whom? _____
Sibling relationships _____
Issues in the daily routine _____

_____

_____

Treatment history/effectiveness _____

_____

_____

_____

The Clinician's Practical Guide to Attention-Deficit/Hyperactivity Disorder
by Marianne Mercugliano, Thomas J. Power, and Nathan J. Blum ©1999 by Paul H. Brookes Publishing Co.

Additional notes from parent _____

_____

_____

_____

_____

_____

_____

_____

_____

_____

_____

_____

Summary

ADHD (type) _____

Learning problems _____

Externalizing problems _____

Internalizing problems _____

Etiology _____

Other issues that are not diagnoses but that will affect treatment:

_____

_____

_____

_____

Further evaluation needed _____

_____

_____

Recommendations/plans _____

_____

_____

_____

_____

_____

Information Request Letters

Date _____

Dear _____:

Your student, _____, presented for evaluation with his/her parent(s)/
guardian(s) with the following concerns:

    1. _____

    2. _____

    3. _____

Your input is very important as part of a comprehensive evaluation. I/we would be grateful if
you could provide the following information:

1. Copies of any psychoeducational testing or individual or group standardized achievement
testing that thas been performed
2. A copy of the most recent report card and comments
3. Completion of the attached behavior rating scale
4. Completion of the attached academic screening questionnaire
5. A brief description of any special assistance/services that the student receives
6. Any other observations, comments, or concerns that you want to report

In addition, we request that this student be referred to the Instructional Support Team to develop
school-based strategies for the main concerns listed above. A report of the team's findings, plan,
and 3-month follow-up status of the intervention is requested. Thank you in advance for your
time and effort.

                        Sincerely,

                        _____

                        _____

                        _____

                        Telephone _____

                        Fax   _____

I agree with the above request and grant permission to personnel at _____
to release the requested documents and information to _____
at the above address/fax.

Legal guardian signature _____ Date _____

The Clinician's Practical Guide to Attention-Deficit/Hyperactivity Disorder
by Marianne Mercugliano, Thomas J. Power, and Nathan J. Blum   ©1999 by Paul H. Brookes Publishing Co.

Date _____

Dear _____:

Your student, _____, presented for evaluation with his/her parent(s)/ guardian(s) with the following concerns:

1. _____

2. _____

3. _____

Your input is very important as part of a comprehensive evaluation. I/we would be grateful if you could provide the following information:

1. Copies of any psychoeducational testing or individual or group standardized achievement testing that thas been performed

2. A copy of the most recent report card and comments

3. Completion of the attached behavior rating scale

4. Completion of the attached brief academic screening questionnaire as it applies to the subject(s) that you teach (please identify them)

5. A brief description of any special assistance/services that the student receives

6. Any other observations, comments, or concerns that you want to report

In addition, we request that this student be referred to the appropriate party to develop school-based strategies for the main concerns listed above. An outline of planned interventions and a 3-month progress report is requested. Thank you in advance for your time and effort.

Sincerely,

_____

_____

_____

Telephone _____

Fax _____

I agree with the above request and grant permission to personnel at _____ to release the requested documents and information to _____ at the above address/fax.

Legal guardian signature _____ Date _____

The Clinician's Practical Guide to Attention-Deficit/Hyperactivity Disorder
by Marianne Mercugliano, Thomas J. Power, and Nathan J. Blum ©1999 by Paul H. Brookes Publishing Co.

D

Physical Examination

PHYSICAL EXAMINATION

Height _____ % _____ Weight _____ % _____ HC _____ % _____
Pulse _____ Blood pressure _____

General   Normal   Not examined   Abnormal (explain)

head _____
eyes _____
ears _____
tympanic membranes _____
optic discs _____
adenopathy _____
thyroid gland _____
chest _____
heart _____
abdomen _____
liver/spleen _____
genitalia _____
spine _____
extremities _____
hands (palmar creases, nailbiting) _____

Interview

view of school—academics _____
view of school—peers _____
concerns at home _____
homework _____
siblings _____
observations about medications (if taking) _____
three wishes _____
eye contact/interaction _____
language _____
thought process _____
insight _____

The Clinician's Practical Guide to Attention-Deficit/Hyperactivity Disorder
by Marianne Mercugliano, Thomas J. Power, and Nathan J. Blum ©1999 by Paul H. Brookes Publishing Co.

Neurological Examination

cranial nerves

    II—vision, visual fields _____

    III, IV, VI—pupillary responses, extraocular movements _____

    V—bite _____

    VII—facial movements _____

    VIII—hearing _____

    IX, X—palate movement _____

    XI—neck strength _____

    XII—tongue movement/strength _____

motor bulk/tone/strength _____

deep tendon reflexes _____

pathological reflexes _____

cortical sensation (stereognosis/graphesthesia) _____

sensation _____

cerebellar (F-N, H-S, Romberg) _____

rapid finger opposition/sequential finger opposition _____

balance _____

gait (toe, heel, tandem, Fog) _____

Using Interviews and Rating Scales to Collect Behavioral Data

with Ricardo B. Eiraldi

Conducting a behavior assessment in clinical practice can be challenging because individuals who are inattentive and/or impulsive may not manifest problems during short visits in structured or unfamiliar settings, such as clinic offices. To understand the nature and function of inattentive and impulsive behavior, the clinician must acquire information about how an individual is performing in naturalistic, or real-life, settings. This chapter describes a variety of techniques that are useful when assessing behavior that is related to attention-deficit/hyperactivity disorder (ADHD) as it occurs in naturalistic contexts.

INTERVIEWS

Interviewing parents and children about family and school concerns is an extremely valuable source of information about problems that are related to ADHD. **Structured interviews** commonly are used to determine whether individuals meet criteria for one or more psychiatric disorders according to classification systems such as the *Diagnostic and Statistical Manual of Mental Disorders, Fourth Edition* (DSM-IV).[1] Structured interviews employ a **categorical approach to assessment:** Disorders are categorized as present or absent based on specific diagnostic criteria derived by a panel of experts after careful consideration of research literature. The format and the item content of structured interviews usually coincide very closely with diagnostic criteria that are delineated in psychiatric classification manuals, such as the DSM-IV.

The most widely used structured interviews for children and adolescents are the Diagnostic Interview for Children and Adolescents–Revised (DICA-R)[2] and the National Institute of Mental Health Diagnostic Interview Schedule for Children, Fourth Edition (DISC-IV).[3] Both of these interviews were revised extensively to reflect changes in diagnostic criteria that are delineated in the DSM-IV. The clinician can administer the module for ADHD and any combination of externalizing (disruptive behavior) and internalizing (anxiety and mood) disorders. For clinicians in primary care, it often is not feasible to administer an entire structured interview because these procedures can be time consuming. To reduce the time that is involved in interviewing, the clinician can administer the module for ADHD and use behavior rating scales to screen for other emotional and behavior problems. Separate child- and parent-report versions have been developed. Both instruments are available in computerized versions that greatly facilitate administration and scoring.

The *Diagnostic and Statistical Manual for Primary Care (DSM-PC) Child and Adolescent Version*[4] is a classification system that enables clinicians to characterize behavioral variants that range from mild to severe, thus enabling physicians in primary care to better evaluate the psychosocial factors that have an impact on youth (see Chapter 1). Although structured interview schedules that are based on the DSM-PC are not available, this manual can serve as an excellent guide to conducting an unstructured clinical interview with the parents and the child. Following is a list of advantages of structured interviews:

1. **Map directly to DSM-IV criteria:** Structured interviews are revised periodically to reflect revisions in the DSM diagnostic criteria.
2. **Provide naturalistic information:** The items provide information about how individuals function in real-life settings based on the reports of informants (self, parent).
3. **Do not require extensive training to administer:** Procedures for administering and scoring structured interviews are delineated clearly so that these instruments can be administered with a high level of integrity without extensive training of clinicians who use them.
4. **Facilitate reliable assessment:** The structured nature of the interview enables clinicians to use these instruments with a high level of reliability. Typically, the correspondence is very high between diagnoses that are derived from structured interviews by one clinician and those that are derived from listening to the interview via audiocassette recorder by another clinician.[5]
5. **Assess functional impairment:** Structured interviews that are based on DSM-IV criteria not only assess whether specific symptoms are present but also provide information about functional impairment across settings. Measuring functional impairment enables clinicians to determine the social impact of symptom clusters on the individual and his or her environment.
6. **Facilitate intervention planning:** Knowing that an individual meets criteria for a disorder often is useful in selecting interventions. For instance, the diagnosis of ADHD often signifies that the use of stimulant medication should be considered.
7. **Are readily available:** Until the 1990s, structured interviews were very difficult to acquire and were not available through publishing companies. Computerized versions that are updated for DSM-IV criteria are available.

Following is a list of limitations of structured interviews:

1. **Are time consuming:** Interview schedules can take as long as 90 minutes to complete, although modules can be administered separately.

2. **Fail to elicit information about family functioning:** Structured interviews are designed to acquire information about emotional and behavior problems and about the impact of these symptoms on an individual's functioning; however, clinicians usually need to ask additional questions to understand patterns of family interaction, methods of parental discipline, and psychosocial problems that may be affecting the family.

3. **Are verbally complex:** The length and the complexity of questions in child versions may not be appropriate for children who are younger than 10 years or for individuals who have developmental disabilities.

4. **May be insensitive to gender, age, and cultural differences:** Structured interviews, such as the DSM-IV, typically employ a unitary set of decision-making rules that may not be applicable equally to males and females from different cultural backgrounds across the life span.

5. **Lack research on psychometric properties:** Although structured interviews have been shown to yield consistent results over time and between interviewers, research regarding the correspondence of these measures with other methods of determining psychopathology still is needed.

6. **Are revised frequently:** To keep pace with the ever-evolving criteria in the diagnostic nomenclature, structured interviews are revised frequently, rendering previous versions obsolete.

7. **Lack utility in planning behavioral interventions:** Structured interviews provide limited information about environmental events that may trigger emotional and behavior problems and about consequences that may maintain maladaptive functioning. Without systemic information about the antecedents and consequences of behavior, it is difficult to design effective behavioral interventions.

RATING SCALES

In contrast to categorical methods, such as structured interviews, a **dimensional approach to assessment** using rating scales provides an analysis of emotional and/or behavior difficulties along a continuum from normal to abnormal, without clear delimitation of the presence or absence of disorder. Informants are asked to rate an individual's functioning in relation to specific behaviors on a scale generally consisting of three to five points (e.g., not at all, just a little, pretty much, very much). Statistical procedures are used to determine the relative standing of an individual in reference to others of similar age and gender.

Rating scales can be classified into those that assess a wide range of behaviors (e.g., disruptive or antisocial behavior, emotional problems, peer relationship problems) and those that evaluate a narrow range of problems. Also, rating scales can be subdivided according to informant: parent, teacher, self, and peer. Table 1 provides a summary of the characteristics of some wide-range and narrow-range measures that commonly are used in assessing children and adolescents for ADHD.

Wide-Range Rating Scales

Wide-range rating scales provide an assessment of many areas of emotional and behavioral functioning from the parents', the teacher's, and the youth's perspectives. The following is a description of some commonly used wide-range rating scales.

Table 1. Wide-range and narrow-range rating scales for children and adolescents

Measure	Informant	ADHD	External	Internal	Peer	Family
Child Behavior Checklist (CBCL)	Parent	X	X	X	X	
CBCL Teacher Report Form	Teacher	X	X	X	X	
CBCL Youth Self-Report Form	Self	X	X	X	X	
Devereux Scales (DSMD)	Parent	X	X	X		
	Teacher	X	X	X		
Behavior Assessment System for Children (BASC)	Parent	X	X	X	X	
	Teacher	X	X	X	X	
BASC Self-Report of Personality	Self	X	X	X	X	
ADHD Rating Scale-IV	Parent	X				
	Teacher	X				
Home Situations Questionnaire	Parent		X			
School Situations Questionnaire	Teacher		X			
Conners' Rating Scales	Parent	X	X	X		
	Teacher	X	X	X		
	Self	X	X	X		
ADD-H Comprehensive Teacher's Rating Scale (ACTeRS)	Parent	X	X		X	
	Teacher	X	X		X	
ADD Evaluation Scale (ADDES)	Parent	X				
	Teacher	X				
ADHD Symptom Checklist-4	Parent	X	X			
	Teacher	X	X			
AD/HD Diagnostic Teacher Rating Scale	Teacher	X	X	X		
Brown ADD Scales	Parent	X				
	Teacher	X				
	Self	X				
Multi-Dimensional Self-Concept Scale	Self			X		
Children's Manifest Anxiety Scale	Self			X		
Children's Depression Inventory	Self			X		
Social Skills Rating System	Parent				X	
	Teacher				X	
	Self				X	
Parenting Stress Index	Parent					X
Issues Checklist	Parent					X
	Self					X

Note: ADHD refers to measures of ADHD; External and Internal refer to measures of externalizing and internalizing problems, respectively; and Peer and Family refer to measures of peer relationships and family functioning, respectively.

Child Behavior Checklist

The most extensively used wide-range scales for children and adolescents are the Achenbach checklists. The Child Behavior Checklist (CBCL),[6] a parent-report scale, and the Teacher Report Form (TRF)[7] have been normed extensively on national samples of children. The CBCL is composed of 112 items that assess behavior problems and several additional items that assess social competence. The TRF was constructed in a similar manner to provide a teacher report of behavior problems and social competence. Both instruments were developed for use with children and adolescents ages 4–18 years. A helpful feature of the Achenbach scales is that they include open-ended questions for informants to describe concerns in their own words, which is especially useful for clinicians who will not be using other methods to collect information from a child's teachers. The CBCL and the TRF yield scores on two broad scales: **Externalizing** (disruptive, oppositional, and aggressive behavior) and **Internalizing** (anxiety, depression, and social withdrawal). In addition, the CBCL and the TRF provide scores on eight narrow subscales (Withdrawn, Somatic Problems, Anxious/Depressed, Social Problems, Thought Problems, Attention Problems, Delinquent Behavior, and Aggressive Behavior). Achenbach also developed a rating scale for adolescents: the Child Behavior Checklist–Youth Self-Report (CBCL-YSR).[8] The CBCL-YSR is very similar to the CBCL and the TRF in terms of item content and subscale structure. Given the structural similarities among the three versions of the CBCL, symptom comparison across raters is obtained easily. The cross-informant computer program[9] facilitates comparison across raters using any combination of the CBCL, the TRF, and the CBCL-YSR.

Behavior Assessment System for Children

The Behavior Assessment System for Children (BASC)[10] is composed of the Parent Rating Scales (PRS) and the Teacher Rating Scales (TRS) for three age groups (Preschool, 4–5 years; Child, 6–11 years; and Adolescent, 12–18 years). Also, a Self-Report of Personality has been developed for children (ages 6–11 years) and adolescents (ages 12–18 years). Each version yields information regarding emotional and behavior problems (e.g., aggression, conduct problems, anxiety, depression, learning problems) and adaptive functioning (e.g., social skills, study skills), in addition to broad-band indices of externalizing and internalizing problems. Unlike the CBCL and the Devereux Scales of Mental Disorders (DSMD)[11] (described in the next section), the BASC provides separate scales for attention problems and hyperactivity, which are useful in assessing DSM-IV subtypes. Because the PRS and the TRS have similar factor structure, comparison of subscale severity across informants is readily available. All three versions have scoring software.

Devereux Scales of Mental Disorders

The DSMD has broad-band scales and narrow-band scales that are similar to those of the CBCL and the BASC and provides separate subscales for anxiety and depression like the BASC. The DSMD has two versions, one that covers ages 5–12 years and another for youth ages 13–18 years. The DSMD uses the same form for parent and teacher, although separate norms for each informant are provided. Computer software is available to facilitate scoring.

Narrow-Range Measures of ADHD and Behavior Problems

Numerous **narrow-range rating scales** are available to assess attention deficits, hyperactivity-impulsivity, emotional and behavior problems that often coexist with ADHD, and family interaction problems that frequently are associated with ADHD (see Table 1).

ADHD Rating Scale-IV

The ADHD Rating Scale-IV[12] was developed to reflect symptoms of ADHD as described in the DSM-IV. Items on this scale were taken directly from the DSM-IV criteria;

however, wording was altered slightly for brevity and clarity. This 18-item scale has been designed for use with children ages 5–18 years as rated by parents and teachers. In addition, an older adolescent and adult self-report version of this measure has been created[13] (see Chapter 14). Respondents are asked to rate each item on a four-point scale (0 [never or rarely] to 3 [very often]) (see Appendix A at the end of this chapter). The ADHD Rating Scale-IV yields scores for both Inattention and Hyperactivity-Impulsivity. Considerable research has demonstrated the reliability and validity of these measures.[14] Normative data on the parent and teacher versions have been collected on a very large national sample that was stratified according to geographical region and ethnic grouping that closely correspond to 1990 census data. The Home and School Versions of this measure are provided in Appendix A. (For normative data and information about the psychometric properties of the ADHD Rating Scale-IV, see DuPaul, Power, Anastopoulos, & Reid, 1999.)

Home and School Situations Questionnaires

The Home Situations Questionnaire (HSQ) is a parent-report scale that assesses behavior problems across 16 home situations (e.g., when watching television, when asked to go to bed). The School Situations Questionnaire (SSQ) is a teacher-report scale that provides an assessment of the extensiveness and severity of behavior problems across 12 common school situations (e.g., during lectures, at lunch). For each situation, the informant is asked to indicate whether the child has a behavior problem and, if so, the severity of the problem. The reliability and the validity of these measures have been demonstrated.[15] Normative data for the HSQ are available for boys and girls separately across the age range of 4–11 years. Normative data for the SSQ are available for children ages 6–11 years.[16] These measures have been adapted for use with adolescents: A parent-report version, a self-report of home problems version, and a self-report of school problems version have been created.[17] The HSQ and the SSQ are very helpful in determining the pervasiveness and the severity of behavior problems at home and in school. Also, these measures can be very useful in delineating targets for behavioral intervention.

Other Measures of ADHD

Numerous norm-referenced measures are available to assess the symptoms of ADHD. Perhaps the most commonly used measures are the Conners' Rating Scales–Revised.[18] The Conners' Rating Scales–Revised, which have parent, teacher, and self-report versions, include a new DSM-IV Symptom Scale that maps directly to DSM-IV criteria for ADHD.

Another commonly used measure is the ADD-H: Comprehensive Teacher's Rating Scale (ACTeRS), which has an accompanying parent form.[19] The ACTeRS yields scores on four factors: attention, hyperactivity, social skills, and oppositional behavior. An extensively normed measure that is available in both parent and teacher forms is the Attention Deficit Disorders Evaluation Scale (ADDES).[20] The ADDES provides a separate assessment of inattention and hyperactivity-impulsivity.

The ADHD Symptom Checklist–4 (ADHD-SC4)[21] helps with the assessment of ADHD and **oppositional defiant disorder,** as defined by the DSM-IV. The inclusion of extensive normative data for children who are younger than 6 years makes this a useful tool for assessing preschool-age children with problems that are related to ADHD (see Chapter 12 for more information about assessing preschool-age children). Another new measure, the AD/HD Diagnostic Teacher Rating Scale (ADTRS),[22] has been normed extensively on teachers of children in kindergarten through grade 5. For assessing adolescents, the Brown Attention-Deficit Disorder Scales[23] are very useful. The Brown scales assess varying dimensions of attention-deficit disorder, including sustaining attention, sustaining effort, organizing work, managing affective interference, and utilizing working memory (see Chapter 13 for more information about assessing adolescents).

Narrow-Range Measures of Emotional Problems

Given that many individuals with problems that are related to ADHD often manifest internalizing difficulties, it is very useful to conduct an assessment of self-esteem, anxiety, and depression. Although parent-report measures have been shown to be more stable indicators of internalizing problems in children than self-report scales[24], the latter may provide additional and nonredundant information about self-esteem, anxiety, and depression.

Multi-Dimensional Self-Concept Scale

Unlike many measures that assess self-esteem as a global construct, the Multi-Dimensional Self-Concept Scale (MSCS)[25] evaluates children's judgments about specific dimensions of self-worth. This measure assesses children's and adolescents' impressions of their competence in six domains: Social, Competence, Affect, Academic, Family, and Physical. Each domain can be assessed independently by administering any of the 25-item scales. The MSCS, which is a well-normed measure with acceptable reliability and validity, has been developed for use with students in grades 5–12.

Revised Children's Manifest Anxiety Scale

A commonly used, well-designed, self-report measure of anxiety is the Revised Children's Manifest Anxiety Scale (RCMAS).[26] This 37-item scale was designed for use with children and adolescents ages 6–17 years. Respondents are asked to respond "yes" or "no" to each of the items. The RCMAS has been normed on a large sample and yields results for the following indices: Physiological Anxiety, Worry/Oversensitivity, Social Concerns/Concentration Problems, Lie Scale, and Total Anxiety. There is evidence that items that are related to Worry/Oversensitivity may be the most indicative of anxiety in children.[27]

Children's Depression Inventory

The most widely used self-report measure of depression in children is the Children's Depression Inventory (CDI).[28] The CDI, a 27-item questionnaire, has been normed extensively on children and adolescents ages 7–17 years. Respondents are asked to rate each item on a three-point scale. The CDI yields an overall index of depression as well as the following scores: Negative Mood, Interpersonal Problems, Ineffectiveness, Anhedonia, and Negative Self-Esteem. Research suggests that items pertaining to Anhedonia may be most related to depression in children.[29]

Beck Depression Inventory-II

The most commonly used measure of depression in older adolescents and adults, the Beck Depression Inventory (BDI), has been updated to reflect features of depression as described in the DSM-IV.[30] The revised BDI (BDI-II) contains norms that extend from age 13 years through adulthood. The psychometric properties of the BDI-II, like its predecessor, are quite favorable. The BDI-II not only is helpful in assessing depression in older adolescents and adults with ADHD-related problems but also may be useful in determining the emotional status of parents of children with ADHD. Given that parental depression has been linked with a bias to rate children as having more behavior problems on behavior rating scales,[31] knowledge of parents' emotional status may be useful to clinicians in interpreting the results of parent-report measures.

Narrow-Range Measures of Peer Relationships

A child's ability to relate to peers can be assessed using parent-, teacher-, peer-, and self-report measures. The following measures are useful for assessing peer relationships.

Social Skills Rating Scale

A well-constructed and widely used measure of peer relationships, the Social Skills Rating Scale (SSRS)[32] assesses social functioning from the perspective of parents, teachers, and children. Separate versions have been developed for use with preschool-age children, school-age children, and adolescents. The SSRS measures peer relationships along five dimensions: Cooperation, Assertiveness, Self-Control, Empathy, and Responsibility.

Peer Ratings

When possible, an assessment of social functioning should include information from peers because peers have been shown to provide information that is different from that provided by parents and teachers.[33] One potentially useful procedure, described by Asher and Dodge (1986), is to ask each child to rate on a five-point scale how much they like to play with each peer in class (1 = "I don't like to"; 5 = "I like to a lot"). Although clinicians may have trouble with collecting these data directly, it may be possible for a school counselor to acquire this information with parental permission.

Narrow-Range Measures of Family Problems

Most individuals with ADHD experience significant problems with family interaction. People with ADHD often engage in behavior patterns that lead to elevated levels of family stress; they, in turn, are highly vulnerable to the effects of family relationship problems. Significant family problems are a major contributing factor to the emergence of comorbid emotional and behavior problems in individuals who are inattentive and impulsive[34]; thus, assessing family interaction problems is an important element of an evaluation of ADHD. The following subsections describe a sample of available family relationship measures.

Parenting Stress Index

The Parenting Stress Index (PSI)[35] is a commonly used measure that assesses the severity and the sources of parenting stress. This 101-item parent-report scale measures stress in two domains: The Child Domain reflects stress that is related to child characteristics, such as hyperactivity, being demanding, and moodiness; the Parent Domain reflects stress that is related to parent variables, such as depression, marital difficulties, and health problems. The PSI also has an optional 19-item Life Stress scale that assesses the level of stress outside the parent–child relationship that may affect the family (e.g., divorce, pregnancy, alcohol problem). The PSI has been used extensively in clinical practice and research and has been shown to have adequate psychometric properties. A brief version of this scale,[36] consisting of 36 items, also exists.

Issues Checklist

The Issues Checklist (IC)[37] is a method for assessing the locus and the extent of conflict between parents and adolescents. Parents and adolescents each respond to the same set of 44 issues that often lead to parent–adolescent conflict (e.g., doing homework, using the telephone, playing stereo or radio too loudly). The respondent indicates whether each subject has been discussed over the past 4 weeks and the anger intensity associated with each situation. The IC yields primarily three indices: the Number of conflictive issues; Anger Intensity, computed as the mean of the endorsed items; and Weighted Anger Intensity, computed as the product of the Number of conflictive issues and the Anger Intensity. Test-retest reliability of the IC is acceptable for mothers, although low for adolescents and fathers.[38] This checklist can be very useful clinically in identifying issues of conflict between parents and adolescents.

Dyadic Adjustment Scale

The Dyadic Adjustment Scale (DAS)[39] is a commonly used measure of marital satisfaction. An advantage of this scale, as compared with other measures of its kind, is the lack of items that may be viewed as intrusive or uncomfortable to complete. This scale assesses four factors: Dyadic Consensus, Dyadic Cohesion, Dyadic Satisfaction, and Affectional Expression. Psychometric properties of this measure are promising. Although extensive normative data are lacking, useful guidelines for interpretation of scores are available.[40]

Interpreting Rating Scales

Clinicians typically experience many challenges in interpreting ratings. The following subsections outline some guidelines for addressing some of the most common issues in interpretation.

Selecting Cutoff Scores

The selection of cutoff scores on rating scales depends on the purpose of the assessment. If an assessment is being conducted primarily for the purpose of screening, then it is important to select a cutoff score that will maximize the detection of true positives. A cutoff score at the 80th percentile on rating scales that measure inattention and hyperactivity-impulsivity often is useful for screening.[41] If rating scales are being used for the purpose of diagnostic assessment, then it is more important to minimize the rate of false positives—that is, the proportion of individuals who fall at or above the cutoff point and who do not have a disorder. A cutoff score at or above the 93rd, 95th, or 98th percentile often is useful for diagnostic purposes.

Choosing an appropriate cutoff score also depends on the extent to which multiple informants are being used to make a determination about diagnostic status. Although it is not recommended that diagnostic decisions be based on information that is derived from a single informant, a stringent cutoff score (e.g., 95th or 98th percentile) usually is indicated in cases in which data from multiple informants are not available. When data are available from two or more informants from different settings (e.g., a parent and a teacher), diagnostic accuracy is optimum at somewhat lower cutoff scores (e.g., 85th or 90th percentile) on each measure.[42] Requiring scores from all informants to be greater than or equal to the 93rd, 95th, or 98th percentile will result in a failure to diagnose many children who have ADHD.

Resolving Differences Between Informants

Informants frequently differ in their ratings of a child's emotional and behavior problems. For instance, parents and teachers often differ in their ratings of ADHD symptoms,[43] as do mothers and fathers.[44] Differences between parent and teacher ratings can

arise because of discrepancies in the child's behavior in the home versus the school setting or differences in informants' perceptions of normal versus deviant behavior. When
a parent and a teacher differ markedly in their ratings, one strategy is to obtain ratings
from the other parent and from different teachers to determine whether there is a similar perception of the child in one setting versus the other. For instance, if all three of a
child's teachers view the child as being very hyperactive but both parents rate the child
as relatively calm, then it is reasonable to hypothesize that the discrepancy is due to
differences in the match between child characteristics and contextual demands. An alternative hypothesis is that both parents are reluctant to rate their child's active behavior as abnormal. It is quite common for teachers to differ among themselves or for a
mother and a father to differ with regard to ratings of ADHD symptoms; these variations may be due to differences in the way in which a child behaves with each adult or
to differences in the informants' criteria for evaluating normal behavior. In these cases,
a useful procedure is to include both parents in the interview and to have a brief discussion with one or more teachers by telephone. An interview often is very helpful in
determining the criteria that informants use to make determinations about the severity
of a child's symptoms.

According to the DSM-IV, the child needs to demonstrate a significant level of
functional impairment in two or more major life settings to be given a diagnosis of
ADHD. Although this criterion often is interpreted as meaning that the child must display functional impairment both at home and in school, the DSM-IV does not state that
impairment in the home and the school is needed for a diagnosis.[45] It is possible for the
child to meet DSM-IV criteria for ADHD by demonstrating functional impairment in
both academic and social settings in school in cases in which there is no significant impairment at home. In situations in which teachers view the child as significantly inattentive and/or hyperactive but parents do not, it is particularly important to acquire
information about the child in multiple situations in the school environment. Also, clinicians should consider the possibility that learning problems are contributing to the
symptoms of ADHD. Similarly, when parents report a significant level of symptomatology but teachers do not, it is critical to establish functional impairment in two or
more settings outside the school. At the same time, it is important to consider the possibility that problems that are related to family stressors or parenting skills may be contributing to the ADHD-like behaviors.

Interpreting Rating Scales in Children with Developmental Disabilities

Clinicians sometimes are asked to evaluate whether a child with a developmental delay or mental retardation meets criteria for ADHD. Although experts commonly recommend that rating scales for a child with a developmental delay be evaluated in relation to peers of similar mental age, the one study that was conducted in this area did
not support the practice of using rating scales in this manner. The study suggested that
using chronological age–based norms is a more accurate procedure than using norms
that are based on developmental age.[46] Although more research is needed, it is recommended that clinicians interview parents carefully to determine their understanding of
the child's disability and the extent to which the parents accounted for the child's
developmental delay in completing the ratings. In cases in which it is clear that the
parents have factored the child's developmental problems into their ratings of
the child's behavior, the use of chronological age–based norms generally is more appropriate; however, in situations in which the parents have not accounted for the

child's disability in completing the scale, the use of developmental age–based norms may be more accurate.

Interpreting rating scales that have been completed by special education teachers also is complicated because it may not be clear whether the teacher has evaluated the child in relation to the general population of children of similar chronological age or has compared the child with peers with developmental problems. It often is useful to collect rating scale data from a teacher who is instructing the child in a general education classroom, if possible. Also, the clinician should strive to confer with the special education teacher to better understand the child's classroom behavior and the perspective being used by the teacher to evaluate the child.

Following is a list of advantages of rating scales:

1. **Are easy to use:** Rating scales are easy to administer, score, and interpret. In addition, computer software is available to facilitate the scoring and interpretation of many of these checklists. The wide-range measures can be scored in about 10 minutes, and the narrow-range scales generally can be scored in less than 5 minutes.
2. **Use multiple informants:** Many rating scales have been developed for use by different informants, including parents, teachers, and self, which permits the required assessment of situational variability.
3. **Are ecologically valid:** Rating scales typically are completed by respondents who are familiar with the functioning of a child, adolescent, or adult in real-life settings. In contrast, office-based measures, such as vigilance tasks, may not be indicative of how a person responds in a naturalistic context.[47]
4. **Are norm referenced:** Many rating scales have been normed for males and females of differing age levels. In some cases, the measures have been standardized on large, normative samples and stratified by geographical region and ethnic grouping (e.g., CBCL, ADHD Rating Scale-IV). Norm referencing permits a determination of the severity of a problem relative to peers of similar age and gender.
5. **Are psychometrically sound:** The leading rating scales, particularly the wide-range measures, yield scores that are relatively stable over time, and most instruments are internally consistent.
6. **Are useful for progress monitoring:** Rating scales can be administered repeatedly to assess changes in functioning in response to intervention.

Following is a list of limitations of rating scales:

1. **Are vulnerable to rater bias:** Ratings often vary greatly depending on the respondent who is completing the scale. For instance, it is not uncommon for one teacher to rate a child very differently from another teacher. Although differences among informants may indicate to some extent variations in behavior across settings, there is considerable evidence that raters differ in their standards for determining when a problem exists and how severe the problem is.[48] In addition, respondents have been shown to exhibit a bias to rate children as hyperactive when they exhibit tendencies to behave in an oppositional manner.[49] Furthermore, maternal depression has been linked to a bias for the mother to rate her child high on externalizing and internalizing problems.[50]
2. **Are limited in diagnostic prediction:** Rating scales are useful for determining the severity of problems that are related to a particular dimension, but it often is difficult to use these measures for diagnostic assessment. Research is being conducted

to determine optimum cutoff scores on rating scales for determining the presence or absence of a disorder,[51] but this information generally is not readily available in rating scale manuals.

3. **Have limited utility in behavioral treatment planning:** Rating scales are useful for identifying the nature and the severity of emotional and behavior problems, but they typically do not provide detailed contextual information, including data about the antecedents and consequences of behavior. Collecting information about events that precede and follow behavior problems can be very helpful in treatment planning. Applied behavior analysis techniques, including interview and direct observation procedures, serve as a helpful complement to rating scales by elucidating possible explanations for behavior problems and leading to suggestions for behavioral intervention.[52]

4. **Have questionable sensitivity to cultural differences:** Many rating scales—and structured interview procedures, for that matter—have been developed with little regard for how constructs, such as hyperactivity, and the language that is used to describe these entities may vary as a function of cultural and ethnic differences. Also, samples from which normative data are derived often are not described in sufficient detail to determine whether a rating scale is appropriate for use with individuals from a particular ethnic or socioeconomic background.[53] Without this information, it is possible that clinicians may use rating scales in a manner that is culturally biased. Until more research is available to guide practice on this issue, clinicians need to be careful about using rating scales to make diagnostic decisions about children who are from ethnic minority groups, particularly those from lower socioeconomic circumstances. In these cases, an interview with the teacher by telephone and a comprehensive interview with the parents are especially important.

DIRECT OBSERVATION TECHNIQUES

Another approach to behavior assessment that often is used by psychologists and educators is to conduct a direct, systematic observation of behavior. Observation procedures are particularly helpful in assessing children in school. Generally, it is useful to observe children on different days and in several settings, including multiple classrooms and the playground, to obtain a comprehensive understanding of a child's difficulties. Also, observations can be conducted on peers for the purpose of normative comparison. Behavior observations afford data about the nature and the severity of a child's problems and can provide information about situations or consequences that aggravate or ameliorate academic and behavior problems.[54] Coding systems that enable clinicians to conduct observations in a reliable and valid manner have been developed.[55]

Although behavior observations are extremely valuable, they are time consuming and often impractical for clinicians to use. Other problems include a lack of representative norms and the effect on a student's behavior of being aware of the observation. Structured or unstructured interviews and behavior rating scales generally are much more feasible for primary care clinicians to use.

CONCLUSION

Primary care providers who want to conduct an evaluation of ADHD symptoms should begin with interviewing the parents and the child and collecting rating scale data. It is advisable to obtain rating scale information from parents and teachers. Wide-range rating scales can be very useful in addition to ADHD-focused rating scales, although they require more time to score. For older children, a wide-range self-report scale also is useful. If this information suggests that problems are related primarily to inattention and/or hyperactivity-impulsivity, if the child meets DSM-IV criteria for ADHD, and if the medical and educational evaluations do not suggest other explanations for the symptoms (see Chapters 1 and 3), then the primary care provider may be in a position to make the diagnosis of ADHD without further consultation. If the interview and the rating scale data suggest significant problems with academic skills, peer functioning, family interaction, or emotional functioning, then a more comprehensive evaluation will be needed. The primary care provider who is skillful in evaluating children with ADHD may then utilize additional rating scales and interview procedures to assess the situation further. Alternatively, the clinician may want to refer the family to a community-based mental health provider or a specialized program that can provide a more comprehensive evaluation.

Ideally, specialists or special programs should strive for the following goals when conducting evaluations:

1. **Include categorical and dimensional measures:** Structured interviews and rating scales have advantages and disadvantages; the combination of both methods appears to be more effective than using either method alone. Indeed, studies of individuals with ADHD have shown that structured interviews and rating scales are complementary and yield valuable information for clinical decision making when used together.[56]

2. **Use multiple informants:** Given that behavior tends to be situation specific, it is important to acquire information about how an individual is functioning in diverse settings. Teachers are an excellent source of information about school behavior, and parents are needed to provide background about home functioning. Individuals who are of preadolescent age and older also can be helpful in providing information about their functioning in various settings.

3. **Assess multiple domains:** Because individuals who are inattentive and/or impulsive often have comorbid externalizing and internalizing difficulties as well as peer and family relationship problems, the evaluation of ADHD symptoms should assess multiple domains of psychosocial functioning. Although wide-range measures provide an assessment of many areas of behavioral and emotional functioning, they frequently need to be supplemented with narrow-range instruments and/or structured interviews.

4. **Select developmentally appropriate measures:** Clinicians need to select measures that contain developmentally appropriate language and that have been normed and validated on a sample of individuals of similar age and developmental level to the referred individual. For instance, many instruments that have been developed for use with school-age children are not appropriate for use with preschool-age children or adults.

5. **Strive to conduct assessment in a culturally sensitive manner:** Clinicians should collect assessment data and interpret this information in a manner that is sensitive to the ethnic and cultural background of the referred individual and his or her family.

ENDNOTES

1. American Psychiatric Association (1994).
2. Reich, Leacock, & Shanfeld (1995).
3. Shaffer & Fisher (1996).
4. American Academy of Pediatrics (1996).
5. Chen, Faraone, Biederman, & Tsuang (1994), Eiraldi, Power, & Nezu (1997).
6. Achenbach (1991a).
7. Achenbach (1991b).
8. Achenbach (1991c).
9. Achenbach (1991d).
10. Reynolds & Kamphaus (1992).
11. Naglieri, LeBuffe, & Pfeiffer (1994).
12. DuPaul, Power, Anastopoulos, & Reid (1999).
13. Murphy & Barkley (1996).
14. DuPaul, Anastopoulos, et al. (1998), DuPaul et al. (1997), DuPaul, Power, McGoey, Ikeda, & Anastopoulos (1998).
15. Altepeter & Breen (1989), Breen & Altepeter (1991).
16. See Barkley (1991).
17. Adams, McCarthy, & Kelley (1995).
18. Conners (1997).
19. Ullman, Sleator, Sprague, & MetriTech Staff (1996).
20. McCarney (1996).
21. Gadow (1997).
22. Wolraich, Feurer, Hannah, Baumgaertel, & Pinnock (in press).
23. Brown (1996).
24. Beidel, Fink, & Turner (1996).
25. Bracken (1991).
26. Reynolds & Richmond (1985).
27. Laurent, Landau, & Stark (1993).
28. Kovacs (1992).
29. Laurent et al. (1993).
30. Beck, Steer, & Brown (1996).
31. Kolko & Kazdin (1993).
32. Gresham & Elliott (1990).
33. Achenbach, McConaughy, & Howell (1987).
34. Barkley (1998), Patterson, Reid, & Dishion (1992).
35. Abidin (1995).
36. Ibid.
37. Robin & Foster (1989).
38. See Robin & Foster (1989).
39. Spanier (1976).
40. Ibid.
41. Power et al. (1998).
42. Ibid.
43. Szatmari, Offord, & Boyle (1989).
44. Achenbach (1991b).
45. Power & DuPaul (1996).
46. Pearson & Aman (1994).
47. Barkley (1991).
48. Reid & Maag (1994).
49. Abikoff, Courtney, Pelham, & Koplewicz (1993).
50. Kolko & Kazdin (1993).
51. Chen et al. (1994), Power et al. (1998).
52. Dunlap et al. (1993).
53. Reid (1995).
54. Dunlap et al. (1993).
55. See Shapiro (1996).
56. Biederman et al. (1995), Eiraldi et al. (1997).

REFERENCES

Abidin, R.R. (1995). *Manual for Parenting Stress Index* (3rd ed.). Odessa, FL: Psychological Assessment Resources, Inc.

Abikoff, H., Courtney, M., Pelham, W.E., Jr., & Koplewicz, H.S. (1993). Teachers' ratings of disruptive behaviors: The influence of halo effects. *Journal of Abnormal Child Psychology, 21*(5), 519–533.

Achenbach, T.M. (1991a). *Manual for the Child Behavior Checklist/4–18 and 1991 Profile.* Burlington: University of Vermont, Department of Psychiatry.

Achenbach, T.M. (1991b). *Manual for the Teacher's Report Form and 1991 Profile.* Burlington: University of Vermont, Department of Psychiatry.

Achenbach, T.M. (1991c). *Manual for the Youth Self-Report and 1991 Profile.* Burlington: University of Vermont, Department of Psychiatry.

Achenbach, T.M. (1991d). *Integrative guide for the 1991 CBCL/4–18, YSR, and TRF profiles.* Burlington: University of Vermont, Department of Psychiatry.

Achenbach, T.M., McConaughy, S.H., & Howell, C.T. (1987). Child/adolescent behavioral and emotional problems: Implications of cross-informant correlations for situational specificity. *Psychological Bulletin, 101,* 213–232.

Adams, C.D., McCarthy, M., & Kelley, M.L. (1995). Adolescent versions of the Home and School Situations Questionnaires: Initial psychometric properties. *Journal of Clinical Child Psychology, 24*(4), 377–385.

Altepeter, T.S., & Breen, M.J. (1989). Situational variation in problem behavior at home and school in attention deficit disorder with hyperactivity: A factor analytic study. *Journal of Child Psychology and Psychiatry, 33*(4), 741–748.

American Academy of Pediatrics. (1996). *Diagnostic and statistical manual for primary care (DSM-PC) child and adolescent version.* Elk Grove Village, IL: Author.

American Psychiatric Association. (1994). *Diagnostic and statistical manual of mental disorders* (4th ed.). Washington, DC: Author.

Asher, S.R., & Dodge, K.A. (1986). Identifying children who are rejected by their peers. *Developmental Psychology, 22,* 444–449.

Barkley, R.A. (1991). *Attention-deficit hyperactivity disorder: A clinical workbook.* New York: Guilford Press.

Barkley, R.A. (1998). *Attention-deficit hyperactivity disorder: A handbook for diagnosis and treatment* (2nd ed.). New York: Guilford Press.

Beck, A.T., Steer, R.A., & Brown, G.K. (1996). *Manual for the Beck Depression Inventory II.* San Antonio, TX: The Psychological Corporation.

Beidel, D.C., Fink, C.M., & Turner, S.M. (1996). Stability of anxious symptomatology in children. *Journal of Abnormal Child Psychology, 24*(3), 257–269.

Biederman, J., Wosniak, J., Kiely, K., Ablon, J.S., Faraone, S., Mick, E., Mundy, E., & Kraus, I. (1995). CBCL clinical scales discriminate prepubertal children with structured interview-derived diagnosis of mania from those with ADHD. *Journal of the American Academy of Child and Adolescent Psychiatry, 34*(4), 464–471.

Bracken, B.A. (1991). *Manual for the Multidimensional Self-Concept Scale.* San Antonio, TX: The Psychological Corporation.

Breen, M.J., & Altepeter, T.S. (1991). Factor structures of the Home Situations Questionnaire and the School Situations Questionnaire. *Journal of Pediatric Psychology, 16*(1), 59–67.

Brown, T. (1996). *Manual for the Brown Attention-Deficit Disorder Scales.* San Antonio, TX: The Psychological Corporation.

Chen, W.J., Faraone, S.V., Biederman, J., & Tsuang, M.T. (1994). Diagnostic accuracy of the Child Behavior Checklist scales for attention-deficit hyperactivity disorder: A receiver-operating characteristic analysis. *Journal of Consulting and Clinical Psychology, 62*(5), 1017–1025.

Conners, C.K. (1997). *Manual for the Conners' Rating Scales–Revised.* North Tonawanda, NY: Multi-Health Systems.

Dunlap, G., Kern, L., dePerczel, M., Clarke, S., Wilson, D., Childs, K.E., White, R., & Falk, G.D. (1993). Functional analysis of classroom variables for students with emotional and behavioral disorders. *Behavioral Disorders, 18*(4), 275–291.

DuPaul, G.J., Anastopoulos, A.D., Power, T.J., Reid, R., McGoey, K.E., & Ikeda, M.J. (1998). Parent ratings of ADHD symptoms: Factor structure, normative data, and psychometric properties. *Journal of Psychopathology and Behavioral Assessment, 20,* 83–102.

DuPaul, G.J., Power, T.J., Anastopoulos, A.D., & Reid, R. (1999). *The ADHD Rating Scale-IV manual*. New York: Guilford Press.

DuPaul, G.J., Power, T.J., Anastopoulos, A.D., Reid, R., McGoey, K.E., & Ikeda, M.J. (1997). Teacher ratings of ADHD symptoms: Factor structure, normative data, and psychometric properties. *Psychological Assessment, 9*, 436–444.

DuPaul, G.J., Power, T.J., McGoey, K.E., Ikeda, M.J., & Anastopoulos, A.D. (1998). Reliability and validity of parent and teacher ratings of attention-deficit/hyperactivity disorder symptoms. *Journal of Psychoeducational Assessment, 16*, 55–68.

Eiraldi, R.B., Power, T.J., & Nezu, C.M. (1997). Patterns of comorbidity associated with subtypes of attention-deficit/hyperactivity disorder among 6- to 12-year-old children. *Journal of the American Academy of Child and Adolescent Psychiatry, 36*(4), 503–514.

Gadow, K. (1997). *Manual for the ADHD Symptom Checklist-4*. Stony Brook, NY: Checkmate Plus.

Gresham, F.M., & Elliott, S.N. (1990). *Manual for the Social Skills Rating System, Parent, Teacher, Self-Report Forms*. Circle Pines, MN: American Guidance Service.

Kolko, D.J., & Kazdin, A.E. (1993). Emotional/behavioral problems in clinic and nonclinic children: Correspondence among child, parent and teacher reports. *Journal of Child Psychology and Psychiatry and Allied Disciplines, 34*(6), 991–1006.

Kovacs, M. (1992). *Manual for the Children's Depression Inventory*. North Tonawanda, NY: Multi-Health Systems.

Laurent, J., Landau, S., & Stark, K.D. (1993). Conditional probabilities in the diagnosis of depressive and anxiety disorders in children. *School Psychology Review, 22*, 98–114.

McCarney, S.B. (1996). *Manual for the Attention Deficit Disorders Evaluation Scale (ADDES): School and home version rating forms*. Columbia, MO: Hawthorne Educational Services.

Murphy, K., & Barkley, R.A. (1996). Prevalence of DSM-IV symptoms of ADHD in adult licensed drivers: Implications for clinical diagnosis. *Journal of Attention Disorders, 1*, 147–161.

Naglieri, J.A., LeBuffe, P.A., & Pfeiffer, S.I. (1994). *Manual for the Devereux Scales of Mental Disorders*. San Antonio, TX: The Psychological Corporation.

Patterson, G.R., Reid, J.B., & Dishion, T.J. (1992). *Antisocial boys*. Eugene, OR: Castalia Press.

Pearson, D.A., & Aman, M.G. (1994). Ratings of hyperactivity and developmental indices: Should clinicians correct for developmental level? *Journal of Autism and Developmental Disorders, 24*, 395–411.

Power, T.J., Doherty, B.J., Panichelli-Mindel, S.M., Karustis, J.L., Eiraldi, R.B., Anastopoulos, A.D., & DuPaul, G.J. (1998). The predictive validity of ADHD symptoms. *Journal of Psychopathology and Behavioral Assessment, 20*, 57–81.

Power, T.J., & DuPaul, G.J. (1996). Attention-deficit hyperactivity disorder: The reemergence of subtypes. *School Psychology Review, 25*, 284–296.

Reich, W., Leacock, N., & Shanfeld, K. (1995). *Diagnostic Interview for Children and Adolescents: Parent version*. St. Louis, MO: Washington University, Division of Child Psychiatry.

Reid, R. (1995). Assessment of ADHD with culturally different groups: The use of behavior rating scales. *School Psychology Review, 24*, 537–560.

Reid, R., & Maag, J.W. (1994). How many fidgets in a pretty much: A critique of behavior rating scales for identifying students with ADHD. *Journal of School Psychology, 32*, 339–354.

Reynolds, C.R., & Kamphaus, R.W. (1992). *Manual for the Behavior Assessment System for Children*. Circle Pines, MN: American Guidance Service.

Reynolds, C.R., & Richmond, B.O. (1985). *Manual for the Revised Children's Manifest Anxiety Scales, What I Think and Feel*. Los Angeles: Western Psychological Services.

Robin, A.L., & Foster, S.L. (1989). *Negotiating parent–adolescent conflict: A behavioral–family systems approach*. New York: Guilford Press.

Shaffer, D., & Fisher, P. (1996). *NIMH Diagnostic Interview Schedule for Children*. New York: New York State Psychiatric Institute.

Shapiro, E.S. (1996). *Academic skills problems: Direct assessment and intervention* (2nd ed.). New York: Guilford Press.

Spanier, G.B. (1976). Measuring dyadic adjustment: New scales for assessing the quality of marriage and similar dyads. *Journal of Marriage and Family, 38*(1), 15–28.

Szatmari, P., Offord, D.R., & Boyle, M.H. (1989). Ontario child health study: Prevalence of attention deficit disorder with hyperactivity. *Journal of Child Psychology and Psychiatry, 30*, 219–230.

Ullman, R., Sleator, S., Sprague, R., & MetriTech Staff. (1996). *Manual for the Comprehensive Teacher's Rating Scale: Parent form*. Champaign, IL: MetriTech.

Wolraich, M.L., Feurer, I.D., Hannah, J.N., Baumgaertel, A., & Pinnock, T.Y. (in press). Obtaining systematic teacher report of disruptive behavior disorders utilizing DSM-IV. *Journal of Abnormal Child Psychology*.

SUGGESTED READINGS

Barkley, R.A. (1998). *Attention-deficit hyperactivity disorder: A handbook for diagnosis and treatment* (2nd ed.). New York: Guilford Press.
DuPaul, J.G., & Stoner, G. (1994). *ADHD in the schools: Assessment and intervention strategies.* New York: Guilford Press.
Mash, E.J., & Terdal, L.G. (1997). *Assessment of childhood disorders* (3rd ed.). New York: Guilford Press.

ORDERING INFORMATION

Structured Interviews

Diagnostic Interview for Children and Adolescents Computer Program (DICA-IV) (Reich, Welner, Herjanic, & MHS Staff, 1997). Multi-Health Systems, 908 Niagara Falls Boulevard, North Tonawanda, NY 14120-2060; (800) 456-3003.
NIMH Diagnostic Interview Schedule for Children (DISC-IV) (Shaffer & Fisher, 1996). New York State Psychiatric Institute, 722 West 168th Street, New York, NY 10032; (888) 814-DISC.

Wide-Range Rating Scales

Behavior Assessment for Children (Parent Rating Scales, Teacher Rating Scales, Self-Report of Personality, ASSIST Software) (Reynolds & Kamphaus, 1992). American Guidance Service, 4201 Woodland Road, Circle Pines, MN 55014-1796; (800) 328-2560.
Child Behavior Checklist (Teacher Report Form, Youth Self-Report Form, Computer Software) (Achenbach, 1991). University Associates in Psychiatry, One South Prospect Street, Burlington, VT 05401-3456; (802) 656-8313.
Devereux Scales of Mental Disorders (DSMD) (Computer Software) (Naglieri, LeBuffe, & Pfeiffer, 1994). The Psychological Corporation, Order Service Center, Post Office Box 839954, San Antonio, TX 78283-3954; (800) 211-8378.

Narrow-Range Rating Scales

ADD-H Comprehensive Teacher's Rating Scale (ACTeRS) (Teacher and Parent Forms) (Ullman, Sleator, Sprague, & MetriTech Staff, 1996). MetriTech, Inc., 4106 Fieldstone Road, Champaign, IL 61821; (800) 747-4868.
AD/HD Diagnostic Teacher Rating Scale (ADTRS) (Wolraich, Feurer, Hannah, Baumgaertel, & Pinnock, in press). Plenum Press, 233 Spring Street, New York, NY 10013; (800) 221-9369.
ADHD Rating Scale-IV (Home and School Versions) (DuPaul, Anastopoulos, Power, & Reid, 1999). Guilford Press, 72 Spring Street, New York, NY 10012; (800) 365-7006.
ADHD Symptom Checklist-4 (ADHD-SC4) (Gadow, 1997). Checkmate Plus, Post Office Box 696, Stony Brook, NY 11790-0696; (800) 779-4292.
Attention Deficit Disorders Evaluation Scale (ADDES) (School and Home Version Rating Forms) (McCarney, 1996). Hawthorne Educational Services, Inc., 800 Gray Oak Drive, Columbia, MO 65201; (800) 542-1673.
Beck Depression Inventory–II (BDI-II) (Beck, Steer, & Brown, 1996). The Psychological Corporation, Order Service Center, Post Office Box 839954, San Antonio, TX 78283-3954; (800) 211-8378.
Brown Attention-Deficit Disorder Scales (Brown, 1996). The Psychological Corporation, Order Service Center, Post Office Box 839954, San Antonio, TX 78283-3954; (800) 211-8378.
Children's Depression Inventory (CDI) (Kovacs, 1992). Multi-Health Systems, 908 Niagara Falls Boulevard, North Tonawanda, NY 14120-2060; (800) 456-3003.
Conners' Rating Scale–Revised (CRS-R) (Parent and Teacher Versions) (Conners, 1997). Multi-Health Systems, 908 Niagara Falls Boulevard, North Tonawanda, NY 14120-2060; (800) 456-3003.
Dyadic Adjustment Scale (DAS) (Spanier, 1976). Multi-Health Systems, 908 Niagara Falls Boulevard, North Tonawanda, NY 14120-2060; (800) 456-3003.

Home Situations Questionnaire and School Situations Questionnaire (in Barkley, 1991). Guilford Press, 72 Spring Street, New York, NY 10012; (800) 365-7006.

Issues Checklist (IC) (In Robin & Foster, 1989). Guilford Publications, 72 Spring Street, New York, NY 10012; (800) 365-7006.

Multi-Dimensional Self-Concept Scale (MSCS) (Bracken, 1991). The Psychological Corporation, Order Service Center, Post Office Box 839954, San Antonio, TX 78283-3954; (800) 211-8378.

Parenting Stress Index–Third Edition (PSI) (Abidin, 1995). The Psychological Corporation, Order Service Center, Post Office Box 839954, San Antonio, TX 78283-3954; (800) 211-8378.

Revised Children's Manifest Anxiety Scale (RCMAS) (Reynolds & Richmond, 1985). Western Psychological Services, Publishers and Distributors, 12031 Wilshire Boulevard, Los Angeles, CA 90025-1251; (800) 648-8857.

Social Skills Rating System (SSRS) (Parent, Teacher, Self-Report Forms) (Gresham & Elliott, 1990). American Guidance Service, Publishers' Building, Circle Pines, MN 55014-1796; (800) 328-2560.

ADHD Rating Scale–IV

ADHD RATING SCALE-IV (HOME VERSION)

Child's name _____ Age _____ Grade _____

Completed by _____

Circle the number that **best describes** your child's home behavior over the past 6 months.

	never or rarely	sometimes	often	very often
1. Fails to give close attention to details or makes careless mistakes in schoolwork.	0	1	2	3
2. Fidgets with hands or feet or squirms in seat.	0	1	2	3
3. Has difficulty sustaining attention in tasks or play activities.	0	1	2	3
4. Leaves seat in classroom or in other situations in which remaining seated is expected.	0	1	2	3
5. Does not seem to listen when spoken to directly.	0	1	2	3
6. Runs about or climbs excessively in situations in which it is inappropriate.	0	1	2	3
7. Does not follow through on instructions and fails to finish work.	0	1	2	3
8. Has difficulty playing or engaging in leisure activities quietly.	0	1	2	3
9. Has difficulty organizing tasks and activities.	0	1	2	3
10. Is "on the go" or acts as if "driven by a motor."	0	1	2	3
11. Avoids tasks (e.g., schoolwork, homework) that require sustained mental effort.	0	1	2	3
12. Talks excessively.	0	1	2	3
13. Loses things necessary for tasks or activities.	0	1	2	3
14. Blurts out answers before questions have been completed.	0	1	2	3
15. Is easily distracted.	0	1	2	3
16. Has difficulty awaiting turn.	0	1	2	3
17. Is forgetful in daily activities.	0	1	2	3
18. Interrupts or intrudes on others.	0	1	2	3

ADHD RATING SCALE-IV (SCHOOL VERSION)

Child's name _____ Age _____ Grade _____

Completed by _____

Circle the number that **best describes** this student's school behavior over the past 6 months (or since the beginning of the school year).

	never or rarely	sometimes	often	very often
1. Fails to give close attention to details or makes careless mistakes in schoolwork.	0	1	2	3
2. Fidgets with hands or feet or squirms in seat.	0	1	2	3
3. Has difficulty sustaining attention in tasks or play activities.	0	1	2	3
4. Leaves seat in classroom or in other situations in which remaining seated is expected.	0	1	2	3
5. Does not seem to listen when spoken to directly.	0	1	2	3
6. Runs about or climbs excessively in situations in which it is inappropriate.	0	1	2	3
7. Does not follow through on instructions and fails to finish work.	0	1	2	3
8. Has difficulty playing or engaging in leisure activities quietly.	0	1	2	3
9. Has difficulty organizing tasks and activities.	0	1	2	3
10. Is "on the go" or acts as if "driven by a motor."	0	1	2	3
11. Avoids tasks (e.g., schoolwork, homework) that require sustained mental effort.	0	1	2	3
12. Talks excessively.	0	1	2	3
13. Loses things necessary for tasks or activities.	0	1	2	3
14. Blurts out answers before questions have been completed.	0	1	2	3
15. Is easily distracted.	0	1	2	3
16. Has difficulty awaiting turn.	0	1	2	3
17. Is forgetful in daily activities.	0	1	2	3
18. Interrupts or intrudes on others.	0	1	2	3

Psychoeducational Assessment for Children with Attention-Deficit/ Hyperactivity Disorder

with James L. Karustis

The overwhelming majority of children with attention-deficit/hyperactivity disorder (ADHD) display problems with academic performance.[1] Their academic problems include learning skills deficits, low rates of task completion and accuracy, homework problems, poor grades in school, grade retention, placement into special education programs, and school dropout.[2] An estimated 25% of children with ADHD meet classification criteria for one or more specific learning disabilities, including disorders of reading, mathematics, and writing[3]; thus, the assessment of ADHD requires an evaluation of learning problems. This assessment should include a determination of the type and the extent of a child's academic deficits, an identification of instructional variables that may be impeding academic progress, and a delineation of potential interventions that may promote academic success. Although an assessment of academic problems is essential to an evaluation of ADHD, it often is not necessary to conduct a comprehensive psychoeducational evaluation. The purpose of this chapter is to describe psychoeducational assessment procedures for evaluating learning difficulties and determining useful academic interventions. In addition, this chapter provides guidelines for interpreting the results of psychoeducational evaluations and discusses the utility of office-based measures for assessing problems with attention and impulse control.

We are grateful to Christa Habboushe, M.D., for her comments and feedback in the preparation of this chapter.

UTILITY OF PSYCHOEDUCATIONAL ASSESSMENT

Psychoeducational assessment can be useful for delineating skills deficits, deriving hypotheses about factors that contribute to academic problems, and developing plans for intervention. Following is a discussion of the utility of psychoeducational assessment.

Identifying Skills Deficits

Standardized, **norm-referenced measures** of achievement are the most commonly used assessment procedures for identifying academic skills deficits. The child's performance on these measures typically is compared with that of children of similar age and/or grade as well as with his or her score on a measure of intellectual performance (IQ) to determine whether a skills deficit exists. Subtests are available to assess a range of skills, including reading word recognition, reading comprehension, math calculation, math applications, spelling, language usage, and written language. These measures can be administered in groups or individually. Individualized batteries, such as the Wechsler Individual Achievement Tests (WIAT)[4] and the Woodcock-Johnson Tests of Achievement,[5] often are preferable to group tests for children with attention problems because of the difficulties that inattentive children have with listening to directions, avoiding distractions, and persisting for relatively long periods of time in large groups.

Alternative methods, such as **curriculum-based assessment** (CBA) procedures, also are useful in assessing academic skills deficits.[6] These methods ensure that what is being measured coincides closely with curriculum expectations in the classroom. With CBA, children are evaluated in relation to established performance criteria, based on research that has identified appropriately challenging curriculum material, instead of in relation to normative standards. CBA procedures are useful for determining the level of instruction in reading, math, writing, and spelling that is optimum for a child.

Identifying Contributing Instructional Factors

A variety of factors, in addition to a child's intrinsic weakness in one or more skills areas, can contribute to academic skills deficits. For instance, the amount of time that children spend actively engaged in instruction (termed **active engaged time**), such as when they are reading orally, participating in class, or performing seat work, has been shown to have a strong impact on academic performance.[7] Active engaged time depends on 1) the number of opportunities that teachers give students to respond actively and 2) the extent to which children take advantage of the opportunities. Typically, less than 15% of the classroom day is devoted to activities that involve children in actively responding to instruction[8]; the rest of the time is spent with classroom organization, behavior management, and passive responding to instruction, such as listening to the teacher or looking at the blackboard. Although this rate of active responding to instruction may be sufficient for competent learners to keep pace with classroom expectations, it is not adequate for children with academic deficits, including most children with ADHD. Furthermore, children with ADHD generally do not take advantage of the opportunities that they have to respond actively; they have lower rates of on-task behavior and work productivity than do their peers.[9]

Classroom observation procedures have been developed to assess children's level of active engagement and instructional variables, such as curriculum materials and teaching strategies, that influence the quantity and the quality of instruction provided. In addition, teacher-report measures can be useful in screening for instructional variables, and parent-report scales have utility for assessing problems that are related to homework.[10]

Planning Intervention

The ultimate purpose of psychoeducational assessment is to devise programs and interventions that will lead to academic progress. Norm-referenced measures can identify skills areas that require intervention. CBA procedures are useful for identifying appropriately challenging instructional materials. Also, CBA techniques have been used extensively to monitor academic progress over time and to evaluate the effectiveness of educational interventions.[11] The assessment of the rates of active and passive engagement in instruction can identify student target behaviors (e.g., on-task behavior during instruction, rates of task completion, rates of task accuracy) that are in need of intervention. Useful behavioral interventions, such as positive reinforcement, response cost, and self-management techniques, have been devised to improve these target behaviors (see Chapter 6). In addition, the assessment of classroom environment and teacher style can yield information that is useful when consulting with teachers about methods to improve instruction and student outcomes.

LEVELS OF ASSESSMENT FOR ACADEMIC PROBLEMS

Because children with problems that are related to ADHD vary greatly with regard to academic problems and because psychoeducational assessment can be time consuming, costly, and in some cases difficult to obtain, administration of a comprehensive psychoeducational evaluation to all children who are suspected of having ADHD is not recommended. The use of a multistage assessment process is a more practical and efficient method of addressing the academic needs of these children. Multistage assessment initially involves screening and/or a brief psychoeducational assessment. When children display significant problems on the screening or the brief assessment, referral for a comprehensive assessment is warranted.

Screening

A screening for academic problems often can be accomplished by a clinician in a community-based practice. The screening consists of having the child's teachers and parents complete brief questionnaires. An example of a teacher-report form that can be useful for screening academic problems is the Academic Performance Questionnaire presented in Appendix A. Teachers are asked to provide information about reading, math, and writing skills, as well as homework problems. In the areas of reading and math, teachers report how the child is performing in the curriculum in relation to his or her classmates. For math and language arts, teachers report the percentage of work that is completed and performed accurately. Academic achievement that is markedly below the average student in the class and/or rates of work completion or accuracy that is below the 80th percentile often are indicative of a problem.

An example of a parent-report form is the Homework Performance Questionnaire presented in Appendix B. Parents are asked to rate the severity of problems that they or their child often encounter with homework and the impact of homework problems on the parent–child relationship. In addition, they are asked to estimate the amount of time that the child spends working on each major subject, the percentage of work completed in each skills area, and the quality of homework completed. This information can be used by the clinician to determine areas of possible skills deficit and behaviors that may need to be targeted for academic and behavioral intervention.

Although information that is derived from a screening such as this may not be sufficient to determine the need for a comprehensive evaluation, this level of assessment can alert parents and educational professionals that the child may be experiencing academic problems that require intervention and further assessment. The clinician then can provide parents with guidance about how to advocate for the academic needs of their child in an effective and respectful manner. For instance, if the screening suggests that the child has problems, then the clinician could encourage the parents to request a referral to the school's **Student Support Team** to provide a more in-depth assessment and to plan useful interventions. In most states, schools are required to have interdisciplinary building support teams, often referred to as **Instructional Support Teams** or **Mainstream Assistance Teams,** to assist with intervention planning. In schools without these teams, the clinician can refer the parents to the counselor or to the principal. (For more information about Mainstream Assistance Teams and strategies for promoting effective collaboration among parents and school professionals, see Fuchs et al., 1990, and Sheridan, Kratochwill, & Bergan, 1996.)

Brief Psychoeducational Assessment

In clinic settings where it is possible to conduct a more thorough screening of academic problems, a brief psychoeducational assessment including the administration of direct measures of performance can provide more specific information than the screening procedures that were described in the previous section. The administration of a brief measure of intelligence, such as the Kaufman Brief Intelligence Test,[12] and brief standardized measures of academic achievement, such as the Reading and Math subtests of the Kaufman Tests of Educational Achievement–Brief Form,[13] yield useful data about level of academic achievement in relation to the child's cognitive ability and compared with peers of similar age and/or grade.

In addition, CBA can provide information about the child's instructional level and whether the child is being taught with the proper instructional materials. Another advantage of CBA is that these procedures are very brief and easy to administer. The following is a description of specific procedures for using CBA methods in clinical practice.

To assess reading using CBA procedures, the child is given three reading passages that are selected at random from his or her reading book or from a set of generic reading passages that are useful for this assessment.[14] The student is asked to read each passage for 1 minute. Errors, including substitutions, omissions, and additions, are recorded; the child is provided the word when he or she pauses for 5 seconds. Passages are scored for the number of words read correctly per minute and the number of errors committed per minute, which have been shown to be valid markers of reading achievement. The median score of the three passages is evaluated in relation to established criteria for determining whether the child's reading is at the instructional level (passages are appropriate), the frustrational level (passages are too challenging), or the mastery level (passages are too easy). The instructional level for children in grades 1 and 2 is 40–60 words correct per minute with four or fewer errors; for children in grades 3–6, the instructional level is 70–100 words correct per minute with six or fewer errors.[15] If time permits, then the evaluation can proceed until the examiner identifies the highest level at which the child can read instructionally and the level at which the child is frustrational; however, for purposes of brief evaluation, determining whether the child can perform at an instructional level with the curriculum that is presented in class is sufficient.

To assess math using CBA procedures, the child is given three worksheets or probes, each of which uses samples from the skills that are being taught to the child during a school semester or unit. For instance, a worksheet for a beginning second grader might consist of one- and two-digit addition and subtraction facts that do not involve regrouping. The child is asked to work on the problems for 2 minutes and is scored on the number of digits that are calculated correctly per minute and the number of errors per minute—valid estimates of math achievement. The median score of the probes is evaluated to established criteria to determine whether the child's performance is at the instructional, frustrational, or mastery level. The instructional level for grades 1–3 is 10–19 digits correct per minute with three to seven errors; for children in grades 4 and above, the instructional level is 20–39 digits correct per minute with three to seven errors.[16]

To assess writing skills, the child is asked to write a story for 3 minutes in response to a sentence stem, which he or she has been asked to think about for 1 minute. An example of a story stem is, "My idea of a great birthday party is…" or, "What I really like about Halloween is…." Often, it is more useful to allow the child to create the story starter to ensure interest and motivation. Passages are scored for the number of words that are written in 3 minutes. Ideally, the child is asked to write three stories, with the median score being compared with scoring criteria, but asking the child to write one or two stories is sufficient for brief assessment. The average numbers of words written in 3 minutes by students according to grade level are the following: 15 for grade 1, 28 for grade 2, 37 for grade 3, 41 for grade 4, 49 for grade 5, and 53 for grade 6.[17]

To assess spelling skills, the child is administered three sets of 20 spelling words that are taken at random from the child's spelling curriculum. Words are presented at the rate of one every 7 seconds. The child's score is the median number of correct letter sequences per minute for each word list. A correct letter sequence is two consecutive letters spelled accurately. In addition, the first and last letters of a word, if spelled accurately, each are counted as a correct letter sequence. For instance, if the word "jail" is spelled "jael," then the child would get two points for spelling the first and last letters correctly as well as a point for the correct sequence of "ja." The child would get no additional credit because the sequences of "ae" and "el" are incorrect. The instructional level for children in grades 1 and 2 is 20–39 correct letter sequences and for children in grades 3–6 is 40–59 correct letter sequences.[18]

Although it may not be feasible to administer CBA procedures in reading, math, writing, and spelling for each child who is being assessed, a review of information on a screening device such as the Academic Performance Questionnaire can identify specific skills areas that need to be investigated more carefully. This brief assessment, which also may include the Homework Problems Questionnaire described previously, can be valuable in providing guidance to parents about educational issues and designing academic interventions; however, it fails to provide a comprehensive assessment of each major skills area and is not sufficient for making determinations about eligibility for special education.

Comprehensive Psychoeducational Assessment

When results of brief assessment procedures suggest the presence of significant deficits in one or more areas of academic skills, a comprehensive psychoeducational assessment is warranted. The comprehensive evaluation can provide useful information about the extent of skills deficits, factors that may be contributing to academic problems, and strategies that may be useful in intervention. Components of a comprehensive assessment should include

- Norm-referenced, individualized measure of cognitive functioning, such as the Wechsler Intelligence Scale for Children, Third Edition (WISC-III)[19] or the Stanford-Binet Intelligence Scale, Fourth Edition[20]
- Norm-referenced, individualized battery of **achievement tests,** such as the WIAT or the Woodcock-Johnson Tests of Achievement
- Teacher report of academic performance in relation to peers for each major subject
- Teacher report of attention and work productivity
- Parent report of homework behavior

In addition, CBA of reading, math, writing, and spelling skills and a direct observation of academic engaged time and classroom environmental factors are valuable. A direct observation of classroom behavior is mandatory for a psychoeducational evaluation that is conducted for the purpose of determining eligibility for special education services.

The use of standardized, norm-referenced measures of cognitive functioning and academic achievement, administered by a certified school psychologist, is required in most states to make decisions about eligibility for special education programming. (For a comprehensive description of norm-referenced cognitive and achievement tests that are useful in psychoeducational evaluation, see Sattler, 1992.) The determination of whether a child has a deficit that is severe enough to be diagnosed as a learning disability and warrant special education placement traditionally has been made on the basis of there being a marked discrepancy between the index of cognitive functioning (IQ) and scores on relevant measures of achievement. For instance, to diagnose a reading disability, there may need to be a marked discrepancy between the child's IQ score and standard score on one or more measures of reading achievement. Similar criteria are used to determine learning disabilities in the areas of math and written language. The operational definition of *marked discrepancy* varies from state to state and might refer to an IQ–achievement score difference of 15 standard score points or to academic functioning that is at least two grade levels below the child's placement. In some states, regression formulas are used to determine the significance of discrepancy scores because a simple discrepancy model can overidentify children with above-average IQ scores and underidentify those with below-average IQ scores.[21] A further explanation for interpreting discrepancy scores is provided later in this chapter.

The use of discrepancy scores on norm-referenced measures to make decisions about special education placement has been challenged, primarily because this method at times is not sensitive to how children function in actual classroom situations. A discrepancy model may exclude from special services students with relatively low levels of cognitive and academic functioning who do not exhibit a marked discrepancy between these two broad areas of performance but who may benefit from intensive academic assistance. Also, this model may not be appropriate for students in first or second grade because achievement tests often are subject to floor effects that limit how poorly students can score, thereby reducing the likelihood of finding a significant discrepancy with these children. The state of Iowa is experimenting with an alternative model, based on CBA and problem-solving procedures, to ensure that determinations about special education correspond to children's performance in the naturalistic setting.[22] Although few states require the incorporation of CBA methods into a comprehensive assessment battery, more and more states are recommending the use of CBA procedures to assist with intervention planning prior to referral for a comprehensive evaluation.

Collecting from the teacher information about a child's academic performance in relation to classmates is an important component of the evaluation. Clinicians should include teacher-report measures, such as the Academic Performance Questionnaire (Appendix A), as well as narrow-range measures of problems that are related to ADHD and wide-range scales of externalizing and internalizing problems (see Chapter 2). In addition, the Academic Performance Rating Scale[23] can be a useful teacher-report measure of academic productivity and accuracy across a range of academic areas. The evaluation also should include a teacher interview; conducting the interview after receiving the teacher-report data is helpful in that the teacher questionnaires can indicate areas that need to be explored in greater depth.

Parent-report information is another essential component of the full evaluation. In addition to the Homework Performance Questionnaire, the Homework Problems Checklist[24] can be useful for eliciting information from parents about factors at home that may be having an impact on academic performance. The clinician will find data from these rating scales very useful for conducting an interview with the family.

A direct observation of the child's performance in the classroom is a critical element of the school psychology evaluation. A direct observation can yield useful information about a student's level of academic engagement in comparison with classmates, as well as instructional and environmental variables that may be contributing to academic skills deficits and low levels of active engagement. Several observation systems have been developed to systematically collect information about relevant classroom variables.[25]

The comprehensive psychoeducational evaluation is not sufficient for some children with ADHD. Many of these children have language problems and need an audiological as well as a speech-language evaluation.[26] Furthermore, some children who present with symptoms of ADHD may have more subtle language-processing difficulties that are related to a **central auditory processing disorder** (CAPD).[27] Clinicians often find it challenging to distinguish CAPD from ADHD. From a neuropsychological perspective, CAPD is characterized by difficulties with the efficient processing of incoming auditory information, whereas ADHD increasingly is becoming recognized as a disorder not of the "input" of information but of the "online management" of information (working memory) and of "output."[28] In cases in which the child appears to have particular problems with listening, especially when there are other indicators of a language-processing problem (reading, spelling, writing, and oral expression deficits), a speech-language evaluation may be indicated, in addition to a thorough assessment of hearing.

For children with marked problems in fine motor coordination and visual-motor integration, an occupational therapy evaluation may be useful. In addition, children with ADHD who have unusual learning profiles, a history or an examination that is suggestive of active neurological disease, or marked organizational and memory problems may benefit from the careful analysis of information processing provided through neuropsychological assessment (for more information about neuropsychological evaluation, see Vanderploeg, 1994). Because neuropsychological evaluations are intensive and time consuming, referral for this service should be limited to children with complex or severe learning problems.

INTERPRETING PSYCHOEDUCATIONAL EVALUATIONS

Clinicians often are asked by parents to interpret the results of psychoeducational evaluations that have been completed by another professional. Psychoeducational evaluations generally consist of measures of cognitive ability and academic achievement in addition to teacher-report data and, in some cases, measures to assess auditory and visual processing as well as visual-motor skills. Following are some general guidelines for interpreting the results of these evaluations. In reviewing these reports, clinicians may have questions about how test findings were derived and interpreted; in these instances, they are encouraged to discuss the case with the professional who conducted the evaluation before sharing concerns with the parents.

Most measures of cognitive functioning yield multiple indices. The most commonly used intelligence test, the WISC-III, yields indices of Verbal IQ and Performance IQ. The WISC-III also produces scores for Freedom from Distractibility and Processing Speed, although these indices are less reliable and valid than the IQ scores. The Freedom from Distractibility and Processing Speed factors have been purported to be useful indices of attention deficits, but research generally has not supported this position.[29] The IQ scores on the WISC-III are given in standard scores with a mean of 100 and a standard deviation (SD) of 15. Because of measurement error, the scores that are provided by IQ tests are estimates of functioning. Using the WISC-III, there is a 95% chance that the child's true IQ score will be his or her standard score ±6 for Verbal functioning, ±8 for Performance functioning, and ±6 for Full Scale functioning. The Verbal and Performance IQ scores each are determined on the basis of functioning on five subtests (Information, Vocabulary, Similarities, Arithmetic, and Comprehension). Each subtest has a mean of 10 and an SD of 3. Although experienced clinicians can draw clinically meaningful inferences from a child's subtest scatter, the validity of interpreting subtest scores on IQ tests has been questioned.[30]

When interpreting IQ scores, the clinician should assess the child's overall level of functioning in relation to his or her peers. Although the mean IQ score in a national sample is 100, the mean score for students in a particular school may be markedly higher or lower than this. In cases in which clinicians do not know the average IQ score for students in the schools that they serve, a brief conversation with some of the local school psychologists may be very useful. Children whose scores on IQ tests are 15 points or more lower than the estimated mean for students in the classroom often experience significant problems in one or more areas of academic functioning. In addition to evaluating children's test scores in relation to their peers, clinicians often find it useful to determine whether there are large discrepancies between different IQ scores. For instance, a discrepancy between Verbal and Performance IQ scores of 15–20 points or more often suggests the presence of relative strengths/weaknesses in language or visuospatial functioning.

Many achievement tests are used in educational practice, but perhaps the most commonly used measure is the WIAT. This measure yields scores in several areas of academic functioning: Basic Reading, Math Reasoning, Spelling, Reading Comprehension, Numerical Operations, Listening Comprehension, Oral Expression, and Written Expression. In addition, this test provides Composite scores for Reading, Mathematics, Language, and Writing. The manual provides both age-based and grade-based norms; grade-based norms are especially useful when there is a marked deviation between a child's age and grade level, which may be due to grade retention. Scores are given in standard score format with a mean of 100 and SD of 15. This measure also provides grade-equivalent scores, but these are very general estimates of how the student is able to perform in relation to peers of similar grade.

As with IQ scores, a student's performance on achievement tests should be evaluated in relation to the estimated performance of students in the classroom. In addition, scores on achievement tests such as the WIAT can be compared with IQ scores to determine whether there is a discrepancy between IQ score and achievement. Using a simple discrepancy model, a difference between Full Scale IQ score on the WISC-III and a subscale score on the WIAT of 12 points or more generally represents a significant difference. The discrepancy between WISC-III and WIAT scores also can be evaluated using a corrected formula that is based on a regression model. Using the WIAT manual, a psychoeducational specialist can determine a child's predicted level of achievement based on his or her Full Scale IQ score. Then the examiner can compare the child's predicted level of achievement with his or her actual level of functioning to determine whether the difference is significant. A difference between predicted and actual level of achievement of 15 points or more generally is needed for significance and is suggestive of a learning disability in a particular skills area. The following case examples illustrate how to use IQ and achievement scores to make decisions about a child's educational functioning. (For additional information, see Wodrich, 1997.)

Darnell, 8 years and 4 months old and in the second grade, was referred by his teacher for psychoeducational testing because of concerns about his reading and spelling skills, in addition to behaviors related to ADHD. His scores on IQ and achievement tests are summarized in Table 1. His Full Scale IQ score on the WISC-III was in the average range as compared with a national sample and the estimated mean IQ score for his school. His Performance IQ score was significantly higher than his Verbal IQ score. Achievement scores in this case were determined from age-based norms. The results of a regression model that was used to evaluate discrepancies between predicted level of achievement, based on the Full Scale IQ score, and actual level of achievement are indicated in Table 1. Although the absolute value of the discrepancy that is significant varies slightly, a discrepancy of about 15 points or more is significant. Darnell's scores in Basic Reading (word recognition), Spelling, Written Expression, the Reading Composite (composed of Basic Reading and Reading Comprehension), and the Writing Composite (composed of Spelling and Written Expression) all were significantly below his Full Scale IQ score. The results clearly support the presence of a learning disability in reading and written expression. Darnell should qualify for special education services at school. Also, results of the IQ test suggested a relative strength in mechanical and spatial reasoning.

Annette, 10 years and 10 months old and in the fifth grade, was referred by her teacher for psychoeducational testing because of disorganization and problems with work completion. Her scores on intelligence and achievement tests are reported in Table 2. Her overall functioning on the WISC-III was in the average range, as compared with national and school norms, with her Performance ability being significantly weaker than her Verbal ability. The 29-point discrepancy between her Verbal and Performance IQ scores is very large and suggestive of a relative weakness in spatial reasoning, visual perception, and visual-motor functioning. Further support for this hypothesis was that her drawings were similar to those of a 7-year-old child. Age-based norms were used to compute achievement scores. Using a regression model, there were no significant discrepancies between Full Scale IQ score and achievement, although scores in the areas of Numerical Op-

Table 1. Results of psychoeducational testing for Darnell

	Standard score	Percentile	95% confidence interval	IQ–achievement discrepancy
IQ Testing				
Full-scale IQ	97	45	92–104	
Verbal IQ	91	27	85–98	
Performance IQ	106	66	97–113	
Achievement Testing				
Basic Reading	76	5	69–83	Significant
Math Reasoning	102	55	92–112	Not significant
Spelling	81	10	73–89	Significant
Reading Composite	86	18	77–95	Not significant
Numerical Operations	98	45	86–110	Not significant
Listening Composite	93	32	81–105	Not significant
Oral Expression	90	25	81–99	Not significant
Written Expression	82	12	68–96	Significant
Reading Composite	75	5	69–81	Significant
Math Composite	101	53	93–109	Not significant
Language Composite	88	21	79–97	Not significant
Writing Composite	76	5	66–86	Significant

erations and Written Expression narrowly failed to reach significance. Although Annette may not meet strict criteria for a learning disability as defined by most states, her pattern of functioning is suggestive of a **nonverbal learning disability,** which often is characterized by marked deficits in visual processing, visual-motor functioning, math calculation, written expression,

Table 2. Results of psychoeducational testing for Annette

	Standard score	Percentile	95% confidence interval	IQ–achievement discrepancy
IQ Testing				
Full-scale IQ	95	37	90–101	
Verbal IQ	110	75	103–116	
Performance IQ	81	10	75–91	
Achievement Testing				
Basic Reading	100	50	93–107	Not significant
Math Reasoning	93	32	85–101	Not significant
Spelling	107	68	99–115	Not significant
Reading Composite	97	42	88–106	Not significant
Numerical Operations	82	12	73–91	Not significant
Listening Composite	89	23	79–89	Not significant
Oral Expression	93	32	85–101	Not significant
Written Expression	76	5	63–89	Not significant
Reading Composite	97	42	91–103	Not significant
Math Composite	86	18	79–93	Not significant
Language Composite	89	23	81–96	Not significant
Writing Composite	98	37	90–106	Not significant

organization, attention, and social skills.[31] Regardless, Annette clearly needs intensive academic intervention in school. In this case, the clinician might advise the parents to work with the school's Instructional Support Team to better understand the nature of the math calculation and writing problems and to devise useful, in-class academic interventions for Annette. Depending on Annette's response to these interventions, a determination can be made later in the year as to whether special education services are warranted.

OFFICE-BASED MEASURES OF INATTENTION AND IMPULSIVITY

Since the early 1970s, numerous attempts have been made to devise office-based procedures to provide objective measurement of inattention and impulsivity. The office measures that have been used most commonly in research and clinical practice to assess variables that are related to ADHD are **continuous performance tests.**

Gordon Diagnostic System Vigilance Task

In one widely used continuous performance test, the Gordon Diagnostic System Vigilance Task,[32] numbers are presented on a screen one at a time at the rate of one per second, and the child is asked to press a button every time a 9 follows the number 1. The task is presented for 9 minutes. Scores are computed electronically. The task yields two primary scores: Total Correct, which is the number of times that the child responds when the target stimuli appear, and Commissions, the number of times that the child responds when the target stimuli do not appear. Research has shown that Total Correct is inversely related to measures of inattention. Commissions scores appear to measure a combination of impulsivity and inattention; the Commissions error that is most related to impulsivity is a response when the number 1 is followed by a number other than 9.[33] Children with ADHD have been shown to perform significantly more poorly on the Gordon Vigilance Task, as well as on most continuous performance tasks, than children without this disorder. The Gordon Task has been normed extensively on school-age children and adolescents. A limitation of the Gordon task is that the electronic system that is needed to administer the test is quite expensive.

Alternative Measures of Continuous Performance

Other versions of the continuous performance task may prove to be more useful and valid than the Gordon task. For instance, the Tests of Variables of Attention (TOVA),[34] a 22-minute continuous performance task that utilizes nonlanguage stimuli, may be useful for discriminating the performance of children with ADHD from those with reading disorders. Visual and auditory versions of this task are available. The TOVA can be administered via computer, thereby reducing the costs of administration. Another widely used version is the Conners' Continuous Performance Test.[35] This is a 14-minute task that also is administered via computer. A unique feature of this task is that the child is asked to respond to each stimulus presented but to inhibit responding when the target stimulus appears. Both of these continuous performance measures have been normed extensively on children and adolescents. Although the TOVA and the Conners' Continuous Performance Test provide noteworthy variations on the standard vigilance task, their validity needs to be established through additional research.

Limitations of Office-Based Measures

Although continuous performance tests are used widely in clinical practice, they have several noteworthy limitations. These tasks generally produce a relatively low rate of false positives, but they appear to generate a high rate of false negatives—that is, they tend to underidentify children with ADHD. False negative rates can vary from 25% to 80%, with higher rates typically being found in older children.[36] Another limitation is that these tasks are relatively poor at discriminating children with ADHD from those with learning disabilities and other clinical disorders.[37] Furthermore, performance on these tasks has been shown to be sensitive to contextual factors, such as whether an examiner is present and when during the course of an assessment the task is administered.[38] The effect of environmental factors raises questions about the reactive effects of taking these tests in contrived, clinical settings as opposed to naturalistic classrooms.

The relationship between performance on these measures and functioning in the classroom as determined by behavior assessment methods has been questioned and appears to be low to moderate.[39] Although most of the research has been conducted on the Gordon Vigilance Task, it is likely that the TOVA and the Conners' Continuous Performance Test will have many of the same limitations as those described in relation to the Gordon task. In particular, the non-naturalistic nature of vigilance tasks likely will continue to present problems with ecological validity.

Office-based measures of attention and impulse control appear to have a limited degree of utility with regard to providing an objective assessment of ADHD; they may be useful for ruling in the disorder but less helpful for ruling it out. Research has raised significant questions about the validity of these instruments. Continuous performance tests and other office-based measures should be considered second-tier instruments for assessing inattention and impulsivity.

CONCLUSION

Given the high incidence of academic problems among children with ADHD, the evaluation of this disorder requires an assessment of functioning in major academic skills areas, an identification of factors that may be contributing to skills deficits, and a delineation of strategies that may be useful for improving academic progress. Questionnaires that are completed by teachers and parents are useful screening devices for uncovering potential academic problems and suggesting areas that are in need of intervention. A brief assessment including direct measures of academic functioning generally is helpful in identifying intervention strategies and determining whether a comprehensive psychoeducational evaluation is needed. CBA procedures may be very useful to clinicians for determining whether the child is able to perform competently with instructional materials that are presented in class and whether more intensive assessment and intervention are needed. The comprehensive psychoeducational evaluation, including a complete battery of norm-referenced cognitive and achievement tests, is needed for investigating the nature and the extent of academic skills deficits and for determining eligibility for special education placement. Additional evaluations, such as speech-language testing and neuropsychological testing, also may be needed for intervention planning. Office-based measures of inattention and impulsivity may have some utility in assessing problems related to ADHD, but their contribution to the assessment of this disorder is secondary to that of clinical interviews, teacher and parent rating scales, and direct observations of the child in multiple contexts.

ENDNOTES

1. Cantwell & Baker (1991).
2. Frick et al. (1991).
3. DuPaul & Stoner (1994).
4. Wechsler (1992).
5. Woodcock & Johnson (1989).
6. Shapiro (1996).
7. Gettinger (1986).
8. Greenwood, Delquadri, & Hall (1984).
9. Abikoff, Gittelman-Klein, & Klein (1977).
10. Anesko, Schoiock, Ramirez, & Levine (1987), Shapiro (1996).
11. Shinn (1997).
12. Kaufman & Kaufman (1990).
13. Kaufman & Kaufman (1985).
14. See Marston & Deno (1995).
15. See Shapiro (1996).
16. Ibid.
17. Ibid.
18. Ibid.
19. Wechsler (1991).
20. Thorndike, Hagen, & Sattler (1986).
21. Frick et al. (1991).
22. Ikeda, Tilly, Stumme, Volmer, & Allison (1996).
23. DuPaul, Rapport, & Perriello (1991).
24. Anesko et al. (1987).
25. See Shapiro (1996).
26. See Wong & Baron (1997).
27. Moss & Sheiffele (1994).
28. Barkley (1997), Denckla (1996).
29. Watkins, Kush, & Glutting (1997).
30. McDermott, Fantuzzo, Glutting, Watkins, & Baggaley (1992).
31. Rourke (1995).
32. Gordon (1987).
33. Halperin, Wolf, Greenblatt, & Young (1991).
34. Greenberg (1988).
35. Conners (1990).
36. DuPaul, Anastopoulos, Shelton, Guevremont, & Metevia (1992), Fischer, Newby, & Gordon (1995).
37. Tarnowski, Prinz, & Nay (1986).
38. Power (1992).
39. Barkley (1991).

REFERENCES

Abikoff, H., Gittelman-Klein, R., & Klein, D. (1977). Validation of a classroom observation code for hyperactive children. *Journal of Consulting and Clinical Psychology, 45,* 772–783.

Anesko, K.M., Schoiock, G., Ramirez, R., & Levine, F.M. (1987). The Homework Problems Checklist: Assessing children's homework difficulties. *Behavioral Assessment, 9,* 179–185.

Barkley, R.A. (1991). The ecological validity of laboratory and analogue assessment methods of ADHD symptoms. *Journal of Abnormal Child Psychology, 19,* 149–178.

Barkley, R.A. (1997). Update on a theory of ADHD and its clinical manifestations. *The ADHD Report, 5,* 10–16.

Cantwell, D.P., & Baker, L. (1991). Association between attention-deficit hyperactivity disorder and learning disorders. *Journal of Learning Disabilities, 24,* 88–95.

Conners, C.K. (1990). *Conners' Continuous Performance Test.* North Tonawanda, NY: Multi-Health Systems.

Denckla, M.B. (1996). Biological correlates of learning and attention: What is relevant to learning disability and attention-deficit hyperactivity disorder? *Developmental and Behavioral Pediatrics, 17*, 114–119.

DuPaul, G.J., Anastopoulos, A.D., Shelton, T.L., Guevremont, D., & Metevia, L. (1992). Multimethod assessment of attention-deficit hyperactivity disorder: The diagnostic utility of clinic-based tests. *Journal of Clinical Child Psychology, 21*, 394–402.

DuPaul, G.J., Rapport, M.D., & Perriello, L.M. (1991). Teacher ratings of academic skills: The development of the Academic Performance Rating Scale. *School Psychology Review, 20*, 284–300.

DuPaul, G.J., & Stoner, G. (1994). *ADHD in the schools: Assessment and intervention strategies.* New York: Guilford Press.

Fischer, M., Newby, R.F., & Gordon, M. (1995). Who are the false negatives on continuous performance tests? *Journal of Clinical Child Psychology, 24*, 427–433.

Frick, P.J., Kamphaus, R.W., Lahey, B.B., Loeber, R., Christ, M.A.G., Hart, E.L., & Tannenbaum, L.E. (1991). Academic underachievement and the disruptive behavior disorders. *Journal of Consulting and Clinical Psychology, 59*, 289–294.

Fuchs, D., Fuchs, L.S., Gilman, S., Reeder, P., Bahr, M., Fernstrom, P., & Roberts, H. (1990). Prereferral intervention through teacher consultation: Mainstream assistance teams. *Academic Therapy, 25*, 263–276.

Gettinger, M. (1986). Achievement as a function of time spent in learning and time needed for learning. *American Educational Research Journal, 21*, 617–628.

Gordon, M. (1987). *The Gordon Diagnostic System.* DeWitt, NY: Gordon Systems.

Greenberg, L. (1988). *Tests of Variables of Attention.* Los Alamitos, CA: Universal Attention Disorders.

Greenwood, C.R., Delquadri, J.C., & Hall, R.V. (1984). Opportunity to respond and student academic performance. In W.L. Heward, T.E. Heron, D.S. Hill, & J. Trap-Porter (Eds.), *Focus on behavior analysis in education* (pp. 55–88). Columbus, OH: Charles E. Merrill.

Halperin, J.M., Wolf, L.E., Greenblatt, E.R., & Young, J.G. (1991). Subtype analysis of commission errors on the continuous performance tests in children. *Developmental Neuropsychology, 7*, 207–217.

Ikeda, M.J., Tilly, D., Stumme, J., Volmer, L., & Allison, R. (1996). Agency-wide implementation of problem solving consultation: Foundations, current implementation, and future direction. *School Psychology Quarterly, 11*, 228–243.

Kaufman, A.S., & Kaufman, N.L. (1985). *Kaufman Tests of Educational Achievement–Brief form.* Circle Pines, MN: American Guidance Service.

Kaufman, A.S., & Kaufman, N.L. (1990). *Kaufman Brief Intelligence Test.* Circle Pines, MN: American Guidance Service.

Marston, D., & Deno, S. (1985). *Standard reading passages: Measures for screening and progress monitoring.* Eden Prairie, MN: Children's Educational Services.

McDermott, P.A., Fantuzzo, J.W., Glutting, J.J., Watkins, M.W., & Baggaley, A.R. (1992). Illusions of meaning in the ipsative assessment of children's ability. *Journal of Special Education, 25*, 504–526.

Moss, W.L., & Sheiffele, W.A. (1994). Can we differentially diagnose an attention deficit disorder without hyperactivity from a central auditory processing problem? *Child Psychiatry and Human Development, 25*, 85–96.

Power, T.J. (1992). Contextual factors in the vigilance testing of children with ADHD. *Journal of Abnormal Child Psychology, 20*, 579–593.

Rourke, B.P. (Ed.). (1995). *Syndrome of nonverbal learning disabilities.* New York: Guilford Press.

Sattler, J.M. (1992). *Assessment of children* (4th ed.). San Antonio, TX: The Psychological Corporation.

Shapiro, E.S. (1996). *Academic skills problems: Direct assessment and intervention.* New York: Guilford Press.

Sheridan, S.M., Kratochwill, T.R., & Bergan, J.R. (1996). *Conjoint behavioral consultation: A procedural manual.* New York: Plenum.

Shinn, M.R. (1997). *Advances in curriculum-based measurement.* New York: Guilford Press.

Tarnowski, K.J., Prinz, R.J., & Nay, S.M. (1986). Comparative analysis of attentional deficits in hyperactive and learning disabled children. *Journal of Abnormal Psychology, 95*, 341–345.

Thorndike, R.L., Hagen, E.P., & Sattler, J.M. (1986). *The Stanford-Binet Intelligence Scale* (4th ed.). Chicago: Riverside.

Vanderploeg, R.D. (Ed.). (1994). *Clinician's guide to neuropsychological assessment.* Mahwah, NJ: Lawrence Erlbaum Associates.

Wang, P.P., & Baron, M.A. (1997). Language: A code for communicating. In M.L. Batshaw (Ed.), *Children with disabilities* (4th ed., pp. 275–292). Baltimore: Paul H. Brookes Publishing Co.

Watkins, M.W., Kush, J.C., & Glutting, J.J. (1997). Prevalence and diagnostic utility of the WISC-III SCAD profile among children with disabilities. *School Psychology Quarterly, 12,* 235–248.

Wechsler, D. (1991). *Wechsler Intelligence Scale for Children* (3rd ed.). San Antonio, TX: The Psychological Corporation.

Wechsler, D. (1992). *Wechsler Individual Achievement Test.* San Antonio, TX: The Psychological Corporation.

Wodrich, D.L. (1997). *Children's psychological testing: A guide for nonpsychologists* (3rd ed.). Baltimore: Paul H. Brookes Publishing Co.

Woodcock, R.W., & Johnson, M.B. (1989). *Woodcock-Johnson Psycho-Educational Battery–Revised.* Allen, TX: DLM Teaching Resources.

RESOURCES FOR CLINICIANS

Sattler, J.M. (1992). *Assessment of children* (4th ed.). San Antonio, TX: The Psychological Corporation. (To order, call [800] 211-8378.)

Shapiro, E.S. (1996). *Academic skills problems: Direct assessment and intervention.* New York: Guilford Press. (To order, call [800] 365-7006.)

Sheridan, S.M., Kratochwill, T.R., & Bergan, J.R. (1996). *Conjoint behavioral consultation: A procedural manual.* New York: Plenum. (To order, call [800] 221-9369.)

Shinn, M.R. (1997). *Advances in curriculum-based measurement.* New York: Guilford Press. (To order, call [800] 365-7006.)

Vanderploeg, R.D. (Ed.). (1994). *Clinician's guide to neuropsychological assessment.* Mahwah, NJ: Lawrence Erlbaum Associates. (To order, call [800] 926-6579.)

Wodrich, D.L. (1997). *Children's psychological testing: A guide for nonpsychologists* (3rd ed.). Baltimore: Paul H. Brookes Publishing Co. (To order, call [800] 638-3775.)

TESTS FOR CLINICIANS

Conners, C.K. (1990). *Conners' Continuous Performance Test.* North Tonawanda, New York: Multi-Health Systems. (To order, call [800] 456-3003.)

Gordon, M. (1987). *The Gordon Diagnostic System.* DeWitt, NY: Gordon Systems. (To order, call [315] 446-4849.)

Greenberg, L. (1988). *Tests of Variable Attention.* Los Alamitos, CA: Universal Attention Disorders. (To order, call [800] 729-2886.)

Kaufman, A.S., & Kaufman, N.L. (1985). *Kaufman Tests of Educational Achievement–Brief form.* Circle Pines, MN: American Guidance Service. (To order, call [800] 328-2560.)

Kaufman, A.S., & Kaufman, N.L. (1990). *Kaufman Brief Intelligence Test.* Circle Pines, MN: American Guidance Service. (To order, call [800] 328-2560.)

Marston, D., & Deno, S. (1985). *Standard reading passages: Measures for screening and progress monitoring.* Eden Prairie, MN: Children's Educational Services. (To order, write to 16650 Baywood Terrace, Eden Prairie, MN 55346.)

RESOURCES FOR PARENTS

Anderson, W., Chitwood, S., & Hayden, D. (1996). *Negotiating the special education maze* (2nd ed.). Bethesda, MD: Woodbine House. (To order, call [800] 843-7323.)

Cutler, B.C. (1993). *You, your child, and special education: A guide to making the system work.* Baltimore: Paul H. Brookes Publishing Co. (To order, call [800] 638-3775.)

Academic Performance Questionnaire

ACADEMIC PERFORMANCE QUESTIONNAIRE

Instructions to teachers: The information provided on this form will assist in assessing this student's learning skills in relation to his or her classroom peers. Please answer the questions listed below. Thank you for your time and cooperation.

Student's name _____ School _____
Grade _____ Teacher's name _____
Type of class _____ Date completed _____

Reading

Compared with the average students in your class, how well is this child able to **read orally**?
____ Well above average   ____ Somewhat below average
____ At or just above average   ____ Well below average

Compared with the average students in your class, how well is this child able to **comprehend what he or she reads**?
____ Well above average   ____ Somewhat below average
____ At or just above average   ____ Well below average

What are this student's specific problems, if any, in reading? _____
_____
_____

Does this child participate in remedial reading?   Yes ____   No ____
If yes, since when? _____ How often and for how long? _____
Type of remediation: ____ Special education out-of-class support
                                         ____ Special education in-class support
                                         ____ Basic skills instruction
                                         ____ Other school-based tutoring

Mathematics

Compared with the average students in your class, how well is this student able to **perform math calculations**?
____ Well above average   ____ Somewhat below average
____ At or just above average   ____ Well below average

Compared with the average students in your class, how well is this student able to **perform math word problems**?
____ Well above average   ____ Somewhat below average
____ At or just above average   ____ Well below average

What are this student's specific problems, if any, in math? _____
_____
_____

The Clinician's Practical Guide to Attention-Deficit/Hyperactivity Disorder
by Marianne Mercugliano, Thomas J. Power, and Nathan J. Blum   ©1999 by Paul H. Brookes Publishing Co.

Please estimate the percentage of written math work *completed* (regardless of accuracy) relative to classmates (circle one)   0–59%   60–69%   70–79%   80–89%   90–100%

Please estimate the *accuracy* of completed written math work (circle one)
   0–59%   60–69%   70–79%   80–89%   90–100%

Does this child participate in remedial math?   Yes ____   No ____

If yes, since when? _____   How often and for how long? _____

Type of remediation: ____ Special education out-of-class support
   ____ Special education in-class support
   ____ Basic skills instruction
   ____ Other school-based tutoring

Writing

Compared with the average students in your class, how well is this child able to **write short stories or essays?**

____ Well above average   ____ Somewhat below average

____ At or just above average   ____ Well below average

What are this student's specific problems, if any, in writing? _____
_____
_____

Please estimate the percentage of written language arts work *completed* (regardless of accuracy) relative to classmates (circle one)   0–59%   60–69%   70–79%   80–89%   90–100%

Please estimate the *accuracy* of completed written language arts work (circle one)
   0–59%   60–69%   70–79%   80–89%   90–100%

Homework

What are this student's specific problems, if any, regarding homework? _____
_____
_____

Please estimate the percentage of homework *completed* (circle one)
   0–59%   60–69%   70–79%   80–89%   90–100%

How would you rate the quality of this student's homework?   A   B   C   D   E   F

Other comments _____
_____
_____

The Clinician's Practical Guide to Attention-Deficit/Hyperactivity Disorder
by Marianne Mercugliano, Thomas J. Power, and Nathan J. Blum   ©1999 by Paul H. Brookes Publishing Co.

B

Homework Performance Questionnaire

HOMEWORK PERFORMANCE QUESTIONNAIRE

Student's name _____ Date of birth ___/___/___ Grade _____

Gender (circle)   Male   Female   Completed by _____

Your relationship to student _____ Date completed ___/___/___

Please check only one for each statement   0   1   2   3

Please rate your child's behavior for each item below.	Never	At times	Often	Very often
1. Leaves necessary homework materials at school				
2. Does not know what the assignments are				
3. Lies about having completed homework at school				
4. Does homework in a distracting location				
5. Needs many reminders to begin homework				
6. Needs constant supervision to remain on task				
7. Argues or complains				
8. Becomes frustrated easily				
9. Rushes through assignments, making careless errors				
10. Fails to submit work to teacher				
11. Homework causes problems in my relationship with this child				
12. Homework with this child causes problems in my relationship with other family members				

The Clinician's Practical Guide to Attention-Deficit/Hyperactivity Disorder
by Marianne Mercugliano, Thomas J. Power, and Nathan J. Blum   ©1999 by Paul H. Brookes Publishing Co.

Average daily *time* (in minutes) spent on homework *OVER THE PAST 2 WEEKS* (circle)

Mathematics	None	1–10	11–20	21–40	41–60	61–90	91–120	more than 2 hrs
Reading assignments	None	1–10	11–20	21–40	41–60	61–90	91–120	more than 2 hrs
Language/spelling	None	1–10	11–20	21–40	41–60	61–90	91–120	more than 2 hrs
Other	None	1–10	11–20	21–40	41–60	61–90	91–120	more than 2 hrs

Percentage of work *completed* for each subject *OVER THE PAST 2 WEEKS* (circle)

Mathematics	0–25%	26–50%	51–70%	71–80%	81–90%	91–100%
Reading assignments	0–25%	26–50%	51–70%	71–80%	81–90%	91–100%
Language/spelling	0–25%	26–50%	51–70%	71–80%	81–90%	91–100%
Other	0–25%	26–50%	51–70%	71–80%	81–90%	91–100%

Quality of your child's homework *OVER THE PAST 2 WEEKS* (circle)

Math accuracy	A	B	C	D	E	F
Reading comprehension	A	B	C	D	E	F
Writing neatness	A	B	C	D	E	F
Writing content	A	B	C	D	E	F
Spelling	A	B	C	D	E	F

The Clinician's Practical Guide to Attention-Deficit/Hyperactivity Disorder
by Marianne Mercugliano, Thomas J. Power, and Nathan J. Blum   ©1999 by Paul H. Brookes Publishing Co.

Treatments for Children with Attention-Deficit/ Hyperactivity Disorder

The impact of attention-deficit/hyperactivity disorder (ADHD) is pervasive: Most children with ADHD underachieve in school, and a significant proportion have disturbed peer relationships and conduct problems. Given ADHD's pervasive nature, multimodal treatment for ADHD generally is the most effective approach. Behavioral interventions and stimulant medication have been demonstrated to be the most effective treatments for the academic, behavior, social, and emotional problems of children with ADHD.[1]

When children with ADHD display behavior and/or emotional problems at home, behavioral approaches to counseling, including parent training and child and family behavior therapy, are needed. To manage the academic problems of these children, educational interventions to address identified skills deficits are necessary. In addition, behavioral interventions to improve on-task behavior and rates of work completion and accuracy are indicated. Social skills training for children who display peer interaction problems and consultation with parents and teachers to guide and reinforce appropriate social behavior should be included.

Applying behavioral interventions at home and in school is not sufficient to enable a majority of children who have ADHD to function appropriately in these settings.[2] Children with a moderate to severe level of impairment, in particular, will need medication to address their difficulties and to help them adapt successfully in home, school, and neighborhood environments.

A guiding principle of the successful management of the symptoms of ADHD that affect children is that intervention is effective to the extent that it occurs at the time and the place in which children are experiencing problems.[3] In the case of behavioral interventions, strategies should be implemented in naturalistic settings, such as the classroom, playground, or home, where children actually have problems with coping. Psychologists have tried repeatedly to use cognitive interventions in office-based settings to teach impulsive children how to control their behavior and relate more effectively with peers, but improvements that are realized in the clinic usually do not generalize to naturalistic settings.[4] At the time when the intervention is needed, children with ADHD may not realize the importance of using a particular strategy or they may find it more reinforcing at the moment to behave in some other manner. Supervising adults need to be trained to observe these children carefully in real-life situations and to prompt and reinforce them for using appropriate strategies.

With pharmacological treatments as well, intervention generally is effective only when the child takes the medication and for the duration of the medication's effect; thus, when children are given methylphenidate before school and at noon, the child's behavior is likely to improve during the time when he or she is in school. When the medication wears off after school, the child's behavior is likely to revert to its baseline state. As another example, children who demonstrate marked improvement in functioning during an academic year when stimulant medication is used are likely to have problems with functioning during the following year without medication unless there is a dramatic difference in the educational and behavioral interventions that are employed.

Because most children with ADHD require multiple treatments to be delivered by several professionals from different settings, it is important that providers collaborate with one another to provide integrated services for children. Unfortunately, in clinical practice, unimodal approaches to treatment (e.g., medication only, parent training only) commonly are implemented in situations in which multimodal approaches are indicated.[5] When multiple methods are used, service providers often do not collaborate with one another, leaving parents in the challenging position of coordinating communications. Regional centers for evaluating and treating children who have ADHD with complex problems, based in tertiary care settings, often are available. These programs generally provide opportunities for multidisciplinary collaboration and parental support regarding children with complex behavior and emotional problems; however, access to these centers often may be inconvenient, and coordination with community-based providers and school personnel may be difficult to arrange. Even for these more challenging cases, it is important that professionals be available in the community to provide treatment services and coordinate care for this population.[6]

The following chapters describe approaches to intervention that can be effective with children who have ADHD in home and school settings. Emphasis is given to intervention approaches that have been shown to improve children's functioning in real-life, naturalistic environments. A chapter on alternative treatments discusses interventions that have been reported by some researchers or clinicians to be useful but that lack empirical data to support their widespread effectiveness. Also included is a chapter that examines issues in the coordination of care for children with ADHD who receive multimodal interventions from many providers in educational and clinical settings.

ENDNOTES

1. Pelham et al. (1993).
2. Ibid.
3. Barkley (1998).
4. Abikoff (1985).
5. Pelham & Murphy (1986).
6. Power, Atkins, Osborne, & Blum (1994).

REFERENCES

Abikoff, H. (1985). Efficacy of cognitive training intervention in hyperactive children: A critical review. *Clinical Psychology Review, 5,* 479–512.

Barkley, R.A. (1998). *Attention-deficit hyperactivity disorder: A handbook for diagnosis and treatment* (2nd ed.). New York: Guilford Press.

Pelham, W.E., Carlson, C., Sams, S.E., Vallano, G., Dixon, M.J., & Hoza, B. (1993). Separate and combined effects of methylphenidate and behavior modification on boys with attention-deficit hyperactivity disorder in the classroom. *Journal of Consulting and Clinical Psychology, 61,* 506–515.

Pelham, W.E., & Murphy, H.A. (1986). Attention deficit and conduct disorders. In M. Hersen (Ed.), *Pharmacological and behavioral treatments: An integrative approach* (pp. 108–148). New York: John Wiley & Sons.

Power, T.J., Atkins, M.S., Osborne, M.L., & Blum, N.J. (1994). The school psychologist as manager of programming for ADHD. *School Psychology Review, 23,* 279–291.

Communicating with Parents, Children, and Teachers

Education about attention-deficit/hyperactivity disorder (ADHD) is the first component of treatment. Clinicians must be able to communicate effectively about ADHD and encourage the people who are important in the life of the child with ADHD to learn more about it to maximize the effectiveness of treatment. Discussing ADHD with parents after the diagnosis is made, discussing ADHD with children who have it, and communicating with school personnel about diagnostic and treatment issues are topics that are included in this chapter. Sources of ongoing education about ADHD for parents, children, and school personnel are provided. (Additional specific areas that require anticipatory guidance and education are covered in Chapters 5, 11, and 13.)

DISCUSSING THE DIAGNOSIS OF ADHD WITH PARENTS

The importance of the clinician's conference with parents following a diagnostic evaluation cannot be overemphasized. It sets the stage for the parents' understanding of ADHD, their incorporation of this facet of their child and family into their approach to parenting, and their understanding of the role that various professionals may play in helping them care for their child. Ideally, it requires at least 30 minutes to discuss the evaluation and next steps. Additional time likely will be required at subsequent visits to further discuss treatment and long-term issues. The clinician frequently does not have as much time available to discuss all aspects of ADHD as he or she and the parents would like. Fortunately, a wide variety of resources are available to provide further education and practical advice.

When the clinician first reviews ADHD with parents, both parents should be present (if appropriate). Ideally, arrangements should be made for child care to eliminate the distractions that the presence of the child would pose. The conference should be set up as a separate appointment whenever feasible, especially when information from other professionals is to be incorporated. The child who is the subject of the evaluation should be told about the purpose of the evaluation at the time that it is conducted and about the outcome in a developmentally appropriate manner, either at the end of the discussion with parents or at a subsequent appointment for follow-up. Older adolescents can participate in the summary discussion with the parents in most cases.

When a parent cannot attend a scheduled conference because of work demands, the clinician should consider arranging to have it at a more suitable time, thereby emphasizing the importance of having both parents present. If this is not possible, then a tape recording or written summary of the conference (see example in Appendix A) may be useful.

Occasionally, animosity between the parents prevents them from attending the summary conference together. Such a situation complicates treatment, especially when legal guardianship is shared. The clinician should address this issue with the parents before or in conjunction with a discussion of the specifics of the evaluation. A parent who was not present for the evaluation should be offered the opportunity to provide input by completing a parent rating scale and providing any other information that he or she wants in the form of a letter. When parents do not have an adequate working relationship, it is likely that a degree of inconsistency will exist in their approaches to the child, which will have a negative impact on the child's functioning. When there is open hostility or conflict that involves the child, emotional issues as well as inconsistency are likely to affect the child. Both parents should be informed that inconsistency and marital discord can have a tremendous negative effect on the well-being of a child with ADHD. They should be informed that a discussion of how the parents will work together to nurture their child with ADHD will need to be held in conjunction with the summary discussion of the diagnosis and treatment. Professional mediation should be recommended in situations in which both parents have legal rights to decision making but cannot agree. The child's clinician, for a variety of reasons, usually is not the best person to serve as a long-term mediator between parents who express significant marital discord. In the meantime, the clinician should make every effort to provide the same information to both parents after the initial evaluation and any subsequent visits. The long-term best interests of the child should be the clinician's guide to treatment recommendations.

One subset of parents who might not attend the summary conference together may differ only in their level of concern related to the diagnosis of ADHD. The most common scenario is a mother who has significant concerns about her child and a father who believes that the behaviors of concern to the mother are "normal" for children of that age. The mother may report that the father is not as involved as she is in the child's day-to-day home and school routines or is, in fact, very similar to the child who is undergoing the evaluation and "in denial" that his own behaviors were or are problematic. In this situation, the parents' difference of opinion, although reported to be restricted to this one issue, *is* likely to be having an impact on other aspects of parenting and family life. Counseling with a marital/family focus is indicated (see Chapters 5 and 14), but this recommendation should wait until the clinician has attempted to hold a conference with both parents. This may require from the clinician an insistent invitation to the reluctant parent, but, ultimately, there is a reasonable chance of getting these parents to work more closely together on their child's behalf by focusing on concerns that both may share rather than discussing a diagnosis or even "the child's problems." Both are likely to have concerns about the child's self-esteem and the impact of the child's receiving "mixed" messages from the parents about his or her behavior or school performance. They also may share concerns about sibling relationships, peer relationships, or declining grades. The clinician may have identified additional concerns that are not linked directly to the presenting parent's chief complaint. In this situation, the clinician provides the most useful long-term benefit to the child by gradually increasing the involvement of the reluctant parent. Generally, nonpharmacological interventions are recommended initially, and counseling, when presented as a means of assisting the child and the family with the issues that the parents have identified together (not as psychotherapy for the child), can be recommended with a greater likelihood of acceptance.

The initial conference about the diagnosis of ADHD can be time consuming. It can be helpful to set a time limit for the conference at the outset and to describe how the time will be allotted (e.g., one third each for the discussion of findings, recommendations, and parents' questions). It generally is useful to cover the child's strengths, weaknesses, and problems; the diagnoses; how and why the diagnoses were made; the reason for any additional evaluations that are recommended; and the nature of the initial steps in treatment. Providing a written outline (as in Appendix A) helps focus the discussion and highlights important points for the family. It also serves as documentation of the discussion for other professionals to whom the family may be referred. A brief but comprehensive overview of relevant information about ADHD is helpful in getting a family started on the journey of caring for their child's ADHD, yet there rarely is time to provide this in practice. Appendix B is a handout ("Summary of Important Information About ADHD") to give families an idea of the kinds of subjects that they may want to learn about in greater depth.

DISCUSSING ADHD WITH CHILDREN

ADHD is a complex condition, and an individual with this disorder usually has many kinds of symptoms. It is difficult enough for adults to understand its impact on relatively abstract components of behavior, such as motivation and persistence; one can only imagine the variety of misconceptions that children can harbor about themselves, their siblings, and their peers. Unfortunately, there has been little research about children's knowledge of and perceptions about ADHD, the functional impact of ADHD, and how involved adults can best empower children with a healthy understanding of ADHD. Talking with adults with ADHD about their childhood experiences is enlightening and sobering. Those who have not had the opportunity to do so may want to read some of the first-person accounts that are listed in the resources at the end of this chapter. Their educational experiences frequently have been overwhelmingly frustrating, confusing, and demoralizing. Their childhoods frequently were characterized by a degree of misery that no child deserves.

Today, ADHD is better understood and more widely discussed than it was even in the 1980s. Although this generally is beneficial for children, especially in terms of their educational experience, the notoriety of ADHD as a subject in the public arena means that misconceptions and misrepresentations also are more widespread. More people, including those with minimal personal or professional exposure, are willing to voice their opinions. Unfortunately, most children still will hear many times in the course of their childhood that "you could do better if you tried" (meaning, "this is your fault") and "ADHD is just an excuse that you/your parents use for your bad behavior or school performance" (meaning, "not only have you disgraced yourself, but you've also disgraced your family" and "you really *are* just bad or stupid").

Clinicians can help children maintain their self-esteem by working with parents in several ways. They can

1. Help the parents to develop successful strategies for treating ADHD
2. Support parents in being effective advocates for their children
3. Provide parents with information about how to support their children's self-esteem
4. Encourage parents to join local and national support and advocacy groups

There also are ways in which the clinician can help the child directly. Primary care clinicians have the opportunity to be role models and respected and trusted adult "friends." When periodic words of confidence and support come from such an individual, the day-to-day impact may not be noticeable, but the long-term impact can be substantial. At the time of an initial evaluation, the clinician can ask the child directly about his or her understanding of the reason for the evaluation. The clinician should provide neutral explanations of the child's difficulties if his or her explanations are self-deprecating. He or she should ask the child and parents about peer and sibling issues and determine whether the child is being victimized in his or her relationships (see Chapter 7). When the diagnosis of ADHD is communicated to the child, it helps the child to hear from clinicians as well as parents that it is not a "disease" or a "defect" but a pattern of thinking and behavior that can have advantages as well as disadvantages, although the disadvantages may be more apparent to the child at first. The clinician should pay careful attention to the interaction between parents and child. Well-meaning parents may undermine their child's self-esteem in ways in which they are unaware. The way in which they discuss the child's strengths and weaknesses, making comparisons with siblings, laughing when the child has difficulties with coordination during the examination, and interrupting or discounting what the child says when the child answers the clinician's questions are some examples. This can be discussed sensitively but directly in the summary conference in the context of the parents' needing to do more than "the average parents" to support their child's self-esteem.

During periodic follow-up visits, the clinician can ask the child what having ADHD means for him or her. Overly negative interpretations may signal the need for more intensive intervention to increase the child's experience of success in a variety of situations. Also during follow-ups, interim peer functioning and interactions with teachers and others at school should be assessed (see Chapter 11 for more detail). Issues with taking medication also should be assessed, and long-acting preparations should be considered when taking medication in the middle of the school day presents a significant social obstacle for the child. Some children will perceive their having to go to the nurse to get medication as the reason why other children tease them when, in fact, a variety of their own behaviors contribute to peer rejection. In this case, multiple social interventions are likely to be necessary (see Chapter 7), and midday medication may be able to be maintained or reintroduced when the other problems have been addressed. Interim history should be obtained about how the parents are managing discipline, the inclusion of positive reinforcement for desired behavior, and the fostering of self-esteem and skill building in areas of strength and weakness. The clinician should ask interim history questions to the child as well as to the parents and indicate that the child's opinion is valued. Adolescents and parents of adolescents should have some opportunity to provide information to the clinician separately, although most of the information collecting and, later, recommendations and plans should be discussed jointly. In some cases, an adolescent will provide to the clinician sensitive information that his or her parents do not know, such as about sexual activity or drug use. How to handle confidentiality issues with adolescents and their parents is an important topic in all fields that are related to the clinical care of children and adolescents, and its in-depth discussion is beyond the scope of this chapter. In general, communication with adolescents should be confidential unless the adolescent's health or safety is in direct jeopardy. The clinician should explain his or her policy to parents and adolescents to-gether when separate interviews are initiated. It should be consistent with the clini-cian's policy in the provision of care to children and adolescents in general; it need not be unique for the provision of care to children and adolescents with ADHD.

The clinician should praise the child's accomplishments and provide reminders about the extra difficulties that individuals with ADHD face and courage that they must demonstrate to accomplish some of the same things that peers do with less effort. Em-phasizing the secondary nature of the role of medication in the child's accomplishments also is important. Clinicians should avoid using ADHD as an adjective (e.g., "the ADHD child") in speaking or in writing; it can suggest that ADHD is the most important thing about the child. Finally, clinicians can provide resources for older children and adoles-cents, in the form of both written materials that they can review with parents and oppor-tunities to receive peer support (local support groups, camps, the World Wide Web).

COMMUNICATING WITH SCHOOL PERSONNEL ABOUT ADHD

Following the assessment, it is useful to provide information to school personnel (with parental permission) as a basis for requesting school-based interventions. Diagnoses, specific functional problems, and recommended interventions that are linked to the specific functional problems are most important because simply having a particular diagnosis does not automatically result in provision of appropriate services (see Chap-ter 8). The format shown in Appendix A may be used to provide this information to the school as well as to the parent. Examples of functional problems that often are encoun-tered by children with ADHD and some of the strategies that can be helpful are listed in Table 1. (A more in-depth presentation of school-based interventions that the clini-cian may want to suggest can be found in Chapters 5–7.) The results of any psychoedu-cational testing obtained during the course of the evaluation should be provided to school personnel. These results often serve as justification for services that are related to learning disabilities and may provide information about instructional modifications that will allow the child to learn more effectively.

CONTINUING TO LEARN ABOUT ADHD

There has been an explosion in the number of books written about ADHD for parents, school professionals, medical and mental health professionals, and children. Many are available in local public libraries and larger bookstores or can be borrowed from the lending libraries of parent support groups. Larger parent support groups, such as Chil-dren and Adults with Attention Deficit Disorders (CH.A.D.D.), and mail-order ser-vices, such as the ADD WareHouse and ADD Plus,[1] are centralized sources of recently published materials from a variety of publishers.

The World Wide Web is an important source of information for both professionals and the public. The common commercial carriers each have forums that are related to ADHD. Through these sites, one can learn about new books, local support groups, up-coming conferences, and new research results. One can communicate with other par-

Table 1. Functional impairments in ADHD and examples of school-based interventions

Cannot keep attention focused on seat work for a sufficient length of time

a. Modify expectations for the length of time that the student is expected to do uninterrupted seat work to allow successful functioning for about 80% of the time.

b. Note the general length of time that the student is able to attend, and give physical breaks and changes in material after this length of time.

c. Give positive reinforcement for work productivity and for the expected length of time spent working; gradually increase expectations when the student is successful at the previously acceptable level for more than 80% of the time.

d. Develop a private "signal," such as a touch on the shoulder, to remind the student to return to task when he or she stops working before the expected length of time.

e. Maximize the use of "hands-on" learning to supplement reading and writing.

Gets distracted easily

a. Seat at the front of the class, near the teacher and students who can serve as role models for appropriate behavior.

b. Limit distractions in the classroom environment.

c. Allow test taking in a modified environment (e.g., the resource room, the office).

Has trouble with getting information on paper

a. Devise ways to allow the child to demonstrate what he or she truly knows in spite of this "output" difficulty, including oral and multiple-choice methods (take into consideration that output difficulty also may include difficulty with oral expression on demand). Substitute other types of projects for some writing assignments (e.g., interviews, picture stories, experiments, computer learning programs).

b. Focus on content (e.g., grade separately for content and mechanics in writing assignments, break longer assignments into two parts [e.g., one night develop content, the next night recopy to focus on spelling, grammar, organization]).

c. Modify writing demands.

d. Allow the use of a word processor if this helps.

e. Assist with note taking by providing instruction in how to abstract important material, provide written as well as verbal information (e.g., overheads of the lecture in outline format), and note the length of time that the student needs to take notes to prevent him or her from consistently falling behind.

f. Limit the effect of weak note-taking skills on learning by providing a written outline or a copy of a peer buddy's notes; allow the use of a tape recorder for lectures.

Exhibits behaviors that are disruptive to the class

a. Use positively oriented behavior management system to encourage desirable behavior and discourage undesirable behavior.

b. Maximize instructional match and hands-on learning.

c. Alternate preferred and nonpreferred activities, and make some preferred activities contingent on previously agreed-on definitions of acceptable behavior.

Has trouble with appropriate social behavior

a. Use positively oriented behavior management system to encourage prosocial behavior and discourage inappropriate social behavior, particularly aggression.

b. Use school-based social skills training, either in a group or individually.

Has trouble with regulating emotions

a. Observe antecedent situations that tend to trigger overreactions (e.g., working on projects in groups, interactions with particular children), and attempt to limit the situations that lead to emotional outbursts or provide additional supervision.

(continued)

Table 1. *(continued)*

b. Provide counseling with a trained, adult advocate, such as a guidance counselor, to learn and practice anxiety- or anger-control strategies, appropriate expression of feelings, and problem solving.

c. If the child and the family are participating in counseling privately, then coordinate with the counselor to reinforce strategies in the school setting.

d. Have a "cooling down" place or activity to assist the child in resuming composure.

Has trouble with keeping desk and belongings organized

a. Establish regular, predictable classroom routines and places to keep belongings.

b. Limit changes in rooms, teachers, and schedules as much as possible.

c. Collaborate with parents to organize notebook (e.g., copy of schedule or day planner, color-coded dividers for each class, a place to copy homework, a folder for storing items or homework sheets to bring home and back).

d. Have a "check-in" with mentor at the end of the day to help ensure that everything that needs to be in the bookbag is in the bookbag.

e. Have an extra copy of books at home.

Has trouble with doing or turning in homework

a. Collaborate with parents to organize the notebook so that parents and teachers are aware of what the child needs to do and has done.

b. Collaborate with parents to develop a positively oriented behavior management system to increase homework production and compliance.

c. Accept homework at the end of the class or later the same day if the student cannot find it at the beginning of class.

d. Assign a "homework buddy" to be called in case of questions about assignment instructions in the evening.

e. Address writing problems as described above.

f. Address organizational problems as described above.

---

ents about ADHD or "listen" to professionals discuss their work and answer questions. Adolescents are finding the World Wide Web a good way to "chat" with other adolescents about ADHD. Several relevant support groups and other sources of information now have web sites on the World Wide Web, which also can be accessed through commercial carriers. The best way to find a variety of ADHD-related sites is to enter "attention deficit disorder" as the key words into the browser function of the commercial carrier or into any of the World Wide Web search engines, such as Excite, Infoseek, Lycos, or Yahoo.

Parents who use on-line services to learn about ADHD may be exposed to new information about causes and treatments before their primary clinician. They should be encouraged to bring such information to the clinician for review, however, because anyone can post information on-line and, thus, there are no guarantees that it is accurate. The clinician should ascertain the source of the material to help the parents put in context its relevance to their child.

Following are some of the references that are available for parents and children; those that are for or specific to adolescents are listed at the end of Chapter 13. Increasing numbers of references also are available on videotape.

ENDNOTE

1. ADD WareHouse, 300 Northwest 70th Avenue, Suite 102, Plantation, FL 33317; (800) 233-9273, (954) 792-8944; http://www.addwarehouse.com. ADD Plus (800) VIP-1-ADD ([800] 847-1233); fax (503) 364-7454.

RESOURCES FOR PARENTS

Barkley, R.A. (1995). *Taking charge of ADHD: The complete authoritative guide for parents.* New York: Guilford Press. (To order, call [800] 365-7006.)

Fowler, M.C. (1990). *Maybe you know my kid.* New York: Birch Lane Press, Carol Publishing Group. (To order, call [201] 866-0490.)

Garrison, J.R. (1996). *Living with a challenging child.* Ann Arbor, MI: Servant Publications. (To order, call [800] 458-8505.)

Hallowell, E. (1996). *When you worry about the child you love: Emotional and learning problems in children.* New York: Simon & Schuster. (To order, call [800] 223-2336.)

Koplewicz, H. (1996). *It's nobody's fault: New hope and help for difficult children and their parents.* New York: Random House. (To order, call [800] 733-3000.)

Murray, I. (1993). Looking back: Reminiscences from childhood and adolescence. In G. Weiss & L.T. Hechtman (Eds.), *Hyperactive children grown up: ADHD in children, adolescents, and adults* (2nd ed., pp. 301–325). New York: Guilford Press. (To order, call [800] 365-7006.)

Parker, H.C. (1994). *The ADD hyperactivity workbook for parents, teachers, and kids.* Plantation, FL: Specialty Press, Inc. (To order, call [800] 233-9273.)

Phelan, T.W. (1996). *All about attention deficit disorder.* Glen Ellyn, IL: Child Management, Inc. (To order, call [800] 442-4453.)

Silver, L.R. (1993). *Dr. Larry Silver's advice to parents on attention deficit hyperactivity disorder.* Washington, DC: American Psychiatric Press. (To order, call [800] 368-5777.)

Taylor, J.F. (1994). *Helping your hyperactive attention deficit child.* Rocklin, CA: Prima Publishing. (To order, call [800] 632-8676.)

Wodrich, D.L. (1994). *Attention deficit hyperactivity disorder: What every parent wants to know.* Baltimore: Paul H. Brookes Publishing Co. (To order, call [800] 638-3775.)

RESOURCES FOR CHILDREN

Amen, D.G. (1995). *A child's guide to attention deficit disorder.* Fairfied, CA: MindWorks Press. (To order, call [800] 626-2720 x400.)

Dunn, K.B., & Dunn, A.B. (1993). *Trouble with school: A family story about learning disabilities.* Bethesda, MD: Woodbine House. (To order, call [800] 843-7323.)

Galvin, M.R. (1995). *Otto learns about his medicine.* New York: Magination Press. (To order, call [800] 374-2721.)

Gehret, J. (1996). *Eagle eyes: A child's guide to paying attention.* Fairport, NY: Verbal Images Press. (To order, call [716] 377-3807.)

Gehret, J. (1992). *I'm somebody too.* Fairport, NY: Verbal Images Press. [For siblings] (To order, call [716] 377-3807.)

Gordon, M. (1993). *Jumpin' Johnny get back to work!* DeWitt, NY: GSI Publications, Inc. (To order, call [315] 446-4849.)

Levine, M. (1990). *Keeping ahead in school: A student's book about learning abilities and learning disorders.* Cambridge, MA: Educators Publishing Service. (To order, call [800] 225-5750).

Nadeau, K.G., & Dixon, E.B. (1997). *Learning to slow down and pay attention: A book for kids about ADD* (2nd ed.). New York: Brunner/Mazel. (To order, call [800] 825-3089.)

Quinn, P.O., & Stern, J.M. (1991). *Putting on the brakes: Young people's guide to understanding attention deficit hyperactivity disorder.* New York: Magination Press. (To order, call [800] 374-2721.)

Stern, J.M., & Quinn, P.O. (Eds.). *Brakes: The interactive newsletter for kids with ADD.* New York: Brunner/Mazel. (To order, call [800] 825-3089.)

Thompson, M. (1992). *My brother Matthew.* Bethesda, MD: Woodbine House (for siblings of a child with a disability, but not specifically about ADHD). (To order, call [800] 843-7323.)

RESOURCES FOR TEACHERS

Barkley, R.A. (1994). *ADHD in the classroom: Strategies for teachers* [Videotape]. New York: Guilford Press. (To order, call [800] 365-7006.)

Brooks, R. (1991). *The self-esteem teacher.* Circle Pines, MN: American Guidance Service. (To order, call [800] 328-2560.)

Davis, L., Sirotowitz, S., & Parker, H.C. (1996). *Study strategies made easy: A practical plan for school success*. Plantation, FL: Specialty Press, Inc. (To order, call [800] 233-9273 [also available on videotape].)

Dornbush, M.P., & Pruitt, S.K. (1995). *Teaching the tiger: A handbook for individuals involved in the teaching of students with attention deficit disorder, Tourette syndrome, or obsessive compulsive disorder*. Duarte, CA: Hope Press. (To order, call [800] 321-4039.)

DuPaul, G., & Stoner, G. (1994). *ADHD in the schools*. New York: Guilford Press. (To order, call [800] 365-7006.)

Fowler, M., Barkley, R.A., Reeve, R., & Zentall, S. (1995). *The educator's in-service program and manual: Attention deficit disorders*. Plantation, FL: CH.A.D.D. (To order, call [305] 587-3700.)

Goldstein, S. (1994). *Understanding and managing children's classroom behavior*. New York: John Wiley & Sons. (To order, call [800] 225-5945.)

Gordon, S.B., & Asher, M.J. (1994). *Meeting the ADD challenge: A practical guide for teachers*. Champaign, IL: Research Press. (To order, call [800] 519-2707.)

Parker, H.C. (1992). *The ADD hyperactivity handbook for schools*. Plantation, FL: Specialty Press, Inc. (To order, call [800] 233-9273.)

Reif, S.F. (1993). *How to reach and teach ADD/ADHD children*. West Nyack, NY: Center for Applied Research in Education. (To order, call ADD WareHouse [800] 233-9273.)

Shapiro, E.S., & Cole, C.L. (1994). *Behavior change in the classroom: Self-management interventions*. New York: Guilford Press. (To order, call [800] 365-7006.)

RESOURCES FOR CLINICIANS

Anastopoulos, A.D. (1995). Facilitating parental understanding and management of attention-deficit/hyperactivity disorder. In A. Reinecke, F.M. Dattilo, & A. Freeman (Eds.), *Cognitive therapy with children and adolescents* (pp. 327–343). New York: Guilford Press. (To order, call [800] 365-7006.)

DuPaul, G.J., & Stoner, G. (1994). Communication with parents, professionals, and students. In *ADHD in the schools: Assessment and intervention strategies* (pp. 199–216). New York: Guilford Press. (To order, call [800] 365-7006.)

FOR MORE INFORMATION ABOUT LEARNING DISABILITIES

International Dyslexia Association (formerly the Orton Dyslexia Society), Suite 382, Chester Building, 8600 LaSalle Road, Baltimore, MD 21286-2044; (410) 296-0232.

Learning Disabilities Association of America, 4156 Library Road, Pittsburgh, PA 15234; (412) 341-8077.

National Center for Learning Disabilities, 381 Park Avenue South, Suite 1420, New York, NY 10016; (212) 545-7510.

ON-LINE RESOURCES

American Academy of Child and Adolescent Psychiatry
http://www.aacap.org/
(for information about a variety of neurodevelopmental/neuropsychiatric disorders in children)
Attention Deficit Disorder Help Page http://members.aol.com/addisorder/4help/

CH.A.D.D.
http://www.chadd.org/
(for information about support groups, ordering materials, conferences, new research)

Internet Mental Health
http://www.mentalhealth.com
(for information specifically about psychopharmacology, add the following to the above address: /p30.html)

National Institutes of Health
http://www.nih.gov/
(for information about research)

United States Department of Education
http://www.ed.gov/
(for information about educational services and educational law)

United States Food and Drug Administration
http://www.fda.gov/fdahomepage.html
(click on Foods, then Dietary Supplements for information about alternative treatments)

Evaluation Summary

EVALUATION SUMMARY

Evaluation Summary for _____

Date of birth _____

Date of Evaluation Summary _____

Clinician's name _____

Signature _____

Telephone _____

Presenting concerns: 1. _____

2. _____

3. _____

4. _____

Additional issues: 1. _____

2. _____

3. _____

4. _____

5. _____

6. _____

Strengths: 1. _____

2. _____

3. _____

4. _____

Diagnoses: 1. _____

2. _____

3. _____

4. _____

The Clinician's Practical Guide to Attention-Deficit/Hyperactivity Disorder
by Marianne Mercugliano, Thomas J. Power, and Nathan J. Blum   ©1999 by Paul H. Brookes Publishing Co.

Additional assessments
needed:

1. _____
2. _____
3. _____
4. _____

Recommendations:

1. _____
2. _____
3. _____
4. _____
5. _____
6. _____
7. _____
8. _____

Referrals:

1. _____
2. _____
3. _____
4. _____

Summary of Important Information About Attention-Deficit/Hyperactivity Disorder

I. **Definition and characteristics of ADHD**
   A. There are specific diagnostic criteria; they all are based on behavior.
   B. Core features are short attention span, distractibility, impulsivity, and hyperactivity.
   C. Other commonly associated characteristics include inconsistency in behavior, noncompliance, feeling easily bored, and not responding as easily as others to rewards and punishments.
   D. It is divided into inattentive type, hyperactive-impulsive type, and combined type.
   E. Associated problems include low motivation, easy boredom, forgetfulness, confusion, social difficulties, difficulties with certain subjects in school (especially writing), and difficulties with regulating emotions.
   F. Some children with ADHD also have learning problems, argumentative or defiant behavior, excess anxiety, depression, and/or tics.

II. **How ADHD is diagnosed**
   A. Information is collected from parents and teacher(s) through interviews and/or rating scales to determine that the symptoms of ADHD are present to a degree that causes functional impairment, have been present for a long time, and are present in multiple situations.
   B. Additional history, rating scales, examinations, and/or tests may be used to diagnose other conditions and factors that may cause similar symptoms or make the symptoms more severe.
   C. Laboratory tests and physical examinations do not confirm or exclude ADHD, but the doctor may conduct them to look for contributing factors or other disorders.

III. **What causes ADHD**
   A. There is evidence that ADHD is the result of how the brain processes information between when it comes in and when it is used to make a response, especially when things need to be "remembered" in the process of using them (e.g., following a direction accurately, comprehending a reading passage, writing a sentence or solving a math word problem).
   B. The connections between the frontal lobes of the brain (the "executive control") and other parts of the brain, particularly the basal ganglia (where things that we have learned to do automatically are stored) are suspected to be the most important brain areas related to ADHD, although more study is required to be certain.
   C. Brain scans do not show sufficient differences to be used diagnostically, although researchers are looking at the structure and function of specific parts of the brain in much greater detail and have found some differences in some studies. More information is likely to come from this line of investigation in the future.
   D. "Brain damage" is a rare cause of ADHD; many children with ADHD have "inherited" it, and some have it with no clear cause. Bad parenting and bad teaching do not cause ADHD, even though they can cause bad behavior, but excellent parenting and teaching skills can help children with ADHD do their best. In other words, the environment at home and in school has an important influence on the severity of symptoms.

The Clinician's Practical Guide to Attention-Deficit/Hyperactivity Disorder
by Marianne Mercugliano, Thomas J. Power, and Nathan J. Blum   ©1999 by Paul H. Brookes Publishing Co.

IV. **The four most important things that the parent of a child with ADHD can do**
   A. Become a careful observer of your child so that you can figure out how to help him or her the most. This also will help you know what to tell teachers and counselors to help them help your child.
      1. Determine what your child does well and what is hard for him or her (at home, at school, in the community).
      2. Determine the conditions that prevent your child from doing his or her best.
      3. Determine the conditions that make it easier for your child to do something that requires effort.
   B. Foster your child's self-esteem
      1. Make sure that your child knows that your love and support are unconditional. (This does not mean that you support everything that your child does or that you do not set limits or provide discipline.)
      2. Find ways to showcase your child's talents.
      3. Create an environment in which your child is likely to experience success.
      4. Give your child self-esteem and a sense of responsibility by helping him or her to contribute.
      5. Help him or her learn to solve problems and not fear mistakes.
   C. Learn everything that you can about ADHD
      1. Read books and articles.
      2. Join support groups, such as Children and Adults with Attention Deficit Disorders (CH.A.D.D.).
      3. Participate in your child's school and in local support and advocacy groups.
      4. If you have never thought of parenting as a "career" that requires preparation, hard work, organization, persistence, and self-discipline, then begin to do so now!
   D. Take care of yourself and your marriage
      1. If you think that you have ADHD, then get help for yourself.
      2. You have a "new job" now; consider saying "no" to some other things.
      3. Get support for yourself and your family.
      4. Learn to work as a team with your spouse.
V. **The long-term effects of ADHD**
   A. ADHD makes accomplishing the tasks of daily life harder for your child.
   B. If your child has additional diagnoses such as a learning disability or oppositional defiant disorder, then accomplishing the tasks of daily life will be harder still for your child.
   C. Children with ADHD are at greater risk for academic and occupational underachievement, a difficult time during adolescence, social and antisocial problems, difficulty with relationships and jobs, driving accidents, substance abuse, and depression than otherwise similar children without ADHD.
   D. These are *risks*, not prophecies! You are the most important person in your child's life, and what you do to help make your child's day-to-day life successful is important in helping your child to have a good rather than a bad

The Clinician's Practical Guide to Attention-Deficit/Hyperactivity Disorder
by Marianne Mercugliano, Thomas J. Power, and Nathan J. Blum   ©1999 by Paul H. Brookes Publishing Co.

outcome (see Item IV). If your child knows that you will never give up on him or her and you do the things that show it, then it will make a difference in the long run, even if you do not see it on a daily basis.

VI. **How ADHD is treated**
    A. Education for you, your child, and your child's siblings and teachers about ADHD and how it relates to your child's particular symptoms
    B. Educational and behavioral interventions and accommodations in school
    C. Family-oriented training in behavior management strategies and home–school coordination
    D. Medication

VII. **More about behavior management**
    A. Behavior management (or behavior modification) is a system of setting up the environment to maximize your child's chance of success. It involves studying the antecedents and consequences of your child's behavior and then changing them to increase the likelihood of desirable behaviors. This involves reminding strategies coupled with positive reinforcement for desired behavior and punishment for undesirable behavior.
    B. Most people think of star charts and happy face stickers when they hear the words "behavior management" or "behavior modification." These are some of the *tools*, but you must understand the *principles* of behavior management in order to use it successfully.
    C. Behavior management systems should be used consistently at home and be coordinated with what is done at school.
    D. You will need the help of books and (usually) an experienced professional to learn enough about the principles of behavior management to use it effectively at home and to advocate for its appropriate use at school.
    E. Find a professional who has experience with behavior management systems for children who have ADHD and with consulting with both parents and schools, if difficulties are present in both settings.

VIII. **The role of other kinds of counseling for children with ADHD**
    A. "Play therapy" and individual psychotherapy for your child do not help ADHD symptoms directly but may be recommended in some cases to address the child's emotional needs.
    B. "Family therapy" also does not specifically treat ADHD symptoms but may be helpful when marital, parent–child, or other family issues prevent progress in other areas under treatment.
    C. Social skills counseling may be recommended to help your child practice and use more adaptive behaviors in social situations. This may be done as part of a school program or privately. Private therapists will need to work with the school to help your child generalize what is learned to the school environment.

IX. **School interventions for ADHD**
    A. Material should be taught at the level at which your child is ready and able to learn.
    B. Gaps in your child's academic skills need to be filled by tutoring or specialized instruction.
    C. Your child may need extra supervision or special assistance with certain educational tasks that are particularly difficult for children with ADHD. These

The Clinician's Practical Guide to Attention-Deficit/Hyperactivity Disorder
by Marianne Mercugliano, Thomas J. Power, and Nathan J. Blum   ©1999 by Paul H. Brookes Publishing Co.

include copying from the blackboard, completing work independently, completing long-term assignments, and taking tests.

D. Your child may require the use of certain techniques to get and maintain his or her attention during the school day.

E. Assistance with study skills and organization is important.

F. Peer buddies, mentors, homeroom or special education teachers, and counselors or school psychologists can assist.

G. Foolproof home–school communication is critical.

H. Grade retention, which sometimes is recommended because the student seems "immature" compared with peers or is behind academically, is not usually an appropriate intervention for ADHD.

X. Medication for ADHD

A. Medication is used when behavioral and educational interventions do not result in sufficient progress in the family, at school, and with peers or when the child is able to make progress but at too great a personal cost.

B. The first-line medications for ADHD are stimulants.

C. Stimulants work by increasing the amount of certain neurotransmitters used by brain cells to communicate, especially dopamine and norepinephrine, which play an important role in regulating the activity of the areas of the brain that seem to be involved in ADHD.

D. They can be very helpful for increasing attention span and focusing and reducing distractibility and impulsivity; they do not simply suppress your child's activity.

E. Some side effects (from most common to least common) include appetite suppression, rebound (worsening of symptoms for a period of time as the medication wears off), slightly increased pulse and blood pressure, insomnia, anxiety, increased repetitive behaviors (including tics), and slowed growth.

F. Most children either do not have side effects or have some that are mild and can be managed with changes in dosage, timing, or a change in the particular stimulant used.

G. Other kinds of medication, especially antidepressants, also treat ADHD symptoms and might be recommended if your child does not tolerate stimulants.

H. The use of alternative medications is most common when the child has additional diagnoses such as a tic disorder, an anxiety disorder, or depression.

XI. Alternative treatments for ADHD

A. Many unproven treatments for ADHD have been advocated; the most common are elimination diets, dietary supplements, and EEG biofeedback.

B. Some alternative treatments benefit some children, but there is no way to know which one(s) will help a particular child.

C. Beware of alternative treatments that are recommended by a group or an individual who will derive financial profit from your purchasing a product.

D. If you elect to use an alternative treatment, then it should be monitored for safety and effectiveness with your physician, just as though you were using standard medications.

XII. Many kinds of professionals may be involved with a child with ADHD

A. A physician should be involved in your child's assessment and will continue to be involved if you elect to use medication for your child.

The Clinician's Practical Guide to Attention-Deficit/Hyperactivity Disorder
by Marianne Mercugliano, Thomas J. Power, and Nathan J. Blum   ©1999 by Paul H. Brookes Publishing Co.

B.	Many different kinds of physicians take care of children with ADHD, including pediatricians, family doctors, neurologists, psychiatrists, and developmental/behavioral pediatricians (pediatricians with extra training in the areas of developmental disorders and child behavior).

C.	Child psychologists can help with evaluation, psychoeducational testing, school consultation, behavior management training, and other types of counseling. Not all psychologists have expertise in the types of interventions that are required for ADHD.

D.	The school psychologist may be involved in evaluation and testing and in helping the teacher to develop educational, behavioral, and social interventions for your child at school.

E.	The special education teacher or the reading specialist may help in devising educational interventions for your child in the general classroom or may work with your child individually or in a small group to assist with academic skills.

F.	The guidance counselor may meet with your child for individual counseling or social skills help. He or she may serve as the coordinator of interventions when your child has multiple teachers. Alternatively, the school psychologist, special educator, or school nurse may fulfill this role.

G.	The guidance counselor may be involved with your child when it is time to learn and make decisions about secondary school programs and postsecondary education.

H.	The speech-language pathologist may be involved with your child for the assessment and treatment of speech or language problems.

I.	The occupational therapist may be involved with your child for the assessment and treatment of fine motor, perceptual, or sensory problems.

XIII.	**Being an advocate for your child**

A.	Federal laws that pertain to special education and educational rights for individuals with disabilities help to safeguard basic rights for students who need individualized interventions in school.

B.	State law may lend additional supports and describe how the process of obtaining special services works.

C.	Parents and school personnel need to work together to design effective strategies and coordinate home and school interventions.

D.	Conflicts between parents and school personnel sometimes arise because educational law is not entirely comprehensive and specific and because schools often are short on resources for students with ADHD (which generally are personnel- and time-intensive).

E.	Parents need to be knowledgeable not only about educational law but also about the specifics of what works for their child and what the child's strengths and weaknesses are so that they can verbalize clearly what the child needs in order to achieve.

F.	Advocating also means creating at home and in other settings an environment that maximizes the child's success and self-esteem.

G.	Parent support and advocacy groups and federal sources of information about educational law can be extremely helpful.

The Clinician's Practical Guide to Attention-Deficit/Hyperactivity Disorder
by Marianne Mercugliano, Thomas J. Power, and Nathan J. Blum   ©1999 by Paul H. Brookes Publishing Co.

XIV. **Learning more about ADHD**
  A. There are many books available about all aspects of ADHD; they can be obtained from local libraries and bookstores, from the lending libraries of parent support groups, from mail-order sources, and at conferences about ADHD.
  B. There also are many videotapes available from the same sources; some are videotape versions of books.
  C. Parent support groups are an important way to continue to learn.
  D. The World Wide Web has a variety of sites for those interested in ADHD; some relate specifically to ADHD, and others are more general but may include information about it.
  E. Because the World Wide Web does not require specific credentials of the individuals who provide information or verification of what is printed, you cannot assume accuracy.

The Clinician's Practical Guide to Attention-Deficit/Hyperactivity Disorder
by Marianne Mercugliano, Thomas J. Power, and Nathan J. Blum   ©1999 by Paul H. Brookes Publishing Co.

Counseling for Children and Families Who Are Coping with Attention-Deficit/Hyperactivity Disorder

Growing up as a child with attention-deficit/hyperactivity disorder (ADHD) is a difficult and often painful process. Parenting a child with ADHD is a continuous challenge. Having ADHD increases the likelihood that the child will engage in disruptive and aggressive behaviors and experience emotional problems. The problems manifested by children with ADHD and parents' reaction to them vary greatly from family to family. Sometimes the difficulties that the family faces represent a relatively specific or isolated problem that is occurring in the context of generally positive parent–child interactions. In these cases, brief counseling that consists primarily of education about ADHD and behavior management strategies may be sufficient. In other cases, conduct problems in school, rejection by peers, highly conflictive parent–child interactions, and heightened levels of moodiness on the part of the child are present. In these instances, counseling will need to take an intensive and multifaceted approach that may include the child and the family in behavior and supportive therapy.

The purpose of this chapter is to describe counseling strategies that are useful for working with children and families who are coping with problems that are related to ADHD. This chapter highlights behavioral approaches for increasing desired behaviors and for decreasing inappropriate behaviors. Brief counseling interventions that may be provided by a primary care provider as well as more intensive behavioral family therapy approaches are presented. (For a summary of the extensive research demonstrating the effectiveness of behavior therapy in working with this population, see Barkley, 1998.)

PROVIDING EMOTIONAL SUPPORT

ADHD has a significant emotional impact on children as well as on their families. At various times in their lives, children with ADHD can experience failure in many aspects of their lives: Teachers may reprimand these children much more frequently than they praise them; peers may view these children as bossy and intrusive, which frequently results in peer rejection; parents can become frustrated, annoyed, and rejecting in response to the demanding nature of these children; and siblings may become resentful of the child with ADHD for occupying so much of their parents' time. It is not surprising that some children with ADHD come to view themselves as incompetent, unlikable, or even intrinsically bad. At the same time, these children are frustrated and angered by the many negative experiences that they encounter each day, which results in strong tendencies to be defiant of their parents and aggressive with siblings.

Many parents of children with ADHD become overwhelmed by the needs and demands of these children. Parents often are confronted by school professionals who are frustrated with their child's indiscretions and misdeeds. Complicating the situation is the insinuation by some teachers that the child's problems are the result of a disorganized home life or poor parenting. Ironically, as the parents' need for the support of family and friends intensifies, they may become increasingly isolated within their family and community.[1] Their own relatives may criticize them for being too permissive and for failing to heed their advice: "Spare the rod, spoil the child." Neighbors may keep their distance because gatherings with the family of a child with ADHD may be stressful.

Families who are coping with the problems of ADHD typically need high levels of emotional support. The child and his or her parents need to feel that someone understands the magnitude of the challenges that they face each day in coping with this disorder and related problems. Furthermore, because of the chronic nature of this disorder and its impact on family life, children and families who are coping with ADHD need from professionals emotional support on an ongoing basis. Providing emotional support is not sufficient to bring about change in child behavior and the quality of parent–child interactions; but unless professionals provide emotional support, they cannot be effective agents of behavior change.

PROVIDING INFORMATION ABOUT ADHD

In the early stages of counseling, parents and children often benefit from a discussion about the specific ways in which ADHD affects the child's functioning and family interaction patterns. This discussion often starts at the time of the summary conference following the evaluation for ADHD (see Chapter 4), but most families will need to discuss these issues in greater depth at follow-up meetings or in counseling. Many parents and children enter counseling with a frame of reference that leads to unproductive and self-defeating patterns of behavior. The task of the clinician is to help the parents develop a different frame of reference, one that will lead to greater understanding of the child's difficulties and increase the use of positive methods of discipline. For instance, parents who view the child as manipulative may become angry easily and be quick to reprimand the child when he or she insists on doing things a certain way. In contrast, parents who understand that their child has to work very hard to control his or her impulses are more likely to be supportive and to use positive methods of behavior management to assist the child in gaining self-control.

IMPROVING THE PARENT–CHILD RELATIONSHIP

In coping with the stresses that are associated with ADHD, parents and children often engage in conflictive, mutually rejecting relationships with each other. Much of their interaction time may be spent attempting to change each other through coercive and manipulative statements and actions,[2] which are discussed in more detail in Chapter 12. When this occurs, brief counseling generally is not effective because parents have trouble with applying behavior management strategies in an effective manner. More intensive counseling that begins with interventions to improve the parent–child relationship often is needed.

A useful strategy for changing a coercive pattern of interacting is to schedule daily parent–child play periods of roughly 20 minutes in length.[3] It is important to adhere to the following rules when conducting these sessions. First, the parent and the child need to choose a time that is mutually convenient; often the best time is when homework is completed and both the parent and the child have some time to relax. Generally, one parent plays with the child during each play session. To involve both parents, the mother and the father can play with the child on alternate days. Second, the child is given the choice of which game to play. It usually is preferable to engage in a game that does not involve rough play or a stringent set of rules, so parents may need to limit the choices that are provided to the child. One way to limit the range of choices without engendering resentment from the child is for the parent to find a time when the child is cooperative and together create a list of fun but appropriate games for them to play with each other. When it is playtime, the child is allowed to choose any of the items on this list. Third, the parents should establish a fixed time limit for the play period by setting a countdown timer. Without clear time limits, children will attempt to extend the length of the play period, often using coercive methods. The parents, in turn, may become resentful and reluctant to conduct play sessions in the future.

Fourth, during the session, it is imperative that the parents refrain from controlling the child's play. Many parents, even those who engage in healthy, mutually supportive relationships with their child, have difficulties with refraining from controlling the agenda of their child's play. Parents control play in subtle ways, such as by making suggestions for what the child should do; teaching the child how to perform a task; or asking leading questions, such as, "Do you want to make a car with the blocks?" An important rule for parents is to observe the child's play carefully, describe what the child is doing as a "play-by-play announcer," and praise the child for creative ideas. The parent should refrain from making suggestions, asking questions, and criticizing the child. If the child's play becomes aggressive or highly disruptive, then the parent can provide a brief command for the child to play cooperatively. If the negative behavior continues, then the parent should discontinue the play period.

With older children, playing a game together may not be appropriate. Instead, the parents should strive to be available at a time when the youth is relaxed and comfortable. During these times, it is important for the parents to listen attentively and allow the child to dictate the direction of the conversation. This is not a time to teach; the main purpose is for the parent to demonstrate an appreciation of the child.

Many parents have problems with conducting play or listening sessions with their children. Clinicians may need to model effective strategies and then coach the parents as they conduct these sessions in the office. (Strategies for conducting these training sessions are described in detail in Barkley, 1997, and Forehand & McMahon, 1981.)

BEHAVIOR CHANGE STRATEGIES

The basic premise of behavior modification is that the likelihood that a specific action will occur is determined by what takes place prior to the behavior (antecedents) and following the behavior (consequences). To change behavior, clinicians can work with families to change the antecedents and the consequences of a child's problem behaviors.

Changing the Antecedents of Behavior

Antecedents refer to the context in which behavior occurs. There are a wide range of variables that can be considered in describing the context of behavior, including environmental and family factors as well as child characteristics.

Modifying the Environment

Changing environmental factors that contribute to problem behaviors can be one of the most effective ways of decreasing these behaviors. For instance, if a child has trouble with completing homework because he or she is distracted easily, then providing a quiet work place may improve attention and productivity. Also, the way in which parents make requests of their children is related to whether the children will comply.[4] When parents frame the request as a wordy question (e.g., "Would you mind turning off the TV and helping to set the table so that I don't have to do everything myself?"), then they are much less likely to gain compliance than when they state the command in a clear, forthright manner (e.g., "I need you to set the table now"). The strategies that were described previously for improving the parent–child relationship also can be used to change the antecedents of noncompliant, defiant behavior, which may lead the child to behave in a more cooperative and respectful manner.

Even in situations in which the antecedents of a problem behavior are difficult to alter, identifying the antecedents is important because it will help parents predict problematic situations, thus enabling parents to be more prepared to cope with them. For instance, it is common for a child to respond differently to requests from different parents. Similarly, the child may respond differently to requests from parents versus from adults outside the home, such as teachers or grandparents. Variations in the way in which children respond to adults may reflect differences in the behavior management strategies that adults have used in the past or differences in the roles that adults play in the lives of children. If one parent assumes primary responsibility for getting the child to comply with demanding tasks such as homework and household chores while the other generally engages in enjoyable activities with the child, then the child may be more likely to resist a request from the more demanding parent. Identifying these situations can make a child's behavior more understandable and can be useful in developing an intervention plan.

Accounting for the Child's Temperament

Another antecedent for problem behaviors is the child's temperament. *Temperament* refers to a child's intrinsic behavioral style. Table 1 presents the temperament characteristics identified by Thomas, Chess, Birch, Hertzig, and Korn (1963) in their longitudinal study of children. Many aspects of temperament, such as the child's attention span, activity level, distractibility, and persistence, are related to ADHD, but other aspects of the child's temperament also may contribute to behavior problems. For example, children who have problems with adaptability often have trouble with adjusting to changing demands. It is important to prepare these children for transitions and to in-

Table 1. Developmental considerations in behavior management

Age	Common behavior problems	Behavior change strategies	Sample reinforcers
Preschool	Temper tantrums Noncompliance with rules Aggression (hitting, biting) Overactivity Sleep problems Food selectivity Worries and fears	Modifying environment Increasing parental praise Distraction Immediate tangible reinforcers Extinction Time-out	Adult attention • Verbal praise • Hug or pat • Thumbs-up sign or wink Stickers Access to toys or games Edible items
School age	Noncompliance with rules Peer problems Aggression Failure to complete chores, school work, or homework Overactivity Disorganization	Modifying environment Increasing parental praise Token reinforcement systems Loss of privileges Time-out	Adult attention Access to privileges • Later bedtime • Computer or TV time • Trip to a special location Access to toys or games • Special game with parents • Grab bag of small toys
Adolescence	Noncompliance with rules Risk-taking behaviors Peer problems Failure to complete chores, school work, or homework Disorganization	Modifying environment Increasing praise from significant adults Token reinforcement systems Self-management Loss of privileges Grounding	Access to privileges • Later curfew • Special trip with friends Money • Additions to allowance • Shopping trip

troduce changes gradually. With variations in temperament, it often is the mismatch between the child's temperament and the expectations of adults that causes the problem.[5] For example, some parents are tolerant of children who respond very intensely to disappointment by having a brief tantrum, whereas other parents view this type of response as intolerable. Identifying dimensions of child temperament can help parents predict situations that are likely to be problematic and develop useful strategies to help their child.

Understanding and, when possible, changing the antecedents of problem behavior are critical in the treatment of a child with ADHD; these types of interventions can be effective and often do not require much additional effort from parents; however, changing the antecedents of behavior may not be sufficient for bringing about the desired degree of improvement in child behavior and parent–child interactions. Counseling generally needs to focus on modifying the consequences of behavior as well.

Modifying the Consequences of Behavior

Consequences are **reinforcers** when they increase the likelihood that the behavior will occur in the future and are **punishers** when they decrease the probability that the behavior will occur in the future. Determining whether a consequence is a reinforcer or a punisher depends on the effect of the response on future behavior as opposed to the intent of the person who is delivering the consequence. The significance of this point was demonstrated in a study by Madsen, Becker, Thomas, Koser, and Plager (1968) in a first-grade classroom. They found that the more that teachers told children to sit down, the more frequently children stood up at inappropriate times; thus, although the teachers intended to decrease the frequency of standing-up behavior, the sit-down command inadvertently provided attention to the child and served as a reinforcer for the standing-up behavior. The following section describes strategies for increasing appropriate behaviors and decreasing inappropriate behaviors of children with ADHD.

Increasing Appropriate Behaviors

When parents come for counseling, their primary objective often is to reduce their child's disruptive behaviors that occur at home and in school. The temptation for clinicians is to suggest behavior reduction or punishment strategies at the outset, but this approach often is counterproductive because it may result in increased frustration and anger in the child. A more sensible approach is to redirect the request for behavior reduction to focus on increasing a behavior that is incompatible with the problem behavior of primary concern. For instance, if the parents are concerned about their child's habit of talking back and being disrespectful when asked to do something, then a useful strategy is to work on gaining the child's compliance with home rules in a timely and respectful manner.

Selecting the Appropriate Behavior to Change

At the outset of counseling, parents typically present a long list of concerns about home and school behavior. Choosing the appropriate target behavior is critical for counseling to be successful. The initial target for intervention should be a behavior that is of strong concern to the parents and the child and one that presents a reasonable probability of success given the quality of the parent–child interaction and the parents' level of behavior management skills. Behaviors that are difficult to treat at the outset for most families are sleep problems and sibling conflict. Target behaviors that usually are responsive to behavioral interventions are increasing compliance with parents' requests and with the family's rules. An advantage of targeting compliance with parents' requests is that improvements in this area often result in a reduction in inappropriate behaviors such as aggression and disruptiveness.[6]

Most children with ADHD have problems with complying with rules several times during the course of a day. Clinicians find it helpful to focus interventions on one period of the day at a time. For instance, it often is useful to establish a morning routine and an after-school homework protocol. As a rule of thumb, clinicians should start with a period of the day when there is a relatively high probability of success to build the parents' and the child's confidence that they can be successful in working together on an intervention plan.

Providing Positive Parental Attention

Once a behavior has been framed in positive terms as a target for intervention, the next step is to develop a set of consequences that will increase the occurrence of the behavior. Research has shown convincingly that adult attention is a powerful motivation for child behavior and can result in the strengthening of desirable and undesirable behaviors.[7] Helping parents provide positive attention to their children in a strategic manner can be very useful for improving targeted behaviors. For instance, paying attention to and praising children for complying with rules and systematically ignoring children for not following rules generally will result in more obedient behavior. As a rule, the more positive the interaction between the parent and the child, the more likely it is that parental attention will improve targeted behaviors.[8] Also, praise is more effective when parents specify the behavior that is being reinforced (e.g., "I really appreciate your emptying the trash cans") than when they offer vague, nonspecific feedback (e.g., "Thanks for helping out").[9]

Using Tangible Reinforcers

The strategic use of positive attention, although helpful, generally is not sufficient to produce the desired level of behavior change in children with ADHD.[10] A more powerful intervention is to supplement verbal praise with more tangible reinforcers, such as privileges, material objects, or in some cases snacks. Tangible reinforcers fall along a continuum: Privileges are the most preferable, food is the least preferable, and material objects (e.g., toys, money) are at an intermediate level of acceptability. As a rule, clinicians should advise parents to use the highest level of reinforcer that will be effective with the child. In general, the older the child, the higher the level of reinforcer that will be effective; however, developmental age and impulsivity level are important factors to consider when determining the most appropriate reinforcer.

It is important to provide children who have ADHD with positive reinforcement frequently and as soon as possible after the desired behavior occurs.[11] Generally, it is not feasible to provide a privilege or a toy every time a child performs the targeted response. Instead, token systems of reinforcement can be very useful. A child is given a token or a chip when the desired behavior occurs. At designated times, the child is able to cash in the chips for back-up reinforcers, such as privileges or toys. (See Barkley, 1997, for a detailed description of how to design effective token systems for children with ADHD and related behavior problems.)

Maintaining the Value of Reinforcers

A potential problem with using concrete reinforcement systems when treating children who have ADHD is that reinforcers may lose their value over time. For this reason, it is helpful to vary the reinforcer frequently and perhaps to introduce an element of uncertainty. For instance, if the child earns a reinforcer, then he or she could roll dice to determine what the reward will be. Another strategy is to use a "mystery motivator"; at the beginning of a specified period of time (e.g., week), the parents decide what the reinforcer will be, write it down, seal it in an envelope, and place it in a location where the child cannot sneak a look at it. Throughout the course of the week, the parents and the child can refer often to the mystery motivator. At the end of the week, if the child has earned a sufficient number of points, then he or she gets to open the envelope and find out the prize.[12]

Reinforcing versus Bribing

Parents and clinicians often are confused about the distinction between reinforcing desirable behavior and bribing children to behave appropriately, yet understanding this difference is important for effective behavior management. Most adults do not have difficulties with identifying a bribe in their own lives. If an individual is offered money for doing something that is improper, such as breaking the law, then the money is considered a bribe; in contrast, receiving a salary for performing a job is not considered a bribe. In behavioral terminology, the distinction is based on whether the reinforcer is being offered for appropriate or inappropriate behavior.

In managing a child's behavior, the distinction between reinforcing appropriate behavior and bribing is similar. For instance, if parents tell their children in the grocery store that they will get snacks at checkout for staying with their parents and not touching objects on the shelves, then the parents are offering the children an opportunity to earn a reinforcer for appropriate behavior. In contrast, if a child starts to have a tantrum in the check-out line and the parent offers a candy bar if the child stops, then the parent is bribing the child. In the latter case, the parent is offering a payoff that is contingent on the performance of inappropriate behavior (temper tantrum); thus, having a tantrum is being reinforced. Another way to conceptualize the difference is that reinforcements are positive consequences that are provided as part of a proactive, strategic plan, whereas bribes are rewards that are offered in a defensive posture as a response to a problem or a crisis that has already arisen.

Bribes are only one mechanism by which inappropriate behavior is reinforced. As mentioned previously, inappropriate behavior often is very effective for eliciting adult attention or allowing a child to escape from task demands. When inappropriate behaviors have been reinforced in any of these ways, it is crucial that this be identified and that the clinician counsel parents to manage the problem in ways that do not unwittingly reinforce the behavior.

Punishment

Punishment refers to responses to behavior that decrease the likelihood that the behavior will occur in the future. Punishment procedures include the loss of adult attention, privileges, or desired objects, as well as the introduction of an aversive consequence. When used in isolation, punishment procedures often are not effective for improving behavior as they do not teach desired ways of behaving as positive reinforcement systems do. For some children with ADHD, however, positive reinforcement systems will not result in a sufficient decrease in inappropriate behavior.[13] In these cases, the behavior management plan will need to incorporate both positive reinforcement and punishment.

Removing Adult Attention

Parents sometimes inadvertently reinforce inappropriate behavior. One way of decreasing the occurrence of these behaviors is to discontinue providing positive reinforcement for the unwanted behavior. The process of stopping the reinforcement of previously reinforced behaviors is referred to as **extinction.** Clinicians who counsel others to use extinction to decrease inappropriate behaviors need to be aware of certain problems with the use of this strategy. Because the child has had multiple experiences of being reinforced for the inappropriate behavior, it is likely that the use of extinction procedures will worsen the problem behavior at the outset. For example, if a child has learned that a tantrum will result in the parents' allowing him or her to go outside without completing homework, then the first few times that the parents refuse to let the child go outside until the homework is finished are likely to result in an intense and prolonged tantrum. It may take several trials before the child learns that the tantrums no longer will be effective and the frequency and the intensity of the tantrums decrease. Because of the tendency for extinction to worsen problem behaviors initially, this technique is best utilized for problem behaviors that are irritating but not dangerous or destructive. In these latter cases, more restrictive methods of punishment may need to be used.

Removing Privileges

Loss of privileges, or **response cost,** can be a very effective consequence for inappropriate behavior, especially when the privilege that is removed is connected logically with the inappropriate behavior. For example, a child who has not completed homework may not be allowed to watch television. If siblings are fighting over a toy, then both may lose the opportunity to play with the toy for a period of time. An adolescent who stays out past curfew may be grounded for a few nights. In other situations, logical consequences may not be available. This often is the case when there is time pressure to get an activity done or when trying to get a child to go to sleep. If a child is taking a long time to get ready for school in the morning, then it is not reasonable to prevent the child from going to school until he or she is ready. In these instances, clinicians may develop a token system whereby the child can earn points for engaging in the desired behaviors and lose points for inappropriate behaviors. Points then can be exchanged for back-up reinforcers after school or on weekends.[14]

When response cost procedures are being used, clinicians need to determine the length of time that privileges are to be removed. It usually is best for privileges to be removed for a short period of time or in a graded manner. For instance, if an inappropriate behavior results in the loss of television time for the entire evening, then the parents have used up a valuable reinforcer for appropriate behavior and an effective punisher for other inappropriate behaviors that may occur that evening. In contrast, if the child is allowed 1 hour of television per night and loses 10 minutes of television time for each episode of misbehavior, then he or she would have to misbehave six times before losing all of the television time.

Another problem with the use of punishers for an extended or indefinite period of time is that it may discourage the child, exacerbate the child's level of defiance, or lead to an escalating spiral of punishment that cannot be enforced. For instance, an adolescent who wants to see friends but is grounded for weeks may feel that there is nothing left to lose for sneaking out to see friends. The parents, in turn, may feel that they have no other choice but to threaten the adolescent with even longer, rather meaningless, intervals of punishment. Grounding the adolescent for one night quickly affords him or her an opportunity to demonstrate the ability to behave responsibly and allows the parents to utilize this consequence again if the adolescent behaves irresponsibly the next day. One alternative to time-based grounding is "job-grounding." With job-grounding, children must stay home until they complete a chore that is not routinely their responsibility. In this way, the child determines the length of the punishment. Continued misbehavior can be punished by a graded increase in the difficulty of the chores or in the number of chores that must be completed.

If the loss of privileges is graded or of short duration and does not seem to be decreasing inappropriate behavior, then clinicians should inquire about what the child is doing while the punishment is in effect and how well the parents enforce the punishment. If the child has many other equally desirable activities available while being punished, then the loss of a privilege may not have much effect on the child's behavior. Similarly, if the parents do not enforce the punishment consistently, then it is not likely to alter the child's behavior.

Time-Out

The power of adult attention to reinforce appropriate behavior has been discussed previously. The systematic removal of the child from the opportunity to get adult attention is referred to as *time-out*, and it can be a powerful punishment for inappropriate behavior. For time-out to be effective, procedures must be followed carefully and consistently.

The first step is to determine whether it is appropriate for the family to be taught a time-out procedure. The effectiveness of time-out is based on the child's experiencing a decrease in adult attention and other reinforcements when placed in time-out. If the child is receiving little adult attention during the day, then time-out is not likely to be effective. In these instances, the clinician must focus on increasing the positive attention that the adults provide to the child before teaching a time-out strategy.[15] In addition, the clinician must identify whether the misbehavior is occurring as a way of escaping chores or responsibilities. If the child often engages in problem behaviors to avoid certain tasks, then time-out may not be effective because it allows the child to continue to avert these responsibilities. If time-out is used in this situation, then the child must be required to complete the task as soon as the time-out is over.

Once the decision to teach time-out has been made, the clinician should help the family identify the behaviors that will result in time-out. It is best to start with only one or two problem behaviors that will result in time-out to ensure that the procedure is not being overused, which could be counterproductive and result in increased hostility in the child. Also, limiting the use of time-out makes it more likely that adults will follow through with the procedure because time-out can be difficult to implement and may result in prolonged tantrums. When implementing this technique, parents should not provide more than one brief warning before placing the child in time-out. Multiple warnings or prolonged discussions with the child provide attention and may reinforce the problem behavior.[16]

In theory, time-out can occur in any location that does not provide entertainment for the child and in which it is safe not to provide the child with adult attention. In practice, a chair in the living room or the dining room most frequently is used. After the child misbehaves and a warning is given, the adult should issue a brief, firm, but not harsh statement of the infraction (e.g., "No hitting, time-out") and calmly place the child in the time-out chair. The child should be required to sit in the chair for a short period. A common recommendation is 1 minute for each year of age to a maximum of 10 minutes; however, the child should show signs of calming before being allowed out of the chair. Time-out could last for 30–60 minutes (or more, in rare cases) if it results in a prolonged tantrum. After time-out, the parent should observe the child and offer positive attention as soon as the child acts in a cooperative manner; if the child continues to have a tantrum, then he or she is directed back to the chair for another few minutes of time-out.

The most common problem that is encountered when using time-out is that the child leaves the chair before being given permission to do so. If the child leaves too soon, then he or she should be placed back in the chair with 1 or 2 minutes added to the timer. If the child continues to leave the chair before time-out is over, then the situation is more complicated. Attempts to keep the child in the chair inadvertently may provide the child with adult attention that subverts the purpose of time-out. In this situation, there are a number of alternatives:

1. **Send the child to his or her room:** A child's room can be used as a time-out location as long as the most desired toys and television are not in the child's room. If the child leaves the room, then the parents can shut the door and hold it shut (but not lock the door) until the child stops struggling to get out. The parents should start

the timer when the child stops trying to open the door and reset the timer if the child opens the door before being told that time-out is over.

2. **Loss of a privilege:** The child could lose a privilege in a graded manner each time that he or she leaves the time-out chair. For this to be effective, the parents need to identify a highly desired privilege that the child gets on a regular basis (e.g., bike riding, visiting a friend).

3. **Restraint procedures:** There are procedures for holding a child in a chair while providing minimal attention to the child. Clinicians should learn these procedures from professionals who are experienced in their use. The inappropriate use of restraints can result in the inadvertent reinforcement of inappropriate behavior at best and injury to the child at worst.

4. **Spanking:** Some experts have recommended spanking as a procedure to be used when the child will not stay in time-out; however, concerns about possible adverse effects of spanking (discussed in the next section) have raised serious questions about using this method to enforce a time-out procedure.

When children are in time-out, they often engage in behaviors that are designed to elicit adult attention. Children commonly state that parents are mean or that they hate their parents. Parents should recognize these as attempts to get their attention but may need reassurance that ignoring these statements is appropriate and necessary for time-out to be effective. Statements that the child is not feeling well or has to go to the bathroom may be more difficult for parents to ignore; however, unless there is evidence that the child was sick prior to being put in time-out, parents should ignore these statements. If they do not, then children are likely to say similar things each time they are put in time-out. The brief nature of time-out makes it easier for parents to ignore these statements. Rarely will children wet themselves or vomit when they are in time-out. Of course, parents need to monitor their children while they are in time-out, but, as a rule, they should continue the course of the intervention if these events occur. Parents must be prepared to ignore these events and then have the child help clean up the mess after time-out is over. Although this is rare, it is important to consider these possibilities when selecting the time-out site. Furthermore, discussion of these possibilities will help parents to feel prepared to manage the "worst-case scenario."

Spanking

Perhaps no parenting strategy has engendered more controversy than the use of spanking. (For an in-depth discussion of the effectiveness and harmful effects of spanking, see Friedman & Schonberg, 1996.) In brief, data suggest that spanking adolescents is both ineffective and associated with aggression later in life.[17] In addition, elimination of corporal punishment in school is not associated with an increase in behavior problems in that setting. Furthermore, corporal punishment in schools has been associated with negative effects on self-concept; both short- and long-term symptoms of stress; and, at times, physical injuries.[18] Spanking is not appropriate in schools or when it involves adolescents or very young children.

The greatest ongoing controversy exists about the appropriateness of parents' spanking preschool- and elementary school–age children. Spanking is widely used, at least on an occasional basis, by parents of children in these age ranges[19]; yet parents generally find it to be the least acceptable form of punishment,[20] and most parents would prefer not to spank their children if effective alternatives were available.[21] Furthermore, at least some studies have shown that the use of corporal punishment is associated with an increase in aggressiveness among children.[22] Given these findings and the effectiveness of alternative ways of disciplining children, clinicians will be able to help virtually all families by educating them about alternatives to corporal punishment.

DEVELOPMENTAL CONSIDERATIONS

Determining which behavior strategies to use in a particular situation depends greatly on the developmental level of the child. In general, the younger the child, the more important it is for consequences to be delivered immediately after the target behavior occurs. Also, as children mature, particularly when they become adolescents, the introduction of self-management interventions becomes important. Examples of behavior change strategies and possible reinforcers to be used with children at varying levels of development are displayed in Table 1. (For additional information about the application of behavior change strategies in the preschool and adolescent years, see Chapters 6, 12, and 13.)

ROLE OF THE CHILD IN COUNSELING

As implied in the previous sections, it is critical for parents to have a central role in the process of counseling to help a child with ADHD. The role of the child will vary as a function of the child's developmental level and degree of impulsivity. With children of any age, clinicians should seek to determine the child's main concerns and perceptions of the problems, potential reinforcers for desirable behaviors, and the emotional concerns of the child. Preschoolers and elementary school–age children, particularly those who are very impulsive, may rapidly become bored and uncomfortable with verbal counseling, requiring that the clinician collect information from them in an efficient manner. In these situations, it is important that the clinician involve children for only brief periods of time and provide them with enjoyable, developmentally appropriate games to play while the clinician works with the parents. As children mature, their ability to sustain attention as well as to reflect on and share their experiences develops so that they can assume a more central role in planning behavioral strategies. By the time that children enter adolescence, it is important that they be active in identifying the goals and strategies of intervention.[23] In fact, without their participation, it is quite likely that adolescents will resist the parents' efforts to help them.

The role of the child in counseling also depends on the level of internalizing problems of the child. Some children with ADHD are very anxious and/or depressed about family, school, and peer problems. In addition, some children are coping with emotional problems that are related to abusive parenting practices. When children are struggling with emotional issues, it is important for clinicians to understand the problems and provide support to them. Often, young, impulsive children will become relatively calm, albeit for brief periods, when discussing problems that are emotionally upsetting to them. Offering children opportunities to reveal concerns and receive emotional support in the context of brief periods of play therapy also can be useful. Although play therapy generally is not a helpful strategy for addressing the behavioral concerns of children with ADHD, this mode of treatment can be beneficial when addressing the emotional issues of young children with this disorder.

BRIEF VERSUS EXTENDED CHILD AND FAMILY COUNSELING

Determining whether a child and a family need brief or more extended counseling depends on many factors, including the range and the extent of the functional impairments that the child faces, the quality of the parent–child interaction, the skill level of the parents, and the level of stress that the family experiences. Clinicians in primary care settings may be able to address adequately the concerns of the child and the family in situations in which

- The child's problems are mild to moderate and related to one or two specific areas of concern (e.g., arguing with parents, fighting with a younger sibling, failing to complete homework)
- The parents and the child generally engage in mutually supportive and reinforcing relationships
- The parents have at least an average level of parenting skill and are not experiencing any other unusual family stressors

In these cases, several brief counseling sessions during which the clinician can offer support, provide information about ADHD, and collaborate with the parents and the child to devise behavior management strategies may be sufficient to resolve the main concerns. The handouts that are provided in Appendixes A and B describe positive reinforcement and time-out strategies for children with ADHD and may be particularly useful in the context of brief counseling.

Many families who are coping with ADHD will not be able to get their needs met through brief counseling. A primary care provider should refer the family to a specialist in behavioral family therapy as soon as it becomes clear that extended counseling is needed. Clinicians who provide intensive behavioral family therapy or parent training will find the programs developed by Barkley (1997) and Forehand and McMahon (1981) very useful in working with families.

REFERRAL FOR MARITAL AND ADULT THERAPY

In some situations, the counseling strategies described in this chapter will not be sufficient for addressing the problems of children with ADHD and their families. For instance, parents with significant marital problems often have problems with working together to design and implement effective intervention strategies for these children. In addition, research has shown that parental psychopathology (e.g., maternal depression, paternal antisocial behavior), maternal isolation from family and friends who can provide emotional support, and socioeconomic disadvantage are predictors of failure to respond to behaviorally oriented counseling.[24]

Before providing counseling, the clinician should screen for family stress factors that may have an effect on the effectiveness of behavioral intervention. An interview with the parents will help to reveal family issues that may have an impact on the course of counseling. In addition, rating scales have been developed to help screen for family stress variables (see Chapter 2). In families in which the parents are experiencing mild problems with marital interaction and/or adjustment in their own lives, these concerns often can be addressed in the context of extended child and family counseling using many of the strategies described in this chapter; however, when parents are coping with moderate to severe marital and/or adult issues, referral to marriage and family therapy or to a clinician who specializes in psychotherapy with adults may be indicated.

CONCLUSION

Parenting a child with ADHD is a challenge. Clinicians should be a source of information, understanding, and support for these parents. When there generally is a supportive parent–child relationship, brief counseling to identify methods for preventing the inadvertent reinforcement of problem behaviors and to educate families about positive reinforcement and response cost strategies often will result in significant improvement in the child's behavior. When there are high levels of family stressors and parents or children have difficulties with working together, longer-term counseling will be needed.

ENDNOTES

1. Barkley (1995).
2. Patterson (1982).
3. Forehand & McMahon (1981).
4. Ibid.
5. Carey & McDevitt (1995).
6. Parrish, Cataldo, Kolko, Neef, & Egel (1986).
7. Patterson (1982).
8. Barkley (1997).
9. Bernhardt & Forehand (1975).
10. Pfiffner & O'Leary (1993).
11. Ibid.
12. See Moore, Waguespack, Wickstrom, Witt, & Gaydos (1994).
13. Pfiffner & O'Leary (1993).
14. Rapport, Murphy, & Bailey (1982).
15. Shriver & Allen (1996).
16. Blum, Williams, Friman, & Christophersen (1995).
17. Larzelere (1996).
18. Hyman (1996).
19. Graziano, Hamblen, & Plante (1996).
20. Socolar & Stein (1996).
21. Graziano et al. (1996).
22. Straus, Sugarman, & Giles-Sims (1997).
23. Robin & Foster (1989).
24. Wahler & Dumas (1989).

REFERENCES

Barkley, R.A. (1995). *Taking charge of ADHD: The complete authoritative guide for parents*. New York: Guilford Press.

Barkley, R.A. (1997). *Defiant children: A clinician's manual for parent training* (2nd ed.). New York: Guilford Press.

Barkley, R.A. (1998). *Attention-deficit hyperactivity disorder: A manual for diagnosis and treatment* (2nd ed.). New York: Guilford Press.

Bernhardt, A.J., & Forehand, R. (1975). The effects of labeled and unlabeled praise upon lower and middle class children. *Journal of Experimental Child Psychology, 19*, 536–543.

Blum, N.J., Williams, G.E., Friman, P.C., & Christophersen, E.R. (1995). Disciplining young children: The role of verbal instructions and reasoning. *Pediatrics, 96*, 336–341.

Carey, W.B., & McDevitt, S.C. (1995). *Coping with children's temperament: A guide for professionals*. New York: Basic Books.

Forehand, R., & McMahon, R. (1981). *Helping the non-compliant child: A clinician's guide to parent training.* New York: Guilford Press.

Friedman, S.B., & Schonberg, S.K. (Eds.). (1996). The short and long term consequences of corporal punishment. *Pediatrics, 98,* 803–860.

Graziano, A.M., Hamblen, J.L., & Plante, W.A. (1996). Subabusive violence in child rearing in middle class American families. *Pediatrics, 98,* 845–848.

Hyman, I.A. (1996). Using research to change public policy: Reflections on 20 years of effort to eliminate corporal punishment in schools. *Pediatrics, 98,* 818–821.

Larzelere, R.E. (1996). A review of the outcomes of parental use of nonabusive or customary physical punishment. *Pediatrics, 98,* 824–828.

Madsen, C.H., Becker, W.C., Thomas, D.R., Koser, L., & Plager, E. (1968). An analysis of the reinforcing function of "sit-down" commands. In R.K. Parker (Ed.), *Readings in educational psychology* (pp. 265–278). Needham Heights, MA: Allyn & Bacon.

Moore, L.A., Waguespack, A.M., Wickstrom, K.F., Witt, J.C., & Gaydos, G.R. (1994). Mystery motivator: An effective and time efficient intervention. *School Psychology Review, 23,* 106–118.

Parrish, J.M., Cataldo, M.F., Kolko, D.J., Neef, N.A., & Egel, A.L. (1986). Experimental analysis of response covariation among compliant and inappropriate behaviors. *Journal of Applied Behavior Analysis, 19,* 241–254.

Patterson, G.R. (1982). *Coercive family process.* Eugene, OR: Castalia.

Pfiffner, L.J., & O'Leary, S.G. (1993). School-based psychological treatments. In J.L. Matson (Ed.), *Handbook of hyperactivity in children* (pp. 234–255). Needham Heights, MA: Allyn & Bacon.

Rapport, M.D., Murphy, A., & Bailey, J.S. (1982). Ritalin versus response cost in the control of hyperactive children: A within subject comparison. *Journal of Applied Behavior Analysis, 15,* 205–216.

Robin, A.L., & Foster, S.L. (1989). *Negotiating parent–adolescent conflict: A behavioral–family systems approach.* New York: Guilford Press.

Shriver, M.D., & Allen, K.D. (1996). The time-out grid: A guide to effective discipline. *School Psychology Quarterly, 11,* 67–74.

Socolar, R.R.S., & Stein, R.K. (1996). Maternal discipline of young children. *Journal of Developmental and Behavioral Pediatrics, 17,* 1–8.

Straus, M.A., Sugarman, D.B., & Giles-Sims, J. (1997). Spanking by parents and subsequent antisocial behavior of children. *Archives of Pediatric and Adolescent Medicine, 151,* 761–767.

Thomas, A., Chess, S., Birch, H.G., Hertzig, M.E., & Korn, S. (1963). *Behavioral individuality in early childhood.* New York: New York University Press.

Wahler, R.G., & Dumas, J.E. (1989). Attentional problems in dysfunctional mother–child interactions: An interbehavioral model. *Psychological Bulletin, 105,* 116–130.

RESOURCES FOR CLINICIANS

Barkley, R.A. (1997). *Defiant children: A clinician's manual for parent training* (2nd ed.). New York: Guilford Press. (To order, call [800] 365-7006.)

Forehand, R., & McMahon, R. (1981). *Helping the non-compliant child: A clinician's guide to parent training.* New York: Guilford Press. (To order, call [800] 365-7006.)

Robin, A.L., & Foster, S.L. (1989). *Negotiating parent–adolescent conflict: A behavioral–family systems approach.* New York: Guilford Press. (To order, call [800] 365-7006.)

RESOURCES FOR PARENTS

Barkley, R.A. (1995). *Taking charge of ADHD: The complete authoritative guide for parents.* New York: Guilford Press. (To order, call [800] 365-7006.)

Becker, W. (1971). *Parents are teachers: A child management program.* Champaign, IL: Research Press. (To order, call [800] 519-2707.)

Blechman, E.A. (1985). *Solving child behavior problems at home and at school.* Champaign, IL: Research Press. (To order, call [800] 519-2707.)

Clark, L. (1996). *SOS help for parents: A practical guide for handling common everyday behavior problems* (2nd ed.). Bowling Green, KY: Parents Press. (To order, call [800] 576-1582; also available on videotape.)

Patterson, G.R. (1976). *Living with children: New methods for parents and teachers.* Champaign, IL: Research Press. (To order, call [800] 519-2707.)

Parker, H.C. (1996). *The ADD hyperactivity workbook for parents, teachers, and kids* (2nd ed.). Plantation, FL: Impact. (To order, call ADD Warehouse [800] 233-9273.)

Phelan, T.W. (1997). *1-2-3 magic: Training your child to do what you want!* (2nd ed.). Glen Ellyn, IL: Child Management, Inc. (To order, call [800] 442-4453; also available on videotape.)

Improving Your Child's Behavior Using Positive Reinforcement Strategies

The following steps are recommended for helping your child behave in a more appropriate manner:

1. **Review your child's behavior on a typical day.** Make a schedule of your child's activities on a typical day, usually a school day, and identify the periods of the day that are most problematic.
2. **Select a period of the day on which to focus.** Choose a time of the day that is problematic, but try not to select the most difficult time of the day until you gain confidence in your behavior management skills. Remember that sleep problems often are difficult to change.
3. **Select an appropriate behavior to change.** Children often demonstrate many behaviors that need to be changed. Focus on one behavior at a time. Often, an improvement in one behavior is associated with a change in other behaviors as well. Improving children's compliance with household rules and parental requests is a good behavior to focus on for intervention.
4. **Identify potential reinforcers for your child's appropriate behavior.** Make a list of privileges, toys, and snacks that your child would like to have. Talking with your child will help you create this list. Review the list, and eliminate items that are not feasible to give your child. Remember that the best reinforcers are ones that the child really likes and that you are comfortable administering. Produce a short list of potential reinforcers that you would feel comfortable giving your child for appropriate behavior during the period of the day that you are targeting for intervention.
5. **Create a system for earning reinforcements.** Most parents find that it is not practical to give the child a privilege or a toy every time the child does something appropriate. Giving children stickers, stars, chips, or points for good behavior typically is more feasible. These tokens then can be exchanged for valuable reinforcers following an exchange system that you develop (e.g., 10 points may earn the child 1 hour of television). It is useful to have reinforcers with different levels of value. The child then has the choice of cashing in tokens quickly for less-valuable reinforcers or saving up tokens to acquire more valuable items.
6. **Discuss with your child ways to earn the reinforcers.** Tell your child that you would like to find a way for him or her to earn some special treats. Present the short list of reinforcers, and find out which ones the child would like to have the most. Then discuss what your child has to do to earn the reinforcers. Explain to your child the token and exchange systems that you have designed, and use the child's feedback to improve the system.
7. **Observe your child carefully, and catch your child being good.** During the time of the day that is designated for intervention, remind your child of the reinforcers and what the child must do to earn them. Observe your child carefully, and look for examples of appropriate behavior. When you see appropriate behavior, praise your child for the specific behavior and offer the child a token to be cashed in later for a reinforcer.
8. **Keep track of your child's progress.** To evaluate progress, record how your child is doing before intervention begins and compare these data with your child's performance at various points during the intervention. For instance, if you are work-

ing on improving your child's compliance with rules in the morning before school, then you could collect data on how long it takes your child to get out of bed, get dressed, and eat breakfast. By comparing your child's behavior on these tasks during baseline and at several times during intervention, you can see whether the strategy that you are using is working.

9. **Make modifications in your strategy.** If your child's behavior is not changing or stops changing after a brief period of improvement, then refine your strategy. Changes to consider are being more generous in offering tokens to the child and varying the reinforcers.

10. **When the child's behavior improves, consider adding a mild punishment technique.** When you see progress but not to an acceptable level, you can take away tokens when your child exhibits behavior that clearly is inappropriate. It is very important that you do not take away points at a faster rate than you give them. A useful rule of thumb is to give at least three times as many points as you take away. Also, if your child shows signs of becoming frustrated or discouraged, then decrease your use of punishment for a short period.

The Clinician's Practical Guide to Attention-Deficit/Hyperactivity Disorder
by Marianne Mercugliano, Thomas J. Power, and Nathan J. Blum   ©1999 by Paul H. Brookes Publishing Co.

B

Time-Out Procedures

Time-out is a way of disciplining your child for misbehavior. It involves removing your child from parental attention and fun activities for a brief period. It is effective because most children get a lot of adult attention and do a lot of fun activities; thus, when they are placed in time-out and cannot do fun things or get adult attention, they do not like it. If you are not able to spend much time with your child or most of your interactions with your child are negative, then discuss this with the clinician who is caring for your child before using time-out.

1. **Select the behaviors that will result in time-out.** Make a list of the behaviors that you think should result in time-out. From this list, select only one or two to start with so that your child is not in time-out too often. Remember that for each of the targeted behaviors, it is important to use time-out on each occasion that the problem behavior occurs.
2. **Select a location for time-out.** As your child learns the rules of time-out, you will be able to use the strategy in many locations. In the beginning, it is best to pick a chair in a convenient location where the child cannot watch television or play with toys. Dangerous or fragile objects should be removed from the area. (See "Prepare for the worst" below.)
3. **Inform your child.** Tell your child that from now on when the targeted behaviors occur, he or she will receive one warning (no warnings for aggression). If your child keeps acting the same way after the warning, then he or she will have to sit in the time-out chair.
4. **Beginning to use time-out.** When your child engages in one of the selected behaviors, briefly state the rule (e.g., "No hitting, time-out") and calmly but firmly instruct your child to go to the time-out chair. If your child does not go toward the chair within 5–10 seconds, then take him or her to the chair.
5. **Prepare for the worst.** When you begin to use time-out, especially with older children, your child may not believe that you are actually going to do it. Often, children get quite upset and may yell, scream, or say nasty things to you. This is okay! If the child is staying in the chair, then ignore these statements. Remember, your child should not get any attention from you when he or she is in time-out. If your child says that he or she does not feel well or has to go to the bathroom, then ignore these statements. Rarely will a child urinate or vomit in time-out. In the event that this does occur, ignore the child, and have him or her help you clean up when time-out is over.
6. **How long should time-out last?** Generally, time-out should not last longer than 1 minute for each year of the child's age (e.g., 2 minutes for 2-year-olds, 5 minutes for 5-year-olds) to a maximum of 10 minutes. Set a timer so that you and the child know when time-out is over. If the child is still screaming and yelling when the timer goes off, however, then do not end time-out until he or she has begun to calm down. This may mean that the child initially remains in time-out for 30 minutes or more because it takes this long for the child to begin to calm down.
7. **What if the child leaves the chair before time-out is over?** This is a common problem when time-out is first implemented. Calmly and without saying anything, take the child back to the chair and add 1 or 2 minutes to the timer. If the child continues to get out of the chair, then consider sending the child to his or her room as long as

The Clinician's Practical Guide to Attention-Deficit/Hyperactivity Disorder
by Marianne Mercugliano, Thomas J. Power, and Nathan J. Blum ©1999 by Paul H. Brookes Publishing Co.

the television and the child's favorite toys are not in the room. If the child tries to leave the room, then you may hold the door shut. Do not start the timer until the child stops trying to get out of the room. If you have tried these procedures and still are having trouble, then contact the clinician who is working with you and your child.

8. **What should happen when time-out is over?** Give the child permission to leave the chair. If you requested that the child do something such as clean up before being placed in time-out, then the child should complete this task when time-out is over. If the child created a mess while in time-out, then he or she should help clean up when time-out is over. Do not talk to the child about why you put him or her in the chair. If you feel that you must talk with the child about the situation, then wait until later in the day or the next day after a period of good behavior. When the child gets out of time-out, look for an opportunity to praise the child for good behavior.

Remember: Be consistent, be calm, and do not give your child attention in time-out.

The Clinician's Practical Guide to Attention-Deficit/Hyperactivity Disorder
by Marianne Mercugliano, Thomas J. Power, and Nathan J. Blum   ©1999 by Paul H. Brookes Publishing Co.

Educational Interventions for Students with Attention-Deficit/Hyperactivity Disorder

The effects of attention-deficit/hyperactivity disorder (ADHD) are pervasive, but this disorder's most profound impact often is on the educational lives of students. A majority of students with ADHD are underachievers and have academic skills deficits. About 25% of these students have either a reading or a math disability, although a much higher percentage underachieve in reading, math, and writing to a lesser degree than meets criteria for a classification of having a learning disability.[1] Students with ADHD are at high risk for grade retention, placement into special education, and dropout from school. Research has shown that chronic school failure can result in serious problems with social relationships and occupational functioning in adolescence and adulthood.[2]

There are many reasons that students with ADHD have academic difficulties, but two factors are particularly important. First, students with ADHD are less actively engaged in academic instruction than their classmates. Students with ADHD typically display lower rates of on-task behavior during instruction and are less productive when responding to academic assignments.[3] Second, students with ADHD who have academic skills deficits require more instruction and practice to keep pace with their peers who do not have learning difficulties.[4] Unfortunately, educational systems often are not prepared to provide these students with the additional instruction and practice that they need, and students with ADHD often resist attempts to provide them with extra instruction.

Many strategies are available to assist students with ADHD who have academic and behavior problems in educational settings. Approaches to intervention can be classified into those that are directed primarily by teachers (teacher mediated), parents (parent mediated), peers (peer mediated), and students themselves (self-directed). The following is a brief description of the various types of interventions. Although it may not be feasible for clinicians to implement many of these interventions, knowledge of the strategies is useful when consulting with parents and school professionals.

TEACHER-MEDIATED STRATEGIES

Teachers can have an effect on student performance and behavior in two general ways: 1) by using instructional interventions—that is, by modifying methods of teaching students—and 2) by implementing behavioral interventions—that is, by managing the consequences for productive and unproductive behavior.

Instructional Interventions

Children with ADHD are more likely to pay attention when teachers use proper instructional materials and present instruction in a clear, organized, and novel manner. Following are some guidelines for designing instructional interventions.

Instructional Match

A student's ability to pay attention and learn is affected greatly by **instructional match**—that is, the correspondence between the individual's academic skills and the level of difficulty of instructional materials. In a study of young elementary school students with significant reading problems, Gickling and Armstrong (1978) found that attentive behavior and rate of productivity on academic assignments were very low when students were asked to work on curriculum materials that clearly were too difficult for them. In contrast, when students were taught at the proper instructional level, their attention and productivity improved dramatically. Furthermore, when students were provided with material that was too easy for them, their task completion and comprehension were high but their attention declined dramatically.

Altering instructional materials so that there is a more favorable match between student skills and curriculum can improve the attention of students with ADHD[5]; thus, when evaluating children who have attention and academic problems, teachers should assess instructional match and make modifications in instructional procedures and learning materials when students are not sufficiently familiar with curriculum material. Most schools have Instructional Support Teams or Student Support Teams to conduct a brief screening of academic skills. Requesting that these teams collect information about a student's ability to adapt to curriculum materials that are used in the classroom may be useful in addressing the issue of instructional match.

Often, changes in curriculum materials and methods of instruction in the general education classroom are not sufficient to enable students to keep pace with peers and learn effectively. In these cases, special education services may be warranted. Traditionally, students have been removed from classrooms to receive special education services, but many schools are implementing a model of inclusion by having special education teachers work collaboratively with general education teachers, thereby providing in-class support. Research has shown, however, that the provision of special education services does not guarantee that students will learn better[6]; therefore, it is imperative that students be provided with specialized learning interventions and that progress be monitored carefully to ensure that the students are acquiring skills at an acceptable rate.[7]

Giving Instructions

The key to increasing the likelihood that students will understand classroom instructions lies in what teachers do before giving the directive.[8] Moving close to the student, providing prompts (e.g., using the student's name, touching the student's shoulder), and making eye contact will help prepare students to receive the instruction. Next, the instruction should be communicated in clear, concise language, with emphasis on key words. Often, it is useful for the teacher to alter slightly the volume or the cadence of speech to highlight that an important instruction is being given. Finally, the teacher needs to check for signs that the student has understood the direction (e.g., making sure that the student is performing the assigned task).

Using Novel, Hands-on Learning Materials

Students with ADHD are able to sustain attention for longer periods of time when tasks are presented in a novel manner. For instance, Zentall and colleagues have shown that students with ADHD were able to pay attention longer and were less hyperactive under conditions in which information was presented in color as opposed to black and white.[9] In addition, attention span can be improved and hyperactivity can be reduced by providing students with tasks that require an active, motoric response[10] and frequent opportunities to receive high-interest feedback for performance, such as computer-assisted learning activities. Computer-assisted instruction generally has been found to improve on-task behavior and academic skills of students with learning problems and is a promising avenue of intervention for individuals with ADHD.[11] For instance, computer programs can make practicing math computation skills and word recognition skills fun and rewarding for students. (For information about the selection of appropriate software for children with attention and learning problems, see Dailey & Rosenberg, 1994.)

Varying the Rate of Presentation

The rate at which teachers present information to students also appears to be critical to the instruction of students with ADHD. In general, neither a consistently slow nor a consistently rapid rate of presentation is optimum for students with ADHD. Students appear to learn best when the rate of presentation is flexible and varies in response to their skills and interests.[12]

Teaching Organizational Skills

Students with ADHD typically have problems with the organization of their work. Strategies have been designed to train students in test taking, the organization of writing assignments, and note taking. For instance, teaching students with ADHD a systematic approach to taking notes has been shown to improve the quality and the organization of students' notes as well as their on-task behavior and academic performance.[13] Because many students with ADHD have a deficit not only in their knowledge of organizational skills but also in their application of known skills, ongoing monitoring of note taking by the instructor and perhaps an external reinforcement system may be needed to improve performance.

Classroom Accommodations

Students with ADHD often need specialized accommodations in the classroom to learn effectively. For instance, sitting near the teacher so that prompts and reinforcements can be provided frequently can be useful. Also, seating the student with ADHD next to students who can model productive and cooperative behavior may help. At the junior and senior high school levels, students may benefit from having an assigned note taker or from tape-recording lectures. Furthermore, these students may perform better when tested orally as opposed to in writing or when given extra time to complete an examination.[14]

Behavioral Interventions: Positive Reinforcement Techniques

A student's ability to pay attention can be affected by changing the consequences of his or her behavior. Following are strategies of positive reinforcement to improve attention to task and self-control.

Selective Attention

Manipulating the consequences of behavior can be a powerful tool for improving the attention and performance of students with ADHD. The selective use of teacher praise and attention has been found repeatedly to improve the behavior of students in classrooms. More specific, providing **positive reinforcement** by praising students frequently for behaving appropriately and ignoring them consistently for behaving inappropriately generally will improve the performance of students with learning and conduct problems; however, the use of praise and attention as positive reinforcers with students who have ADHD is not sufficient.[15] Students with ADHD require more intensive programs of behavior modification that involve a combination of concrete positive reinforcers and the strategic use of negative consequence interventions.

Concrete Reinforcement and Token Systems

As indicated in Chapter 5, one method of enhancing the effects of a positive reinforcement system is to provide concrete reinforcers (e.g., access to special privileges or activities) that are contingent on the performance of a specified target behavior, such as paying attention during class instruction or completing 80% of seat work. Often, it is impractical to offer concrete reinforcers frequently and immediately after a student performs the desired target behavior. A more efficient means of providing enhanced positive reinforcement is to introduce tokens (e.g., stars, stickers, points) that can be accumulated and exchanged for back-up reinforcers of greater value (e.g., 10 points can be exchanged for 20 minutes of computer time at the end of the school day). The advantage of **token reinforcers** is that they can be distributed frequently, immediately, and inexpensively.[16]

The effects of token systems can be enhanced by using group contingencies, which involves providing positive reinforcement to a group of students when the targeted student achieves an established goal.[17] Particularly when a student's behavior problem inadvertently is being reinforced and maintained by responses from peers, group contingencies can help the peers understand what they are doing wrong and change the reinforcers so that they encourage appropriate behavior. When these interventions are used, however, it is important to check whether peers are placing too much pressure on the student with ADHD to achieve his or her goals.

Deciding on the specific targets for intervention is very important when designing systems of behavior modification. When academic productivity and accuracy are targeted for intervention, token systems often result in an improvement in academic performance and a reduction in disruptive behavior; however, when disruptive behavior is the target of treatment, improvements often are demonstrated in behavior but not in academic performance.[18] Designing interventions that focus on changing one or two pivotal or key target behaviors can result in improvement in a whole class of related behaviors; thus, identifying critical target behaviors can enable clinicians to design treatments that are maximally effective and efficient to use.

Teachers frequently report that token systems work for short periods of time and then lose their effectiveness. One reason for this is that the value of reinforcements declines when they are used repeatedly, and reinforcements typically lose their value more rapidly with students who have ADHD. Behavior modification plans should include provisions for varying reinforcements frequently and randomly.[19] One way to do this is to ask the student and the teacher to generate a menu of possible reinforcements. Each reinforcement can be assigned a different number. When the student attains the established goal, he or she is permitted to spin a wheel, roll dice, or pick a number from a hat to determine which reward is earned.

Behavioral Interventions: Negative Consequence Techniques

Behavior can be changed by applying negative consequences. Following are some useful strategies for applying negative consequences.

Corrective Feedback

The use of an all-positive system of behavior modification usually is not sufficient to improve the performance and the behavior of students with ADHD. The strategic provision of negative consequences generally is a useful component of a behavior modification program for these students. Corrective feedback, or verbal reprimands, a mild form of punishment, commonly is used by teachers and can be effective when delivered properly. Correction is helpful when it is delivered in a brief, firm, matter-of-fact manner that indicates to the student what to do instead of what he or she is not doing (e.g., better to say, "Billy, back to work," than, "Billy, you're not paying attention"). Also, corrective feedback is most helpful to the student when it is provided immediately after the problem behavior has occurred and on a consistent basis.[20] A note of caution is that it is easy to overuse corrective feedback with a student who is impulsive and/or inattentive, and corrective feedback if provided at the wrong time could unwittingly become a reinforcer for problem behavior. One helpful rule of thumb for teachers is to provide positive reinforcement at least three times more often than correction or other forms of punishment. There needs to be a clear distinction between the positive reinforcement that teachers provide when the student follows a rule and the verbal correction offered when the student is not complying with the rule.

Response Cost

As discussed in Chapter 5, one method of enhancing a system of negative consequences is **response cost,** which involves the withdrawal of a reinforcer that is contingent on inappropriate or unproductive behavior. Rapport, Murphy, and Bailey (1982) found that response cost was very effective for improving the on-task behavior and academic performance of students with ADHD. In their study, students lost 1 minute of recess each time the teacher observed them to be off-task. Response cost procedures should be embedded in a system of behavior modification that is primarily positive. It is essential that students earn points at a faster rate than they lose them.

Time-Out

Time-out has been demonstrated repeatedly to be effective in reducing the occurrence of inappropriate behaviors. Time-out involves the systematic withdrawal of sources of positive reinforcement (e.g., teacher attention, peer attention, curricular materials) contingent on maladaptive behavior. Time-out procedures vary in their level of restriction. Examples of time-out ordered from least restrictive to most restrictive are the following: ignoring, removal of reinforcing stimuli, exclusion from the group, and removal from class. In general, it is recommended that teachers employ the least restrictive method of time-out that is effective and that they refrain from using isolation by removal from the classroom if possible.[21] Time-out is effective only when there is a clear contrast between the positive reinforcement received when a student is behaving appropriately (time-in) and the lack of positive reinforcement experienced when the child misbehaves (time-out). Time-out is not effective when the student receives as much or more positive reinforcement in the time-out area as in the general classroom setting. The duration of time-out can be relatively brief (e.g., 1–4 minutes); for many students with ADHD, long time-outs can be difficult to enforce and may be counterproductive. (See Appendix B in Chapter 5 for an explanation of time-out procedures.)

Strategies for Adolescents

It is important to engage adolescents in the process of delineating targets for intervention and devising behavioral plans. Contracting and mentoring should be considered when working with adolescents with ADHD.

Contracting

Behavioral contracting is a process of negotiation between a student and a teacher that specifies 1) behaviors targeted for change, 2) goals for behavior, and 3) consequences for attaining goals. Contracts are designed mutually by the student and the teacher through a process of collaboration, and they generally result in written agreements.[22] Contracting is particularly well suited for adolescents and adults who want to have some measure of control over decisions that are made about their lives. Behavioral interventions with adolescents are much more likely to be effective when students 1) express a willingness to change certain behaviors, 2) have input into goals for future behavior, and 3) specify short- and long-term positive consequences that they can earn for attaining goals. Contracts sometimes fail to be effective with students who have ADHD when goals are stated in general, ambiguous terms or are too lofty to be attained most of the time. Also, delays in providing consequences for achieving goals as stated in the contract can reduce the effectiveness of contracts.

Mentoring

Designing educational interventions for adolescents with ADHD can be complicated in that these students usually interact with several teachers during the course of a day. Teachers in middle schools, high schools, and colleges may have fewer opportunities to observe students and understand their unique learning needs than teachers in preschool and elementary environments. In addition, teachers in middle school and beyond often expect a level of autonomy, responsibility, and organization that is difficult for many students with ADHD to achieve.[23] One method that has been used to help adolescents with ADHD to adjust in school is to establish a mentoring system. The mentor is an adult within the school (e.g., instructor, counselor, coach) who the student believes could be helpful and who has the time and the willingness to commit to the mentoring process. The roles of the mentor include

- Developing a supportive relationship with the student
- Designing organizational strategies with the student

- Negotiating behavioral contracts with the student
- Monitoring student performance carefully by meeting with the student and checking with teachers frequently
- Holding the student to the terms of the behavioral contract
- Assisting teachers with the design of useful classroom interventions

Although many high schools and colleges have a system of advising for students, the typical relationship between a student and an advisor is not sufficient to address the needs of students with ADHD. Consultation with clinicians who are outside the system may be needed to design mentoring programs that can really make a difference for these students.

PARENT-MEDIATED STRATEGIES

Parents can assist children with their education in several ways, including providing homework strategies, home-based consequences for school performance and behavior, and parent tutoring.

Homework Strategies

Students with ADHD frequently have problems with completing homework; they often forget assignments, avoid doing the work, take too long to complete assigned tasks, make careless mistakes, and engage in conflict with their parents. Several interventions have been designed to assist students with homework problems, including having students complete homework assignment sheets and requesting that teachers verify these assignment sheets for accuracy, structuring the home environment (e.g., deciding on the proper time and place for homework, reducing distractions), and providing positive reinforcement that is contingent on cooperative behavior and the completion of homework.[24] An approach to homework intervention that is particularly promising is **goal setting** with contingency contracting. In a study conducted by Kahle and Kelley (1994), each parent–child dyad was trained to divide homework assignments into small, manageable units of work. For each unit, the child and the parent were asked to agree on a goal for the number of items to be completed, the number of items to be completed accurately, and the time spent on-task. The child was instructed to work for a specified amount of time and, upon expiration of the time limit, to evaluate performance with regard to work completion and accuracy (see Figure 1). The child was reinforced for goal attainment in accordance with a contract that had been negotiated by the parent and the child. This intervention can be effective for improving rates of homework completion and accuracy, and parents usually report that the procedures are useful and easy to implement.

School–Home Notes with Home-Based Reinforcement Systems

A commonly used and potentially effective intervention for improving children's performance and behavior in school is a **school–home note** with consequences administered at home by parents.[25] This intervention involves having teachers evaluate students on one or more target behaviors at least once per day. Target behaviors might include 1) completes work, 2) pays attention to instruction, and 3) speaks at appropriate times. Teachers often use a four-point scale to evaluate each behavior (0 = work harder, 1 = OK, 2 = good work, 3 = great job!). At the end of the school day, the student is instructed to take the note home for parental review. Parents are trained to set

HOMEWORK GOAL SHEET

Name _____ Date _____

Subject _____

Directions: Before starting the assignment, set reasonable goals. When the time limit is over, check how well you performed. Evaluate whether your performance reached the goal, and have your parents check to make sure that you made the correct decision. Talk to your parents about setting up an incentive system to reward you for reaching your goals.

Goal Setting

	Goal	Actual performance
Number of items completed	_____	_____
Number of items correct	_____	_____
Time	_____	_____

Evaluation

	Student	Parent
Better than goal	_____	_____
Met goal	_____	_____
Just missed goal	_____	_____
Did not meet goal	_____	_____

The Clinician's Practical Guide to Attention-Deficit/Hyperactivity Disorder
by Marianne Mercugliano, Thomas J. Power, and Nathan J. Blum   ©1999 by Paul H. Brookes Publishing Co.

Figure 1.   Homework goal sheet.

reasonable goals for performance—that is, goals that ensure student success at least 80% of the time. Also, parents are given instruction about how to determine effective reinforcers. In general, it is recommended that reinforcers be provided to students on a daily and a weekly basis. For instance, a student could earn 30 minutes of extra television time in the evening if he or she attained the daily goal, and the student could earn a trip to the movies on the weekend for reaching the goal on four of five days during the week. When using this intervention with students who have ADHD, it often is necessary to have teachers provide feedback to students several times during the course of the day (e.g., at the end of each class period) (see Figure 2). Delaying reinforcement may diminish its effectiveness. It may be helpful to supplement home-based contingencies with a school-based system of consequences.

To enhance the effects of a school–home note, clinicians could consider incorporating a response cost component (see Figure 3). For instance, the teacher could provide ratings of the student's behavior and performance after each class period. In addition, every time the teacher notices that the student is not paying attention to instruction for 15 seconds or more at a time, the teacher could take a point away from the student. As described previously, the parents are instructed to set a reasonable goal for teacher ratings; if the student attains the goal, then he or she is eligible for a daily reinforcement (e.g., 30 minutes of playing a video game in the evening). For each point lost on the school–home note, the child loses 1 minute of video game playing time.

Parent Tutoring

Parent tutoring has been found to be effective for enhancing student performance in reading, math, and spelling.[26] Some communities have developed programs to enlist volunteers to provide tutoring. Schools, parent–teacher associations, parent advocacy organizations, university student affairs offices, and other community volunteer groups may provide tutoring services when parents are unable to do so themselves. During tutoring sessions with students with ADHD, the use of reinforcement procedures to enhance attention and motivation often is necessary. Because parent tutoring entails making additional demands on the child for academic work, these techniques generally are not recommended until the child is able to complete homework in a reasonable amount of time.

PEER-MEDIATED STRATEGIES

Involving a student's peers in interventions can be useful for improving the on-task behavior and social performance of a student with ADHD. Following are some guidelines for incorporating peers into the intervention process.

Peer Tutoring

As indicated previously, overcoming academic skills deficits requires that students be provided substantially more opportunities to learn and practice than those typically afforded in the classroom. Most schools lack the resources to hire additional educators or teacher aides to provide students with the extra learning opportunities that they need. One potentially effective and efficient method of increasing instructional time is peer tutoring. Many versions of peer tutoring have been developed, but the **classwide peer tutoring** (CWPT) procedures formulated by Greenwood, Delquadri, and Carta (1988) have been described most often in the literature. In CWPT, students in a classroom are paired randomly to work on an academic subject. Each student in the pair takes a turn

DAILY REPORT

Name _____ Date _____

Directions: Rate the student at the end of each class period on the behaviors listed below using the following scale:

0 = Work harder

1 = OK

2 = Good work

3 = Great job!

	Reading	Math	Lang. Arts	Soc. Studies	Science
1. Completes assignments	____	____	____	____	____
2. Speaks at appropriate times	____	____	____	____	____

TOTAL POINTS EARNED   ____

The Clinician's Practical Guide to Attention-Deficit/Hyperactivity Disorder
by Marianne Mercugliano, Thomas J. Power, and Nathan J. Blum   ©1999 by Paul H. Brookes Publishing Co.

Figure 2.   Daily report.

DAILY REPORT

Name _____ Date _____

Directions: Rate the student at the end of each class period on the behaviors listed under numbers 1 and 2 below using the following scale. On item 3 below, each time the student is off-task for 15 seconds or more, cross out the highest number remaining for each class.

0 = Work harder

1 = OK

2 = Good work

3 = Great job!

	Reading	Math	Lang. Arts	Soc. Studies	Science
1. Completes assignments	_____	_____	_____	_____	_____
2. Speaks at appropriate times	_____	_____	_____	_____	_____
3. Off-task	5 4 3 2 1	5 4 3 2 1	5 4 3 2 1	5 4 3 2 1	5 4 3 2 1

TOTAL TEACHER RATINGS _____

TOTAL POINTS LOST _____

POINTS EARNED (Teacher ratings – Points lost) _____

The Clinician's Practical Guide to Attention-Deficit/Hyperactivity Disorder
by Marianne Mercugliano, Thomas J. Power, and Nathan J. Blum ©1999 by Paul H. Brookes Publishing Co.

Figure 3.   Daily report.

being tutor and tutee. The tutor is instructed to follow a script that contains questions and answers to a series of items. Points are administered by the tutor to the tutee for correct responses to items. Points then are recorded on a cumulative basis throughout the week as a visual display of progress. As an additional incentive, concrete rewards can be offered for the attainment of goals. CWPT procedures have been applied successfully in the areas of reading, math, and spelling. Moreover, CWPT has been shown to improve the on-task behavior of students with ADHD and, in some cases, to enhance their acquisition of academic skills.[27]

Peer Coaching

Students with ADHD often experience on a daily basis problems with planning and organization. Although helpful, meeting with a mental health professional weekly may not be sufficient to address their day-to-day struggles. One method of responding to this need is to develop a peer coaching service, which is similar in many ways to the mentoring strategy described previously with the exception that a peer instead of an adult provides guidance to the student with ADHD. The student with ADHD is assigned to a peer coach—that is, a contemporary who understands the problems that students with ADHD encounter and who wants to help. The roles of the coach may include providing emotional support, helping the student with ADHD to develop two or three specific objectives for the day, developing plans to achieve each objective, and reviewing performance from the previous day.[28] For students with ADHD, it may be critical to formalize the intervention procedures; apply them consistently on a day-to-day basis; and, in some cases, include external consequences for attaining specified goals. For middle school and high school students, peer coaching might take the form of meeting each morning before school begins; for adults, coaching might entail speaking on the telephone at the end of the day. Although peer coaching has been described in the literature, research has yet to validate this procedure with students who have ADHD.

SELF-DIRECTED STRATEGIES

Several strategies have been developed for use by students with ADHD themselves; two approaches that have been used most commonly with students who have ADHD are self-monitoring and self-evaluation.

Self-Monitoring

Self-monitoring involves having a student observe him- or herself to determine whether a specific behavior (e.g., paying attention) has occurred or how well a behavior (e.g., accuracy on an academic assignment) has been performed. In general, students are asked to record on a checklist whether the behavior has happened. For instance, a self-monitoring procedure could be used to help a student pay attention during a 20-minute seat work task. With the assistance of an audiocassette recorder, a tone is presented to the student via headphones at random intervals. The average time interval between tones can vary; clinicians need to determine the interval that maximizes self-awareness and minimizes distraction. Each time the tone sounds, the student is instructed to observe whether he or she is paying attention and to record this determination on a checklist (see Figure 4). The student also could be asked to monitor and record how much work has been performed accurately since the last tone sounded. There is some evidence that suggests that self-monitoring academic accuracy may be

WAS I PAYING ATTENTION?

Name _____   Date _____

1. Yes _____   No _____

2. Yes _____   No _____

3. Yes _____   No _____

4. Yes _____   No _____

5. Yes _____   No _____

6. Yes _____   No _____

7. Yes _____   No _____

8. Yes _____   No _____

9. Yes _____   No _____

10. Yes _____   No _____

PERCENTAGE OF TIME PAYING ATTENTION   _____ %

The Clinician's Practical Guide to Attention-Deficit/Hyperactivity Disorder
by Marianne Mercugliano, Thomas J. Power, and Nathan J. Blum   ©1999 by Paul H. Brookes Publishing Co.

Figure 4.   Self-monitoring attention.

superior to self-monitoring on-task behavior.[29] In cases in which the student has ADHD, particularly predominantly impulsive type, it may be important for the teacher to check frequently to make sure that the student is complying with intervention procedures. Self-monitoring is more likely to be effective with students who are middle school age or older than with younger children.

Self-Evaluation

Self-evaluation requires that students evaluate how well they have complied with an established rule (e.g., listening to instructions, completing assigned tasks). At the end of a specified interval, students are requested to indicate their rating on a recording sheet.

During the initial stages, self-evaluation procedures usually involve an external evaluation component to teach students how to use the intervention and to make sure that they are evaluating themselves accurately. Once a student demonstrates improvement and is able to match his or her ratings to those of the teacher, the external evaluation component is faded.

The following steps are adapted from self-evaluation procedures that were developed by Rhode, Morgan, and Young (1983). These procedures have been developed primarily for students in middle school and high school.

1. The intervention is initiated in one of the student's classes. The teacher and the student meet to identify target behaviors, a scale for rating each behavior, a daily goal for performance, and a menu of reinforcements. An example of a checklist that is used as part of a self-evaluation intervention is depicted in Figure 5. In the example, two target behaviors are identified: 1) follows classroom rules and 2) works accurately. The classroom period is divided into quarters, and the student is asked to evaluate him- or herself at the end of each quarter using a six-point rating scale from 0 (unacceptable) to 5 (excellent). After the student evaluates him- or herself, the teacher provides an external evaluation. At the end of the class period, the student determines the total points earned, which is the sum of the teacher ratings plus the sum of the match points (a match point is earned when the student's rating is within one point of the teacher's rating). If the student's daily performance reaches the established goal, then he or she is eligible for a reinforcer.
2. When the student is performing at an acceptable level on a consistent basis, the number of external evaluations gradually is reduced (e.g., from four to one per period). During this stage, the student still is eligible for a reinforcer if the goal is attained.
3. If the student still is performing at an acceptable level, then the student continues to evaluate him- or herself every day; the teacher further reduces the frequency of checks on a random interval basis (e.g., checking on an average of once every 2 days and then checking on an average of once every 3 days). During this phase, external reinforcement is provided only on the days when the teacher checks the student.
4. Assuming that the student still is performing within an acceptable range, the faded intervention that is described in Step 3 can be applied in one or more other classrooms.
5. If the student begins to manifest problems at any point, then the teacher should go back to the least intensive and least intrusive intervention needed to recapture the desired effect.

DAILY REPORT CARD

Name _____   Date _____

5 = Excellent	Followed all classroom rules. Work 100% accurate.
4 = Very good	Only a minor infraction of rules (e.g., a call out). Work at least 90% accurate.
3 = Average	A couple of minor infractions, but no serious offenses. Work at least 80% accurate.
2 = Below average	Followed rules part of the time, but one or more major rule violations (e.g., aggressive, disturbed classmates). Work approximately 60%–80% correct.
1 = Poor	Engaged in a high degree of inappropriate behavior most of the time. Work between 10% and 60% correct.
0 = Unacceptable	Broke one or more major rules for the entire time. Did not work at all, or all work incorrect.

Behavior	1st Quarter		2nd Quarter		3rd Quarter		4th Quarter	
	S	T	S	T	S	T	S	T
1. Follows classroom rules	____	____	____	____	____	____	____	____
2. Works accurately	____	____	____	____	____	____	____	____

Note: A match point is given each time the student's rating is within one point of the teacher's rating.

Total teacher ratings ____

Total match points ____

Grand total ____

The Clinician's Practical Guide to Attention-Deficit/Hyperactivity Disorder
by Marianne Mercugliano, Thomas J. Power, and Nathan J. Blum   ©1999 by Paul H. Brookes Publishing Co.

Figure 5.   A self-evaluation form.

Self-evaluation procedures such as those just described have been used successfully with adolescents who have attention and behavior problems; preliminary evidence has shown that they can be effective with adolescents who have ADHD.[30]

COMBINING EDUCATIONAL INTERVENTIONS WITH MEDICATION

Educational and behavioral interventions usually are helpful in working with students who have ADHD, but the behavior and performance of these children generally cannot be normalized with behavioral interventions alone.[31] Stimulant medication often is needed to enable children with ADHD to function adaptively in educational settings. By the same token, stimulant medication alone often is not sufficient to normalize the academic and behavioral functioning of children with ADHD. Rapport, Denney, DuPaul, and Gardner (1994) examined the effects of four dosages of methylphenidate (5, 10, 15, and 20 milligrams). They found that the optimum dosage of medication normalized approximately 75% of the students with regard to teacher ratings of behavior and direct observations of attention; however, the optimum dosage of medication normalized productivity on academic assignments in only approximately 50% of the cases. These findings highlight the limits of medication particularly with regard to improving academic performance. Addressing students' academic needs is a complex process that often requires the instructional and behavioral interventions that are outlined in this chapter in addition to medication. (See Chapter 9 for an extensive overview of medications.)

IMPLEMENTING EDUCATIONAL INTERVENTIONS

Although many of the interventions that are described in this chapter are not feasible for clinicians to implement, there clearly is a role for clinicians in the educational treatment of students with ADHD. An important role for clinicians is collaborating with school administrators and counselors to advocate for the needs of these students. For instance, the clinician could speak with the principal by telephone to advocate for the selection of an appropriate teacher. It is not likely that the clinician would know who the most appropriate teacher would be, and, indeed, most principals probably would prefer that clinicians not recommend a specific teacher. Instead, the clinician could recommend placement with a teacher who has a set of qualities that are likely to lead to success, such as a teacher who is

- Warm and caring
- Clear about setting rules
- Quick to offer verbal praise for following rules
- Willing to use concrete reinforcement systems
- Open to collaboration with health and mental health professionals within and outside the school
- Experienced in collaborating effectively with parents

Similarly, for students in middle school, high school, or college, the clinician could advocate for assignment to a mentor who can relate effectively to the student, collaborate with the student to develop specific behavioral contracts, and hold the student to the terms of the contract. Furthermore, the clinician could recommend that the selected teacher and/or mentor collaborate with a teacher who was successful with the student in earlier grades to learn about useful methods of intervention.

Another role for the clinician is consulting with teachers to design specific educational strategies. Teachers differ markedly in their perceptions of the utility of various educational interventions, so it is important for clinicians to quickly assess teacher attitudes prior to making specific recommendations. In general, teachers are more accepting of interventions that utilize primarily positive consequences and that are not time consuming to implement. For instance, they may be more willing to use a school–home note system with home-based rewards than a relatively time-intensive token economy system that they have to implement on their own in the classroom.[32]

In general, it is not feasible for clinicians to consult with educational professionals face to face; therefore, it is critical that clinical and educational professionals find a way to collaborate by telephone. Identifying a mutually convenient time to collaborate can be a major obstacle to school consultation; clinicians should identify the specific times that are best to contact the teacher. In general, teachers are most likely to be available before and after school, and some teachers are willing to collaborate by telephone in the evening. Often, parents can be helpful to clinicians in determining the optimum times for telephone consultation with the teacher by acting as a liaison.

Clinicians can play a significant role in the education of students with ADHD by providing consultation to parents. Parents often need advice about useful homework strategies and methods for tutoring their child. When school–home notes are being used, parents usually need consultation with regard to setting appropriate goals for performance and providing salient daily and weekly reinforcers. Moreover, parents could benefit from consultation about how to approach school professionals to advocate effectively for their child. Providing parents with specific tips about whom to contact at school, how to approach the teacher to elicit a helpful response, how to cope with teachers who utilize negative consequence interventions too frequently, how to show appreciation to teachers when they use helpful strategies, and how to approach an administrator when their child is performing poorly in school may be extremely useful to parents. In some cases, informing parents about provisions in education law that pertain to their child (see Chapter 8) and providing parents with referrals to non-profit educational advocacy organizations may be needed. Also, referring parents to local ADHD support groups may help them become more effective advocates for their child's educational needs.

The educational difficulties of students with ADHD can be very complex and often cannot be addressed sufficiently by a clinician who is able to consult only briefly with parents and educational professionals. It may be necessary for the clinician to make a recommendation to an educational specialist, school psychologist, or child clinical psychologist to work more intensively with the family and the school. Effective educational specialists or psychologists have

- Advanced knowledge about ADHD and related problems
- Expertise in behavior therapy
- Understanding of school ecology
- Well-developed teacher consultation skills
- Knowledge of education law

In many cases, recommendation to the school psychologist is an excellent idea, given his or her easy access to teachers and school administrators; however, in some districts, the role of the school psychologist is restricted primarily to testing and making determinations about eligibility for special education. In these cases, referral to another school professional or to an external consultant may be preferable. Many child clinical psychologists are knowledgeable about ADHD and behavior therapy, but their expertise regarding educational matters varies markedly. Clinicians will find that professionals who are associated with local ADHD support groups can provide a wealth of valuable information about school-based and clinic-based professionals who can be helpful with students who have ADHD.

COLLABORATION BETWEEN CLINICAL AND EDUCATIONAL PROFESSIONALS

Because students with ADHD usually require a multimodal approach to intervention to succeed in educational settings, successful treatment generally involves professionals from many disciplines, including pediatrics, psychiatry, psychology, nursing, general education, special education, and educational administration. Coordination of professionals, who may work in diverse settings, is essential to ensure a comprehensive and well-integrated approach to treatment.

Historically, treatment for ADHD has been provided primarily in clinic settings. A clinic-based model has some clear strengths: Clinical specialists often have a high degree of knowledge and experience about ADHD and its comorbidities, a mechanism for coordinating health and mental health already may be established, and rights to privacy can be protected readily in clinics. Clinic-based programs for ADHD face several limitations, however, including problems with acquiring naturalistic information about school functioning; difficulties with collaborating with educators on an ongoing basis; and the inaccessibility of clinic services to some families because of problems with payment, scheduling, and transportation.[33]

The need to develop a school-based model for the delivery of services to students with ADHD has become apparent. In 1991, the U.S. Department of Education affirmed the importance of a school-based model of programming for students with ADHD by mandating school-based services for individuals with ADHD who display impairments in educational settings. School-based models of service delivery have some clear strengths: Naturalistic information about school functioning can be obtained readily, ongoing collaboration between educators and school-based consultants (e.g., school psychologist, school nurse) is feasible to arrange, and school-based services are readily accessible to families who live in the community. School-based models of service delivery are not without limitations, however, and these may include a lack of expertise with regard to ADHD and its comorbidities, failure of clinic-based health professionals and school personnel to collaborate, and questions about the degree of privacy afforded when clinical services are offered in the public world of the school.[34]

Because clinic- and school-based models of programming for students with ADHD each have their strengths and limitations, a model of service delivery that integrates both approaches has been advocated.[35] Coordinating clinic-based and school-based services requires close collaboration between professionals in each of these settings. Through ongoing collaboration between clinical and school professionals, clinicians can acquire more information about how students function in school settings and can have an influence on teachers by working through school-based mental health consultants; school professionals can obtain valuable medical and psychological information pertaining to students and can further develop their expertise in working with students who have ADHD and related difficulties.

CONCLUSION

Students with ADHD usually have difficulties with coping in educational settings because of a lack of engagement in academic work and insufficient opportunities to learn and practice academic skills. A multimodal intervention plan usually is needed to successfully treat the educational problems of these individuals. Multimodal interventions may consist of a combination of teacher-, parent-, peer-, and self-mediated strategies, often in conjunction with stimulant medication. Self-directed approaches to intervention are particularly useful when students become adolescents, although incorporating components of self-management interventions is recommended with younger students. Traditionally, programs for students with ADHD have been based in clinic settings, but a movement to establish school-based systems of care for these individuals has been gaining momentum. The integration of clinic-based and school-based programs of intervention is needed to successfully manage the educational problems of students with this disorder.

ENDNOTES

1. Barkley, DuPaul, & McMurray (1990).
2. Weiss & Hechtman (1993).
3. Barkley (1998).
4. Becker & Carnine (1981).
5. Gickling & Thompson (1985).
6. Kavale (1990).
7. Shinn (1989).
8. DuPaul & Stoner (1994).
9. Zentall & Dwyer (1988).
10. Zentall & Meyer (1987).
11. DuPaul & Stoner (1994).
12. Conte, Kinsbourne, Swanson, Zirk, & Samuels (1987).
13. Evans, Pelham, & Grudberg (1995).
14. McCormack & Leonard (1994).
15. Pfiffner & O'Leary (1993).
16. Ibid.
17. Rosenbaum, O'Leary, & Jacob (1975).
18. Pfiffner & O'Leary (1993).
19. Rhode, Jenson, & Reavis (1992).
20. See Abramowitz & O'Leary (1991).
21. Lentz (1988).
22. Rhode et al. (1992).
23. Shapiro, DuPaul, Bradley, & Bailey (1996).
24. Olympia, Jenson, Clark, & Sheridan (1992).
25. Kelley (1990).
26. Bowen, Olympia, & Jenson (1994).
27. DuPaul, Hook, Ervin, & Kyle (1995).
28. Hallowell (1995).
29. Lam, Cole, Shapiro, & Bambara (1994).
30. Bradley & Shapiro (1997).
31. Pelham et al. (1993).
32. Power, Hess, & Bennett (1995).
33. Power, Atkins, Osborne, & Blum (1994).
34. Ibid.
35. Ibid.

REFERENCES

Abramowitz, A.J., & O'Leary, S.G. (1991). Behavioral interventions for the classroom: Implications for students with ADHD. *School Psychology Review, 20,* 220–234.

Barkley, R.A. (1998). *Attention-deficit hyperactivity disorder: A handbook for diagnosis and treatment* (2nd ed.). New York: Guilford Press.

Barkley, R.A., DuPaul, G.J., & McMurray, M.B. (1990). A comprehensive evaluation of attention deficit disorder with and without hyperactivity as defined by research criteria. *Journal of Consulting and Clinical Psychology, 58,* 775–789.

Becker, W.C., & Carnine, D.W. (1981). Direct instruction: A behavior therapy model for comprehensive educational intervention with the disadvantaged. In S.W. Bijou & R. Ruiz (Eds.), *Behavior modification: Contributions to education* (pp. 145–210). Mahwah, NJ: Lawrence Erlbaum Associates.

Bowen, J., Olympia, D., & Jenson, W.R. (1994). *Study buddies: A parent-to-child tutoring program in reading, math, and spelling.* Longmont, CO: Sopris West.

Bradley, K.L., & Shapiro, E.S. (1997, April). *The effects of a self-management intervention on the classroom behavior of young adolescents with attention deficit/hyperactivity disorder.* Paper presented at the annual convention of the National Association of School Psychologists, Anaheim, CA.

Conte, R., Kinsbourne, M., Swanson, J., Zirk, H., & Samuels, M. (1987). Presentation rate effects on paired associate learning by attention deficit disordered children. *Child Development, 57,* 681–687.

Dailey, E.M., & Rosenberg, M.S. (1994, Fall). ADD, computers, and learning. *Attention!,* 8–16.

DuPaul, G.J., Hook, C.L., Ervin, R., & Kyle, K. (1995, August). *Effects of classwide peer tutoring on students with attention deficit hyperactivity disorder.* Paper presented at the annual convention of the National Association of School Psychologists, New York.

DuPaul, G.J., & Stoner, G. (1994). *ADHD in the schools: Assessment and intervention strategies.* New York: Guilford Press.

Evans, S.W., Pelham, W.E., & Grudberg, M.V. (1995). The efficacy of notetaking to improve behavior and comprehension of adolescents with attention deficit hyperactivity disorder. *Exceptionality, 5,* 1–17.

Gickling, E., & Armstrong, D.L. (1978). Levels of instructional difficulty as related to on-task behavior, task completion, and comprehension. *Journal of Learning Disabilities, 11,* 559–566.

Gickling, E., & Thompson, V.P. (1985). A personal view of curriculum-based assessment. *Exceptional Children, 52,* 205–218.

Greenwood, C.R., Delquadri, J., & Carta, J.J. (1988). *Classwide peer tutoring.* Seattle: Educational Achievement Systems.

Hallowell, E.M. (1995, August). Coaching: An adjunct to the treatment of ADHD. *The ADHD Report, 3*(4), 7–9.

Kahle, A.L., & Kelley, M.L. (1994). Children's homework problems: A comparison of goal setting and parent training. *Behavior Therapy, 25,* 275–290.

Kavale, K. (1990). The effectiveness of special education. In T.B. Gutkin & C.R. Reynolds (Eds.), *The handbook of school psychology* (2nd ed., pp. 868–898). New York: John Wiley & Sons.

Kelley, M.L. (1990). *School–home notes: Promoting children's classroom success.* New York: Guilford Press.

Lam, A.L., Cole, C.L., Shapiro, E.S., & Bambara, L.M. (1994). Relative effects of self-monitoring on-task behavior, academic accuracy, and disruptive behavior in students with behavior disorders. *School Psychology Review, 23,* 44–58.

Lentz, F.E. (1988). Reductive procedures. In J.C. Witt, S.N. Elliott, & F.M. Gresham (Eds.), *Handbook of behavior therapy in education* (pp. 439–468). New York: Plenum.

McCormack, A., & Leonard, F. (1994). Learning accommodations for ADD students. In P.O. Quinn (Ed.), *ADD and the college student* (pp. 75–84). New York: Magination Press.

Olympia, D., Jenson, W.R., Clark, E., & Sheridan, S. (1992). Training parents to facilitate homework completion: A model for home–school collaboration. In S.L. Christenson & J.C. Conoley (Eds.), *Home–school collaboration: Enhancing children's academic and social competence* (pp. 309–331). Silver Spring, MD: National Association of School Psychologists.

Pelham, W.E., Carlson, C., Sams, S.E., Vallano, G., Dixon, M.J., & Hoza, B. (1993). Separate and combined effects of methylphenidate and behavior modification on boys with attention-deficit hyperactivity disorder in the classroom. *Journal of Consulting and Clinical Psychology, 61,* 506–515.

Pfiffner, L.J., & O'Leary, S.G. (1993). School-based psychological treatments. In J.L. Matson (Ed.), *Handbook of hyperactivity in children* (pp. 234–255). Needham Heights, MA: Allyn & Bacon.

Power, T.J., Atkins, M.S., Osborne, M.L., & Blum, N.J. (1994). The school psychologist as manager of programming for ADHD. *School Psychology Review, 23,* 279–291.

Power, T.J., Hess, L.E., & Bennett, D.S. (1995). The acceptability of interventions for attention-deficit hyperactivity disorder among elementary and middle school teachers. *Developmental and Behavioral Pediatrics, 16,* 238–243.

Rapport, M.D., Denney, C., DuPaul, G.J., & Gardner, M.J. (1994). Attention deficit disorder and methylphenidate: Normalization rates, clinical effectiveness, and response prediction in 76 children. *Journal of the American Academy of Child and Adolescent Psychiatry, 33,* 882–893.

Rapport, M.D., Murphy, A., & Bailey, J.S. (1982). Ritalin vs. response cost in the control of hyperactive children: A within subject comparison. *Journal of Applied Behavior Analysis, 15,* 205–216.

Rhode, G., Jenson, W.R., & Reavis, H.K. (1992). *The tough kid book: Practical classroom management strategies.* Longmont, CO: Sopris West.

Rhode, G., Morgan, D.P., & Young, K.R. (1983). Generalization and maintenance of treatment gains of behaviorally handicapped students from resource rooms to regular classrooms using self-evaluation procedures. *Journal of Applied Behavior Analysis, 16,* 171–188.

Rosenbaum, A., O'Leary, S.G., & Jacob, R.G. (1975). Behavioral interventions with hyperactive children: Group consequences as a supplement to individual contingencies. *Behavior Therapy, 6,* 315–323.

Shapiro, E.S., DuPaul, G.J., Bradley, K.L., & Bailey, L.T. (1996). A school-based consultation model for service delivery to middle school students with attention deficit disorder. *Journal of Emotional and Behavioral Disorders, 4,* 73–81.

Shinn, M.R. (Ed.). (1989). *Curriculum-based measurement: Assessing special children.* New York: Guilford Press.

Weiss, G., & Hechtman, L. (1993). *Hyperactive children grown up: ADHD in children, adolescents, and adults* (2nd ed.). New York: Guilford Press.

Zentall, S.S., & Dwyer, A.M. (1988). Color effects on the impulsivity and activity of hyperactive children. *Journal of School Psychology, 27,* 165–174.

Zentall, S.S., & Meyer, M.J. (1987). Self-regulation of stimulation for ADD-H children during reading and vigilance task performance. *Journal of Abnormal Child Psychology, 15,* 519–536.

RESOURCES FOR PARENTS

Bowen, J., Olympia, D., & Jenson, W.R. (1994). *Study buddies: A parent-to-child tutoring program in reading, math, and spelling.* Longmont, CO: Sopris West. (To order, call [800] 547-6747.)

Cutler, B.C. (1993). *You, your child, and special education: A guide to making the system work.* Baltimore: Paul H. Brookes Publishing Co. (To order, call [800] 638-3775.)

Gordon, M. (1990). *ADHD/hyperactivity: A consumer's guide.* DeWitt, NY: GSI Publications. (To order, call [800] 233-9273.)

Parker, H.C. (1988). *The ADD hyperactivity workbook for parents, teachers, and kids* (2nd ed.). Plantation, FL: Impact. (To order, call [800] 233-9273.)

RESOURCES FOR TEACHERS

Gordon, S.B., & Asher, M.J. (1993). *Meeting the ADD challenge: A practical guide for teachers.* Champaign, IL: Research Press. (To order, call [800] 233-9273.)

Fowler, M. (1992). *The CH.A.D.D. educator's manual.* Plantation, FL: Impact. (To order, call [800] 233-9273.)

Olympia, D., Andrews, D., Valum, L., & Jenson, W. (1994). *Homework teams: Homework management strategies for the classroom.* Longmont, CO: Sopris West. (To order, call [800] 547-6747.)

Parker, H.C. (1992). *The ADD hyperactivity handbook for schools.* Plantation, FL: Impact. (To order, call [800] 233-9273.)

Rhode, G., Jenson, W., & Reavis, H.K. (1992). *The tough kid book: Practical classroom management strategies.* Longmont, CO: Sopris West. (To order, call [800] 547-6747.)

RESOURCES FOR CLINICIANS

DuPaul, G.J., & Stoner, G. (1994). *ADHD in the schools: Assessment and intervention strategies.* New York: Guilford Press. (To order, call [800] 365-7006.)

Kelley, M.L. (1990). *School–home notes: Promoting children's classroom success.* New York: Guilford Press. (To order, call [800] 365-7006.)

Kendall, P.C., & Braswell, L. (1993). *Cognitive–behavioral therapy for impulsive children.* New York: Guilford Press. (To order, call [800] 365-7006.)

Shapiro, E.S., & Cole, C.L. (1994). *Behavior change in the classroom: Self-management interventions.* New York: Guilford Press. (To order, call [800] 365-7006.)

Understanding and Treating the Peer Problems of Children with Attention-Deficit/ Hyperactivity Disorder

with Stephen S. Leff and Tracy E. Costigan

Inattention and hyperactivity-impulsivity place children with attention-deficit/hyperactivity disorder (ADHD) at risk for social problems and peer rejection. In fact, more than half of children with ADHD have significant social relationship difficulties.[1] Because early peer relationship problems are predictive of rejection by the peer group, high rates of school dropout, juvenile delinquency, and psychopathology in adolescence and adulthood,[2] understanding and addressing the peer interaction difficulties of children with ADHD is extremely important.

Children with ADHD have trouble with initiating and maintaining peer friendships for many reasons[3]:

1. They often make inappropriate attempts to enter groups.
2. They have trouble with following the rules to games.
3. They have difficulties with making transitions.
4. They get frustrated easily.
5. They are prone to losing their temper.
6. They may become aggressive when conflicts arise.

Peers often react negatively to children with ADHD, in part because of their intrusive and irritating social behavior. Inappropriate social behaviors often cause children with ADHD to be rejected and bullied by others.[4] Unfortunately, the sequence of events that leads to peer rejection is difficult to interrupt; many children with ADHD who are rejected remain unaccepted by their peers as they advance through the school grades.[5]

FACTORS THAT AFFECT CHILDREN'S SOCIAL BEHAVIOR

Because many children with ADHD can articulate clearly how they should act in social situations, the social problems of these children can be difficult for parents and teachers to understand. Children with ADHD often are able to explain, select, and demonstrate appropriate behaviors in hypothetical situations[6] but often do not engage in the same behaviors in real-life social interactions. For example, Brian, a 9-year-old with ADHD, wants to join a group of children in a game. He previously has told both his parents and his teacher that he is most likely to be successful when he asks to participate before entering the group, thus demonstrating adequate **social knowledge.** When Brian encounters the same situation on the playground, however, he attempts to join in by interrupting and trying to change the rules, demonstrating inadequate **social performance.** As a result, he is ignored or rejected by the peer group. Given his adequate social knowledge, his parents and teachers do not understand why he cannot act appropriately in social situations and conclude that he is socially immature.

Many factors can contribute to the performance deficits of children with ADHD. One factor is a problem with impulsivity or response inhibition.[7] Children's impulsivity may result in inappropriate social goals—that is, the consequences that they hope to achieve when they approach social situations.[8] Impulsivity also is associated with a strong desire to seek immediate gratification and with a failure to consider the long-term consequences of behavior. For instance, Brian's goal, like that of many impulsive children, may be to become a member of the group as quickly as he can. He wants so much to engage with his peers that he may resort to using an inappropriate strategy, such as barging in, and fail to consider the consequences of being intrusive with others.

Another factor that can influence children's social behavior is how children interpret events. For example, suppose that Sharlene, an aggressive girl with ADHD, is bumped from behind by a peer and it is unclear whether this happened on purpose or by accident. Sharlene must interpret the peer's intentions. Children with ADHD often infer hostile intentions in ambiguous social situations[9] (e.g., "She bumped into me on purpose and to be mean"). This tendency has been termed a **hostile attributional bias.**[10] If Sharlene exhibits a hostile attributional bias when bumped into from behind, then she is very likely to shove or push the child back.

A child's level of **emotional regulation** is another factor that can influence social behavior. *Emotional regulation* refers to a child's ability to control his or her emotional responses to a social event.[11] Many children with ADHD have trouble with controlling their emotions in social situations; they become hurt and angry very easily, and their anger often is extreme. Their emotional response, in turn, can affect their ability to interpret a situation in an accurate manner.

There are many factors that may lead a child with ADHD to exhibit inappropriate social behavior. Although it is instructive to examine each factor separately, it is important to understand that these factors interact to determine a child's behavior response. For example, Ricardo is a child with ADHD who frequently exhibits aggressive behavior during lunchtime. He will react aggressively when a peer accidentally kicks him or spills milk on him because he views the action as intentional. When the counselor speaks to him, she can tell that he has little understanding of how he gets himself into trouble with his peers, but he is able to think of some useful ideas for coping with situations that arise in the lunchroom. Ricardo's social goal of being in charge of others and his strong desire for immediate gratification contribute to his social problems. His impulsivity, his tendency to become angry easily, and his predisposition to exhibit a hostile attributional bias lead Ricardo to misinterpret other children's intentions and react aggressively. Ricardo mistakenly assumes that the children bump him and spill milk on him on purpose, and he quickly responds by punching and kicking.

ASSESSING CHILDREN'S SOCIAL SKILLS

Children with ADHD can vary greatly in the nature and the severity of their social problems. Four issues are important to consider when determining the severity of a child's social difficulties and the level of intervention that is needed:

1. Whether the child has been able to maintain a close friendship over an extended time period
2. The child's level of impairment in school caused by peer relationship problems
3. The extent to which the child is bothered by his or her social difficulties
4. The child's response to previous attempts at intervention

A brief interview with the parents and the child may be useful for determining whether to offer guidance to the family or to refer the child to a school- or clinic-based mental health professional who can provide more intensive social skills intervention.

Table 1 provides examples of questions that could be used in an interview with parents and children to determine the level of intervention that is needed. For instance, if Sally, a child with ADHD, has difficulties with making new friends and gets teased occasionally but has two or three close friends and does not appear highly concerned about peer relationships, then the clinician may want to offer guidance to the family regarding strategies to address the problems. If Sally has few, if any, friends; gets teased every day to the point that it causes her to feel sad and to withdraw from others; and has not responded well to various attempts by her parents to address the problems, then more intensive social skills programming may be warranted. Of course, there are many borderline situations in which it may be difficult to determine whether to refer a child for specialized help. One approach may be to offer advice to the parents, get the school counselor involved, and arrange for a follow-up appointment in roughly 1 month to determine the response to intervention.

Many tools, in addition to parent and child interviews, are available to assist mental health professionals with the assessment of children's social problems. For instance, teacher and parent rating scales, such as The Social Skills Rating System[12] and the Walker-McConnell Scale of Social Competence,[13] can be useful for identifying the type and the severity of social skills problems that children exhibit. Alternatively, direct observations of children's behavior on the playground[14] and peer ratings of children's acceptance in school[15] may be the most comprehensive and accurate ways to assess social skills, but these methods may not be practical because they are time consuming and labor intensive.

SOCIAL SKILLS INTERVENTIONS

Several approaches are useful for improving the social skills of children with ADHD. Consulting with parents, providing social skills training, and involving school person-

Table 1. Brief family interview to assess peer relationship problems

Questions for parents:

1. Friendships
   - How easily does your child make friends?
   - Does your child have a lot of friends?
   - Does your child have a best friend?
   - What are your child's friends like? Are they popular, unpopular, aggressive, passive, and so forth?
   - How well does your child get along with his or her siblings?
2. Impairment in school
   - How does your child get along with peers in school?
   - Does your child have any trouble on the playground?
   - Does your child bully or tease others?
   - Does your child get bullied or teased on the playground?
3. Impact on child
   - How does your child feel about his or her peer relationships?
   - Have you noticed that your child is getting frustrated with his or her peers?
   - Have you noticed that your child is withdrawing from peers?

Questions for child:

1. Friendships
   - How easily do you make friends?
   - Do you have a lot of friends?
   - Do you have a best friend?
   - What do you like to do with your friends?
   - How well do you get along with your brothers or sisters?
2. Impairment in school
   - How do you get along with students in school?
   - How do things go for you on the playground?
   - Is anyone mean or unfair to you in school?
   - Are you ever unfair or mean to others in school?
3. Impact on child
   - How do you feel about the children in your school? in your neighborhood?
   - Do you ever get frustrated with the other kids?
   - Do you feel like it is easier just to stay by yourself on the playground?

nel and peers in the intervention process can contribute to positive outcomes in peer relations.

Consultation with Parents

Parents have a critical role to play in helping children develop effective social skills. When children have mild social problems, a clinician can consult with parents and offer guidance. For instance, when a child experiences peer problems at school, clinicians can empower parents to serve as advocates to make sure that the child gets the needed assistance from teachers and counselors. If the child does not have many playmates, then the clinician can urge the parents to arrange for a student from the school to visit their home. It is critical that these encounters be brief, well organized, and enjoyable so that the friend will want to visit again. If the child with ADHD has problems with playing with others away from home, then the parents will need to work closely with the parents of the other child to design a successful visit.

Involvement in organized activities and sports generally is very useful in developing social skills. Children with ADHD often have difficulties with organized activities, perhaps because of their impatience, problem with taking turns, and underdeveloped fine and gross motor skills. Parents should be encouraged to find an activity that matches the child's skills and interests. Sometimes these children perform more competently in sports that emphasize the development of individual skills, such as karate and fencing, as opposed to team sports. In addition, it may be helpful for parents to get involved as coaches, den leaders, and mentors to provide guidance to their child, to advocate for their child's needs in the group, and to provide support for other adults who work with their child. Close supervision and supportive coaching often are required to prevent negative interactions and to promote positive social behavior.

Social Skills Programming

Improving the social behavior and reducing peers' rejection of children with ADHD can be a complex process. In cases in which the child with ADHD is experiencing moderate to severe social problems, the involvement of a school- or clinic-based mental health specialist may be indicated. Following are descriptions of critical components of social skills intervention programs that can be useful. These components address the underlying factors that often lead to inappropriate social behavior, including inadequate knowledge, inappropriate goals, negative expectations for success, a hostile attributional bias, and problems with regulating anger.

Determine how the student becomes the object of peer rejection. Children with ADHD get into trouble with their peers in a variety of ways (e.g., teasing others, not keeping their hands to themselves, failing to take turns, insisting on being in charge of games). Clinicians need to understand the specific ways in which the child sets up himor herself for rejection. Assessment procedures such as parent and teacher ratings and direct observations can be useful in this regard.

Engage the child in a problem-solving process. Social problem solving consists of five main steps:

1. Problem identification
2. Generation of alternative solutions
3. Consideration of the consequences of each alternative
4. Selection and use of a specific strategy
5. Evaluation of efficacy of the strategy[16]

The social problem-solving process is designed to improve the child's knowledge of how to behave in specific social situations. Although children with ADHD typically rush through the problem-solving process, it is important to prompt and reinforce them to slow down and take each step seriously, particularly the step involving generation of potential solutions to the problem.

Provide instruction and modeling. Children with social problems usually need instruction in how to implement the strategies that they decide to use in solving a social problem. **Modeling,** particularly from a peer who is perceived by the child as having high status, can be very effective for teaching children social skills and helping them to develop positive expectations for success. Self-modeling, which involves the child's viewing him- or herself on videotape performing a social skill effectively, also is useful for enhancing expectations for success.[17] In the initial stages of modeling, the model should demonstrate mastery or ideal performance. Later in the training, children can benefit from observing a coping model, who illustrates some of the problems that typically arise when using the strategy. The coping model can provide important points of discussion for the clinician and the child.[18]

Provide opportunities for role playing. Once instruction has been given, the child needs to practice using the strategy. **Role-play** situations can be staged with the child and one or more peers. Having the child play several roles, not just the one that he or she is accustomed to assuming, may enable the child to acquire a useful perspective on the problem. For instance, if the child is learning a strategy for coping with peer teasing, then he or she could be encouraged to play the role of the bully as well as that of the victim. In this way, the child's tendency to exhibit a hostile attributional bias may become evident. Role-play scenarios should reflect actual situations with which the child is having trouble coping in school and at home.

Assign homework. Knowing how to behave in a social situation and having the skills to perform a useful strategy often are not sufficient to change behavior. Children, particularly those who are impulsive, have significant problems with generalizing social skills to naturalistic settings, such as the playground and the lunchroom. One potentially useful approach to improving **generalization** is to give students a homework assignment that requires them to implement the learned strategy, write down how the strategy was used and the outcome that was derived, and report back to the clinician within a short interval (see Figure 1). Because many students with ADHD often do not comply with rules and instructions, the student and the clinician should devise a behavioral contract that stipulates the assignment and the consequences of fulfilling and not fulfilling the contract. (See Chapter 6 for further discussion of behavior contracts.)

Teach adults and peers to prompt and reinforce appropriate social behavior. Because impulsive children have significant problems with applying learned skills in diverse social settings, it is important for adults (e.g., teachers, playground aides, parents) to observe these children carefully, prompt them to use specific skills, and reinforce effective use of the strategies.[19] Also, because many children with ADHD have trouble with regulating their emotions in social situations, they may need adults to help them relax and deal with their emotions in an adaptive manner. In some cases, a peer can be enlisted to serve as a buddy to the child with ADHD. The role of the peer buddy, like that of the adult mentor, includes prompting and reinforcing the effective use of strategies and control of emotions. It is important, however, that the child with ADHD be able to offer his or her buddy some assistance (e.g., in reading or math) so that the relationship is mutually helpful and not hierarchical. Assisting children with social problems on the playground and in the lunchroom is not easy; adult mentors and peer buddies need training and ongoing consultation to make sure that they indeed are being helpful to the child.

Provide training to nontarget peers. Children who annoy others can acquire bad reputations that are difficult to change. Research has shown that peers who interact with aggressive children continue to view these children as aggressive even in situations in which their behavior is not aggressive by objective standards.[20] To change a pattern of social behavior, it is not sufficient to work solely with the aggressive child; peers who are not impulsive or aggressive also need training to identify ways that they "set up" the child to behave in an aggressive manner.[21]

PEER INTERACTION DIARY

Date _____

1. Which strategy did you use? (Be specific.)

_____

_____

2. When did you use the strategy? (Describe the situation.)

_____

_____

_____

3. How did the strategy work?

_____

_____

_____

4. What or who helped you to do a good job?

_____

_____

5. What made it hard for you to do a good job?

_____

_____

The Clinician's Practical Guide to Attention-Deficit/Hyperactivity Disorder
by Marianne Mercugliano, Thomas J. Power, and Nathan J. Blum   ©1999 by Paul H. Brookes Publishing Co.

Figure 1.   Peer interaction diary.

Design social environments that promote positive social behavior. Many children, not just those with ADHD, exhibit problems with peer functioning when the environment is not organized properly. For instance, playgrounds that are poorly supervised and that do not provide students with age-appropriate games often facilitate highly aggressive behavior.[22] In schools, it is recommended that the principal and the physical education teacher work with playground aides to supervise carefully all sections of the playground, to design developmentally appropriate activities, and to ensure that supervision is offered and games are available to the students on a daily basis.

Importance of School-Based Group Intervention

School-based programs of group intervention have several advantages over clinic-based interventions. First, involving peers in the process of social skills intervention is very important. Organizing social skills intervention groups with children who are of similar age is much more feasible in schools than in clinics. Second, in clinics, children are likely to be involved in groups with peers from different communities; thus, clinic-based groups may have a limited effect on peer relationships in the child's own community. Third, consultation between the teacher and the school mental health professional is important to promoting the student's generalization of intervention effects. It is more feasible for school-based professionals to collaborate with teachers than it is for clinic-based providers. Fourth, school professionals can change the natural environments in which peers interact (e.g., playground, lunchroom), whereas clinic-based professionals have limited control over contextual factors in the child's natural environment.

School professionals sometimes have trouble with implementing recommendations for school-based social skills group interventions on behalf of students with ADHD and related problems. One reason for this is that arranging group interventions is difficult and time consuming. Nonetheless, if a student with ADHD experiences social impairments as a result of this condition, then he or she is entitled to appropriate interventions (see Chapter 8). If a school fails to provide the social skills interventions that a student needs, then the parent should speak to the principal about writing an individualized education program, as outlined in the Individuals with Disabilities Education Act (IDEA) of 1990 (PL 101-476) and its amendments of 1997 (PL 105-17), which mandate the use of these approaches. Another reason for problems with the implementation of group interventions is that school professionals may lack the necessary training. In these instances, a professional from outside the school (e.g., child clinical psychologist, clinical social worker) can be enlisted to provide consultation. Also, excellent resources are available to assist school professionals with providing social skills interventions to students with ADHD and related problems (see "Resources for Professionals" at the end of this chapter).

CONCLUSION

Children with ADHD often have social relationship difficulties that are the result of inadequate social knowledge, problems with regulating impulsivity and emotional responses, unrealistic goals and expectations for success, and inaccurate interpretations of social events. The strategies that were described in this chapter can be useful in assisting a child who has problems with relating to peers.

When children with ADHD experience relatively mild problems with peer relationships, the clinician often can be helpful by consulting with parents about ways in which they can establish and support meaningful social experiences for their child. When the social problems result in a greater degree of impairment, enrolling the child in a social skills training program that is conducted by a trained mental health professional may be needed. Office-based social skills training can provide a child with opportunities to practice specific peer relationship strategies, but this type of intervention generally must be supplemented with strategies that change the social context for the child's behavior to change. For instance, reorganizing the playground context, providing training to playground aides, and involving one or more peers in the intervention process usually are necessary. The school is the ideal setting for conducting group social skills training, but school professionals often need the consultation of mental health providers outside the school to design an effective program of peer relationship intervention.

ENDNOTES

1. Pelham & Bender (1982).
2. Parker & Asher (1987).
3. DuPaul & Stoner (1994).
4. Pelham & Bender (1982).
5. Coie & Dodge (1983).
6. Hoza & Pelham (1995).
7. Barkley (1997).
8. Melnick & Hinshaw (1996).
9. Costigan, Zupan, Hinshaw, & McGuffin (1995).
10. For a review, see Crick & Dodge (1994).
11. Whalen & Henker (1992).
12. Gresham & Elliott (1990).
13. Walker & McConnell (1988).
14. Murphy, Hutchison, & Bailey (1983).
15. E.g., Kupersmidt, Leff, & Patterson (1996).
16. Shure & Spivack (1978).
17. Dowrick (1991).
18. Kendall & Braswell (1993).
19. Sheridan (1995).
20. Dodge & Frame (1982).
21. Guevremont (1990).
22. Murphy et al. (1983).

REFERENCES

Barkley, R.A. (1997). Behavioral inhibition, sustained attention, and executive functions: Constructing a unifying theory of ADHD. *Psychological Bulletin, 121,* 65–94.

Coie, J.D., & Dodge, K.A. (1983). Continuities and changes in children's social status: A five-year longitudinal study. *Merrill-Palmer Quarterly, 29,* 261–282.

Costigan, T.E., Zupan, B.A., Hinshaw, S.P., & McGuffin, P.W. (1995, November). *Peer instigators and social-information processing: Effects of behavioral characteristics on attribution and response decision.* Poster presented at the 29th annual meeting of the Association for the Advancement of Behavior Therapy, Washington, DC.

Crick, N.R., & Dodge, K.A. (1994). A review and reformulation of social information-processing mechanisms in children's social adjustment. *Psychological Bulletin, 115,* 74–101.

Dodge, K.A., & Frame, C.L. (1982). Social cognitive biases and deficits in aggressive boys. *Child Development, 53*, 620–635.

Dowrick, P.W. (1991). *Practical guide to using video in the behavioral sciences.* New York: Wiley Interscience.

DuPaul, G.J., & Stoner, G. (1994). *ADHD in the schools: Assessment and intervention strategies.* New York: Guilford Press.

Gresham, F.M., & Elliott, S.N. (1990). *The Social Skills Rating System.* Circle Pines, MN: American Guidance Service.

Guevremont, D. (1990). Social skills and peer relationship training. In R.A. Barkley (Ed.), *Attention-deficit hyperactivity disorder: A handbook for diagnosis and treatment* (pp. 540–572). New York: Guilford Press.

Hoza, B., & Pelham, W.E. (1995). Social-cognitive predictors of treatment response in children with ADHD. *Journal of Social and Clinical Psychology, 14*, 23–35.

Individuals with Disabilities Education Act (IDEA) of 1990, PL 101-476, 20 U.S.C. §§ 1400 *et seq.*

Individuals with Disabilities Education Act Amendments of 1997, PL 105-17, 20 U.S.C. §§ 1400 *et seq.*

Kendall, P.C., & Braswell, L. (1993). *Cognitive-behavioral therapy for impulsive children.* New York: Guilford Press.

Kupersmidt, J.B., Leff, S.L., & Patterson, C. (1996, August). *Teacher and peer reports of bullying and victimization.* Poster presented at the 14th biennial meeting of the International Society for the Study of Behavioral Development, Quebec City, Quebec, Canada.

Melnick, S.M., & Hinshaw, S.P. (1996). What they want and what they get: The social goals of boys with ADHD and comparison boys. *Journal of Abnormal Child Psychology, 24*, 169–185.

Murphy, H.A., Hutchison, J.M., & Bailey, J.S. (1983). Behavioral school psychology goes outdoors: The effect of organized games on playground aggression. *Journal of Applied Behavior Analysis, 16*, 29–35.

Parker, J.G., & Asher, S.R. (1987). Peer relations and later personal adjustment: Are low-accepted children at risk? *Psychological Bulletin, 102*, 357–389.

Pelham, W.E., & Bender, M.E. (1982). Peer relationships in hyperactive children: Description and treatment. In K.D. Gadow & I. Bialer (Eds.), *Advances in learning and behavioral disabilities* (Vol. 1, pp. 365–436). Greenwich, CT: JAI Press.

Sheridan, S.M. (1995). *The tough kid social skills book.* Longmont, CO: Sopris West.

Shure, M.B., & Spivack, G. (1978). *Problem-solving techniques in childrearing.* San Francisco: Jossey-Bass.

Walker, H., & McConnell, S. (1988). *Walker-McConnell Scale of Social Competence.* Austin, TX: PRO-ED.

Whalen, C.K., & Henker, B. (1992). The social profile of attention-deficit hyperactivity disorder: Five fundamental facets. *Attention-Deficit Hyperactivity Disorder, 1*(2), 395–410.

RESOURCES FOR PROFESSIONALS

Kendall, P.C., & Braswell, L. (1993). *Cognitive-behavioral therapy for impulsive children.* New York: Guilford Press. (72 Spring Street, New York, NY 10012; [800] 365-7006)

Goldstein, A.P., Sprafkin, R.P., Gershaw, N.J., & Klein, P. (1985). *Skillstreaming the adolescent.* Champaign, IL: Research Press. (Department 97, Post Office Box 9177, Champaign, IL 61826; [800] 519-2707)

McGinnis, E., & Goldstein, A.P. (1984). *Skillstreaming the elementary school child: A guide for teaching prosocial skills.* Champaign, IL: Research Press. (Department 97, Post Office Box 9177, Champaign, IL 61826; [800] 519-2707)

Sheridan, S.M. (1996). *The tough kid social skills book.* Longmont, CO: Sopris West. (1140 Boston Avenue, Longmont, CO 80501; [303] 651-2829)

Shure, M.B. (1992). *I Can Problem Solve: An interpersonal cognitive problem solving program.* (ADD Warehouse, 300 Northwest 70th Avenue, Suite 102, Plantation, FL 33317; [800] 233-9273)

Walker, H.M., McConnell, S., Holmes, D., Todis, B., Walker, J., & Golden, N. (1988). *The ACCEPTS Program: A curriculum for children's effective peer and teacher skills.* Austin, TX: PRO-ED. (8700 Shoal Creek Boulevard, Austin, TX 78757-6897; [512] 451-3246)

RESOURCES FOR CHILDREN AND YOUTH

The Good Behavior Game. (To order, call A.D.D. Warehouse [800] 233-9273.)
The Social Skills Game. (To order, call A.D.D. Warehouse [800] 233-9273.)

ASSESSMENT TOOLS

Gresham, F.M., & Elliott, S.N. (1990). *The Social Skills Rating System.* Circle Pines, MN: American Guidance Service. (4201 Woodland Road, Post Office Box 99, Circle Pines, MN 55014-1796; [800] 328-2560)
Walker, H., & McConnell, S. (1988). *Walker-McConnell Scale of Social Competence.* Austin, TX: PRO-ED. (8700 Shoal Creek Boulevard, Austin, TX 78757-6897; [512] 451-3246)

Advocacy and Legal Issues

8

Students with attention-deficit/hyperactivity disorder (ADHD) may receive special services at school under federal and state laws that govern special education and the civil rights of individuals with disabilities; however, the actual implementation of such services in the community may be compromised by several factors. The application of legal provisions to children with ADHD has occurred relatively recently; thus, school personnel, clinicians, and families may not be familiar with them. School personnel may not have training in school-based interventions for students with ADHD or in implementing them effectively. Alternatively, they may have the prerequisite knowledge but not the resources to provide additional assistance. As a result, parents often have difficulties with communicating with school personnel and obtaining the help that is needed to address ADHD-related difficulties in the educational setting.[1] It is important for clinicians to have a basic knowledge of educational law at the federal, state, and local levels as it applies to ADHD so that they are able to provide to parents anticipatory guidance and referral as well as the most useful written reports. Parents will be better-equipped advocates if they are familiar with this subject matter *before* they become embroiled in the process. In this chapter, the essential features of federal and state laws as they apply to the education of students with ADHD are reviewed, and information for the support and anticipatory guidance of parents is provided.

FEDERAL LAWS THAT GOVERN SPECIAL EDUCATION SERVICES

There are five main federal laws that relate to the education of children with disabilities (see Table 1). In the aggregate, these laws provide for a free appropriate public educa-

The authors gratefully acknowledge Ellen Mancuso, of The Educational Law Center of Pennsylvania, for her thorough and helpful review of this chapter.

Table 1. Federal laws related to special education

- **Section 504 of the Rehabilitation Act of 1973 (PL 93-112)**
  A civil rights law that relates to educational and workplace issues, includes students with ADHD, and applies to recipients of federal funds
- **Education for All Handicapped Children Act of 1975 (PL 94-142)**
  Established the provision of specialized education in the least restrictive environment for students with disabilities
- **Education of the Handicapped Act Amendments of 1986 (PL 99-457)**
  Extended PL 94-142's eligibility for special services to children at risk from birth through the preschool years
- **Americans with Disabilities Act (ADA) of 1990 (PL 101-336)**
  A civil rights law that provides broad protections from discrimination against individuals with disabilities and includes school settings
- **Individuals with Disabilities Education Act (IDEA) of 1990 (PL 101-476)**
  Further amended PL 94-142 by changing the name, adding categories of qualifying students, and providing for transitional services to promote postsecondary education functioning

tion for all children. Each child's unique learning needs must be met, including needs for both specialized instruction and the related services that are deemed necessary to allow the student to take full advantage of specialized instruction. Such a program is to take place within the least restrictive environment possible and to be developed within a framework of **due process** procedures to protect the parents' right to provide input into the educational plan. When disagreements cannot be settled at the school level, federal laws provide for an impartial hearing officer, arranged for but not selected by the school district, to review the case. The wording of these laws is broad to encompass the needs of a diverse group of students, but this broad language also creates problems with interpretation. Some definitions are provided, although they may differ between the Individuals with Disabilities Education Act (IDEA) of 1990 (PL 101-476) and Section 504 of the Rehabilitation Act of 1973 (PL 93-112) (see Table 2).

Individuals with Disabilities Education Act

IDEA is the central federal law related to special education. In addition to appropriating funds for special education services, IDEA spells out the procedures for identifying and evaluating a disability and implementing services. To be eligible for services under IDEA, two important criteria must be met. First, the disability must be shown to have an *educational* impact; simply having a disability does not qualify a student. What constitutes an educational impact is not spelled out, but a low IQ score, an **IQ–achievement discrepancy,** and declining grades or achievement test scores typically are used as evidence. Second, a student must be diagnosed as having one of a particular list of disabilities:

- Hearing impairments (including deafness)
- Speech or language impairments
- Visual impairments (including blindness)
- Serious emotional disturbance
- Orthopedic impairments
- Autism
- Traumatic brain injury
- Other health impairments
- Specific learning disabilities

Table 2.   Definitions used in Section 504 and IDEA

- Under Section 504, *disability* refers to a condition that substantially limits a major life activity including learning, behavioral, emotional, social, and vocational development; under IDEA, *disability* is defined as one of a list of eligible diagnoses, with specific criteria for each one.
- *Free* means at no cost to the parents.
- Under IDEA, *appropriate* means an individualized, planned program that allows the child to make meaningful progress; under Section 504, *appropriate* means education to the same extent as that available to students without disabilities.
- *Meaningful progress* means progress toward the ability to live independently as an adult and to be a fully participating member of the community.
- *Specialized instruction* may include different methods of teaching the same material and skills as are taught to general education students or different material and skills (e.g., study and organizational skills).
- *Related services* refers to transportation, counseling, and therapies.
- *Due process* is a series of safeguards at each step of the process of assessment for and implementation of special education services to ensure that parents are fully informed and in agreement with the services provided. Due process includes protection of parents' right to understand each step of the process and its alternatives, the right to disagree, the right to impartial mediation for disputes that cannot be resolved at the school level, the right to obtain records and have them explained, and the right to recover certain costs for privately obtained evaluations and attorney's fees.

ADHD is not on this list. Students with ADHD may qualify, however, if they also have one of the disabilities on the list; the two that most frequently coexist with ADHD are learning disabilities and serious emotional disturbance.

In a Joint Policy Memo dated September 16, 1991, the U.S. Department of Education issued a statement clarifying that students with ADHD may qualify for services under IDEA through the "other health impairments" category,[2] defined as any acute or chronic condition that results in limited alertness and thereby impairs educational performance. In individual legal cases, ADHD has been argued to limit alertness through increased alertness to irrelevant stimuli (distractibility) and through decreased metabolic activity in attention-related parts of the brain, as shown by positron emission tomography scan studies.[3] Finally, IDEA mandates the school to provide what is *necessary* for the child's educational success, not what may be considered *optimum.*

Service provision under IDEA focuses on evaluation of the child and development of the individualized education program (IEP), which must be conducted by a multidisciplinary team (MDT)[a] that consists of, at minimum, the school psychologist, the child's teacher, and the parent(s); others may be included as deemed necessary. Parents or school personnel may initiate the process. If a parent believes that his or her child needs special services, then the parent must write a dated letter to the school principal requesting an evaluation for such services (see Appendix A for an example of such a letter). The school then has "a reasonable time" to complete this evaluation, limited to a specific number of days in some states. If the MDT evaluation is delayed or refused, then the parent should request a hearing (again, by dated letter) and send a copy of this request to the special education director for the school district. In some states, the parents may request a prehearing conference, which is an additional opportunity to address the situation between parents and school before proceeding with due process.

---

[a]In particular school districts, a different name may be used for the MDT, such as Child Study Team or Student Support Team.

The evaluation must consist of classroom observation, a thorough review of educational and medical records, consideration of any relevant independent evaluations, and information provided by parents. No specific tests are mandated at the federal level, but MDT evaluations frequently include IQ and academic achievement tests. Unfortunately, a statistically significant IQ–achievement discrepancy sometimes is the only measure that is used to determine educational impairment. Although this measure generally is required for the diagnosis of learning disability, it is not designed to detect the academic skills deficits, social difficulties, and frustrations that affect the educational life of the student with ADHD. In certain instances, a psychiatric evaluation may be included (e.g., for the designation of serious emotional disturbance). If the MDT requests additional evaluations, such as psychiatric or speech-language evaluations, then these must be provided by the school district at no charge to the parents. The diagnosis of a disability that qualifies for services under IDEA may be made through a school-based or an independent evaluation. Although the MDT is required to consider information from independent evaluations, it is not required to accept the conclusions from these evaluations. When independent evaluations are used in place of required components of the MDT evaluation, parents may be eligible for reimbursement.

If school personnel want to initiate an MDT evaluation, then they must notify the parents in writing and explain

- The reasons for the evaluation
- What the evaluation will consist of and why
- What specific information is sought
- What the subsequent process and its time line will be
- The parents' options and rights at each step in the process

Parents must give written permission for such an evaluation; although they have the right to refuse it, it usually is unwise to do so. Referral by the school team usually occurs when a child is experiencing substantial academic or behavior difficulties. The information that is provided by such an evaluation should be useful to parents in determining how best to support their child. Permitting the evaluation does not constitute an agreement to subsequent recommendations.

Once the evaluation is completed, the MDT writes a summary report of its findings and recommendations. This report must be made available to the parents. If the parents disagree with the conclusions of the report or believe that further evaluation is necessary in order to write the IEP, then they should make a written request for a hearing promptly. Within 30 days of the generation of this report, a conference must be scheduled to write the IEP. Parents should be present at this meeting and participate in the development of the IEP, although, unfortunately, the MDT often has written the IEP prior to the meeting and presents it to the parents for their signature as a formality. Because their signature on the IEP signifies agreement with its contents, parents should insist that they be given the opportunity to provide their input in the development of the IEP and may want to have their clinician review it as well. If parents disagree with the contents of the IEP, in terms of either the recommended placement or the services to be provided, then they should be made aware of the legally mandated options for dispute resolution.

Often, the IEP focuses on specialized educational instruction; parents should be prepared to insist on the inclusion of other components that are relevant to their child with ADHD, such as behavior management strategies, social skills programming, the teaching of organizational and study skills, and methods for measuring and documenting academic progress. (Behavior management strategies are described more specifically in Chapters 5 and 6.) These components should be described specifically in the IEP, including who is responsible for carrying out the required components.

An IEP may include the goal *Johnny will correctly copy homework assignments from the board*; however, if this is something that Johnny has been unable to do independently, then simply including it as a goal in the IEP will not correct Johnny's problem. The IEP should state the type of help that Johnny is to receive in order to be able to copy his assignments from the board successfully, who is responsible for providing it, and what the next level of intervention will be if the described plan is unsuccessful. Likewise, outcomes measurement for each of the stated goals, including what constitutes success and the lack thereof, how and how often it will be assessed, and the steps that will be taken in the event of a lack of progress, should be clarified in the IEP. When these components are missing, there is less chance that the IEP will meet the child's needs and result in an improvement in the child's ability to function and achieve.

Once a child has an IEP, an annual review is required in which parents also should participate. This does not mean that a review cannot be requested sooner: A lack of progress or a lack of service provision as described in the IEP should prompt a written request for early review. If a change in placement is recommended after a review and the parents disagree with this conclusion or the recommended placement itself, then the parents can invoke IDEA's "stay put" clause, which requires that the child remain in the present placement until all due process procedures are completed and a decision is reached. In addition, a major review is required every 3 years to reevaluate eligibility. IDEA was reauthorized by Congress during 1997 without substantial change to its provisions in regard to ADHD.

Section 504 of the Rehabilitation Act

Section 504 is part of a civil rights law that has some important components that are relevant to the education of children with ADHD. It has both similarities to and differences from IDEA. Like IDEA, Section 504

- Applies primarily to public schools
- Provides for parental involvement and due process procedures
- Requires that there be a functional impact of the disability, not simply its existence
- Provides for services that may extend beyond those that are related directly to specialized instruction
- Requires what is *necessary* for the child's educational success, not what may be considered *optimum*

Its central importance for children with ADHD is that, unlike IDEA, Section 504 does not identify specific disabilities for eligibility and it allows for classroom accommodations for students whose disability may be causing significant problems that are not specifically academic in nature. Thus, it can be used as the basis for the provision of a variety of services to children with ADHD who are experiencing social, emotional, and behavior problems but not necessarily academic problems (i.e., those who do not need *specialized instruction* but who may benefit from other types of modifications within the educational setting). States and local school districts have more freedom to determine how to implement this law compared with IDEA. Some states use the same procedure as for IDEA, but others have developed a simpler process. The educational plan that is developed under Section 504 guidelines is identified as a *service plan* (SP) rather than as an IEP. Another difference is that there is no "stay put" clause to prevent a change in placement during due process proceedings. Table 3 provides some examples of the types of accommodations that may be implemented under Section 504. These accommodations also may be included in an IEP under IDEA. (See Chapter 6 for additional types of educational interventions that may be included in the IEP or the SP for students with ADHD.)

Americans with Disabilities Act

The Americans with Disabilities Act (ADA) of 1990 (PL 101-336) is a general civil rights law with some aspects that relate to education and related services. It applies to all public and private—but not parochial—institutions. It is divided into three titles. All titles support accommodations that allow a person with disabilities to take full advantage of opportunities. The definition of a *person with a disability* is a person with a physical or a mental health impairment that substantially limits a major life activity (e.g., learning, caring for oneself, seeing, hearing, walking). Title I is designed to prevent discrimination in employment and describes guidelines for employment practices for businesses that employ 15 people or more. It is enforced by the Equal Employment Opportunity Commission (EEOC). Title I includes information that may be relevant to the adolescent or adult with ADHD who believes that he or she has been denied a job because of ADHD or who has a job and seeks accommodations in the workplace (see Chapter 14). Title II is designed to prevent discriminatory practices in employment and in the programs and services that are offered by government agencies. It is enforced by the EEOC and the U.S. Department of Justice. Title III applies to privately owned businesses that are open to the public, including private schools, nursery schools, community colleges,

Table 3. Accommodations for students with ADHD

1. Consultation with teacher by an ADHD expert
2. Providing structure to the learning environment (e.g., seating location, role models, reducing distractors, teacher standing near student while lecturing or giving directions)
3. Repeating and simplifying directions, making eye contact before giving directions, and using both verbal and visual instructions
4. Using behavior management techniques and giving frequent, immediate, positive feedback
5. Adjusting class schedules
6. Using modified tests or workbooks, modifying how tests are given, and tailoring homework assignments
7. Using computer and other audiovisual equipment–related instruction
8. Pairing students, peer tutoring, or mentoring
9. Writing key points on an overhead projector, providing guided lecture notes or outlines, and allowing use of tape recorders
10. Providing extra time to complete tasks and homework and breaking them down into smaller segments
11. Teaching methods of self-monitoring and organizational skills
12. Allowing assignments to be typed or word-processed rather than handwritten
13. Assisting student and parent with keeping a homework assignment book and/or using methods to ensure that homework assignments are recorded properly and necessary materials are brought home
14. Participating in other forms of school–home communication
15. Allowing a student to have a set of books at home

and preparation courses for national entrance examinations. Titles II and III include regulations that are relevant to individuals with ADHD in terms of both access to programs and modifications that may be requested in order to derive full benefit from the programs. Reasonable modifications might include a quiet room for testing, increased time allotment for testing, allowing the tape recording of lectures, and providing an extra aide in a recreational setting.

ADHD AND DISCIPLINE

There are relatively few clear-cut guidelines about discipline in special education law, but a growing body of case law may help to shape future policies. Under both Section 504 and IDEA, the nature of disciplinary action permitted depends on whether the behavior requiring discipline is deemed related to the disability. This determination obviously can be quite controversial, and there are no specific guidelines as to how it should be made. Furthermore, this determination is made by school personnel, and there are no guidelines as to how disagreements between school personnel and parents or external professionals should be handled. Technicalities in addition to ambiguity also can affect this process. For example, if a child with ADHD (who is designated as having an "other health impairment" and has an IEP under IDEA) who is known to be especially impulsive in overwhelming and unstructured social situations hits another child during an escalating altercation on the playground, then school personnel may deem this behavior related to the disability. If the *same child* instead is classified on the basis of a learning disability rather than ADHD, even if both disorders are present, then the impulsive behavior may be deemed unrelated to the disability. For most forms of disciplinary action, this determination is not an issue. For reasons described next, discipline for a child with an IEP or an SP becomes an issue primarily when the disciplinary action to be taken involves a significant exclusion from the educational program.

If a child is classified and receives services under IDEA, then he or she may not be excluded from the planned educational program for disciplinary reasons without alternative educational plans (however, alternative educational plans may be defined so loosely as to consist of suspension and sending work home). If the behavior that requires disciplinary action is deemed related to the disability, then it must be dealt with through the IEP process rather than through the school's disciplinary procedures. In particular, any exclusion from the planned educational program for *greater than 10 consecutive days* constitutes a change in placement. A change in placement can be accomplished only through the standard IEP process, meaning that school personnel must present the parents with a plan for the proposed change as well as reasons and expectations regarding how the change will improve the student's conduct and a time line within IEP guidelines. Parental involvement and agreement is required for the change in placement to occur. If the parents do not agree and a due process procedure is instituted, then the "stay put" clause is invoked. If the behavior that requires disciplinary action is deemed unrelated to the disability, then the disciplinary policies for general education apply, but parents retain the right to due process and "stay put" safeguards. Essentially, a child with an IEP may not be suspended from school for more than 10 consecutive days without parental consent unless it is ordered by the hearing officer. The only exceptions to this are if a child brings a firearm to school and if the child presents an immediate danger to him- or herself or others. In the former case, the child can be suspended for up to 45 days in spite of due process but must receive some services during exclusion. In the latter case, the school may obtain a court order to proceed with the change of placement while due process is in progress.

Under Section 504, if the behavior that requires disciplinary action is deemed related to the disability, then exclusion cannot be instituted for greater than 10 days without some form of alternative service; however, there is no "stay put" clause, which means that a proposed change in placement still can proceed when a due process procedure has been initiated. If the behavior that requires disciplinary action is not deemed related to the disability, then any disciplinary policies that apply to students in general education can be applied to the student who is receiving services under Section 504, including suspension for more than 10 days. Nevertheless, some constitutional protections and due process procedures exist for students in general education as well: Under both IDEA and Section 504, if a student's placement is changed midyear, then he or she cannot be suspended for another 10 days (i.e., the suspension limit is per school year, not per placement). The federal Office of Civil Rights and the Office of Special Education Programs have supported the concept that several shorter suspensions, which are greater than 10 days in aggregate and occur over a "short" period of time, also may trigger the "10-day rule."

As individual cases are tried in court, a developing body of case law provides guidelines for the interpretation of the rather vague federal law in individual situations. Overall, this body of case law has tended to favor increased rights for students. For example, the courts often have supported external professional opinion when there is a disagreement with school personnel as to whether the behavior that requires discipline is related to the student's disability. In several cases, it has been determined that insufficient behavior management plans have been included in the IEP or the SP and that the behavioral infraction must be dealt with through the educational plan rather than through disciplinary procedures. *Insufficient* generally refers to a situation in which excessive onus is placed on the student for behavioral control rather than having sufficient adult involvement in the supervisory and behavior management procedures. Also, part-day or in-school suspensions that interrupt the typical educational program also may be included in the 10-day aggregate. Finally, there is some precedent that children who are not yet identified as needing special services but who *should* be also are protected by the same due process procedures as special education students.

STATE LAW

Although state laws cannot override the principles of federal laws, they frequently add specifics regarding the implementation of various procedures that can be extremely important for parents to know. For example, some states have laws that specify the amount of time that may elapse between sequential steps in the IEP process. In addition, state laws often provide additional services, rights, and safeguards above and beyond those described in federal law (e.g., in the areas of guidelines for disciplinary action and services for gifted students).

WHAT CLINICIANS SHOULD DO

Clinicians should obtain, read, and clarify any federal, state, and local documents that relate to special education law. Copies of the federal and state documents usually can be obtained through the state special education office or another related state office to which the special education office can refer. Copies of local policy can be obtained from the relevant school district. Someone at these offices may be available to answer questions about the material. Alternatively, every state has an umbrella office that can provide information about all of the state advocacy agencies, and either this office or the special education office should be able to direct a caller to the organization that primarily is involved with educational advocacy to answer questions about the laws. In addition, every state has a Parent Information Center (PIC), established by the Education of the Handicapped Act Amendments of 1983 (PL 98-199). PICs can provide copies of federal and state laws. A list of PICs is available in Cutler (1993) and the annual January resource guide issue of *Exceptional Parent* magazine. (Additional resource centers at the state level are listed in *Exceptional Parent* and in Anderson, Chitwood, & Hayden, 1990.) Finally, the federal Office of Special Education and Rehabilitative Services (listed under "Resources") can provide copies of relevant federal laws. Clinicians may want to make this information available to their patients' parents or provide them with the numbers to call to obtain their own copies. Most of the state-level advocacy offices provide pamphlets that translate the original language of the laws into more readable form for the public. It is important to encourage parents of children who are or are likely to become involved in special education to be familiar with this information in advance. It should be emphasized that due process procedures that exist under federal and state law are designed to protect parents' right to involvement but are not designed to assist parents who are unprepared to participate in the process.

Clinicians should play a role in the provision of diagnostic and recommended treatment information to MDTs either from their direct involvement in assessment and treatment or through provision of records from consultants, with written parental permission. Clinicians, especially primary care providers, also often are in a unique position to provide the team with information that is acquired through their long-term relationships with families. As an example, family problems such as the loss of a job may create stress on a family that has an impact on a child's behavior or performance at school. When parents meet with a concerned teacher or a school psychologist at the beginning of a school year and report information about family issues, school personnel may conclude erroneously that home stress is the primary cause of the school difficulty because the two occurred simultaneously in their experience with the child. Family counseling, therefore, may be recommended; however, the primary provider may know that this child has had the same difficulties at the beginning of each school year and that particular school-based strategies help to get him on track if applied quickly and intensively during the first quarter, thus resulting in a recommendation for a somewhat different intervention focus.

One very important point must be kept in mind when writing reports that may be used to support the need for school-related services. A report that provides only a diagnosis will not be helpful for obtaining specific services. It is critical that the report also focus on the functional effects of the diagnosis and the types of school services that are needed to address those functional effects. The link among the child's diagnosis, day-to-day problems, and educational needs must be explicit. Other chapters in this book will assist the clinician with identifying functional effects and describing relevant service needs. Finally, the primary care provider should review with parents all documents that are related to the IEP process, especially the IEP itself, to ensure their understanding of the document and to identify any of the missing components described previously.

WHAT PARENTS SHOULD DO

Clearly, the most important thing that parents can do is be prepared to participate as fully and as knowledgeably as possible in the process of obtaining and monitoring the effectiveness of special services for their child. The day before the IEP meeting is too late to begin learning and preparing. Like the process of learning about ADHD itself, being an effective parent advocate requires a significant time investment to learn both the required factual knowledge and the effective skills for negotiating and working with school personnel. Some parents will choose to read the original federal, state, and local documents as described previously. Others will find that books written on this subject for parents are more understandable, but, of course, they also are more general and will not provide state- or district-specific information. Talking with other parents who have been through the process or are participating in parent advocacy groups may provide a forum for learning how to conduct oneself and interact with school personnel during school-related meetings. There are a variety of specific principles and approaches that may help parents maximize their negotiating effectiveness at the beginning of the special education process, as shown in Table 4.

Some parents will need or want direct assistance with the process and will choose to consult with a person who can function as the student's advocate. Such a person may be a professional (e.g., child psychologist, educational consultant, attorney) or an experienced parent volunteer. As stated previously, advocacy agencies are located in every state and are best located through the state Department of Special Education or the office of state protection and advocacy organizations. Educational consultants (who often function as educational advocates) are professionals who specialize in helping parents work with schools to determine a child's individual educational needs and to implement them. Many have worked as educators, special educators, psychologists, or other professionals in special education. An educational consultant may be located through local ADHD and learning disability support groups or the school system. This is a relatively new profession, and there are no specific federal or state requirements that ensure standards of training or practice as there are for many professions; thus, it is important to know the consultant's training and qualifications, as well as to obtain references from others who have worked with the individual. There is one national group of educational consultants, The Independent Educational Consultants Association (see "Resources"), that can provide referrals throughout the United States; however, this group focuses on helping families identify appropriate schools and school programs for children with special needs rather than on implementation of services within the school that the child attends. Insurance coverage for this type of consultation may not be available as this is likely to be considered an educational rather than a medical consultation. Parent advocates are experienced members of local or state support groups who volunteer to assist other parents with the special education process. Attorneys who specialize in educational law can be found through the advocacy agencies, the local bar association, or local law schools. Several schools, agencies, and firms provide some pro bono work in this area for families who cannot afford legal services. Unfortunately, the process remains quite complex and can become adversarial, even for the most knowledgeable parent. When the knowledgeable layperson senses that things have not proceeded in line with their understanding of the law, then legal assistance is advisable. The most effective use of any type of advocate will require preparatory meeting time among the parent, clinician(s), and advocate to develop a joint understanding of the child's needs and the basis for requesting them. The advocate likely will need to be involved in future meetings with the MDT.

Table 4. Strategies for parents

1. Do not wait until the child is under consideration for special education to begin making connections with school staff. It is very helpful to the teacher, as well as useful in establishing credibility, for parents to speak prospectively with each year's teacher(s) about the child's areas of strength and weakness and what has and has not been helpful in the past. Sometimes asking a previously particularly effective teacher to speak with the new teacher is helpful.

2. Participate in school functions such as PTA and classroom activities. Going the extra mile for the teacher (e.g., giving a presentation to the class in your area of expertise, assisting with field trips and special activities) will indicate appreciation for his or her willingness to go the extra mile for the child. It also is important for the parents to be knowledgeable about how the class is conducted in order to credibly ask for modifications.

3. Keep records of relevant behavior and academic issues (e.g., length of time it takes to complete homework, accuracy of homework and school work, writing samples, grades and written comments).

4. Put all communications in writing, date them, and address them to specific individuals by name (see sample letters).

5. Keep copies of all evaluations, school and medical records, and everything that is given to the school (e.g., letters, reports).

6. Ask for important communications from the school in writing.

7. Keep notes on any conversation with school personnel, including name, position, date, what he or she is going to do and by when, and so forth.

8. Take an advocate, helpful friend, or independent evaluator to school meetings or to court. When possible, both parents should attend school meetings.

9. Think in advance about what should be said and how to best say it. Bring notes, including an outline of what the parent wants to say and questions to ask.

10. Ask for a copy of applicable policies when a process or a procedure is implemented or when told that something cannot be done.

11. Be prepared for the fact that the MDT is likely to have a plan in mind for the child before the IEP meeting occurs. Ask for copies of reports that will be discussed or used in IEP planning beforehand. Know the options for educational interventions, do not be afraid to ask questions, do not be afraid to disagree, and do not be coerced into signing the IEP at the meeting if more information or time to review it is needed.

12. Visit the educational setting, if a new one is under consideration.

13. Remember that "needs" do not simply mean what is needed to achieve passing grades in academic subjects. Difficulties with writing, social skills, copying homework assignments, bringing home necessary materials, and remembering to turn in homework that is lost in the recesses of a bookbag all are common problems that have an impact on motivation, attitude about school and self, and achievement in children with ADHD. Think in advance about what is needed from school personnel as well as the parent to ensure that these issues do not interfere with the child's ability to demonstrate his or her knowledge.

Once the child is involved in special education, parents should

1. Document any of the child's needs that are not being addressed in the IEP, both through the parent's direct experience (through the records kept as per #3 above) and through any independent evaluations.

2. Periodically review the child's classification to be sure that the classification is as appropriate as possible and that the child is not receiving services that are based on the "label" rather than on the child's specific needs.

3. Not let frustration interfere with rational behavior! Sometimes parents are uncooperative or explosive at precisely the wrong time (e.g., when something is really about to be accomplished) because they feel that they are at their wit's end.

4. Not minimize the importance of the annual review. Do not allow it to be treated as a formality. Provide input and any relevant records several weeks in advance, and make it clear that the parent wishes to be an active participant and to be present at the meeting.

5. Attempt to resolve problems or disputes informally by meeting with relevant personnel before requesting due process procedures.

CONCLUSION

In spite of the wealth of information that is available for parents and the mandates of federal and state law to support the educational needs of all children, many feel that they struggle year after year to get school personnel to individualize the educational environment in the ways that will allow their child with ADHD to succeed. Some opt for private schools with smaller class sizes or for private schools that specialize in teaching children with learning differences. A growing number are opting for home schooling. As a result of increasing awareness about ADHD and its educational impact, some school districts are developing policies, procedures, and programs for the school-based evaluation and management of ADHD, which include in-service training in behavioral and educational strategies. It is hoped that the widespread application of such behavioral and educational strategies will be helpful to large numbers of students with ADHD.

ENDNOTES

1. Hokola (1992).
2. Davila, Williams, & McDonald (1991).
3. Zametkin et al. (1990).

REFERENCES

Americans with Disabilities Act (ADA) of 1990, PL 101-336, 42 U.S.C. §§ 12101 *et seq.*

Anderson, W., Chitwood, S., & Hayden, D. (1990). *Negotiating the special education maze: A guide for parents and teachers* (3rd ed.). Bethesda, MD: Woodbine House.

Cutler, B.C. (1993). *You, your child, and special education: A guide to making the system work.* Baltimore: Paul H. Brookes Publishing Co.

Davila, R.R., Williams, M.L., & McDonald, J.T. (1991). *Clarification of policy to address the needs of children with attention deficit disorders within general and/or special education.* Washington, DC: U.S. Department of Education, Office of Special Education and Rehabilitative Services and Office of Civil Rights.

Education for All Handicapped Children Act of 1975, PL 94-142, 20 U.S.C. §§ 1400 *et seq.*

Education of the Handicapped Act Amendments of 1983, PL 98-199, 20 U.S.C. §§ 1400 *et seq.*

Education of the Handicapped Act Amendments of 1986, PL 99-457, 20 U.S.C. §§ 1400 *et seq.*

Hokola, S.R. (1992). Legal rights of students with attention deficit disorder. *School Psychology Quarterly, 7,* 285–297.

Individuals with Disabilities Education Act (IDEA) of 1990, PL 101-476, 20 U.S.C. §§ 1400 *et seq.*

Rehabilitation Act of 1973, PL 93-112, 29 U.S.C. §§ 701 *et seq.*

Zametkin, A.J., Nordahl, T.E., Gross, M., King, A.C., Semple, W.E., Rumsey, J., Hamburger, S., & Cohen, R.M. (1990). Cerebral glucose metabolism in adults with hyperactivity of childhood onset. *New England Journal of Medicine, 323,* 1361–1366.

RESOURCES

American Bar Association Center on Children and the Law
740 15th Street, NW
Ninth Floor
Washington, DC 20005-1009
(202) 662-1720
(202) 662-1755 (fax)
e-mail ctrchildlaw@attmail.com

CH.A.D.D. (Children and Adults with Attention Deficit Disorders)
499 NW 70th Avenue
Suite 101
Plantation, FL 33317
(954) 587-3700
Specific materials include *The CH.A.D.D. Educators Manual* (for examples of educational strategies and modifications), *CH.A.D.D. Facts # 4: Educational Rights for Children with ADHD,* and regular articles as well as a column called "The Advocate" in the members quarterly newsletter/magazine.

Children's Defense Fund
25 E Street, NW
Washington, DC 20001
(202) 628-8787
(202) 662-3520 (fax)

Cohen, M.D. (1997, Summer). Section 504 and IDEA. *Attention!,* 23–27.

Disability Rights Education and Defense Fund
2212 Sixth Street
Berkeley, CA 94710
(800) 466-4232 (voice/TTY)
(510) 644-2555 (voice/TTY)
(510) 841-8645 (fax)

The Educational Law Center, Inc.
155 Washington Street
Room 209
Newark, NJ 07102
(201) 624-1815
(201) 624-7339 (fax)

The Educational Law Center, Inc.
801 Arch Street
Suite 610
Philadelphia, PA 19107
(215) 238-6970
(215) 625-9589 (fax)

Exceptional Parent Magazine
555 Kinderkamack Road
Oradell, NJ 07649-1517
(201) 634-6550
(201) 634-6599 (fax)
Each year, the January issue is a resource directory.

HEALTH Resource Center (The National Clearinghouse on Postsecondary Education for Individuals with Disabilities)
One Dupont Circle, NW
Suite 800
Washington, DC 20036
(800) 544-3284

The Independent Educational Consultants Association
4085 Chain Bridge Road
Suite 401
Fairfax, VA 22030
(703) 591-4850

Judge David Bazelon Center for Mental Health Law
1101 15th Street, NW
Suite 1212
Washington, DC 20005
(202) 467-5730
(202) 467-4232 (TTY)
(202) 223-0409 (fax)

Latham, P.S., & Latham, P.H. (1992). *Attention deficit disorder and the law.* Washington, DC: JKL Communications.

Learning Disabilities Association of America
4156 Library Road
Pittsburgh, PA 15234
(412) 341-1515

National Association of Protection and Advocacy Systems
900 Second Street, NE
Suite 211
Washington, DC 20002
(202) 408-9514
(202) 408-9521 (TTY)
(202) 408-9520 (fax)

National Information Center for Children and Youth with Disabilities
Post Office Box 1492
Washington, DC 20036
(800) 695-0285
(703) 893-8614 (TDD)
(202) 884-8441 (fax)

National Parent Network on Disabilities
1727 King Street
Suite 305
Alexandria, VA 22314
(703) 684-6763 (voice/TTY)
(703) 836-1232 (fax)
Provides addresses for state Parent Training and Information Centers.

Office of Special Education and Rehabilitative Services
U.S. Department of Education
Switzer Building
Room 3132
Washington, DC 20202-2524
(202) 205-8723
A clearinghouse for various types of disability-related information.

Pike Institute on Law and Disability
Boston University School of Law
765 Commonwealth Avenue
Boston, MA 02215-1620
(617) 353-2904 (voice/TTY)
(617) 353-2906 (fax)

Regional Offices of the U.S. Department of Education, Office of Civil Rights
CT, ME, MA, NH, RI, VT . . . . (617) 223-9662
NJ, NY, PR, VI . . . . (212) 637-6466
DC, NC, VA . . . . (202) 260-9225
DE, KY, MD, PA, WV . . . . (215) 596-6772
AL, FL, GA, SC, TN. . . . . (404) 562-6350
IL, IN, MN, WI. . . . . (312) 886-8434
MI, OH . . . . (216) 522-4970
AR, LA, MS, OK, TX . . . . (214) 767-3959
IA, KS, MO, NE, ND, SD . . . . (816) 880-4202
AZ, CO, MT, NM, UT, WY. . . . . (303) 844-5695
CA . . . . (415) 437-7700
AK, HI, ID, OR, WA . . . . (206) 220-7880

A

Request Letter

Analogous letters may be written to request a reevaluation, an independent evaluation, and a prehearing conference.

Date

Your name

Address

Telephone

Principal

School

Address

Dear_____:

My child, _____ , who was born on _____, is a student in your school in the _____ grade. My child has not been doing well at school as demonstrated by _____ . Therefore, I am requesting a comprehensive MDT evaluation to determine his/her eligibility for special services or modifications in his/her education program. I understand that I am to be considered a member of the MDT and intend to participate fully in this process. Please let me know when the MDT will meet so that I may attend. I hereby give my consent for this evaluation to be performed. I understand that the evaluation must be completed within __ days of my consent [depending on state law]. If you have any questions or problems with this request, then please contact me. Thank you.

Sincerely,

The Clinician's Practical Guide to Attention-Deficit/Hyperactivity Disorder
by Marianne Mercugliano, Thomas J. Power, and Nathan J. Blum   ©1999 by Paul H. Brookes Publishing Co.

Medication Treatment for Attention-Deficit/ Hyperactivity Disorder

with Mark C. Clayton

Medication is one of the most commonly used and effective treatments for attention-deficit/hyperactivity disorder (ADHD). This chapter examines the indications for pharmacological treatment of ADHD, important principles in medication trials, and issues in discontinuing medication. Then, categories of drugs and specific medications are reviewed with an emphasis on important information for their clinical use. Several of the medications that are discussed in this chapter are not approved for use for ADHD or for use in children because of insufficient research on efficacy and side effects rather than because of known problems.

INDICATIONS FOR PHARMACOLOGICAL TREATMENT OF ADHD

The decision to start medication for ADHD will depend on the likelihood of the medication's improving problematic symptoms, the severity and the pervasiveness of the symptoms, and the likelihood of side effects from the medication. Stimulants, such as

---

Dosage recommendations come from Food and Drug Administration guidelines, if available, or research studies. Monitoring recommendations are taken from the *Physicians' Desk Reference* (1997), the pediatric psychopharmacology literature, and clinical experience. The lists of side effects and drug interactions included in this chapter are comprehensive but not exhaustive. Drug interactions included focus on medications that commonly are prescribed to children. Clinicians are encouraged to take advantage of the physician consultation service of the relevant drug company, especially when a medical situation or side effect occurs that is not addressed in the literature.

methylphenidate (MPH) and dextroamphetamine, are helpful in 70% of appropriately diagnosed children. Different stimulants and different dosages can increase the response rate to as high as 95%.[1] Although stimulant side effects generally are mild, they are not uncommon. Also, ADHD occurs on a spectrum of severity[2]; therefore, some children may benefit sufficiently from nonpharmacological interventions alone. Professional practice guidelines generally support the concept that medication should be recommended when the ADHD is severe enough to suspect that nonpharmacological strategies alone will be insufficient to improve functional status or when appropriate nonpharmacological treatments have been in place and have not resulted in sufficient improvement.[3] This still leaves the clinician to determine when these criteria are met on an individual basis.

Severity may be difficult to measure because there is no explicit, valid severity scale for ADHD. Pervasiveness may be easier to identify. If a child is functioning adequately in all areas except bringing home the appropriate materials for homework, then concentrating on a nonpharmacological intervention in this area may be feasible; however, if other areas also are suffering, then it is less likely that the child and the child's family will be able to make progress in several areas at once without the primary relief from core symptoms that medication provides.

Other clues to severity can be found in the "cost" to the child of coping with his or her symptoms and in the development of secondary problems. A child may be getting adequate grades and functioning reasonably well in class, but if he or she is demonstrating problematic anxiety or anger about school functioning at home or is spending almost or all of his or her nonschool time doing homework, then one might predict that these secondary problems will escalate. Low self-esteem, self-denigration, increasing problems with behavior or interpersonal functioning at home, and peer rejection often are important indicators of significant functional impairment in the school setting, even if grades are adequate.

In some cases, clinicians are reluctant to introduce medication because insufficient nonpharmacological strategies have been in place. Family interventions range from beginning to educate the family about ADHD and its management (see Chapter 4) to extended family therapy and behavior management counseling (see Chapter 5). Educational interventions range from providing the teacher with materials about ADHD and its management to designing an extensive special education plan to address behavioral and academic concerns (see Chapter 6). Even when family, school, and community resources are limited, the clinician can initiate nonpharmacological interventions by providing education and the tools to pursue more intensive interventions. Unfortunately, in many situations, the resources of the family, the school, and the community take precedence over the child's degree of need in determining the type and the intensity of nonpharmacological interventions that ultimately will be employed. The clinician must decide how long to wait while advocating more intensive nonpharmacological assistance for the child before recommending medication. Considering the cost to the child is helpful in this situation. When the cost is clear, delaying medication treatment is not likely to benefit the child in the long run. An important component of the use of medication in situations in which the clinician believes that other interventions also are necessary is the careful identification of target symptoms and assessment of their response to medication, described further in the next section.

A medication trial should not be used to make a diagnosis because individuals without a diagnosis of ADHD also may show improved focusing and work production while taking a stimulant (although the degree of improvement may be less).[4] In some cases, medication may be used to treat the symptoms of a short attention span and/or overactivity when a child has a different primary diagnosis, such as **central auditory processing disorder** or a **pervasive developmental disorder** (PDD).

IMPORTANT PRINCIPLES IN MEDICATION TRIALS

The specifics of a medication trial depend on the medication in question. Although ideal trials for research purposes include multiple dosages and placebo controls, placebos are not readily available to community clinicians. Several other factors can be taken into account to help ensure an appropriate decision about continued medication treatment in the primary care setting.

1. The clinician and the parents (and the preadolescent or the adolescent) should be clear about the target symptoms. Four or five target symptoms that are most important should be identified in the course of the evaluation. The clinician may need to assist the family with identifying appropriate targets. Having specific, realistic target behaviors helps all involved to focus more accurately on the effects of the medication during the trial period.
2. The clinician should request from parents and teachers on a regular basis written feedback in the form of a rating scale rather than simply ask for an impression of effectiveness. Although impressions are sufficient to indicate a positive response in a dramatic responder, they may be too nonspecific to be helpful in distinguishing optimum dosages. Also, ratings of specific behaviors over a given time period are less likely than general impressions to be skewed by isolated atypical positive or negative behaviors and events. The rating scale can be "homemade" and can be part of the child's daily report (see Chapter 6), or it can be one of the shorter, established, narrow-range rating scales that are described in Chapter 2. If important target behaviors are identified but are not included in the selected rating scale, then they can be added. Rating scales, in order to be optimally useful, should be completed for 1–2 weeks before beginning medication. Having the teacher complete the rating scale once or twice weekly for 4–6 weeks after medication is begun allows for an adequate trial with adjustments of the medication dosage. (Appendix A at the end of this chapter provides a sample cover letter to the teacher requesting questionnaire completion.)
3. Parents need to experience the full range of medication effects in order to be effective participants in decision making. For example, a morning and a lunchtime dose of a short-acting stimulant will not give the parent an opportunity to observe medication effects. When teachers observe positive effects and parents observe only "rebound" (exacerbation of hyperactivity and/or moodiness as medication wears off), they are unlikely to be in agreement about the usefulness of medication, and this disagreement may affect their ability to work together on behalf of the child. One way to ensure sufficient parent exposure is for the parents to give the medication on the weekends during the trial period or to use a third dose for homework and early evening behavior.
4. A range of dosages and, in some cases, different stimulants should be tried in order to identify the optimum regimen. Some children may experience more irritability on a dosage that is too low. A week for each dosage is helpful, not because the medication requires this length of time to be effective (stimulants are effective immediately with the possible exception of magnesium pemoline) but to allow parents and teachers a sufficient, representative observation period. Up to 60% of children will respond better to one stimulant than another,[5] so it is reasonable to try a different stimulant if inadequate results are obtained with the first.

DISCONTINUING MEDICATION

Discontinuing medication may mean a "drug holiday" or permanent discontinuation. For many years, it was standard procedure to prescribe stimulants for use only during school hours. Eventually, however, positive effects on interpersonal functioning with peers and family members were recognized,[6] and clinicians began prescribing stimulants for use during weekends and holidays as well. In addition, in spite of well-documented effects on short-term behavioral and academic functioning, stimulants have not been shown to alter long-term outcome substantially in these areas. It has been hypothesized that one reason for this is a lack of effective treatment during non-classroom hours. Finally, it also has been suggested that more consistent use of medication might reduce some side effects, such as the development of tics, although there is no clear evidence to support or refute this hypothesis. One side effect that does appear to have some relation to cumulative exposure is the slowing of weight gain and linear growth, although this is by no means universal.

If previously identified responsive target behaviors also are an issue on weekends, then it probably is in the child's best interest to take medication on the weekend. It can be helpful for improving homework completion; family relationships; and behavior during sports, social interactions, and religious services. In some cases, a lower dosage than is required for school may be effective. During the summer, sports participation, summer camp, tutoring, and summer school may be more successful if the child remains on medication. A 3- to 4-week summer medication holiday is reasonable if there are growth concerns or if a reassessment of the medication's effect on extracurricular functioning is needed. Some students without significant disruptive behavior may function equally well without weekend medication.

Most children who benefit from medication will do so for several years. It used to be thought that stimulants were ineffective after puberty, but it has been shown clearly that stimulants can be helpful for adolescents and adults.[7] Although symptoms of ADHD may subside with time (especially outwardly apparent hyperactivity), the majority of individuals will continue to experience some symptoms into adulthood.[8] The decision to discontinue medication hinges on whether there are remaining symptoms and, if so, how functionally impairing they are and whether they can be addressed by nonpharmacological interventions.

The prescribing clinician should reassess the medication's effectiveness periodically during the course of medication monitoring and follow-up (see Chapter 11). Often, this occurs informally when a dose is forgotten and parents receive feedback from an unsuspecting teacher. If it the medication's effectiveness is not clear, then a brief trial (e.g., 2–3 weeks) off medication or on a lower dosage may be helpful. It is best not to do this during a time when the student will be at a significant disadvantage if his or her school functioning deteriorates markedly (e.g., just before or during final exams, at the beginning of a new school year, when entering a new school setting).

MEDICATIONS THAT ARE USED TO TREAT ADHD

The following sections describe the types of medications that generally are used to treat ADHD. They include stimulants, tricyclic antidepressants (TCAs), antihypertensives, and selective serotonin reuptake inhibitors (SSRIs). Table 1 lists the chemical and brand names of these medications as well as some additional psychoactive drugs.

Table 1. Brand names and chemical names of psychoactive medications

Adderall (amphetamine, dextroamphetamine)
Anafranil (clomipramine)
Ativan (lorazepam)
BuSpar (buspirone hydrochloride)
Catapres (clonidine—not Klonopin, which is clonazepam!)
Cylert (magnesium pemoline)
Depakene (valproic acid)
Desoxyn (methamphetamine)
Dexedrine (dextroamphetamine)
Dextrostat (dextroamphetamine)
Effexor (venlafaxine)
Elavil (amitriptyline hydrochloride)
Eldepryl (deprenyl, selegiline)
Endep (amitriptyline hydrochloride)
Etrafon (amitriptyline hydrochloride)
Haldol (haloperidol)
Klonopin (clonazepam)
Luvox (fluvoxamine)
Norpramin (desipramine hydrochloride)
Pamelor (nortriptyline hydrochloride)
Paxil (paroxetine)
Pertofrane (desipramine hydrochloride)
Prozac (fluoxetine)
Risperdal (risperidone)
Ritalin (methylphenidate hydrochloride)
Tegretol (carbamazepine)
Tenex (guanfacine)
Tofranil (imipramine hydrochloride)
Valium (diazepam)
Wellbutrin (bupropion)
Ziprexil (olanzepine)
Zoloft (sertraline)

Stimulants

The stimulants that commonly are used for ADHD treatment include MPH (Ritalin), dextroamphetamine (Dexedrine), dextroamphetamine/amphetamine (Adderall), and magnesium pemoline (Cylert). Methamphetamine (Desoxyn) also is available but is used less frequently. The stimulants are well-documented to improve classroom behavior, work production, sustained attention, and parent–child and peer interactions in short-term studies. In the relatively small number of long-term studies, medication treatment does not appear to have resulted in substantial improvements in ultimate educational or interpersonal outcomes.[9] It remains unclear to what degree these negative findings are the result of insufficient nonpharmacological treatment, insufficient duration of medication use, difficulties that are inherent in the adequate completion of long-term outcome studies, or other factors. Stimulants are effective in preschool-age children, school-age children, adolescents, and adults, although school-age children seem to have the most robust effects.[10] Side effects commonly are reported, but many of them also are reported prior to starting the medication or during placebo trials, especially insomnia, poor appetite, headaches, and stomachaches.[11] Preexisting poor appetite usually will worsen while taking stimulants. Preexisting insomnia may either worsen or improve (if it is stress related due to school concerns), but most often it is unchanged. Preexisting headaches (including migraines) and stomachaches (when stress related) often improve while taking stimulants, although migraines sometimes can be exacerbated. One study suggested that growth impairment also may be related to ADHD itself rather than stimulant treatment.[12]

Methylphenidate

It is estimated that 1.5 million students (2.8%) take MPH for attention problems. There has been a 2.5-fold increase in its use between 1990 and 1995, primarily from increased use among girls, adolescents, and students with the predominantly inattentive type of ADHD.[13] MPH is approved for use for ADHD and narcolepsy in individuals who are 6 years of age and older. It also is used for the treatment of depression in older adults. It primarily blocks the reuptake of dopamine into presynaptic neurons but also increases its release. It comes in a regular release form (5-, 10-, and 20-milligram [mg] tablets) and a 20-mg sustained release (SR) capsule-shaped tablet. The 10- and 20-mg regular release tablets are scored. The SR preparation should not be crushed or chewed. Several generic formulations exist, which occasionally cause less effect or more side effects. The regular release preparations have an effective duration of 2.5–4 hours, and the sustained release lasts from 5 to 8 hours. The usual administration schedule is two to three (occasionally four) times per day. Increasing the dosage does not substantially increase the effective duration. Usually, 0.3–0.6 mg per kilogram (kg) of the child's body weight per dose is effective, but titration should be based on effects and side effects because body mass is not predictive.[14] For the trial, 0.3 mg/kg/dose is the usual starting point, although, occasionally, a child (usually predominantly inattentive) will respond to 5 or 10 mg even when it is less than 0.3 mg/kg. Effects occur immediately. Occasionally, a more robust effect is seen on the first day of administration. One week at each dosage level should be sufficient to obtain representative teacher feedback. Anticipated positive effects include improved attention span, increased work completion, accuracy, and organization of writing as well as decreased careless errors, impulsive responding, distractibility, and negative interpersonal interactions.

Common side effects include appetite suppression, stomachache, and rebound. Less common side effects include insomnia, headaches, slowing of growth (weight and height), tics, other perseverative behaviors, and exacerbation of moodiness during the effective period. Rare side effects include **neutropenia** and, possibly, **eosinophilia.** Too large a dose can induce transient thought disorders. Some side effects may be transient, although appetite suppression usually is a concomitant part of effective treatment. To minimize the effects of appetite suppression, the morning dose can be given after breakfast, and more substantial after-school and bedtime snacks should be provided. Dinner may need to be shifted later, and many children who take less medication on the weekend "catch up" on their calories then.

To reduce the symptoms of rebound, food can be given as the medication wears off and the dosing schedule can be adjusted so that rebound does not fall during a time of "high demand." If possible, the child should have a "cooling-off" period with watching television, listening to music, using the computer, taking a bath, or other calming activity during this time. It often is best for children with ADHD to do their homework after school rather than after dinner so that their homework is finished before rebound sets in. Occasionally, there is less rebound with a higher dosage or a different stimulant. Decremental dosages during the course of the day, a mix of sustained and regular release, an additional small dose at the beginning of rebound, or the addition of clonidine or an SSRI can help reduce the effects of rebound. For insomnia, the clinician first should determine whether the problem is caused or exacerbated by the medication, as many children with ADHD are poor sleepers at baseline. If so, then eliminating caffeine, shifting doses to an earlier time, reducing the last dose, using clonidine in the evening, or changing to one of the more sedating antidepressants may help. The possible untoward cardiovascular effects of evening clonidine with daytime stimulants (discussed further) have made clinicians more wary of using this combination to address rebound and insomnia unless other measures are ineffective.

Stomachaches can be reduced by giving the medication with food or a full glass of liquid. If the child with problematic stomachaches also has a history of colic, spitting up, gagging, a very selective appetite, or food texture sensitivity, then the stimulant may exacerbate dyspepsia or gastroesophageal reflux and further gastrointestinal evaluation and a trial of antacid may be informative. For declining height or weight percentiles, add calorie supplements (e.g., commercial "milkshake meals" as a snack), and give medication holidays on weekends or during the summer for "catch-up." If insufficient catch-up occurs or if the child was small for age to start, then a trial of an alternative medication and consideration of a growth evaluation (e.g., family history, growth hormone and thyroid function tests, bone age, and consultation with a specialist) are warranted.

MPH may interfere with the effects of central nervous system (CNS) depressants (e.g., discontinue before sedation or anesthesia). Decongestants that contain stimulants (pseudoephedrine or phenylpropanolamine) may interact to cause increased heart rate, palpitations, flushing, or jitteriness. Warm steam (e.g., from the shower) can be used to decongest the child in the morning, and the decongestant can be used at night, or one half to three fourths of the recommended decongestant dosage can be used as a test to determine the child's response.

Specific monitoring during MPH treatment should include vital signs and growth parameters, and some clinicians will check a complete blood count with differential every 1–2 years. MPH is a Schedule II controlled substance and, as such, requires a monthly written prescription without refills.

Dextroamphetamine

Dextroamphetamine (Dexedrine) is approved for use for ADHD and narcolepsy in individuals who are 3 years of age and older. It increases the release of both norepinephrine and dopamine. It comes as 5-, 10-, and 15-mg capsules (spansules) and a 5-mg regular release tablet. The duration of action is 4–5 hours for tablets and 6–8 hours for spansules. It also is available with a brand name of Dextrostat CII, in 5- and 10-mg scored tablets with a reported effective duration of 4–6 hours. A typical dosing schedule is 5–60 mg/day in two or three doses of regular tablets and one or two doses of spansule. For a trial, common starting dosages are 2.5 mg if younger than 5 years, 5 mg if younger than 12 years, and 10 mg if older than 12 years. One week per dosage should be sufficient. The anticipated positive effects, drug interactions, and side effects and their treatment are the same as for MPH, with the exception that hematologic side effects are not reported. Monitoring includes vital signs and growth. Fruit juice may decrease its absorption. Dextroamphetamine is a Schedule II controlled substance.

Magnesium Pemoline

Magnesium pemoline (Cylert) is approved for the treatment of ADHD in individuals who are 6 years of age and older. It is a weak dopamine reuptake blocker and releaser. It comes in 18.75-, 37.5-, and 75-mg scored tablets and a 37.5-mg chewable tablet. The duration of action is 8–12 hours, and the recommended maximum daily dosage is 112.5 mg. For a trial, 18.75 or 37.5 mg are common starting dosages with increases by 18.75 mg every 2–3 weeks. It is reported to take up to 3 weeks to see the full effects of a given dosage, but this is not common and may be related to inadequate dosing during the initial stages of dose titration. Metabolism slows down in adolescence, and a decrease in dosage may be necessary. The anticipated positive effects, drug interactions, and side effects are the same as for MPH. Pemoline may have less abuse potential[15] and fewer peripheral vascular effects than other stimulants. It may cause insomnia more frequently than other stimulants and may cause other choreoathetoid movements as well as tics.[16] A 1% incidence of elevated liver enzymes (chemical hepatitis) has been reported. A warning has been added to the package insert about several cases of fulminant hepatic failure that have occurred in children, adolescents, and adults who had been on pemoline for longer than 6 months. These cases are under further study, and some may have had predisposing factors.[17] It is not clear specifically who is at risk or whether routine monitoring can prevent this occurrence. Monitoring should include periodic liver enzymes (one suggestion: at baseline, 1 month after starting, 3 months after starting, then every 3–6 months), vital signs, and growth parameters. Some clinicians also do a complete blood count annually. Elevated liver enzymes require prompt discontinuation. Treatment of side effects is otherwise the same as for MPH. Magnesium pemoline is a Schedule IV controlled substance; prescriptions can be telephoned in, and refills can be provided.

Dextroamphetamine/Amphetamine

Adderall is approved for the treatment of ADHD in individuals who are 3 years of age and older. It consists of two salts of dextroamphetamine (dextroamphetamine sulfate and dextroamphetamine saccharate) and two salts of amphetamine (amphetamine sulfate and aspartate), which theoretically give it a longer and more consistent clinical effect. The average length of effect is 5–7 hours. Its mechanism of action includes increased release of norepinephrine and dopamine and some reuptake blockade. It comes as 5-, 10-, 20-, and 30-mg double-scored tablets and generally is given once or twice daily with a usual dosage range of 5–40 mg daily. Recommended starting dosages are 2.5 mg daily for children who are between 3 and 5 years of age and 5 mg once or twice daily in older children. One week at each dosage level should be sufficient for evaluating effects. There is one published study of the effects/side effects of this medication,[18] which indicates that Adderall is effective, in a dose–response pattern between 5 and 20 mg, for improving attention, behavior, and work productivity in students between 7 and 14 years of age with ADHD and a previous positive response to MPH. In addition, this study suggests that increasing the dosage of Adderall over the range employed in this study increases the duration of effects without substantially increasing side effects.

Preliminary reports of studies in progress indicate a favorable efficacy/side effects pattern in comparison with MPH.[19] The package insert is identical to that of dextroamphetamine and notes a warning of the abuse potential of amphetamines. It is classified as a Schedule II controlled substance.

Tricyclic Antidepressants

The TCAs long have been considered second-line medications for the treatment of ADHD.[20] Some clinicians would consider them first line in a child with ADHD and co-existing depression or anxiety. They also have the advantage over stimulants of a stable effect into the evening. They increase the release of all biogenic amine transmitters including dopamine, norepinephrine, and serotonin but are thought to have their most prominent effects on release rather than on reuptake blockade and on norepinephrine rather than on dopamine. Several studies from preschoolers to adults document the efficacy of TCAs for the treatment of ADHD symptoms, although most comparative studies show that they are somewhat less effective than stimulants. The specific TCAs that have been studied include imipramine, desipramine, nortriptyline, amitriptyline, and clomipramine. The dosage ranges studied varied widely, and there does not appear to be a good correlation between dosage and effectiveness or plasma level and effectiveness. Plasma levels still are important, however, for avoiding toxicity. TCAs are less likely than stimulants to exacerbate tic disorders. Like stimulants, a better response may be found with one rather than another, but there are no predictive data to help guide choices for an individual patient. As with stimulants and SSRIs, the TCAs can precipitate or exacerbate mania. There are no long-term studies of TCA treatment of ADHD.

Children appear to need a higher mg/kg dosage to achieve the same plasma levels. Lower dosages generally are required for the treatment of ADHD compared with depression. There is wide inter-individual variability in plasma levels on the same dosage of a given TCA. Approximately 7% of the population are considered "slow metabolizers" and may develop toxic levels on standard dosages; thus, plasma monitoring is crucial. Tolerance to an effective dosage may develop after several weeks to a few months.

CNS side effects may manifest as worsening symptoms of depression, disorientation and decreased memory, thought disorder, ataxia, tremor, and seizures. If withdrawal is abrupt, then a flu-like syndrome with gastrointestinal and generalized symptoms may occur and are believed to result from cholinergic excess. TCAs, therefore, should be withdrawn over approximately 2 weeks. TCAs should not be used within 14 days of the use of a monoamine oxidase inhibitor (MAOI) because their overlap can induce extreme temperature elevation, hypertension, and seizures. TCA overdose potentially is fatal and is more likely to be fatal than an overdose of stimulants or SSRIs; therefore, careful consideration of the ability of the family to keep all of its members safe is necessary before prescribing TCAs.

Cardiotoxicity is the greatest concern as a side effect of taking TCAs. The potential for cardiotoxicity with TCAs is not a new phenomenon, but the sudden death of several children and adolescents (presumed to be the result of tachyarrhythmias, not of overdose) who were taking desipramine for ADHD has increased attention to this concern.[21] Several of the children had potential signs of cardiac vulnerability in their own or their family histories, again highlighting the need to investigate these issues carefully. TCAs can increase PR, QRS, and QTc intervals (slow conduction) on the EKG, cause heart block, and increase the frequency of premature atrial contractions and supraventricular tachycardia, as well as raise heart rate and blood pressure. Several of these findings may predispose to arrhythmia, although the QTc interval probably is of prime importance. Blood pressure and heart rate changes may occur at lower dosages, but conduction abnormalities are uncommon at the lower end of the dosage range (e.g., less than 3.5 mg/kg/day for desipramine). Most of the cardiovascular changes that occur in children who are taking TCAs are of minor clinical significance.[22] Cardiovascular toxicity can be increased when a TCA is used for a condition that also predisposes to cardiotoxicity (e.g., with asthma medication, hyperthyroidism).

Reasons for the association of sudden death with desipramine rather than with other TCAs is unclear, except that it may be the most specific inhibitor of norepinephrine reuptake, which may lead to greater increased sympathetic tone.[23] Desipramine may have a greater potential for prolonging the QT interval than other TCAs, and imipramine may have fewer cardiovascular effects, but these data should be considered preliminary.[24] EKG changes may occur or change after several weeks of treatment[25]; therefore, long-term monitoring is necessary. Table 2 provides recommendations for monitoring patients who are taking TCAs, although it is not yet known whether following such guidelines will prevent adverse occurrences. These recommendations are somewhat stricter than those recommended in the psychiatric literature in that they refer to age-specific norms rather than absolutes (e.g., blood pressure greater than 130/80). Guidelines can help identify children for whom cardiac consultation is appropriate, as well as identify children who may be able to remain on a TCA if needed with additional cardiac monitoring.

In addition to cardiac effects, there are a variety of other side effects that may be caused by TCAs, some of which are sufficiently problematic to lead to discontinuance. These include anticholinergic effects (dry mouth, blurred vision, constipation), blood dyscrasias, drowsiness, sleep changes (insomnia, nightmares), headache, stomachache, anxiety, mania, worsening of psychosis, sexual dysfunction, weight increase or decrease, dizziness or orthostatic hypotension (lightheadedness when getting up or run-

---

Table 2. Cardiac monitoring for children who are taking tricyclic antidepressants

Suggested Monitoring

Baseline: history, family history, vital signs, complete blood count with differential, chemistry panel (including AST, ALT), EKG

Trial: EKG and plasma level repeated upon reaching 1 and 3 mg/kg/day and upon reaching final dosage if greater than the previous level at which these were done. Vital signs with each dose change.

Ongoing: every 3 months, interim history, vital signs, growth parameters, evidence for organomegaly, bleeding, bruising, rash; every 3 months for 6 months, then every 6 months thereafter, EKG, plasma level, complete blood count with differential, chemistry panel.

Suggested Guidelines

Do not use if

1. Prolongation to greater than normal for age of PR, QRS, or QT interval
2. Unstable or unknown cardiovascular disease, recent use of MAOIs
3. Other contraindications under specific medications

Consider cardiac consultation or discontinuance if any of the following occur betwen baseline and monitoring:

1. Prolongation to greater than normal for age of any interval (including QTc)
2. Prolongation of the QRS interval by greater than 0.02 seconds or 20% more than it was at baseline
3. Elevated BP for age
4. Pulse greater than 120 (adolescents) to 130 (children)

ning abruptly secondary to suppression of the body's ability to appropriately increase pulse or blood pressure), rash, and seizures. Divided doses may minimize side effects, and prophylactic treatment of constipation with increased fiber and fluid or mild laxatives is helpful in preventing abdominal discomfort.

Imipramine

Imipramine (Tofranil) is indicated for depression in adolescents and adults and enuresis in children. It also is used for ADHD; ADHD with coexisting mood, anxiety, conduct, or tic disorders; trichotillomania; sleep disorders; depression; and separation anxiety. Individuals with sulfite allergy should not take imipramine as sulfite is one of the inactive ingredients. Imipramine is supplied as 10-, 25-, and 50-mg tablets and 75-, 100-, 125-, and 150-mg capsules (long acting). Long-acting forms are not recommended for children. Divided doses may reduce side effects. A reasonable starting dosage is 10 mg for children who are 6 years and 25 mg for older children with weekly increases of 10–25 mg. The usual effective dosage is 1–2.5 mg/kg/day divided into two or three doses. The maximum recommended dosage is 2.5 mg/kg/day. Interactions include reduced effectiveness of antihypertensives; increased imipramine level when given with MPH, cimetidine, or fluoxetine; and reduced imipramine level when given with barbiturates or phenytoin. (*Note:* It is uncommon to give a TCA with an SSRI because there is very little information available about these combinations and there are potential cardiovascular and nervous system activating effects.)

Desipramine

Desipramine (Norpramin) is indicated for depression in adolescents and adults. It also is used for ADHD; ADHD with coexisting mood, anxiety, conduct, or tic disorders; depression; and enuresis. It is supplied as 10-, 25-, 50-, 75-, 100-, and 150-mg tablets. Divided doses may reduce side effects. Typical starting dosages are 10 mg for children younger than 6 years and 25 mg for older children with weekly increases of 10–25 mg. The usual daily dosage is 2.5–5 mg/kg/day divided into two or three doses. The maximum recommended dosage is 5 mg/kg/day. It may have less anticholinergic side effects than imipramine. Interactions are similar to those listed for imipramine.

Nortriptyline

Nortriptyline (Pamelor) is indicated for depression in adolescents and adults. It also is used for ADHD and ADHD with coexisting mood, anxiety, conduct, or tic disorders. It is supplied as 10-, 25-, 50-, and 75-mg tablets and 10-mg/5-ml oral solution. Side effects may be minimized by dividing into two or three doses daily. Usual starting dosages are 10 mg for children younger than 6 years and 25 mg for older children with increases of 10–25 mg weekly. The usual effective dosage is 0.5–3.0 mg/kg/day divided into two doses. The maximum recommended dosage is not clear because there are no childhood indications. Up to 4.5 mg/kg/day has been reported.

Amitriptyline

Amitriptyline (Elavil) is indicated for depression in adolescents and adults. It is not widely used because of its sedating effects. It also is used for ADHD and ADHD with coexisting mood, anxiety, or tic disorders. It is supplied as 10-, 25-, 50-, 75-, and 100-mg tablets. Side effects may be minimized by dividing into three or four doses daily. A typical starting dosage is 10 mg for children younger than 6 years and 25 mg for older children with increases of 10–25 mg weekly. The usual daily dosage is 25–150 mg. Maximum dosages reported are 150 mg/day for children and 200 mg/day for adolescents.

Clomipramine

Clomipramine (Anafranil) is indicated for **obsessive-compulsive disorder** (OCD) in individuals who are 10 years and older. Although tricyclic in structure, clomipramine has prominent serotonergic effects. It also is used for ADHD; ADHD with coexisting internalizing, externalizing, or tic disorders; and other perseverative behaviors. It is supplied as 10-, 25-, 50-, 75-, and 100-mg tablets. Side effects may be minimized by dividing into three or four doses daily. Typical starting dosages are 10 mg for children younger than 6 years and 25 mg for older children with increases of 10–25 mg weekly. Usual daily dosages are 25–150 mg. The maximum recommended dosage is 3 mg/kg/day or 200 mg (whichever is less). Treatment should be initiated with divided doses (two times daily) given with meals to minimize gastrointestinal side effects. If tolerated, once-daily dosing in the evening may be used for long-term maintenance. Clomipramine may be more sedating than other TCAs.

Bupropion

Bupropion (Wellbutrin) is a stimulant-like antidepressant that is structurally dissimilar to tricyclic and other antidepressants.[26] Its specific mechanism of action is unclear, but it appears to have effects on dopamine, norepinephrine, and serotonin neurotransmitter systems, although to a weaker degree than other antidepressants and stimulants. Its stimulant-like effects may come from weak dopamine uptake blockade, and its mood-related effects may come from its noradrenergic properties.[27] A limited number of both open trials and double-blind, placebo-controlled studies support its effectiveness for ADHD symptoms in children, adolescents, and adults, and it may have better effects on short-term memory than other antidepressants.[28] One study suggests similar efficacy to MPH.[29] It also improves conduct problems.[30] Case reports suggest that it may exacerbate tics similarly to stimulants.[31] It has not been adequately studied to assess its effects on childhood depression. Its indication is for depression in individuals who are older than 18 years.

Bupropion has a higher incidence of associated seizures than other antidepressants (approximately 4 per 1,000). In adults, there is an increase in the risk of seizures once dosages of 450 mg/day are reached, but the equivalent dosage for children is unknown. EEG changes have been reported in a subset of children and adolescents who did not demonstrate seizures.[32]

It is supplied as 75- and 100-mg tablets; 50–75 mg daily is a common starting dosage for children and 75 mg for adolescents, with weekly increases to two or three times daily. In older adolescents and adults, it can be started at 100 mg daily. Optimum dosages for children and young adolescents range from 50 to 250 mg/day, although most are maintained on 100–150 mg/day (or 3–5 mg/kg). A pill cutter may be required to try 50-mg dosages because the tablets are not scored. Full effects may take up to 3–4 weeks to be apparent, and some side effects may diminish over this time. Maximum dosages reported in children are 250 mg (or 6 mg/kg). In adults, seizure frequency increases above dosages of 450 mg/day, although seizures also occur at lower dosages. Taking doses too close together can increase the risk of having a seizure; thus, missed doses should not be "doubled up."

Interactions between bupropion and other medications are complex because its metabolites are biologically active and other medications may have different effects on the metabolites and parent compound. Levels of both may increase when bupropion is combined with lithium or fluoxetine. Like TCAs, bupropion should not be used within 14 days of using MAOIs or with other medications that decrease the seizure threshold. Patients with anorexia nervosa or bulimia also may have an increased risk of seizures. Combined administration with stimulants or other antidepressants has been done occasionally but has not been studied and, thus, cannot be recommended.

Side effects include agitation, dry mouth, insomnia, headache, weight loss, nausea, vomiting, constipation, tremor, rash (including hives), and activation of mania or psychosis. Bupropion may be better tolerated by individuals who develop orthostatic hypotension while taking TCAs. Because of the lack of long-term data on children, the clinician should carefully monitor positive and negative symptoms, vital signs, growth, and physical/neurological signs. Although no clinically significant changes were reported in a short-term study (1 month),[33] the clinician may choose to monitor complete blood counts, chemistry panels, and EKGs during long-term use because data on children are unavailable. The role of EEGs in predicting seizures and the meaningfulness of EEGs that change from normal to abnormal in the absence of seizures is unclear. Further study is needed to determine whether the development of an abnormal EEG while taking bupropion is related to any detrimental cognitive or behavioral effects. Because the role of EEG monitoring is unclear, the clinician may choose to focus on careful clinical rather than EEG monitoring.

Antihypertensives

Several antihypertensive medications, most notably clonidine and guanfacine (but also nadolol, propranolol, and atenolol), have been used to treat symptoms of overactivity, overreactivity, and impulsivity in individuals with ADHD, tic disorders, and other developmental disabilities.

Clonidine

Clonidine (Catapres) is an antihypertensive that first was used for **Tourette syndrome** (TS) and ADHD in the 1970s and came into more common use in the late 1980s.[34] Although it is indicated only for hypertension, in addition to its use in ADHD and tic disorders, it is used for the treatment of overarousal and sleep disturbance associated with a variety of developmental disabilities, posttraumatic stress disorder, anxiety disorders, and drug withdrawal and to increase growth hormone release in children with short stature. It is an agonist at the alpha$_2$ presynaptic norepinephrine receptor, resulting in a decreased release of norepinephrine in the forebrain. It is reported to be effective for overarousal, overreactivity, low frustration tolerance, and hyperactivity and, therefore, is used most commonly for children with ADHD, primarily hyperactive/impulsive or combined types, or for children with ADHD and associated oppositional or conduct problems. Positive effects on attention span, focusing, and distractibility have not been documented clearly.

Clonidine initially was reported to be of benefit in approximately 70% of children with ADHD.[35] It has played an especially prominent role in the treatment of ADHD in the presence of tic disorders because it does not exacerbate repetitive behaviors and may, in fact, suppress them. It also has been used widely in combination with MPH, either throughout the day to decrease residual hyperactivity/impulsivity or to allow a lower dosage of MPH to be used, or in the evening to limit the rebound and insomnia that sometimes is associated with stimulant use.

As clonidine has been used and studied more frequently, its positive effects have been less impressive and its side effects more prominent.[36] In particular, the possible role of clonidine-related cardiovascular effects in several cases of sudden death or syncope reported in children who were taking the combination of MPH and clonidine is of concern (although there appear to be other contributing factors in some of the cases).[37]

Clonidine comes as 0.1-, 0.2-, and 0.3-mg tablets and a transdermal patch (Catapres-TTS 1, 2, or 3 designed to release 0.1, 0.2, or 0.3 mg/day, respectively, for 7 days). The advantage of the patch is continuous dosing (for approximately 5–7 days), but there is a significant incidence of dermatitis and it does not stay on well in humid weather. Clonidine usually is started as a half tablet (0.05 mg) once daily, increasing to three or four times daily, or as a single dose at night (approximately 30–60 minutes prior to the desired bedtime). In children who are younger than 7 years of age, it may be prudent to start with ¼ tablet to avoid hypotension. Two to three weeks at each dosage is reasonable for the trial period. This length is chosen primarily to determine whether side effects dissipate. Potential positive effects include a decreased activity level and reduced impulsivity, reactivity, and frustration. Side effects include lethargy, hypotension, orthostatic signs, headache, dry mouth, constipation, depression,[38] agitation, phobias,[39] EKG changes and arrhythmias,[40] transient exacerbation of tics upon initiation,[41] rebound hypertension when discontinued abruptly or as doses wear off, and night waking (when late-day doses are given). Children with a history of depression, symptoms of depression, or a history of cardiac disease should not receive clonidine. Caution should be exercised in using clonidine for children with anxiety as reports of both improvement and exacerbation exist. Monitoring should include orthostatic blood pressure measurements in addition to growth and vital signs. Laboratory monitoring should include a periodic complete blood count with differential, chemistry panel, and EKG. When clonidine is given at night and stimulants are given during the day, morning measurements should be taken to ensure that the rebound effects from the clonidine in combination with the stimulant do not cause excessive elevations of pulse and blood pressure.

Guanfacine

Guanfacine (Tenex) is an agonist at the alpha$_2$ receptor; however, it is more selective for the alpha$_2$A subtype. It also binds to alpha$_2$A receptors on postsynaptic frontal cortex neurons and has direct effects on working memory in animal studies.[42] It is hoped that the greater neurochemical specificity of guanfacine, as well as its longer half-life, will make it more effective with fewer side effects, but it has not been studied sufficiently to allow more than tentative conclusions. Initial open trials suggest that it may be effective for children with ADHD[43] and ADHD in TS. It also appears to decrease tic severity.[44]

Guanfacine is indicated for hypertension in individuals who are 12 years of age and older. It is available as 1- and 2-mg tablets. It should be started at a dosage of 0.5 mg nightly and increased weekly to a maximum of 4 mg/day in three or four divided doses. The most common maximally effective dosages reported in open studies are 1–3.5 mg/day. The most common side effects are lethargy, headache, stomachache, and decreased appetite, but in most subjects these were resolved or decreased after 2 weeks. No significant changes in pulse or blood pressure have been noted.

Selective Serotonin Reuptake Inhibitors

The SSRIs (fluoxetine, fluvoxamine, paroxetine, and sertraline) have antidepressant, antianxiety, and anti–obsessive-compulsive effects that may be useful adjuncts in the treatment of ADHD.[45] Although serotonin has not been implicated directly in the symptoms of ADHD, it does appear to play a prominent role in depression, anxiety, obsessive-compulsive symptoms, and aggression. The SSRIs work by blocking the reuptake of serotonin. Because they are specific to the serotonin system and do not have significant effects at other neurotransmitter uptake sites or receptors, they have relatively few side effects compared with TCAs. In particular, they do not have significant cardiovascular effects, and they appear to be safe in combination with stimulants or antihypertensives. They increase TCA levels and, thus, generally should not be combined with them. The main side effects of SSRIs include headache, nausea, vomiting, diarrhea, nervousness, sleep disturbance, and sexual dysfunction. Although frequently used in the treatment of aggressive outbursts or temper control problems, some children will show an increase in these problems with one or more of the SSRIs. Behavioral activation/agitation may result in the apparent worsening of ADHD symptoms. The SSRIs can exacerbate mania and psychosis. The individual SSRIs differ in their pharmacokinetic properties (half-life and biological activity of metabolites), drug interactions (because each interacts differently with hepatic P450 metabolizing enzyme subsystems), and effectiveness for individual patients; thus, if one is ineffective or has significant side effects, then it is reasonable to try a different one. SSRIs should not be used within 14 days of taking a MAOI (or longer with fluoxetine, see next section). SSRIs should not be used in combination with other serotonergic agents, such as tryptophan, a serotonin precursor.

Fluoxetine

Fluoxetine (Prozac) is approved for the treatment of depression and OCD in older adolescents and adults. It also is used for ADHD with coexisting internalizing or externalizing features, anxiety disorders, selective mutism, obsessive-compulsive symptoms, any of these disorders with TS, and repetitive behaviors in individuals with mental retardation or autism. One open trial has shown positive effects of fluoxetine alone on ADHD symptoms, in 11 of 19 children, noting that the majority of subjects in the study had coexisting disorders.[46] Gammon and Brown (1993) also documented improvement in children and adolescents with ADHD and coexisting disorders when fluoxetine was added to a stimulant.

Fluoxetine is available as liquid (20 mg/5 ml) and 10- and 20-mg pulvules. Common starting dosages are 2.5–5 mg daily in young children, 5 mg daily in older children, and 5–10 mg daily in adolescents. Maximum dosages in common use are 20–40 mg/day. The lower end of the dosage range may be effective when used in combination with a stimulant, although no specific data are available. If no effect is noted, then an increase by the starting amount after the first week is reasonable; after that, increases should be slower, perhaps only every 2–3 weeks. It may take up to 4 weeks to see full effects because of fluoxetine's long half-life (1–4 days). Its primary metabolite, norfluoxetine, is biologically active and has an even longer half-life (up to 15 days); therefore, it may take up to a few weeks for effects to dissipate once it is stopped. It usually is given once daily if 20 mg or less is used and divided into twice-daily dosing for larger dosages.

In addition to the side effects listed, suicidal ideation and obsessions/compulsions associated with self-harm have been reported. Because of the prolonged half-life, it may be wise to wait longer than 14 days to start a MAOI. Increased levels of both medications may occur when fluoxetine is used with a TCA; it also can increase levels of carbamazepine, diazepam, lithium, and neuroleptics.

Sertraline

Sertraline (Zoloft) is indicated for the treatment of depression in older adolescents and young adults. It has not been studied for ADHD. Some children have less behavioral activation on sertraline as compared with fluoxetine, whereas the reverse is true for others. Sertraline has fewer drug interactions than the other SSRIs, but it does have the same risk when combined with MAOIs. It is available as 50- and 100-mg scored tablets. It can be started at 25 mg daily, either in the morning (if it causes sleep disturbance) or evening (if it causes somnolence). If no effect is apparent at the first dosage, then it can be increased after 1 week. Subsequent increases should be made more slowly.

Paroxetine

Paroxetine (Paxil) is indicated for the treatment of depression in adults. It is reported anecdotally to be effective for the extreme temper outbursts that are associated (most often) with coexisting disorders in children and adolescents with ADHD. It is available as 20- and 30-mg scored tablets. Starting dosages of 10 mg usually are given daily in the morning, with an increase in 1 week and then slower titration subsequently because full effects can take several weeks to become apparent.

Fluvoxamine

Fluvoxamine (Luvox) is indicated for OCD in adults. It also is used for OCD or obsessive-compulsive features in children with other disorders (e.g., ADHD, PDDs, TS). It is available as scored 50- and 100-mg tablets. The starting dosage commonly is 25 mg at bedtime. Dosages have ranged from 100 to 300 mg daily for adolescents with major depressive disorder or TS. It should not be given with astemizole (Hismanal) or cisapride (Propusid) because of the risk of an increased cardiac QT interval. Because of its moderately long plasma half-life of greater than 15 hours, it should be discontinued before using these medications. Of the SSRIs, fluvoxamine interacts with the largest number of other medications, including (in addition to the MAOIs) benzodiazepines, carbamazepine, and theophylline.

Other Medications

A variety of other medications have been reported to be useful for the treatment of ADHD symptoms including the MAOIs; a newer antidepressant, venlafaxine (Effexor); the antianxiety agent buspirone (Buspar); and neuroleptics. The MAOIs that have been reported to be effective for ADHD include clorgyline (not available), tranylcypramine (Parnate), and L-deprenyl (Eldepryl). They are not in common use because of the risk of hypertensive crisis when foods that are high in tyramine or dopamine (e.g., aged cheese, red wine) are ingested and because of a lack of a clear advantage over more standard treatments. They might be considered in a child whose ADHD is resistant to other medications and whose parent has been treated for depression or ADHD with a wide variety of agents without success until the MAOI was used. Deprenyl was effective in an open study for ADHD in individuals with TS with a low incidence of tic exacerbation.[47]

Venlafaxine is a new antidepressant in its own structural category. It blocks the reuptake of both serotonin and norepinephrine. Two open trials of adults showed positive effects in the majority of adults who remained in the trial, but there was a fairly substantial rate of intolerable side effects.[48] An open trial of children and adolescents with ADHD (many with coexisting disorders) showed that 25% discontinued because of side effects; in the majority of these, the side effect was behavioral activation leading to worsening of the ADHD symptoms. Of those who remained in the study, approximately one half showed a significant clinical improvement. There was little effect on conduct or cognitive symptoms, and the study was too small to assess the effects of coexisting disorders on response status. The dosages ranged from 12.5 to 25 mg three times daily.

Buspirone is an agonist at the 1A subtype of serotonin receptor. It is an antianxiety agent without the sedative or tolerance effects of benzodiazepines, and it is indicated for the relief of anxiety in adults. With the exception of MAOIs, little information is available about potential contraindications and interactions. Case reports indicate effectiveness without excessive side effects in anxiety disorders, ADHD, and aggression. Dosages for children typically range from 2.5 to 10 mg three times daily with a maximum of 20 mg/day for children and 30–60 mg/day for adolescents. Side effects include dizziness, drowsiness, nausea, headache, and insomnia.[49]

The neuroleptics have been used as an alternative treatment, sometimes with stimulants, in otherwise treatment-resistant individuals. Side effects of sedation and dyskinesias have, for the most part, resulted in their use being limited to children with TS, mental retardation, or PDDs. Those shown to have some effectiveness for ADHD symptoms include thioridizine (Mellaril), chlorpromazine (Thorazine), and haloperidol (Haldol). In general, lower dosages than those used to treat psychosis were effective. The more recent development of antipsychotic medications with a low risk of inducing dyskinesias (including risperidone [Risperdal] and olanzepine [Ziprexil]) can be expected to lead to renewed study of the role of antipsychotic medications in children with complex neurobehavioral disorders.

Medication Combinations

There has been very little formal study of combinations of medications for ADHD, although their use is not uncommon, especially when coexisting disorders are present. The most common combinations include a stimulant with an antihypertensive, an SSRI, a TCA, or an antipsychotic. The combination of a stimulant with beta-blockers (nadolol, propranolol) also has been reported. Such combinations can be very useful, but careful clinical and laboratory monitoring is required.

Clonidine or guanfacine sometimes are used throughout the day with a stimulant to treat residual impulsivity/hyperactivity or just later in the day to treat rebound or to induce sleep. Hunt, Capper, and O'Donnell (1990) reported that the combined use of MPH and clonidine was effective for children with coexisting oppositional defiant or conduct disorders with residual overarousal or distractibility while taking MPH alone. They also reported that in some children, the combination allows a lower dosage of MPH to be used, resulting in less rebound, appetite suppression, and insomnia. Prince, Wilens, Biederman, Spencer, and Wozniak (1996) reported the effective use of clonidine at night to assist with stimulant-related insomnia.

Gammon and Brown (1993) showed dramatic, positive results in an open trial of MPH and fluoxetine for children and adolescents with comorbid externalizing (oppositional, conduct) and internalizing (anxiety, dysthymia) disorders. The subjects were taking standard dosages of MPH and responded optimally to 2.5–20 mg daily of fluoxetine with improvement in ADHD, conduct, anxiety, and learning symptoms.

The primary advantage of stimulant–tricyclic combinations is the ability to address ADHD symptoms "around the clock" with a maximum level of effectiveness during the school day. The main concern is potentiation of cardiovascular effects. Although desipramine levels generally are not different with or without a concomitant stimulant, cardiac changes and noncardiac side effects are more prominent in children who are taking the combination.[50]

USING MEDICATION IN SPECIAL CIRCUMSTANCES

The presence of additional disorders often complicates the pharmacological management of ADHD in that individuals with coexisting disorders may be more prone to side effects and may need more than one medication. Consultation with a physician who has additional expertise in the use of alternatives (to stimulants) or medication combinations may be useful.

Tic Disorders

Tics are brief, staccato, repetitive, semi-involuntary movements or sounds that are believed to be due primarily to dopaminergic dysfunction in the **basal ganglia.** Tic disorders are commonly seen in pediatric practice, commonly coexist with ADHD, and have important implications for the medical management of ADHD.[51] Tic disorders include transient tic disorder of childhood, chronic motor tic, chronic vocal tic, and TS. Tics are designated simple or complex. Examples of common simple motor tics include eye blinking, facial grimacing, and shoulder shrugging. Common simple vocal tics include sniffing, grunting, and throat clearing. Complex motor tics involve a series of movements such as repetitive touching, squatting, or rituals. Complex vocal tics include the repetition of words and phrases. Coprolalia, the repetition of curse words, occurs in only a small percentage of individuals with TS.

Genetic studies indicate that TS, chronic tic disorders, and OCD are genetically transmitted together in families; therefore, if a relative is identified as having TS, OCD, or a chronic tic disorder, then a child has a greater risk of developing a tic disorder. Stuttering and ADHD also occur more frequently in families with tic disorders than in the general population, but the nature of their relationship still is controversial.[52] On average, about 50% of children with a chronic tic disorder or TS have ADHD.[53]

Stimulants can induce or exacerbate a variety of repetitive behaviors, including tics, TS, perseverative thinking, and compulsive behaviors.[54] Many clinicians have considered the history of a tic or the family history of a tic as a contraindication to stimulant use. Since the recognition that the genetic predisposition for tic disorders is much more common than previously realized, however, it has become apparent that many individuals who developed tics while taking stimulants may have had such a predisposition.[55] Because the majority of tic disorders are mild and the coexisting ADHD often is more function impairing, many clinicians do prescribe stimulants for children with tic disorders.

In the population as a whole, the incidence of developing a tic while taking stimulants has been reported to range from 1%–2%[56] to as high as 9%.[57] If a careful history of the child and the family is negative, then the risk probably is at the lower end of this range. Unfortunately, family history research indicates that individuals often are unable to provide an accurate report about tics in relatives. Precise figures for the risk of developing a tic when there is a previous history in the child or a positive immediate family history for a tic disorder or OCD are unclear but may be as high as 50%.[58] Children with anxiety disorders and ADHD also seem to have an increased frequency of developing tics.

For the majority of children who develop a tic while taking stimulants, the tic will resolve when the dosage is decreased or when the medication is discontinued. A small percentage of children will be left with a persistent tic disorder, but it is believed that these children have a predisposition for a tic disorder that is unmasked by the stimulant. Approximately 25% of children with a preexisting tic disorder will have an increase in severity with the addition of a stimulant.[59] Their tics also likely will decrease when the stimulant is withdrawn or when the dosage is decreased.[60]

Stimulants are effective for ADHD symptoms in children with tic disorders,[61] but there is little clear evidence for the preference of one stimulant over another. Some clinicians report informally that longer-acting stimulants have less risk of tic exacerbation, whereas others have found MPH less problematic than dextroamphetamine or magnesium pemoline.[62] There is no evidence for or against the hypothesis that the continued use of stimulants in the presence of a tic disorder will permanently increase the severity of the disorder.

Many clinicians first will try an alternative medication for ADHD treatment in a child with a tic disorder, such as the antihypertensives guanfacine and clonidine or a TCA. Clonidine appears to be somewhat less effective for ADHD and for tic reduction than initially suggested.[63] TCAs that have been investigated for their effectiveness include nortriptyline[64] and desipramine.[65] Preliminary results also suggest that deprenyl (or selegilene) may be effective with a low incidence of exacerbating tics,[66] whereas bupropion has been reported to exacerbate tics.[67]

Many children with moderate to severe tic disorders will benefit from a combination of medications to treat ADHD and the tics. When the dosage of a stimulant that is required to treat significantly function-impairing ADHD exacerbates tics to an unacceptable degree and alternative medications are not effective for the ADHD, a tic suppressant should be considered. Clonazepam, guanfacine, clonidine, and even SSRIs may decrease tics, but the most clearly documented, commonly used tic suppressants are the neuroleptics pimozide and haloperidol. The newer neuroleptics, risperidone and olanzapine, have less risk of inducing dyskinesias and are effective in preliminary reports.[68]

Learning Disorders

Stimulants are well documented to improve classroom work productivity,[69] but their effects on learning are less clear. Many studies over the years have examined the effectiveness of stimulant medication for ADHD on reading achievement. Although controversy in this area continues, it appears that improved scores on measures of reading achievement are correlated with and likely mediated by behavior improvement.[70] This suggests that stimulants should not be anticipated to improve reading achievement in the absence of coexisting ADHD symptoms. A related issue is whether stimulants are more effective for improving cognitive symptoms at a lower dosage than that required for improvements in disruptive behavior. Although an early, often-quoted study suggested this,[71] subsequent studies have reported parallel improvements in both learning and behavior with increasing dosages.[72]

The use of stimulant medication in children with **mental retardation** (MR) and ADHD also has been studied. In regards to diagnosing ADHD in the presence of mental retardation, criteria that are listed in the *Diagnostic and Statistical Manual of Mental Disorders, Fourth Edition* (DSM-IV)[73] require that the characteristics be present beyond what would be expected for the child's mental age. There is, however, some controversy as to whether it is appropriate to specifically interpret rating scale data for ADHD according to the norms for the child's mental or chronological age.[74] It may be prudent to withhold a diagnosis of ADHD until the child is placed into an appropriate classroom and can be reevaluated in a setting with realistic expectations. In this setting, a teacher who is experienced with children with cognitive impairment should be able to provide useful information about behavior in comparison with peers and functional impairment.

Children with MR show improvements in attention span, activity level, disruptive behavior, and work production but not learning or prosocial behavior in response to stimulants.[75] These findings parallel those in cognitively normal children. Overall, research suggests that in mild to moderate MR, the positive response rate is similar to that in children with typical cognitive abilities and the positive response rate declines as the severity of MR increases. Children with MR (as well as children with PDDs) have a higher rate of side effects, however, including an approximately 20% incidence of emergent tics.[76] Clonidine and thioridizine have shown some positive effects on hyperactivity in children with MR and may be useful alternatives.

Internalizing Disorders

Most studies of stimulant effectiveness for ADHD with coexisting internalizing disorders (e.g., anxiety, depression) suggest that the positive response rate of ADHD symptoms may be somewhat lower and the frequency of side effects somewhat higher than in uncomplicated ADHD.[77] Side effects may include increased anxiety, insomnia, or tics. Occasionally, anxiety improves, especially when the anxiety relates to ADHD-related difficulties (but, in most cases, anxiety that is restricted to ADHD-related issues will not result in a diagnosis of an anxiety disorder).

Stimulants sometimes can make depression worse; this may be true to a greater extent for dextroamphetamine than MPH.[78] Children with an underlying mood disorder may seem excessively withdrawn during the effective period of the stimulant and may cry easily, be overly anxious, or be labile during the rebound period. They may become increasingly withdrawn or irritable the longer that they are taking the stimulant. Alternative regimens in children and adolescents with internalizing disorders include the addition of an SSRI to the stimulant or the use of bupropion or a TCA instead of the stimulant. SSRIs and buspirone may be useful for anxiety but should not be expected to have direct effects on ADHD symptoms. Clonidine proba-bly should not be used for children with internalizing disorders because of its risk of causing/exacerbating them.[79]

Early-onset bipolar disorder often presents with prominent ADHD symptoms. These children often have chronic, severe irritability and tantrums; depressive symptoms; and oppositional/conduct symptoms and infrequently have clear cycling between depression and mania.[80] Medications may appear to be only briefly effective; and stimulants, TCAs, and SSRIs all may exacerbate the irritability and lability. Psychiatric referral is indicated for consideration of mood stabilization with carbamazepine, valproate, or lithium.[81]

Externalizing Disorders

Externalizing disorders include **oppositional defiant disorder** (ODD) and conduct disorder (CD). There has been little specific study of the effects of stimulants and other medications used to treat ADHD on ODD, but in studies that have targeted some of the symptoms of ODD (such as noncompliance),[82] it appears that stimulants and TCAs are helpful. Several studies have examined medication effects in children with CD, but most target aggression, a cardinal but nonspecific symptom of CD.[83] In addition, few studies distinguish different types of aggression—for example, the impulsive aggression often seen in ADHD from the premeditated or predatory aggression that may be part of CD.

A key consideration when choosing a medication for a child with ODD or CD is coexisting disorders. Most will have coexisting ADHD; some also will have coexisting mood disorders. Treating the coexisting disorder may be critical to improving the externalizing symptoms. Medications that have been shown to be effective in CD or aggression (and in coexisting ADHD) in controlled studies include stimulants, TCAs, and neuroleptics (although they generally are considered a last choice because of the risk of cognitive blunting and dyskinesias).[84] Lithium carbonate also has been shown to be superior to placebo in the treatment of aggression and explosiveness, but most studies have been of subjects with psychiatric diagnoses in addition to or instead of ADHD.[85] Medications for which there is some preliminary evidence of effectiveness for CD or aggression in open studies or case reports include buspirone, bupropion, clonidine, and propranolol.[86] The usefulness of the anticonvulsant carbamazepine continues to be controversial, with positive and negative results reported in different studies.[87] (For further review of medications that are used in the treatment of aggression in a range of neuropsychiatric disorders, see Fava, 1997.)

Seizure Disorders

ADHD and seizures frequently co-occur because both are common, both may be related to a similar underlying pathology, and antiepileptic medications may contribute to ADHD symptoms. Excitation of the CNS with medications that enhance **catecholamine** neurotransmission, such as stimulants and antidepressants, should, theoretically, lower the seizure threshold. There have been only a few studies of the safety and the efficacy of medications that are used to treat ADHD in children with seizures.[88] MPH appears to be effective and does not induce seizures in children whose seizures are controlled with antiepileptic medications prior to starting the stimulant. Seizure frequency may increase when MPH is added for children who continue to have seizures while taking antiepileptic medication.[89] There are no studies that specifically address the issue of the symptomatic treatment of ADHD-like symptoms that are thought to be caused by a necessary antiepileptic medication, rather than by ADHD, perhaps because the diagnostic distinction is difficult.

The TCAs lower the seizure threshold and interact pharmacologically with several anticonvulsants.[90] Seizures can be induced by TCAs, with a direct dosage–response relationship. The SSRIs fluoxetine, sertraline, paroxetine, and fluvoxamine are thought to be less likely to induce seizures than other antidepressants.[91] Bupropion is known to have a higher risk of causing a seizure than any of the other medications mentioned thus far, although this appears to occur primarily at dosages larger than those generally used in children. Seizures are reported to occur in 0.4% of adults who take bupropion as opposed to 0.1% of adults who take TCAs.[92]

Medication interactions are an important consideration when treating ADHD and seizures and are shown in Table 3. The alterations in effectiveness shown in this table arise from various mechanisms including lowering the seizure threshold, altering intestinal absorption, or influencing the activity of metabolic enzymes. With medications for which blood levels are unavailable, such as stimulants and SSRIs, careful clinical monitoring of the effects of introducing an antiepileptic medication on the baseline ef-

Table 3. Medication interactions in the treatment of ADHD and seizures

Adding...	May change the effectiveness/side effects of... in this direction[a]
Methylphenidate	Phenobarbital (I), phenytoin (I), primidone (I)
Dextroamphetamine	Ethosuximide (D), phenobarbital (I), phenytoin (I)
Magnesium pemoline	Carbamazepine (D), ethosuximide (D), felbamate (D), lamotrigine (D), phenobarbital (D), phenytoin (D), primidone (D), valproic acid (D)
Nortriptyline	Phenobarbital (NC)
Imipramine	Diazepam (I), lorazepam (I), phenobarbital (I)
Desipramine	Diazepam (I), lorazepam (I), phenobarbital (I)
Amitriptyline	Diazepam (I), lorazepam (I), phenobarbital (I)
Clonidine	Diazepam (I), lorazepam (I), phenobarbital (I)
Guanfacine	Diazepam (I), lorazepam (I), phenobarbital (I), phenytoin (D)
Carbamazepine	Clomipramine (I), bupropion (D)
Ethosuximide	NR
Phenobarbital	Imipramine (D), desipramine (D)
Phenytoin	Imipramine (D)
Primidone	NR
Sodium valproate	NR

[a]I = increase, D = decrease, NC = expected effects not clear, NR = none reported.

Note: This table does not describe all reported interactions of all medications mentioned in this chapter. For example, the addition of fluoxetine can increase carbamazepine levels, and the combination of carbamazepine and pimozide can cause neuroleptic malignant syndrome. The information provided here is limited to specific effects of anticonvulsants on medications commonly used to treat ADHD and vice versa. Each time medication combinations are considered, possible interactions should be reviewed.

fectiveness of these medications is required. Most often, the dosage of stimulant or SSRI will need to be increased, secondary either to increased hepatic metabolism after the addition of the antiepileptic medication or to an exacerbation of symptoms.

Cardiovascular Disease

The stimulants and the SSRIs appear to have relatively mild cardiovascular effects, whereas TCAs and antihypertensives may have more significant effects. In otherwise healthy children, the stimulants tend to cause relatively minor increases in heart rate and blood pressure.[93] Young children who have significant increases in blood pressure while taking stimulants still should be investigated for treatable causes of hypertension, even if their hypertension resolves when they stop taking stimulants, because this rare occurrence may signal an underlying contributing factor, such as renal vascular disease. In adolescents, elevation in blood pressure while taking stimulants may reflect the unmasking of a predisposition to essential hypertension.[94] Excess caffeine intake, in combination with the stimulant, may lead to excessive pulse or blood pressure elevation. Stimulants in combination with other medications that may predispose to increased blood pressure, such as TCAs, also can cause hypertension,[95] and stimulants in combination with antihypertensives may predispose to ventricular arrhythmia.[96] A thorough cardiovascular history and family history related to cardiovascular disease, especially of early onset, is important when considering pharmacological treatment.

There is little information about medication effects in children with known cardiovascular disease, but studies of MPH use in older, depressed adults following stroke or cardiac surgery suggest that cardiac changes on MPH are mild and less significant than those that occur with TCAs. In children with structural heart disease that may predispose to arrhythmia or with a history of arrhythmias without structural heart disease, stimulants may be a safer option than other available medications, but close coordination with the child's cardiologist and careful monitoring (with a Holter monitor or possibly even admission to the hospital for medication initiation) will be required. Theoretically, MPH and magnesium pemoline may be safer choices than dextroamphetamine because they have less noradrenergic effect, but this has not been proved clinically.

The antihypertensive agent clonidine can cause hypotension and bradycardia, rebound hypertension, and tachyarrhythmias (primarily in combination with a stimulant).[97] Bupropion may be a good choice for children with cardiovascular disease, although there has been relatively little study of its cardiovascular effects relative to other medications.

Asthma

A substantial number of children have both asthma and ADHD, although it is not clear that there is a specific relationship.[98] Stimulant medications appear to be quite safe in combination with asthma medications, although several tend to increase heart rate. Hyperactivity has been reported with beta-agonists or theophylline, particularly in younger children. Increased irritable behavior sometimes occurs in children who are taking MPH and who begin a course of oral steroids.

TCAs have been reported to cause increased side effects in approximately 10% of children who are treated for anxiety or depression and who chronically take multiple medications for asthma. These side effects have included increased activity and impulsivity, insomnia, postural hypotension, diastolic hypertension, tachycardia, premature atrial contractions, and generalized seizures.[99] The alternative medications have not been studied specifically in combination with medications for asthma in children. A small percentage of asthmatic children react to the yellow dye tartrazine or other inactive medication ingredients, which should be kept in mind if increased respiratory symptoms occur with the introduction of a new medication.

CONCLUSION

Medication is one of the mainstays of treatment for ADHD, and the vast majority of individuals with this disorder are treated effectively with stimulants. Stimulants are, in general, the most effective category of medications for the core symptoms of ADHD. Alternative medications exist for use instead of or in addition to stimulants. Some individuals are stimulant nonresponders, but most often other medications are needed secondary to intolerable stimulant side effects or the presence of coexisting disorders. Continued research is needed related to several aspects of the use of alternative medications for children and adolescents.

ENDNOTES

1. Elia, Borcherding, Rapoport, & Keysor (1991).
2. Levy, Hay, McStephen, Wood, & Waldman (1997).
3. American Academy of Child and Adolescent Psychiatry (1997), Committee on Children with Disabilities and Committee on Drugs, American Academy of Pediatrics (1996).
4. Rapoport et al. (1978).
5. Reviewed in Richters et al. (1995).
6. Cantwell (1996), Richters et al. (1995).

7. Spencer et al. (1996a).
8. Reviewed in Cantwell (1996).
9. Reviewed in Richters et al. (1995).
10. Ibid.
11. Ahmann et al. (1993), Effron, Jarman, & Barker (1997).
12. Spencer, Biederman, Harding, et al. (1996).
13. Safer, Zito, & Fine (1996).
14. Rapport & Denney (1997).
15. Riggs, Thompson, Mikulich, Whitmore, & Crowley (1996).
16. Stork & Cantor (1997).
17. Shevell & Schreiber (1997).
18. Swanson et al. (1998).
19. Kutcher (1996).
20. Reviewed in Green (1995a, 1995b), Spencer, Biederman, Wilens, et al. (1996).
21. Reviewed in Wilens et al. (1996).
22. Wilens et al. (1996).
23. Walsh, Giardina, Sloan, Greenhill, & Goldfein (1994).
24. Wilens et al. (1996).
25. Leonard et al. (1995).
26. Reviewed in Gardner (1996), Green (1995a).
27. Conners et al. (1996), Gardner (1996).
28. Green (1995a).
29. Barrickman et al. (1995).
30. Conners et al. (1996).
31. Spencer, Biederman, Steingard, & Wilens (1993).
32. Conners et al. (1996).
33. Ibid.
34. Reviewed in Garland (1996), Green (1995a).
35. Hunt, Capper, & O'Connell (1990), Hunt, Minderaa, & Cohen (1985).
36. Singer et al. (1995).
37. Swanson et al. (1995).
38. McCracken & Martin (1997).
39. Mercugliano, Batshaw, Steinberg, & Wang (n.d.).
40. Cantwell, Swanson, & Connor (1997).
41. Huk (1989); Mercugliano, personal observation.
42. Arnsten, Steere, & Hunt (1996), Coull (1994).
43. Horrigan & Barnhill (1995), Hunt, Arnsten, & Asbell (1995).
44. Chappell, Riddle, et al. (1995).
45. Reviewed in Goodnick (1994), Green (1995a), Leonard, March, Rickler, & Allen (1997).
46. Barrickman, Noyes, Kuperman, Schumacher, & Verda (1991).
47. Jankovic (1993).
48. Adler, Resnick, Kunz, & Devinsky (1995), Hedges, Reimherr, Rogers, Strong, & Wender (1995).
49. Reviewed in Green (1995a).
50. Reviewed in Green (1995b).
51. Reviewed in Power & Mercugliano (1997).
52. Reviewed in Tobin & Riddle (1993).
53. Reviewed in Commings (1990a), Tobin & Riddle (1993).
54. Borcherding, Keysor, Rapoport, Elia, & Amass (1990); reviewed in Riddle et al. (1995).
55. Commings (1990b).
56. Golden (1993).
57. Lipkin, Goldstein, & Adesman (1994).
58. Commings (1990b).
59. Golden (1993).
60. Riddle et al. (1995).
61. Gadow, Sverd, Sprafkin, Nolan, & Ezor (1995), Nolan & Gadow (1997).
62. Borcherding et al. (1990), Castellanos et al. (1997).
63. Singer et al. (1995).

64. Spencer, Biederman, Wilens, Steingard, & Geist (1993).
65. Singer et al. (1995), Spencer, Biederman, Kerman, Steingard, & Wilens (1993).
66. Jankovic (1993).
67. Spencer, Biederman, Steingard, & Wilens (1993).
68. Lombroso et al. (1995).
69. Swanson, Cantwell, Lerner, McBurnett, & Hanna (1991).
70. Richardson, Kupietz, Winsberg, Maitinsky, & Mendell (1988).
71. Sprague & Sleator (1977).
72. Rapport & Kelly (1991).
73. American Psychiatric Association (1994).
74. Pearson & Aman (1994).
75. Reviewed in Handen (1993).
76. Handen, Feldman, Gosling, Breaux, & McAuliffe (1991).
77. Reviewed in Greenhill (1995), Spencer, Biederman, Wilens, et al. (1996).
78. Effron, Jarman, & Barker (1997).
79. McCracken & Martin (1997).
80. Geller & Luby (1997).
81. Ibid.
82. Lufi, Parish-Plass, & Gai (1997), Pliszka (1989), Schachar, Tannock, Cunningham, & Corkum (1997).
83. Reviewed in Klein (1993), Klein et al. (1997), Spencer, Biederman, Wilens, et al. (1996).
84. Reviewed in Green (1995a), Greenhill (1995), Spencer, Biederman, Wilens, et al. (1996).
85. Green (1995a).
86. Green (1995a), Simeon & Sponst (1996).
87. Cueva et al. (1996), Silva, Munoz, & Alpert (1996).
88. E.g., Feldman, Crumrine, Handen, Alvin, & Teodori (1989), Gross-Tsur, Manor, van der Meere, Joseph, & Shalev (1997).
89. Gross-Tsur et al. (1997).
90. Brodie (1992).
91. Rosenstein, Nelson, & Jacobs (1993).
92. Physicians' Desk Reference (1997).
93. Safer (1992).
94. Brown & Sexson (1989).
95. Flemenbaum (1972).
96. Swanson et al. (1995).
97. Ibid.
98. Daly et al. (1996).
99. Wamboldt, Yancey, & Roesler (1997).

REFERENCES

Adler, L.A., Resnick, S., Kunz, M., & Devinsky, O. (1995). Open-label trial of venlafaxine in adults with attention deficit disorder. *Pychopharmacology Bulletin, 31*, 785–788.

Ahmann, P.A., Waltonen, S.J., Olson, K.A., Theye, F.W., Van Erem, A.J., & LaPlant, R.J. (1993). Placebo-controlled evaluation of Ritalin side effects. *Pediatrics, 91*, 1101–1106.

American Academy of Child and Adolescent Psychiatry. (1997). Practice parameters for the assessment and treatment of children, adolescents, and adults with attention-deficit/hyperactivity disorder. *Journal of the American Academy of Child and Adolescent Psychiatry, 36S*, 85S–121S.

American Psychiatric Association. (1994). *Diagnostic and statistical manual of mental disorders* (4th ed.). Washington, DC: Author

Arnsten, A.F.T., Steere, J.C., & Hunt, R.D. (1996). The contribution of a 2-noradrenergic mechanisms to prefrontal cortical cognitive function. *Archives of General Psychiatry, 53*, 448–455.

Barrickman, L.L., Noyes, R., Kuperman, S., Schumacher, E., & Verda, M. (1991). Treatment of ADHD with fluoxetine: A preliminary trial. *Journal of the American Academy of Child and Adolescent Psychiatry, 30*, 762–767.

Barrickman, L.L., Perry, P.J., Allen, A.J., Kuperman, S., Arndt, S.V., Herrmann K.J., & Schumacher, E. (1995). Bupropion versus methylphenidate in the treatment of attention-deficit hyperactivity disorder. *Journal of the American Academy of Child and Adolescent Psychiatry, 34*, 649–657.

Borcherding, B.G., Keysor, C.S., Rapoport, J.L., Elia, J., & Amass, J. (1990). Motor/vocal tics and compulsive behaviors on stimulant drugs: Is there a common vulnerability? *Psychiatry Research, 33,* 83–94.

Brodie, M.J. (1992). Drug interactions in epilepsy. *Epilepsia, 33*(Suppl. 1), S13–S22.

Brown, R.T., & Sexson, S.B. (1989). Effects of methylphenidate on cardiovascular responses in attention deficit hyperactivity disordered adolescents. *Journal of Adolescent Health Care, 10,* 179–183.

Cantwell, D.P. (1996). Attention deficit disorder: A review of the past 10 years. *Journal of the American Academy of Child and Adolescent Psychiatry, 35,* 978–987.

Cantwell, D.P., Swanson, J., & Connor, D.F. (1997). Case study: Adverse response to clonidine. *Journal of the American Academy of Child and Adolescent Psychiatry, 36,* 539–544.

Castellanos, F.X., Giedd, J.N., Elia, J., Marsh, W.L., Ritchie, G.F., Hamburger, S.D., & Rapoport, J.L. (1997). Controlled stimulant treatment of ADHD and comorbid Tourette's syndrome: Effects of stimulant and dose. *Journal of the American Academy of Child and Adolescent Psychiatry, 36,* 589–596.

Chappell, P.B., Riddle, M.A., Scahill, L., Lynch, K.A., Schultz, R., Arnsten, A., Leckman, J.F., & Cohen, D.J. (1995). Guanfacine treatment of comorbid attention-deficit hyperactivity disorder and Tourette's syndrome: Preliminary clinical experience. *Journal of the American Academy of Child and Adolescent Psychiatry, 34,* 1140–1146.

Commings, D.E. (1990a). ADHD in Tourette syndrome. In *Tourette syndrome and human behavior* (pp. 99–104). Duarte, CA: Hope Press.

Commings, D.E. (1990b). ADHD secondary to a Gts gene. In *Tourette syndrome and human behavior* (pp. 259–262). Duarte, CA: Hope Press.

Committee on Children with Disabilities and Committee on Drugs, American Academy of Pediatrics. (1996). Medication for children with attention disorders. *Pediatrics, 98,* 301–304.

Conners, C.K., Casat, C.D., Gualtieri, C.T., Weller, E., Reader, M., Reiss, A., Weller, R.A., Khayrallah, M., & Ascher, J. (1996). Bupropion hydrochloride in attention deficit disorder with hyperactivity. *Journal of the American Academy of Child and Adolescent Psychiatry, 35,* 1314–1321.

Coull, J.T. (1994). Pharmacological manipulations of the alpha 2-noradrenergic system: Effects on cognition. *Drugs & Aging, 5,* 116–126.

Cueva, J.E., Overall, J.E., Small, A.M., Armenteros, J.L., Perry, R., & Campbell, M. (1996). Carbamazepine in aggressive children with conduct disorder: A double-blind and placebo-controlled study. *Journal of the American Academy of Child and Adolescent Psychiatry, 35,* 480–490.

Daly, J.M., Biederman, J., Bostic, J.Q., Maraganore, A.M., Lelon, E., Jellinek, M., & Lapey, A. (1996). The relationship between childhood asthma and attention deficit hyperactivity disorder: A review of the literature. *Journal of Attention Disorders, 1,* 31–41.

Effron, D., Jarman, F., & Barker, M. (1997). Side effects of methylphenidate and dextroamphetamine in children with attention deficit hyperactivity disorder: A double-blind, crossover trial. *Pediatrics, 100,* 662–666.

Elia, J., Borcherding, B.G., Rapoport, J.L., & Keysor, C.S. (1991). Methylphenidate and dextroamphetamine treatments of hyperactivity: Are there true nonresponders? *Psychiatry Research, 36,* 141–155.

Fava, M. (1997). Psychopharmacologic treatment of pathologic aggression. *Psychiatric Clinics of North America, 20,* 427–451.

Feldman, H., Crumrine, P., Handen, B.L., Alvin, R., & Teodori, J. (1989). Methylphenidate in children with seizures and attention-deficit disorder. *American Journal of Diseases of Children, 143,* 1081–1086.

Flemenbaum, A. (1972). Hypertensive episodes after adding methylphenidate (Ritalin) to tricyclic antidepressants. *Psychosomatics, 13,* 265–268.

Gadow, K.D., Sverd, J., Sprafkin, J., Nolan, E.E., & Ezor, S.N. (1995). Efficacy of methylphenidate for attention-deficit hyperactivity disorder in children with tic disorder. *Archives of General Psychiatry, 52,* 444–455.

Gammon, G.D., & Brown, T.E. (1993). Fluoxetine and methylphenidate in combination for treatment of attention deficit disorder and comorbid depressive disorder. *Journal of Child and Adolescent Psychopharmacology, 3,* 1–10.

Gardner, D. (1996). Bupropion: Pharmacologic and clinical update. *Child and Adolescent Psychopharmacology News, 1,* 1–3.

Garland, E.J. (1996). Clonidine: Finding its place in child psychiatry. *Child and Adolescent Psychopharmacology News, 1,* 8–9.

Geller, B., & Luby, J. (1997). Child and adolescent bipolar disorder: A review of the past 10 years. *Journal of the American Academy of Child and Adolescent Psychiatry, 36,* 1168–1176.

Golden, G.S. (1993). Treatment of attention deficit disorder. In R. Kurlan (Ed.), *Handbook of Tourette's syndrome and related tic and behavioral disorders* (pp. 423–430). New York: Marcel Dekker.

Goodnick, P.J. (1994). Pharmacokinetic optimisation of therapy with newer antidepressants. *Clinical Pharmacokinetics, 27,* 307–330.

Green, W.H. (1995a). *Child and adolescent clinical psychopharmacology* (2nd ed.). Baltimore: Williams & Wilkins.

Green, W.H. (1995b). The treatment of attention-deficit hyperactivity disorder with non-stimulant medications. *Child and Adolescent Psychiatric Clinics of North America, 4,* 169–195.

Greenhill, L.L. (1995). Attention-deficit hyperactivity disorder: The stimulants. *Child and Adolescent Psychiatric Clinics of North America, 4,* 123–168.

Gross-Tsur, V., Manor, O., van der Meere, J., Joseph, A., & Shalev, R.S. (1997). Epilepsy and attention deficit hyperactivity disorder: Is methylphenidate safe and effective? *Journal of Pediatrics, 130,* 670–674.

Handen, B.L. (1993). Pharmacotherapy in mental retardation and autism. *School Psychology Review, 22,* 162–183.

Handen, B.L., Feldman, H., Gosling, A., Breaux, A.M., & McAuliffe, S. (1991). Adverse side effects of methylphenidate among mentally retarded children with ADHD. *Journal of the American Academy of Child and Adolescent Psychiatry, 30,* 241–245.

Hedges, D., Reimherr, F.W., Rogers, A., Strong, R., & Wender, P.H. (1995). An open trial of venlafaxine in adult patients with attention deficit hyperactivity disorder. *Psychopharmacology Bulletin, 31,* 779–783.

Horrigan, J.P., & Barnhill, L.J. (1995). Guanfacine for treatment of attention-deficit hyperactivity disorder in boys. *Journal of Child and Adolescent Psychopharmacology, 5,* 215–223.

Huk, S.G. (1989). Transient exacerbation of tics in treatment of Tourette's syndrome with clonidine. *Journal of the American Academy of Child and Adolescent Psychiatry, 28,* 583–586.

Hunt, R.D., Arnsten, A.F.T., & Asbell, M.D. (1995). An open trial of guanfacine in the treatment of attention-deficit hyperactivity disorder. *Journal of the American Academy of Child and Adolescent Psychiatry, 34,* 50–54.

Hunt, R.D., Capper, L., & O'Connell, P. (1990). Clonidine in child and adolescent psychiatry. *Journal of Child and Adolescent Psychopharmacology, 1,* 87–101.

Hunt, R.D., Minderaa, R.B., & Cohen, D.J. (1985). Clonidine benefits children with attention deficit disorder and hyperactivity: Report of a double-blind placebo-controlled crossover study. *Journal of the American Academy of Child and Adolescent Psychiatry, 24,* 617–629.

Jankovic, J. (1993). Deprenyl in attention deficit associated with Tourette's syndrome. *Archives of Neurology, 50,* 286–288.

Klein, R.G. (1993). Clinical efficacy of methylphenidate in children and adolescents. *Encephale, 19,* 89–93.

Klein, R.G., Abikoff, H., Klass, E., Ganeles, D., Seese, L.M., & Pollack, S. (1997). Clinical efficacy of methylphenidate in conduct disorder with and without attention deficit hyperactivity disorder. *Archives of General Psychiatry, 54,* 1073–1080.

Kutcher, S.P. (1996). Adderall, a possible medication for ADHD. *Child and Adolescent Psychopharmacology News, 1,* 6.

Leonard, H.L., March, J., Rickler, K.C., & Allen, A.J. (1997). Pharmacology of the selective serotonin reuptake inhibitors in children and adolescents. *Journal of the American Academy of Child and Adolescent Psychiatry, 36,* 725–736.

Leonard, H.L., Meyer, M.C., Swedo, S.E., Richter, D., Hamburger, S.D., Allen, A.J., Rapoport, J.L., & Tucker, E. (1995). Electrocardiographic changes during desipramine and clomipramine treatment in children and adolescents. *Journal of the American Academy of Child and Adolescent Psychiatry, 34,* 1460–1468.

Levy, F., Hay, D.A., McStephen, M., Wood, C., & Waldman, I. (1997). Attention-deficit hyperactivity disorder: A category or a continuum? Analysis of a large-scale twin study. *Journal of the American Academy of Child and Adolescent Psychiatry, 36,* 737–744.

Lipkin, P.H., Goldstein, I.J., & Adesman, A.R. (1994). Tics and dyskinesias associated with stimulant treatment of attention-deficit hyperactivity disorder. *Archives of Pediatric and Adolescent Medicine, 148,* 859–961.

Lombroso, P.J., Scahill, L., King, R.A., Peterson, B.S., Lynch, K.A., & Leckman, J.F. (1995). Risperidone treatment of children and adolescents with chronic tic disorders: A preliminary report. *Journal of the American Academy of Child and Adolescent Psychiatry, 34,* 1147–1152.

Lufi, D., Parish-Plass, J., & Gai, E. (1997). The effect of methylphenidate on the cognitive and personality functioning of ADHD children. *Israeli Journal of Psychiatry and Related Sciences, 34,* 200–209.

McCracken, J.T., & Martin, W. (1997). Clonidine side effect [Letter]. *Journal of the American Academy of Child and Adolescent Psychiatry, 36,* 160.

Mercugliano, M., Batshaw, M., Steinberg, A., & Wang, P. (n.d.). *Case series: Phobias, obsessions, compulsions, and hallucinations as side effects of clonidine and guanfacine treatment.* Manuscript submitted for publication.

Nolan, E.E., & Gadow, K.D. (1997). Children with ADHD and tic disorder and their classmates: Behavioral normalization with methylphenidate. *Journal of the American Academy of Child and Adolescent Psychiatry, 36,* 597–604.

Pearson, D.A., & Aman, M.G. (1994). Ratings of hyperactivity and developmental indices: Should clinicians correct for developmental level? *Journal of Autism and Developmental Disorders, 24,* 395–411.

Physicians' desk reference. (1997). Montvale, NJ: Medical Economics Data.

Pliszka, S.R. (1989). Effect of anxiety on cognition, behavior, and stimulant response in ADHD. *Journal of the American Academy of Child and Adolescent Psychiatry, 28,* 882–887.

Power, T.J., & Mercugliano, M. (1997). Tic disorders. In G.G. Bear, K.M. Minke, & A. Thomas (Eds.), *Children's needs: II. Development, problems, and alternatives* (pp. 887–896). Bethesda, MD: National Association of School Psychologists.

Prince, J.B., Wilens, T.E., Biederman, J., Spencer, T.J., & Wozniak, J.R. (1996). Clonidine for sleep disturbances associated with attention-deficit hyperactivity disorder: A systematic chart review of 62 cases. *Journal of the American Academy of Child and Adolescent Psychiatry, 35,* 599–605.

Rapoport, J.L., Buchsbaum, M.S., Zahn, T.P., Weingartner, H., Ludlow, C., & Mikkelson, E.J. (1978). Dextroamphetamine: Cognitive and behavioral effects in normal prepubertal boys. *Science, 199,* 560–563.

Rapport, M.D., & Denney, C. (1997). Titrating methylphenidate in children with attention-deficit/hyperactivity disorder: Is body mass predictive of clinical response? *Journal of the American Academy of Child and Adolescent Psychiatry, 36,* 523–530.

Rapport, M.D., & Kelly, K.L. (1991). Psychostimulant effects on learning and cognitive function: Findings and implications for children with attention deficit hyperactivity disorder. *Clinical Psychology Review, 11,* 61–92.

Richardson, E., Kupietz, S.S., Winsberg, B.G., Maitinsky, S., & Mendell, N. (1988). Effects of methylphenidate dosage in hyperactive reading-disabled children: II. Reading achievement. *Journal of the American Academy of Child and Adolescent Psychiatry, 27,* 78–87.

Richters, J.E., Arnold, L.E., Jensen, P.S., Abikoff, H., Conners, C.K., Greenhill, L.L., Hechtman, L., Hinshaw, S.P., Pelham, W.E., & Swanson, J.M. (1995). NIMH collaborative multisite multimodal treatment study of children with ADHD: I. Background and rationale. *Journal of the American Academy of Child and Adolescent Psychiatry, 34,* 987–1000.

Riddle, M.A., Lynch, K.A., Scahill, L., DeVries, A., Cohen, D.J., & Leckman, J.F. (1995). Methylphenidate discontinuation and reinitiation during long-term treatment of children with Tourette's disorder and attention-deficit hyperactivity disorder: A pilot study. *Journal of Child and Adolescent Psychopharmacology, 5,* 205–214.

Riggs, P.D., Thompson, L.L., Mikulich, S.K., Whitmore, E.A., & Crowley, T.J. (1996). An open trial of pemoline in drug-dependent delinquents with attention-deficit hyperactivity disorder. *Journal of the American Academy of Child and Adolescent Psychiatry, 35,* 1018–1024.

Rosenstein, D.L., Nelson, J.C., & Jacobs, S.C. (1993). Seizures associated with antidepressants: A review. *Journal of Clinical Psychiatry, 54,* 289–299.

Safer, D.J. (1992). Relative cardiovascular safety of psychostimulants used to treat attention-deficit hyperactivity disorder. *Journal of Child and Adolescent Psychopharmacology, 2,* 279–290.

Safer, D.J., Zito, J.M., & Fine, E.M. (1996). Increased methylphenidate usage for attention deficit disorder in the 1990s. *Pediatrics, 98,* 1084–1088.

Schachar, R.J., Tannock, R., Cunningham, C., & Corkum, P.V. (1997). Behavioral, situational, and temporal effects of treatment of ADHD with methylphenidate. *Journal of the American Academy of Child and Adolescent Psychiatry, 36,* 754–763.

Shevell, M., & Schreiber, R. (1997). Pemoline-associated hepatic failure: A critical analysis of the literature. *Pediatric Neurology, 16,* 14–16.

Silva, R.R., Munoz, D.M., & Alpert, M. (1996). Carbamazepine use in children and adolescents with features of attention-deficit hyperactivity disorder: A meta-analysis. *Journal of the American Academy of Child and Adolescent Psychiatry, 35,* 352–358.

Simeon, J., & Sponst, W. (1996). Propranolol in aggressive children and adolescents. *Child and Adolescent Psychopharmacology News, 1,* 5–10.

Singer, H.S., Brown, J., Quaskey, S., Rosenberg, L.A., Mellits, E.D., & Denckla, M.B. (1995). The treatment of attention-deficit hyperactivity disorder in Tourette's syndrome: A double-blind placebo-controlled study with clonidine and desipramine. *Pediatrics, 95,* 74–81.

Spencer, T., Biederman, J., Harding, M., O'Donnell, D., Faraone, S.V., & Wilens, T.E. (1996). Growth deficits in ADHD children revisited: Evidence for disorder-associated growth delays? *Journal of the American Academy of Child and Adolescent Psychiatry, 35,* 1460–1469.

Spencer, T., Biederman, J., Kerman, K., Steingard, R., & Wilens, T. (1993). Desipramine treatment of children with attention-deficit hyperactivity disorder and tic disorder or Tourette's syndrome. *Journal of the American Academy of Child and Adolescent Psychiatry, 32,* 354–360.

Spencer, T., Biederman, J., Steingard, R., & Wilens, T. (1993). Bupropion exacerbates tics in children with attention-deficit hyperactivity disorder and Tourette's syndrome. *Journal of the American Academy of Child and Adolescent Psychiatry, 32,* 211–214.

Spencer, T., Biederman, J., Wilens, T., Harding, M., O'Donnell, D., & Griffin, S. (1996). Pharmacotherapy of attention-deficit hyperactivity disorder across the life cycle. *Journal of the American Academy of Child and Adolescent Psychiatry, 35,* 409–432.

Spencer, T., Biederman, J., Wilens, T., Steingard, R., & Geist, D. (1993). Nortriptyline treatment of children with attention-deficit hyperactivity disorder and tic disorder or Tourette's syndrome. *Journal of the American Academy of Child and Adolescent Psychiatry, 32,* 205–210.

Spencer, T., Wilens, T., & Biederman, J. (1995). Psychotropic medication for children and adolescents. *Child and Adolescent Psychiatric Clinics of North America, 4,* 97–121.

Sprague, R.L., & Sleator, E.K. (1977). Methylphenidate in hyperkinetic children: Differences in dose effects on learning and social behavior. *Science, 198,* 1274–1276.

Stork, C.M., & Cantor, R. (1997). Pemolin induced choreoathetosis: Case report and review of the literature. *Clinical Toxicology, 35,* 105–108.

Swanson, J.M., Cantwell, D., Lerner, M., McBurnett, K., & Hanna, G. (1991). Effects of stimulant medication on learning in children with ADHD. *Journal of Learning Disabilities, 24,* 219–230, 255.

Swanson, J.M., Flockhart, D., Udrea, D., Cantwell, D., Connor, D., & Williams, L. (1995). Clonidine in the treatment of ADHD: Questions about safety and efficacy. *Journal of Child and Adolescent Psychopharmacology, 5,* 301–304.

Swanson, J.M., Wigal, S., Greenhill, L.L., Browne, R., Waslik, B., Lerner, M., Williams, L., Flynn, D., Agler, D., Crowley, K., Fineberg, E., Baren, M., & Cantwell, D.P. (1998). Analog classroom assessment of Adderall in children with ADHD. *Journal of the American Academy of Child and Adolescent Psychiatry, 37,* 519–526.

Tobin, K.E., & Riddle, M.A. (1993). Attention deficit hyperactivity disorder. In R. Kurlan (Ed.), *Handbook of Tourette's syndrome and related tic and behavioral disorders* (pp. 89–109). New York: Marcel Dekker.

Walsh, B.T., Giardina, E.-G.V., Sloan, R.P., Greenhill, L., & Goldfein, J. (1994). Effects of desipramine on autonomic control of the heart. *Journal of the American Academy of Child and Adolescent Psychiatry, 33,* 191–197.

Wamboldt, M.Z., Yancey, A.G., Jr., & Roesler, T.A. (1997). Cardiovascular effects of tricyclic antidepressants in childhood asthma: A case series and review. *Journal of Child and Adolescent Psychopharmacology, 7,* 45–64.

Wilens, T.E., Biederman, J., Baldessarini, R.J., Geller, B., Schleifer, D., Spencer, T.J., & Birmaher, B. (1996). Cardiovascular effects of therapeutic doses of tricyclic antidepressants in children and adolescents. *Journal of the American Academy of Child and Adolescent Psychiatry, 35,* 1491–1501.

RESOURCES

Garber, S.W., Garber, M.D., & Spizman, R.F. (1997). *Beyond Ritalin.* New York: HarperCollins. (For parents; to order, call [800] 242-7737.)

Green, W.H. (1995). *Child and adolescent clinical psychopharmacology* (2nd ed.). Baltimore: Williams & Wilkins. (To order, call [800] 638-0672.)

Greenhill, L.L., & Osman, B.B. (1991). *Ritalin: Theory and patient management.* Larchmont, NY: Mary Ann Liebert, Inc. (To order, call [800] 654-3237.)

PDR guide to drug interactions, side effects, indications, contraindications. (1997). Montvale, NJ: Medical Economics Data.

Physicians' desk reference. (1997). Montvale, NJ: Medical Economics Data.

Werry, J.S., & Aman, M.G. (1993). *Practitioner's guide to psychoactive drugs for children and adolescents.* New York: Plenum. (To order, call [800] 221-9369.)

VIDEOTAPES

Biederman, J., Spencer, T., & Wilens, T. (1997). *Medical management of attention deficit hyperactivity disorder.* Plantation, FL: Specialty Press. (To order, call [800] 233-9273.)

Phelan, T.W., & Bloomberg, J. (1990). *Medication for attention deficit disorder.* Glen Ellyn, IL: Child Management, Inc. (To order, call [800] 442-4453.)

A Cover Letter

Date _____

Dear _____ :

Your student, _____ , is beginning a trial period of intervention for attention-deficit/hyperactivity disorder. Because your observations about the effectiveness of treatment on functioning in the school setting are critical, I am writing to ask if you would be willing to complete a brief questionnaire (copies attached) on a regular basis. The specifics are described below. Please date and sign each one. Thank you in advance for your time.

A. Title of questionnaire _____

B. Frequency of completion

_____ weekly

_____ twice weekly

_____ daily

C. Duration of completion _____

D. Disposition of questionnaires

_____ return to parent

_____ mail to me each week (envelopes attached)

_____ mail to me at end of trial (envelopes attached)

E. Special instructions

_____ note the class and time when you have this student

_____ rate A.M. behavior only

_____ rate entire day but note any consistent A.M./P.M. difference

_____ rate class time only

_____ rate class and unstructured time (lunch/recess) but note any consistent class/unstructured time differences

F. Other

_____

_____

The Clinician's Practical Guide to Attention-Deficit/Hyperactivity Disorder
by Marianne Mercugliano, Thomas J. Power, and Nathan J. Blum   ©1999 by Paul H. Brookes Publishing Co.

10

Alternative Treatments for Attention-Deficit/ Hyperactivity Disorder

Alternative (nonstandard) treatments for attention-deficit/hyperactivity disorder (ADHD) abound and are reported widely in the media. A treatment approach may be considered "nonstandard" when it is adopted and practiced before adequate trials of safety and efficacy are completed or when documentation of effectiveness in the peer-reviewed medical literature is absent or unclear. For these reasons, the treatment is not widely accepted by the medical community. Parents frequently bring their questions about alternative treatments to their clinicians, who must be sufficiently knowledgeable to provide guidance in this area. This chapter covers the most common alternative treatments for ADHD, including nutritional supplements, herbal and homeopathic remedies, elimination diets, treatment of yeast overgrowth, electroencephalographic (EEG) biofeedback, vestibular treatment, and vision therapy.

NUTRITIONAL SUPPLEMENTS

Vitamin and Mineral Supplements

It has been hypothesized that some individuals have a need for many times the normal requirement of a vitamin or a mineral for normal physiological or cognitive functioning because of an unknown genetic/metabolic abnormality, analogous to the condition of **pyridoxine-responsive seizures.** This hypothesis underlies the approach to diagnosis and treatment in the field known as *orthomolecular psychiatry,* a term coined by Linus Pauling in the late 1960s. A corollary of the orthomolecular approach is that every individual is biochemically unique; thus, different patterns of relative vitamin and mineral deficiencies might cause the same "final common pathway" of cognitive/behavioral effects in different individuals.

Usually, 10 times the recommended dietary allowance is considered a "megadose" of a vitamin or a mineral, but, often, dosages far in excess of this are used. Initial studies of the effectiveness of "megadoses" of vitamins and minerals were conducted with adults with schizophrenia, but the American Academy of Psychiatry ultimately concluded that this was not an effective method for treating schizophrenia. Studies of children with mental retardation[1] and with reading and behavior problems[2] reported improved outcomes, but the results were confounded by the use of combined treatments that were not taken into account in the control groups.

In studies of hyperactive children, there were no consistent positive results from large dosages of vitamin/mineral supplements[3] and side effects included possible interference with the absorption of other nutrients[4] and elevated liver enzymes.[5] In one study, a higher-protein/lower-sugar diet was used without controls; thus, improvements noted could have been related to the altered diet rather than to the supplements.[6]

In 1976, the American Academy of Pediatrics concluded that there was no basis for the use of high-dosage vitamin/mineral supplements for childhood behavior disorders, following a similar decision by the American Academy of Psychiatry[7]; no subsequent, well-designed studies of children with ADHD have challenged this position effectively. This approach cannot be considered safe because of the potential for liver enzyme abnormalities and because high dosages of certain vitamins and minerals may interfere with the levels and functions of others, and high dosages of even the water-soluble vitamins and minerals can have significant side effects.[8]

Zinc deficiency may be related to ADHD in a subgroup of children. Several groups of researchers have found lower zinc levels in children with ADHD compared with controls, using either serum[9] or urine[10] measurements. Several animal studies also support a possible relationship between zinc deficiency and attention/behavior deficits.[11] Because of its relationship to fatty acid metabolism, Bekaroğlu et al. (1996) hypothesized, zinc deficiency may be the primary cause of low free fatty acid levels, which also have been found in children with ADHD (see next section). Arnold et al. (1990) hypothesized that zinc deficiency might be related to suboptimum stimulant responsiveness because of a positive correlation between baseline zinc levels and the degree of change during a double-blind, placebo-controlled trial of amphetamine treatment in school-age males with ADHD. This is a very preliminary finding because of methodological limitations.

Studies support the role of iron deficiency, even to a degree that is not sufficient to cause anemia, in decreased concentration and mood regulation in children.[12] The clinician can help to support parents in providing a nutritionally adequate diet for children, including a breakfast that includes both protein and carbohydrates, and a daily multivitamin and multimineral supplement because many children with ADHD do not, in fact, consume an adequate diet. Screening for iron sufficiency in addition to anemia should be considered, and aggressive treatment with replacement levels of iron supplementation should be administered when laboratory studies indicate iron deficiency, even in the absence of anemia. The role for routine measurement of serum zinc is less clear because studies of its correlation with zinc intake and change with supplementation in children with ADHD have not been conducted.

Essential Fatty Acids and ADHD

Dietary fats are divided into the saturated, monounsaturated, and polyunsaturated groups based on their chemical structures. One subset of polyunsaturated fats is called *essential fatty acids* (EFAs) because they cannot be synthesized in the body from precursors.[13] There is one absolute EFA, cis-linoleic acid, although some consider alpha-linolenic acid essential as well. Several other important fatty acids are synthesized from these.

EFAs influence a wide variety of bodily functions via their two main structural roles: They are important components of cell membranes, influencing fluidity, permeability, and electrical transmission; and they are precursors to the synthesis of prostaglandins, which are involved in vascular, immunological, gastrointestinal, and central nervous system functions. Symptoms of EFA deficiency in animals and humans include dry skin and hair, eczema, dandruff, brittle nails, excessive thirst and urination, asthma, allergies, and cognitive and emotional changes.[14]

EFAs can be divided into two groups—omega-3s (linolenic acid and its derivatives) and omega-6s (linoleic acid and its derivatives). The omega-6s are found throughout the body, but the omega-3s are highly concentrated in the brain. Several different research groups have found lower levels of EFAs in children with ADHD compared with controls.[15] Reductions were found in plasma levels of specific EFAs (some omega-3s and some omega-6s) as well as total concentration. An inverse relationship was found for EFA levels and clinical symptoms of EFA deficiency.[16] More specific, higher rates of behavior problems, temper tantrums, and sleep problems were associated with low omega-3 levels, and higher rates of upper-respiratory infections and antibiotic use were associated with low omega-6 levels.[17] The lower concentration of EFAs in the plasma of children with ADHD does not appear to be due to decreased dietary intake, although more in-depth measurements are needed before this can be concluded.[18] Possible differences in absorption, synthesis, or metabolism also should be explored. Fatty acids in the *trans* configuration, partially hydrogenated fats, and saturated fats can interfere with the function of EFAs such that an optimum balance and not just quantitatively sufficient intake ultimately may be important.[19]

Colquhoun and Bunday (1981) found positive effects of EFA supplementation with evening primrose oil on ADHD symptoms in an uncontrolled study. Two subsequent controlled studies found no overall significant effects but some positive effects on specific rating scale items[20]; however, evening primrose oil is primarily an omega-6 supplement, and behavior disturbances may be more closely linked to deficient omega-3 EFAs. Further study is needed in this area before specific supplements or dietary modifications can be recommended. Fish and vegetable oils are good sources of dietary EFAs and should provide adequate amounts.

Other Supplements

Nutritional supplements in the form of neurotransmitter precursors have not been shown to be effective for ADHD symptoms. In particular, the dopamine and norepinephrine precursors tyrosine[21] and phenylalanine[22] and the serotonin precursor tryptophan[23] have been studied. In the Nemzer et al. (1986) study, tryptophan supplementation improved some parent behavior ratings but not teacher behavior ratings. In the late 1980s, supplementation with tryptophan was associated with several cases of eosinophilia-myalgia syndrome, a serious inflammatory disorder. This highlighted the fact that "natural" does not equal "safe."

The compound dimethylaminoethanol (DMAE) is being actively promoted for the treatment of ADHD. DMAE is found in small amounts in the brain, where it promotes the formation of choline. Choline is important for the production of lecithin, a component of cell membranes and regulator of lipid metabolism. It also is a precursor to the neurotransmitter acetylcholine. Increasing acetylcholine transmission in the brain has been shown to improve cognitive performance and to slow the memory loss in individuals with Alzheimer's disease,[24] but no studies of the safety or the cognitive effects of DMAE or choline in individuals with ADHD are available. DMAE can have side effects including insomnia, muscle tension, headaches, and diarrhea. The lack of studies supporting safety or effectiveness make this approach insupportable at this time.

HERBAL TREATMENTS

Ginkgo biloba extract (GBE) and pycnogenol are two plant derivatives that are reported anecdotally to be effective for ADHD symptoms. GBE is an extract from the leaf of the ginkgo tree, which contains a high concentration of specific flavonoids—plant-derived small molecular weight compounds with a wide variety of biological effects based on their ability to inhibit the enzymes involved in many cellular metabolic processes. Certain flavonoids, at appropriate dosages, have antiallergenic, anti-inflammatory, antiviral, and anticarcinogenic effects. Their basic biology has been studied widely, they have been used in Eastern medicine for many years, and they are used in conventional medical practice in many European countries. Ginkgolides (the particular subgroup of flavonoids of interest from the ginkgo leaf) are extracted, purified, concentrated, and standardized for activity level to make GBE. GBE acts as an **antioxidant, free radical scavenger,** and microcirculatory stimulant. It appears to work by stabilizing red blood cell membranes and lowering blood viscosity.[25] It may be effective for a variety of vascular diseases, primarily in older adults. There also is some interest in its use for dementia and brain injury. One study (in the French literature) reported positive effects of GBE on the mental functioning of young, healthy adults.[26]

GBE is not recommended by its manufacturers for ADHD; in fact, there are no reported indications for its use with children except for asthma (it can inhibit bronchial constriction).[27] No controlled studies of GBE's effectiveness in individuals with ADHD or of its safety and pharmacokinetics in children are available in standard medical search databases. Because the specific neurobiological cause of ADHD remains unknown, it is unclear whether a microcirculatory stimulant is a sensible treatment.

GBE appears to be safe for healthy adults in commonly recommended dosages. Its effects are reported to be cumulative, with improvements taking 3–6 weeks to become evident, and long-term use usually is recommended.[28] Side effects that have been reported in individuals who take excessive dosages include irritability, restlessness, headache, diarrhea, nausea, and vomiting.[29] Although GBE appears thus far to be relatively safe, parts of the ginkgo plant are extremely toxic and should not be confused.[30]

Pycnogenol, a flavonoid compound extracted from the bark of the Maritime pine tree that grows in southern France, is advertised for the treatment of ADHD. It has been less well-studied for its medical uses than GBE and, like GBE, has not been studied specifically for safety in children or for efficacy in individuals with ADHD. Pycnogenol is made up of more than 40 individual flavonoids in two categories—proanthocyanidins and catechins. Proanthocyanidins are powerful antioxidant and free radical scavengers, and catechins are antioxidants and **collagen** stabilizers. Pycnogenol is reported to have an impressive array of positive effects including protection and rejuvenation of the skin, prevention of heart disease, reduction of the inflammation associated with arthritis, and reduction of peripheral vascular symptoms such as phlebitis, edema, and varicose veins. In terms of neurological function, pycnogenol is reported to protect against strokes, diabetic retinopathy, and symptoms of Parkinson's and Alzheimer's diseases, as well as generally improve mental function and visual acuity.

Pycnogenol does not appear to contain the specific flavonoids that have caused adverse reactions,[31] and safety studies in up to 6 months of regular usage in adults show loose stools as the only reported side effect. The primary concerns with safety are the lack of study in children and the lack of control over specific composition of different preparations. Different preparations of pycnogenol are reported to differ in their bioavailability by as much as four times; thus, dosing recommendations are not uniform. Pycnogenol preparations that also contain ginkgo biloba, beta carotene, vitamin E, zinc, selenium, and other flavonoids also exist. In the United States, GBE and pycnogenol (like DMAE, tryptophan, and vitamin/mineral preparations) are considered dietary supplements rather than medications. As such, they are available over the counter, most commonly in health food stores, and are not monitored by the U.S. Food and Drug Administration.[32] Although these products appear to be safe, their lack of study with children and for ADHD makes their recommendation for this purpose premature.

HOMEOPATHY

Homeopathy is a program of treatment with origins in ancient times. It is based on ideas that are very different from those of modern medicine. According to homeopathy, natural substances from plant, animal, and mineral sources that cause specific profiles or clusters of symptoms in large amounts can inhibit the same symptoms when taken in very small amounts. Because individual substances treat multiple rather than single symptoms, a homeopathic practitioner may treat two individuals who have the same disorder with different substances based on their associated symptoms. Symptoms are reported to show gradual but significant and lasting improvement over long periods of time, unlike the symptom-treating (rather than curative) effects of standard medications for ADHD. Although self-help information is available for parents and some homeopathic substances are available at health food stores, homeopathic practitioners recommend working with an experienced practitioner to determine which treatment should be used first and how much should be given.[33] There are no available published studies of the safety or effectiveness of this approach with ADHD, but reports of its effectiveness are appearing increasingly in the lay press.

ELIMINATION DIETS

The Feingold Diet

The Feingold diet eliminates artificial colors, flavorings, preservatives, and naturally occurring **salicylates.** Benjamin Feingold, M.D. (1900–1982), was an allergist who noted that several of his adult patients with asthma who reacted with respiratory symptoms to tartrazine (yellow dye FD & C #5) and the chemically related salicylates also had improvements in mood and other behavioral/psychiatric symptoms when they adhered to a salicylate-free diet. He extended his work to include children and found that they also showed improvements with the elimination of these substances. In addition to all artificial colors and flavors, the eliminated substances include the preservatives butylated hydroxyanisole (BHA), butylated hydroxytoluene (BHT), and tertiary butylhydroquinone (TBHQ), as well as fruits and vegetables that contain naturally occurring salicylates (see Table 1).

Feingold noted improvements in attention span, impatience and impulsivity, hyperactivity, aggression, risk taking, reading, writing, drawing, coordination, eye disorders such as **strabismus** and **nystagmus,** tics, seizures, enuresis and daytime wetting,

Table 1. Stages of the Feingold diet

Stage 1

Eliminate the following from the diet:

BHT, BHA, and TBHQ

Synthetic (artificial) colors

Synthetic (artificial) flavors

Naturally occurring salicylates:

- Vegetables: cucumbers (also pickles), tomatoes, peppers
- Fruits: apples (also cider and vinegar), apricots, all berries, cherries, currants, grapes, raisins (also wine, wine vinegar), nectarines, oranges, peaches, plums, prunes, tangerines
- Other: coffee, tea, cloves, oil of wintergreen, paprika, almonds, aspirin and related medications

Stage 2

Reintroduce the naturally occurring salicylates (fruits and vegetables) one at a time to assess tolerability.

Note: Additional items that were not eliminated by Dr. Feingold but to which some members report the same types of adverse reactions include monosodium glutamate, sodium nitrite, sodium benzoate, calcium propionate, corn syrup, excess sugars, chocolate, and allergenic foods.

headaches, stomachaches, otitis media, hives, and asthma. His hypothesis, published in the popular book *Why Your Child Is Hyperactive*,[34] was based on extensive clinical observation rather than on scientific research. Noting that the offending substances were not proteins and thus could not be inducing a classical allergic reaction, Feingold proposed that these substances might be either forming complexes with proteins to induce an allergic reaction or, because they are small molecules, crossing the blood–brain barrier and interfering with neurotransmitter function more directly. Over the years, the term food or chemical "sensitivity" has been applied to the as-yet-unexplained mechanism for these reported behavioral reactions.

A number of studies have been conducted to test Feingold's hypothesis. Several different methods have been used, each with advantages and disadvantages. The two main types of studies include exposing subjects to the diet or a placebo diet and putting all subjects on a baseline diet and challenging them with either colors or preservatives or a placebo. These "challenge" studies are not actually tests of the effectiveness of the Feingold diet as they usually test only a single substance.

Initial open studies provided substantial support and generated much enthusiasm; however, subsequent controlled studies have not been as supportive. Because overall results in group studies that compared the effects of a baseline or placebo and the experimental elimination diet have not shown statistically significant results, it often has been concluded that the Feingold diet is not an effective treatment.[35] In most cases, the studies have shown some positive results, but they were not consistent (e.g., improvement has been shown in some cases on parent but not teacher rating scales, the results were confounded by order effects).[36] Nonetheless, in almost all of the studies, a minority (approximately 10%) of children had consistently positive effects[37]; in one study, all 10 of the preschool-age children who were included in the study of 46 children had a positive response to the diet.[38] (The details of several of the early studies are reviewed in Conners, 1989a.)

Studies using a baseline elimination diet and studying children's responses to a challenge with blinded placebo controls also showed mixed results. In children who had been on the Feingold diet for 1 month and whose parents believed them to be responders, Conners (1989c) found a brief deterioration in functioning on parent ratings and a tracking task after challenge with a cookie that contained artificial colors in a concentration that was believed to reflect the 90th percentile of children's daily intake, but not after a placebo cookie. Attempts to replicate the results with a less selective group did not show the same results. Williams, Cram, Tausig, and Webster (1978) used a similar protocol with a lower concentration of artificial coloring and also included a comparison with medication. Depending on the criteria used, between 10% and 35% of the children were diet responders, although medication was consistently more effective. Rowe and Rowe (1994) used a baseline diet that was free of colorings only and found a dose response curve with increasing irritability, restlessness, and sleep disturbance in approximately 50% of participants in response to a challenge with the yellow dye tartrazine, but not the placebo.

The book *Why Can't My Child Behave?*[39] provides a current overview from the Feingold Association, a national organization primarily of parents with some professional support with the mission of assisting families who want to try this approach. An important item provided to members is a comprehensive list of prepared/brand items that have been researched and found not to contain artificial preservatives, colors, flavors, or other "hidden" unacceptable ingredients. Food labeling practices make it impossible for even the most educated shopper to discern the presence of preservatives, in particular, in prepared items; thus, an adequate trial of this diet without a Feingold Association guide generally is not feasible. When starting the diet, it is recommended to continue for several weeks before expecting to see an effect, although some families have noted improvements in only a couple of days. After a positive response is seen, it is possible for some children to resume eating some or all of the salicylate-containing foods (see Table 1). In some cases, other disabilities including Tourette syndrome and autism have been reported to respond to the diet.

It is not easy to adhere to the Feingold diet; it requires a significant commitment of time and motivation as well as some investigative skill on the part of parents. It limits a family's ability to eat in restaurants and prevents a child from eating the same things as his or her peers at social gatherings. It is not necessarily nutritionally inadequate, which is a common criticism. When one undertakes any type of elimination diet, there is a risk for nutritional deficiency, especially when the child eats a limited variety of foods or is unwilling to try new foods that can be substituted for those eliminated.

Although overall evidence does not support dramatic effectiveness of the Feingold diet for large numbers of the children studied, careful review of the original research suggests that 1) some studies contained design flaws that may have contributed to negative results; 2) moodiness, irritability, sleep problems, and perseveration may be important target symptoms that generally were not assessed; and 3) a small proportion of children were clear responders. Because there are many similarities between the Feingold diet and the food allergy elimination diet (discussed next), consideration of how the clinician should counsel parents regarding elimination diets follows the next section.

Food Allergies

The role of food allergies in behavior dysfunction has been under discussion for several decades. The "allergic-tension fatigue syndrome" was characterized by fatigue, listlessness, nasal congestion, dark circles under the eyes, and mental/emotional symptoms; and one of the most common culprits was believed to be milk. The mental/emotional symptoms included irritability; restlessness; anxiety; poor concentration; tearfulness; compulsiveness; oppositionality; and, sometimes, psychotic features.[40] In 1991, Dr. Doris Rapp, a pediatrician and classically trained allergist, wrote *Is This Your Child? Discovering and Treating Unrecognized Allergies in Children and Adults* to describe her clinical experiences in the assessment and treatment of children's allergies and their relationship to a variety of behavior and medical disorders. She hypothesized that some food allergies are caused by a different immunological mechanism than the type 1, histamine-mediated reactions that typically cause dermatological, mucous membrane, and respiratory symptoms and that this immune response can trigger a variety of behavioral and medical symptoms. She used a testing method that involved placing extracts of the allergen under the tongue and measuring physical and behavior responses. The most common foods to trigger adverse behavior responses were, for the most part, the same ones that cause most "classic" food allergies, including milk, wheat, corn, eggs, soy, and peanuts but also chocolate, cane sugar, and food additives. There would be no argument among allergists about the first part of the hypothesis (for reviews of current thinking about several aspects of food allergy, see Ferguson, 1992, and Sampson, 1997). Gastrointestinal allergic symptoms may be caused by foods that do not lead to wheezing, hives, and so forth in the same individual, and standard allergy testing may not detect a gastrointestinal allergen. The controversy arises in the number of children for whom this is pertinent, the nature of the relationship between the immune response and behavior, and the method that Dr. Rapp used to test for allergies. Like Dr. Feingold, she reported that children can have either immediate or delayed (up to 3 days) reactions that can take up to 3 days to resolve. Finally, she reported that children seem to develop cravings for the foods for which they test positive, creating a cycle of more selective eating and more severe behavior and health problems.

Many studies over the years have identified a relationship between ADHD-related symptoms and colic, allergies, asthma, congestion, and recurrent infections, especially otitis media. "Choosy" eating (eating a limited number of foods) has been reported to be associated with externalizing behavior disorders.[41] In a study of the relationship between allergies and behavior, gastrointestinal allergies were more highly associated with behavioral symptoms than allergies were with respiratory symptoms.[42] Tryphonas and Trites (1979) used an accepted allergy testing method (the **RAST test**) and found high rates (40%–77%) of food allergies among children with hyperactivity, learning disabilities, or emotional disorders. There was a direct relationship between parent ratings of hyperactivity and number of allergies. These reports indicate that studies that are designed to assess the nature of this relationship are warranted.

Several placebo-controlled studies have suggested that elimination of a combination of allergenic foods and colors/preservatives may be helpful for some children. Egger, Carter, Graham, Gumley, and Soothill (1985) placed 76 unmedicated hyperactive children on an "oligoantigenic diet" for 4 weeks, which included only two foods from each food group and vitamin/mineral supplements. Sixty-two were believed to improve in the open phase based on parental reports on the short form Conners rating scale.[43] Twenty-eight of these underwent a confirmatory reintroduction phase followed by a placebo-controlled challenge phase. Although most of the results did not reach statistical significance, 9 of the 11 outcome measurements were better during placebo than active challenge phases. The most common reactive items were tartrazine, benzoate (the only color and preservative, respectively, assessed), soy, cow milk, chocolate, grapes, wheat, oranges, eggs, peanuts, and corn. Very few children reacted to only one food. The presence of physical symptoms such as headaches, stomachaches, and seizures also improved during the elimination phase and worsened during the challenge period when the suspected food was eaten every day for 1 week.

Kaplan, McNicol, Conte, and Moghadam (1989) provided all food for the families of 24 unmedicated hyperactive preschool boys for 10 weeks. The study was divided into a 3-week baseline, 3-week placebo diet, and 4-week elimination diet with data used from only the last 2 weeks of each period. The experimental diet eliminated colors, flavors, preservatives, chocolate, monosodium glutamate, caffeine, and any other substance that a family thought suspect (e.g., 15 eliminated cow milk) and included a color- and additive-free vitamin, calcium supplements if milk was eliminated, and a decrease in simple sugars compared with baseline. More than half of the sample reported a significant (25%) improvement in behavior, including sleep, rated by parents and child care providers that could not be explained by placebo or order effects. Boris and Mandel (1994) also found that a substantial percentage of children with ADHD responded to a diet in which colors, preservatives, and allergenic foods were eliminated. After a 2-week open trial of a diet that was free of dairy products, wheat, corn, yeast, soy, citrus, egg, chocolate, peanuts, artificial colors, and preservatives, 19 responders (73%) underwent a 4-week double-blind, placebo-controlled challenge in which one challenge item or its placebo was added to the diet daily for 1 week. Complete data on 16 subjects indicated a significant difference between Conners parent rating scale[44] scores on challenge days versus placebo days. Scores also were higher during the original diet than on the one-item challenge days. Finally, there was no difference in scores between the baseline elimination diet and the placebo challenge days.

Taken together, studies examining Feingold's hypothesis and the role of allergenic foods indicate that a small but significant proportion of children with ADHD, especially preschool-age children, and those with sleep disturbance or classic allergy symptoms may show some behavior improvement while on diets that eliminate colors and preservatives and/or selected commonly allergenic foods. Most children are reported to react to multiple foods/additives, but the colors/preservatives consistently are the most common offenders. Preschool-age children, particularly those who have allergic symptoms, have sleep or additional problems, and eat an adequate variety of foods, may be suitable candidates for a trial of an elimination diet because they may be more responsive and because their parents retain more control over their diets.

Available are books that guide parents in undertaking a trial of an elimination diet for allergenic substances.[45] Clinicians may assist parents with devising a home and school monitoring system to measure effectiveness, just as one might do during a medication trial, to assess effects as objectively as possible. In addition, if deemed effective, strategies to minimize impact on the child of having a different or restricted diet will be needed. Many support groups for families coping with diet modifications (e.g., those related to allergy, celiac disease, and diabetes mellitus; the Feingold Association) can provide guidance in this area. In addition, just as with medication, the clinician should help families devise a plan for the periodic reassessment of effectiveness. Nutritional counseling will be needed for families who eliminate a wide variety of foods or for children who are selective eaters and do not have a wide variety of substitutes. Any child who does not drink milk requires calcium supplementation because most daily vitamin/mineral supplements do not contain a sufficient amount. Finally, because a positive response does not necessarily mean a complete response, the clinician may need to assist families with combining traditional and nontraditional interventions.

SUGAR AND OTHER SWEETENERS

Parents often report that their child becomes "hyper" after ingesting sugar. Both the sugar load itself and the resultant reactive hypoglycemia have been hypothesized to cause undesirable behaviors. Three types of studies have been used to examine the effects of sugar on behavior. In one type, the amount of sugar in the diet is correlated with behavior. In the second type, a diet that is low or high in sugar is maintained for a period of time and behavior is compared across diets. In the third type, sugar or another sweetener is used as a challenge during a baseline diet. The advantage of the first approach is that it is naturalistic, but it can identify only an association and cannot be used to draw conclusions about causation. The advantage of the second type is that it is naturalistic and, depending on the control of other relevant variables, may allow conclusions about causation. The advantage of the third approach is that, assuming that the study is otherwise methodologically sound, it can detect a causative role in any subsequent behavior change. The disadvantage is that children usually do not eat in the form of single large challenges; a specific baseline diet must be selected, which may be quite different from the child's normal diet, and the appropriate dosage for the challenge is empirically selected. In addition, the placebo for comparative and challenge studies often is an artificial sweetener that also has been hypothesized to alter behavior in some children. Some studies have examined the effects of sugar in children with ADHD, whereas others have examined behaviors that are characteristic of ADHD in children without behavioral diagnoses. Most often, attention, hyperactivity, and aggression, using a variety of different measures, have been studied.

Correlative studies showed that children with high sugar intake had poorer attention, had more psychiatric disorders, and were more aggressive. In adults, high sugar intake and abnormal glucose tolerance tests correlated with juvenile delinquency and antisocial behaviors.[46] Subsequent challenge studies showed mixed results but, overall, did not support a causative role for sugar in ADHD. Wolraich, Wilson, and White (1995) performed a meta-analysis of 23 double-blind, placebo-controlled studies of the effects of sugar on behavior in children and found no overall effects on behavior or cognition; however, this type of study would not allow for the detection of small effects on a subset of children.

Some studies have suggested, however, that sugar may have more complex effects on behavior than those mediated only by the degree of rise and fall in blood sugar. For example, studies of younger children are more likely to show an effect; the type of sugar and placebo may play a role, and the outcome measure used (e.g., teacher observation, parent observation, laboratory measure of attention) may make a difference in the results.[47] Conners (1993) and colleagues also found that what was consumed with the sugar had an important effect on subsequent behavior. A protein-containing meal plus a sugar challenge resulted in improved attention and behavior, but a carbohydrate meal plus sugar challenge resulted in a deterioration in behavior. Wender and Solanto (1991) found a similar result with respect to the deterioration in behavior when a sugar challenge was accompanied by carbohydrate.

Some studies of children with ADHD have revealed altered neuroendocrine responses to a sugar challenge. Hyperactive children failed to show the normal suppression of cortisol and growth hormone in response to the sugar challenge.[48] The hyperactive group had higher glucose levels than controls both pre- and postchallenge. Girardi et al. (1995) compared children with and without ADHD on several behavioral, metabolic, and neuroendocrine measures following an oral glucose tolerance test. Unlike Conners's study, they found similar glucose and growth hormone levels in the two groups but found that the epinephrine rise that was stimulated by the fall in glucose after its initial rise was only half as great in the group with ADHD compared with the control group. Additional clarification of neuroendocrine differences between children with and without ADHD clearly is needed. Then, the relationship of these differences to the behavioral effects of sugar can be evaluated further.

There are several reports of altered behavior in response to sugar substitutes, particularly aspartame. Aspartame is a sugar substitute in the form of a protein that is digested into its component amino acids L-aspartic acid and L-phenylalanine. L-Aspartic acid is a form of aspartate, an excitatory amino acid neurotransmitter that may contribute to excitotoxic brain damage during ischemia and other forms of metabolic derangement. Using an amount of aspartame estimated to be at the 99th percentile of daily consumption as a loading dose, infants and adults, as well as individuals with **phenylketonuria,** have been found to metabolize aspartame similarly and to have only modest rises in plasma phenylalanine levels, which still are within the normal range. Because of placental concentrating ability, excessive use of aspartame should be discouraged during pregnancy. Those with phenylketonuria must limit their total phenylalanine intake but do not appear to be at any greater risk from aspartame than any other source of phenylalanine.[49]

Several studies have looked for behavioral toxicity of aspartame in children, each using a slightly different methodology. Among the studies that are reasonably methodologically sound (in that they include a placebo control and multiple outcome measures), none found consistent or significant results,[50] although some found elevations in activity level as one of several outcome measures.[51] In the studies by Shaywitz et al. (1994) and Wolraich et al. (1994), concomitant biochemical measures provide reassurance that levels of potentially detrimental metabolic products of artificial sweeteners were not elevated and did not alter plasma levels of the neurochemical markers studied. A recent study suggests that adults who are diagnosed with depression ($n = 8$) may experience more neurobehavioral side effects from aspartame than nonpsychiatric controls ($n = 5$). Two of the eight experimental subjects also experienced eye pain/complications. The side effects were sufficiently prominent that the institutional review board elected to discontinue the study prior to enrollment of the anticipated number of subjects. They did not appear to relate to whether the subjects were taking antidepressants, but the number of subjects involved was too small to draw firm conclusions about this.[52]

Further research regarding the neuroendocrine responses of individuals with ADHD to sugar will be of interest, and further research is needed to determine whether children with ADHD eat differently than controls and, if so, why and how it is related to symptoms. The possible role of nutrition in the functional *severity* of symptoms in individuals with ADHD has not been studied. Some of the studies described throughout the earlier parts of this chapter also suggest that a study of the effects on ADHD symptoms of a diet that is higher in protein and lower in sugar would be of interest. In support of this approach, Conners (1989b) showed that children concentrate much better following a breakfast consisting of carbohydrate plus protein than one of carbohydrate alone. The role of coexisting disorders in the individual's response to foods/additives also warrants further research as suggested by the preliminary study by Walton et al. (1993).

From the clinician's point of view, there is no evidence to indicate that there is unique advice for parents of children with ADHD regarding dietary sugar. A diet that is high in simple sugars and products that are artificially sweetened can be discouraged for all children for a multitude of reasons. When parents express the concern that their child has extreme negative behavioral reactions to sugar, the clinician may want to consider working with the parents to

1. Improve the entire family's diet by substituting complex carbohydrates and fruits for overly frequent highly sweetened desserts and snacks
2. Assess the role of the environmental contributions to the observed behavior
3. Consider what is ingested with the sugar that may contribute to the observed reaction (e.g., colors, preservatives, caffeine)
4. Determine whether ingesting protein before or with the sugar is helpful and, if so, then smaller, more frequent meals and snacks containing a combination of protein and carbohydrate may be useful

YEAST IN BEHAVIOR AND HEALTH PROBLEMS

A sensitivity to yeast (*candida albicans*) has been hypothesized to cause a wide range of physical and mental symptoms in adults and children, including (but not limited to) fatigue/irritability, digestive disorders, muscle pain, menstrual disorders, allergic symptoms, hypoglycemia, depression, hyperactivity, and problems with attention span and learning. It has been proposed that yeast overgrowth in the gastrointestinal and genitourinary tracts, occurring as a result of multiple contributing factors including antibiotic use, a diet high in carbohydrates and sugar, and/or the chronic use of corticosteroids or birth control pills, leads to two conditions that result in symptoms. First, it disrupts the lining of the gastrointestinal tract, allowing proteins that are not fully digested to be absorbed, thereby increasing the likelihood of the development of food allergies. Second, it results in circulating toxins that suppress immune system function, creating a vicious cycle of increased susceptibility to infection and other noxious agents. This hypothesis was first proposed by Dr. C. Orion Truss in the 1970s and has been written about most widely by Dr. William G. Crook, a pediatrician, allergist, and specialist in environmental medicine. There are anecdotal reports of success with this approach.

There are no reliable methods for the laboratory assessment of yeast overgrowth; thus, the diagnosis is based on clinical history. Some laboratories report that they can detect yeast metabolic products by chromatography of the serum, but much work must be done before valid methods for distinguishing the effects of normal yeast colonization from those that are related to yeast overgrowth can be established.

Treatment is based on restoring conditions that are conducive to a normal balance of bowel flora (low carbohydrate/sugar diet and vitamin, garlic, and "good" bacteria supplements), reducing yeast growth (low sugar diet, no yeast/mold-containing foods, antifungal medication such as nystatin), and eliminating other irritants to the immune system (allergenic foods, dyes, preservatives, chemical exposures, antibiotics to the degree possible, other medications). The dietary and exposure modifications must be considered permanent lifestyle changes, whereas the use of nystatin, although prolonged, may not need to be indefinite. The assessment and treatment are thoroughly described in Crook (1986).

Although some of the basic tenets of this approach are well documented (antibiotics that lead to yeast overgrowth and yeast infections that influence subsequent immune system function), there are no peer-reviewed studies of this approach to assessment or treatment of ADHD symptoms. Systematic research in adults with this proposed disorder is needed before this treatment approach can be recommended for children, even on an experimental basis. The chronic use of nystatin can cause mild side effects such as diarrhea, and it is reported that some individuals can experience malaise and a worsening of symptoms at the beginning of treatment secondary to the rapid dying off of large numbers of yeast with an increase in the release of toxins.

EEG BIOFEEDBACK

EEG biofeedback training has attracted widespread attention as a treatment approach for ADHD. Different brain wave patterns with characteristic EEG appearances are associated with alertness/attention and drowsy/daydreaming mental states, respectively. If given feedback about the brain wave pattern that is being generated, an individual can "learn" to increase the amount of time in the desired state. During EEG monitoring, the brain wave activity patterns are transformed by a computer program into different signals in either a visual or an auditory form so that the subject knows whether he or she is producing the desired brain wave pattern. Children can be "trained," using positive feedback, to generate the "good" (beta) brain waves for longer periods of time.[53] This treatment was developed in the 1970s by Dr. Joel Lubar, a professor of psychology.[54] While working with another investigator on the use of this technique in children with seizures, he noted that behavior as well as seizures often improved.

A few studies of this treatment for children with ADHD report improvements on parent and teacher behavior rating scales and tests of IQ and achievement; however, small numbers of children have been studied, and there are no control groups or controls for placebo effects.[55] Biofeedback has been used to treat a variety of disorders, and there certainly is some rationale to investigate its use in ADHD; however, it seems premature to accept it as an effective treatment. It is a time-consuming and expensive treatment. Training sessions require about 40 minutes, two or three times per week for up to several months.[56] No specific adverse effects have been reported, and no children have been reported to show declining test scores after treatment.[57] Further research is required to determine which, if any, subgroups of children or adolescents with ADHD respond to this treatment. EEG biofeedback training is carried out in combination with counseling; tutoring; and, sometimes, medication; thus, its specific role in clinical improvement is not clear. The combined treatment package has been reported to produce persistent positive effects after the discontinuation of treatment, but scientific documentation of this is necessary.

VESTIBULAR DYSFUNCTION

Vestibular dysfunction was first proposed as a cause of learning disabilities (particularly in reading and writing) in the 1970s. Dr. Harold Levinson was working as a psychiatrist and neurologist in the New York City public schools and incorporated previous work about the role of the **vestibular-cerebellar system** in eye movement control with his observations that many of the children with learning disabilities whom he was called upon to evaluate had problems with eye movements, spatial orientation, coordination, and balance. In an initial paper, Frank and Levinson (1973) proposed a subtype of dyslexia (affecting approximately 2% of first graders) called dysmetric dyslexia whereby children demonstrate signs of cerebellar dysfunction on examination including dysmetric ocular pursuit, have subclinical nystagmus detected by electronystagmography, and show asymmetric vestibular function. Unfortunately, the actual examination methods and findings are barely described, so it is impossible to determine whether the results justify the conclusions. A subsequent series of studies led to a more detailed theory[58]:

1. Children with dysmetric dyslexia have a primary cerebellar-vestibular disorder that leads to nystagmus (not always clinically detectable) and ocular dysmetria.
2. This results in a dysfunction in directional control of eye movements, ocular fixation, and sequential scanning.
3. This results in skipping, reversing, and scrambling of letters, words, and sentences and symptoms during reading, including blurred or double vision, photophobia, **oscillopsia,** vertigo, nausea, fatigue, and headache.
4. The visual problem, because it is present during development, leads to a secondary central processing deficit for memory or conceptual function if adequate compensation does not occur.

There are methodological strengths and weaknesses in these studies, and attempts by a small number of other researchers to find vestibular dysfunction in children with learning disabilities have resulted in virtually equal numbers in either camp. Two additional authors report signs of vestibular dysfunction in children with learning disabilities (LD),[59] but the author of a more scientifically rigorous study[60] reported their absence. In addition, this author compared academic performance in children with and without vestibular signs and found no correlation. There continues to be discussion as to the appropriate specific procedures for eliciting vestibular-related ocular motor abnormalities.[61]

Subsequently, Levinson reported that children with ADHD often have similar findings to those with learning disabilities[62] and even that phobias and other anxiety disorders can result from cerebellar-vestibular dysfunction.[63] Based on the belief that vestibular-cerebellar dysfunction underlies LD/ADHD in a substantial subpopulation, combinations of anti–motion sickness medications such as meclizine (Antivert) and antihistamines have been recommended to "stabilize" the vestibular system. They are used in combination with the more commonly used psychostimulants; thus, the role of the former is unclear. There has been little systematic study of efficacy and no study of potential negative effects of these medication combinations.

The lack of several pieces of information render this theory and its treatment approach experimental. First, the presence of vestibular-related ocular-motor abnormalities remains controversial. Second, if present, then their role in the causation of ADHD symptoms is unknown but doubtful based on available information on the neurobiological correlates of ADHD. Third, the effects of meclizine alone on ADHD symptoms has not been reported. Fourth, the combination of meclizine and standard medications has not been shown to be more effective than standard medications alone.

VISION THERAPY

Vision therapy sometimes is recommended for children with reading difficulties. Because reading difficulties commonly are associated with ADHD, vision therapy often is recommended for children with both reading difficulties and ADHD. Most of the studies of vision therapy are found in the optometry literature; technical terminology that may not be familiar to the primary clinician is used commonly. Vision therapy encompasses many different specific treatments. In addition, subject selection criteria, assessment procedures, and treatment modalities differ from center to center. These factors make it particularly difficult to draw conclusions from this literature and for clinicians to provide guidance to families about this type of treatment.

Using its broadest definition, *vision therapy* refers to treatment for a range of problems in three areas: visual acuity (eye health, eye development, and refractive status); visual skill efficiency including oculomotor (tracking), accommodative (focusing), and binocular (eye coordination) functions; and visual-perceptual–motor skills (recognition, discrimination, organization, and interpretation of visual input). Therapy is targeted to correct problems in the preceding order. A focus on the efficiency of binocular function rather than on purely structure or acuity is characteristic of the vision therapy approach. *Orthoptics* is one aspect of vision therapy, which refers to the use of devices such as lenses and prisms. *Visual training* refers to programs of exercises and activities to address visual skill and visual-perceptual–motor deficiencies.[64] Sometimes when the term "vision therapy" is used, the author is referring to the "visual training" component. The key questions are 1) can visual training improve visual function in the areas found to be deficient, and 2) does improved visual function lead to improved reading?

Many studies have provided support for the idea that students with various types of academic problems have a higher incidence of visual abnormalities compared with controls.[65] These abnormalities include control of ocular movement; near- and farsightedness; deficits in convergence, accommodation, and binocular fusion; and deficits in systematic search strategies and visual-perceptual skills.[66] The frequency of visual abnormalities in children with learning disorders has been reported to range from 20% to 90%, or from approximately 2 to 10 times the incidence in control populations.[67] Studies using functional magnetic resonance imaging indicate that individuals with dyslexia have abnormalities of rapid visual processing involving cortical–subcortical pathways.[68]

The views among ophthalmology and optometry professionals range from one end of the spectrum (visual skill deficits cause reading disorders) to the middle ground (visual skill deficits may cause unpleasant symptoms during reading) to the opposite end of the spectrum (reading disorders are caused primarily by altered phonological awareness at the cortical level,[69] and disorders of the eyes have little bearing on this condition). In fact, it is known that overly difficult reading material can cause abnormal eye movement patterns in normal readers, suggesting that, to some degree, the abnormalities of oculomotor functioning in children with reading disorders may be a result, rather than a cause, of their reading difficulty.[70]

The American Academies of Ophthalmology and Pediatrics and the American Association of Pediatric Ophthalmology and Strabismus issued policy statements in 1984 indicating that there was no clear evidence supporting a role for vision therapy in the remediation of learning disabilities. Many studies have addressed the effectiveness of vision therapy, and approximately equal numbers have found positive and negative results. This suggests that some important factors are not being taken into account in the experimental design that may relate to the matching of carefully selected subjects to specific treatments. In general, the effectiveness of vision therapy in improving visual perception and reading ability is not well documented[71]; however, there is some support for vision therapy effects on binocular visual efficiency and the symptoms that the lack of good binocular function can cause. Therefore, vision therapy may be helpful for a subgroup of children with fatigue, headaches, blurring, and complaints of "words jumping around" and skipping lines.[72] Even within this group, more information about predictors of successful or unsuccessful outcome (e.g., age, cognitive and attention skill prerequisites, specific visual abnormalities) would be helpful.

One orthoptic approach, the use of Irlen, or colored lenses, has been advocated for individuals with learning disabilities. Based on her clinical experience, Dr. Irlen described "scotopic sensitivity syndrome" whereby several aspects of color detection including light source, luminosity, wavelength, and contrast impair perception. She believed that scotopic sensitivity syndrome was common among individuals with dyslexia. Although there are case reports that this approach improves uncomfortable symptoms during reading when used in combination with other vision therapy approaches,[73] the scientific basis for this approach and its effectiveness are questionable.[74]

Families should be advised that it still is not clear who will benefit from vision therapy and that there is little standardization from program to program. It may be a useful adjunctive therapy for some children with the symptoms described previously. They should be wary of programs that present this approach as more than a treatment for the relief of symptoms that may add to reading difficulties. Some programs, recognizing that remediation of reading problems is a multidisciplinary undertaking, may offer additional services such as psychoeducational evaluation, tutoring, and even nutritional counseling. Parents should understand what they are paying for, what the length of treatment is expected to be, which components will be practiced at home and which will be done in the office, how effectiveness will be evaluated, and what the likely outcome will be. When additional services are offered, the need for those services in that setting and the qualifications of the individuals who are providing them should be ascertained with advice from the child's physician and school personnel.

CONCLUSION

A variety of nonstandard therapies for ADHD have been developed since the early 1970s. Some, such as the elimination diets, have been shown in methodologically sound studies to be effective for some children, but it is not clear in advance who those children are. Other approaches have not been subject to sufficient studies of effectiveness, and long-term safety issues are a concern in several. As with standard treatments, it is difficult to study the effectiveness of a single treatment that may be helpful when used in combination with others. The fact that the National Institutes of Health considered it important to fund a 5-year, multicenter study of the effectiveness of the more standard treatments for ADHD[75] highlights the complexity of ADHD and its treatment and how much still must be learned.

Clinicians have an important role to play when families consider alternative therapies. First, for all children, clinicians can provide anticipatory guidance about optimum nutrition and support referral to a nutritionist when families need assistance with providing an adequate diet. Some behavior specialists also have expertise in this area and may be helpful when the acceptance rather than the provision of a healthy diet is an issue. Clinicians can assist families with considering the pros and cons of alternative treatments, especially safety factors and issues (e.g., financial) that might have an impact on families' ability to provide additional important treatments. Finally, when a family chooses to pursue an alternative therapy, rather than withdraw from involvement, the clinician should play an important role in assisting the family to assess its effectiveness in much the same way as one would during pharmacological treatment. Information should be collected from multiple sources including parents; teachers; and, whenever possible, objective performance measures. The clinician has an important role in helping families avoid falling prey to misinformation about standard approaches provided by some proponents of alternative therapies. Clearly, there is no "magic" answer for ADHD, among the traditional or nontraditional approaches.

ENDNOTES

1. Harrell, Capp, Davis, Peerless, & Ravitz (1981).
2. Colgan & Colgan (1984).
3. Arnold, Christopher, Huestis, & Smeltzer (1978), Brenner (1982), Haslam, Dalby, & Rade-maker (1984), Kershner & Hawke (1979).
4. Brenner (1982), Kershner & Hawke (1979).
5. Haslam et al. (1984)
6. Kershner & Hawke (1979).
7. Ingersoll & Goldstein (1993a).
8. Liskov, Kerstetter, Baltimore, & Carpenter (1997).
9. Bekaroğlu et. al (1996), Toren et al. (1996).
10. Arnold, Votolano, Kleykamp, Baker, & Bornstein (1990).
11. Sandstead (1986), Golub et al. (1994).
12. Ballin et al. (1992), Bruner, Joffe, Duggan, Casella, & Brandt (1996), Pollitt, Saco-Pollitt, Leibel, & Viteri (1986).
13. Reviewed in Brown & Smith (1995), Linscheer & Vergroesen (1994).
14. Stevens et al. (1995).
15. Bekaroğlu et al. (1996), Mitchell, Aman, Turbott, & Manku (1987), Stevens et al. (1995).
16. Stevens et al. (1995).
17. Stevens, Zentall, Abate, Kuczek, & Burgess (1996).
18. Stevens et al. (1995).
19. Linscheer & Vergroesen (1994).
20. Aman, Mitchell, & Turbott (1987), Arnold et al. (1989).
21. Nemzer, Arnold, Votolano, & McConnell (1986).
22. Wood, Reimherr, & Wender (1985), Zametkin, Karoum, & Rapoport (1987).
23. Nemzer et al. (1986).
24. Muir (1997).
25. Reviewed in McCaleb (1992), Murray (1995).
26. Reviewed in McCaleb (1992).
27. Castleman (1991), McCaleb (1992).
28. McCaleb (1992).
29. Castleman (1991).
30. Becker & Skipworth (1975), Murray (1995).
31. Middleton (1988).
32. McCaleb (1992), Murray (1995).
33. Reichenberg-Ullman & Ullman (1996).
34. Feingold (1974).
35. National Institutes of Health (1982).
36. Conners (1989c), Conners, Goyette, Southwick, Lees, & Andrulonis (1976), Harley et al. (1978).
37. Conners (1989c).
38. Harley et al. (1978).
39. Hersey (1996).
40. Crook, Harrison, Crawford, & Emerson (1961).
41. Rydell & Sundeln (1995).
42. McLoughlin et al. (1983).
43. Goyette, Conners, & Ulrich (1978).
44. Ibid.
45. McNicol (1992), Rapp (1991).
46. Reviewed in Conners (1989d, 1993).
47. Conners (1989d).
48. Conners (1993).
49. Reviewed in Council Report (1985).
50. Kruesi et al. (1987), Saravis, Schachar, Zlotkin, Leiter, & Anderson (1990), Shaywitz et al. (1994), Wolraich et al. (1994).
51. Saravis et al. (1990), Shaywitz et al. (1994).
52. Walton, Hudak, & Green-White (1993).
53. Lubar (1991).
54. Reviewed in Lubar (1989, 1991).

55. Lubar (1991), Lubar & Lubar (1984).
56. Ingersoll & Goldstein (1993b).
57. Lubar (1991).
58. Levinson (1989a).
59. Reviewed in Silver (1991).
60. Polatajko (1985).
61. Levinson (1990).
62. Ibid.
63. Levinson (1989b, 1989c).
64. Reviewed in Hoffman & Rouse (1987), Keogh & Pelland (1985).
65. Hoffman & Rouse (1987), Keogh & Pelland (1985), Lennerstrand & Ygge (1992).
66. Ygge, Lennerstrand, Axelsson, & Rydberg (1993).
67. Keogh & Pelland (1985).
68. Eden et al. (1996), Lennerstrand & Ygge (1991).
69. Reviewed in Church, Lewis, & Batshaw (1997).
70. Keogh & Pelland (1985), Lennerstrand & Ygge (1992).
71. Keogh & Pelland (1985).
72. Atzmon, Nemet, Ishay, & Karni (1993), Duckman (1987), Hoffman & Rouse (1987), Keogh & Pelland (1985).
73. Lightstone & Evans (1995).
74. Menacker, Breton, Breton, Radcliffe, & Gole (1993).
75. Hinshaw et al. (1997).

REFERENCES

Aman, M.G., Mitchell, E.A., & Turbott, S.H. (1987). The effects of essential fatty acid supplementation by Efamol in hyperactive children. *Journal of Abnormal Child Psychology, 15,* 75–90.

Arnold, L.E., Christopher, J., Huestis, R.D., & Smeltzer, D.J. (1978). Megavitamins for minimal brain dysfunction. *Journal of the American Medical Association, 240,* 2642–2643.

Arnold, L.E., Kleykamp, D., Votolano, N.A., Taylor, W.A., Kontras, S.B., & Tobin, K. (1989). Gamma-linoleic acid for attention-deficit hyperactivity disorder: Placebo-controlled comparison to D-amphetamine. *Biological Psychiatry, 25,* 222–228.

Arnold, L.E., Votolano, N.A., Kleykamp, D., Baker, G.B., & Bornstein, R.A. (1990). Does hair zinc predict amphetamine improvement of ADD/hyperactivity? *International Journal of Neuroscience, 50,* 103–107.

Atzmon, D., Nemet, P., Ishay, A., & Karni, E. (1993). A randomized prospective masked and matched comparative study of orthoptic treatment versus conventional reading tutoring treatment for reading disabilities in 62 children. *Binocular Vision & Eye Muscle Surgery Quarterly, 8,* 91–106.

Ballin, A., Berar, M., Rubinstein, U., Kleter, Y., Herschkovitz, A., & Meytes, D. (1992). Iron state in female adolescents. *American Journal of Diseases in Children, 146,* 803–805.

Becker, L.E., & Skipworth, G.B. (1975). Ginkgo-tree dermatitis, stomatitis, and proctitis. *Journal of the American Medical Association, 231,* 1162–1163.

Bekaroğlu, M., Aslan, Y., Gedik, Y., Deger, O., Mocan, H., Erduran, E., & Karahan, C. (1996). Relationships between serum free fatty acids and zinc, and attention deficit hyperactivity disorder: A research note. *Journal of Child Psychology and Psychiatry, 37,* 225–227.

Boris, M., & Mandel, F.S. (1994). Foods and additives are common causes of the attention deficit hyperactive disorder in children. *Annals of Allergy, 72,* 462–468.

Brenner, A. (1982). The effect of megadoses of selected B-complex vitamins on children with hyperkinesis: Controlled studies with long-term follow-up. *Journal of Learning Disabilities, 15,* 258–264.

Brown, W.V., & Smith, D.A. (1995). Fats and cholesterol. In V. Herbert & G. Subak-Sharpe (Eds.), *Total nutrition* (pp. 63–93). New York: St. Martin's Press.

Bruner, A.B., Joffe, A., Duggan, A.K., Casella, J.F., & Brandt, J. (1996). Randomized study of cognitive effects of iron supplementation in non-anemic iron-deficient adolescent girls. *The Lancet, 348,* 992–996.

Castleman, M. (1991). Ginkgo: What's old is new. In *The healing herbs: The ultimate guide to the curative power of nature's medicines* (pp. 190–192). Emmaus, PA: Rodale Press.

Church, R.P., Lewis, M.E.B., & Batshaw, M.L. (1997). Learning disabilities. In M.L. Batshaw (Ed.), *Children with disabilities* (4th ed., pp. 471–497). Baltimore: Paul H. Brookes Publishing Co.

Colgan, M., & Colgan, L. (1984). Do nutrient supplements and dietary changes affect learning and emotional reactions to children with learning difficulties? A controlled series of 16 cases. *Nutrition and Health, 3,* 69–77.

Colquhoun, I., & Bunday, S. (1981). A lack of essential fatty acids as a possible cause of hyperactivity in children. *Medical Hypotheses, 7,* 673–679.

Conners, C.K. (1989a). *Feeding the brain: How foods affect children.* New York: Plenum.

Conners, C.K. (1989b). The first meal of the day. In *Feeding the brain: How foods affect children* (pp. 55–73). New York: Plenum.

Conners, C.K. (1989c). Food additives and food allergies. In *Feeding the brain: How foods affect children* (pp. 157–185). New York: Plenum.

Conners, C.K. (1989d). Sugar and its effects on behavior and mood. In *Feeding the brain: How foods affect children* (pp. 75–100). New York: Plenum.

Conners, C.K. (1993). Nootropics and foods. In J.S. Werry & M.G. Aman (Eds.), *Practitioner's guide to psychoactive drugs for children and adolescents* (pp. 373–389). New York: Plenum.

Conners, C.K., Goyette, C.H., Southwick, D.A., Lees, J.M., & Andrulonis, P.A. (1976). Food additives and hyperkinesis: A controlled double-blind experiment. *Pediatrics, 58,* 154–166.

Council Report. (1985). Aspartame: Review of safety issues. *Journal of the American Medical Association, 254,* 400–402.

Crook, W.G. (1986). *The yeast connection: A medical breakthrough.* New York: Random House.

Crook, W.G., Harrison, W.W., Crawford, S.E., & Emerson, B.S. (1961). Systemic manifestations due to allergy: Report of fifty patients and a review of the literature on the subject (sometimes referred to as allergic toxemia and the allergic tension-fatigue syndrome). *Pediatrics, 27,* 790–799.

Duckman, R.H. (1987). Management of binocular abnormalities: Efficiency of vision therapy, exotropia. *American Journal of Optometry & Physiological Optics, 64,* 421–429.

Eden, G.F., VanMeter, J.W., Rumsey, J.M., Maisog, J.Ma., Woods, R.P., & Zeffiro, T.A. (1996). Abnormal processing of visual motion in dyslexia revealed by functional brain imaging. *Nature, 382,* 66–69.

Egger, J., Carter, C.M., Graham, P.J., Gumley, D., & Soothill, J.F. (1985). Controlled trial of oligoantigenic treatment in the hyperkinetic child syndrome. *The Lancet, 2,* 540–545.

Feingold, B.F. (1974). *Why your child is hyperactive.* New York: Random House.

Ferguson, A. (1992). Definitions and diagnosis of food intolerance and food allergy: Consensus and controversy. *Journal of Pediatrics, 121,* S7–S11.

Frank, J., & Levinson, H.N. (1973). Dysmetric dyslexia and dyspraxia: Hypothesis and study. *Journal of the American Academy of Child Psychiatry, 12,* 690–701.

Girardi, N.L., Shaywitz, S.E., Shaywitz, B.A., Marchione, K., Fleischman, S.J., Jones, T.W., & Tamborlane, W.V. (1995). Blunted catecholamine responses after glucose ingestion in children with attention deficit disorder. *Pediatric Research, 38,* 539–542.

Golub, M.S., Takeuchi, P.T., Keen, C.L., Gershwin, M.E., Hendrickx, A.G., & Lonnerdal, B. (1994). Modulation of behavioral performance of prepubertal monkeys by moderate dietary zinc deprivation. *American Journal of Clinical Nutrition, 60,* 238–243.

Goyette, C.H., Conners, C.K., & Ulrich, R.F. (1978). Normative data on revised Conners parent and teacher rating scales. *Journal of Abnormal Child Psychology, 6,* 221–236.

Harley, J.P., Ray, R.S., Tomasi, L., Eichman, P.L., Matthews, C.G., Chun, R., Cleeland, C.S., & Traisman, E. (1978). Hyperkinesis and food additives: Testing the Feingold hypothesis. *Pediatrics, 61,* 818–828.

Harrell R.F., Capp R.H., Davis D.R., Peerless, J., & Ravitz, L.R. (1981). Can nutritional supplements help mentally retarded children? An exploratory study. *Proceedings of the National Academy of Sciences, USA, 78,* 574–578.

Haslam, R.H.A., Dalby, J.T., & Rademaker, A.W. (1984). Effects of megavitamin therapy on children with attention deficit disorders. *Pediatrics, 74,* 103–111.

Hersey, J. (1996). *Why can't my child behave?* Alexandria, VA: Pear Tree Press.

Hinshaw, S.P., March, J.S., Abikoff, H., Arnold, L.E., Cantwell, D.P., Conners, C.K., Elliott, G.R., Halperin, J., Greenhill, L.L., Hechtman, L.T., Hoza, B., Jensen, P.S., Newcorn, J.H., McBurnett, K., Pelham, W.E., Richters, J.E., Severe, J.B., Schiller, E., Swanson, J., Vereen, D., Wells, K., & Wigal, T. (1997). Comprehensive assessment of childhood attention-deficit hyperactivity disorder in the context of a multisite, multimodal clinical trial. *Journal of Attention Disorders, 1,* 217–234.

Hoffman, L.G., & Rouse, M.W. (1987). Vision therapy revisited: A restatement. *Journal of the American Optometric Association, 58*, 536–541.

Ingersoll, B.D., & Goldstein, S. (1993a). Pills and potions. In *Attention deficit disorder and learning disabilities: Realities, myths and controversial treatments* (pp. 121–148). New York: Doubleday.

Ingersoll, B.D., & Goldstein, S. (1993b). Training approaches to treatment. In *Attention deficit disorder and learning disabilities: Realities, myths and controversial treatments* (pp. 171–198). New York: Doubleday.

Kaplan, B.J., McNicol, J., Conte, R.A., & Moghadam, H.K. (1989). Dietary replacement in preschool-aged hyperactive boys. *Pediatrics, 83*, 7–17.

Keogh, B.K., & Pelland, M. (1985). Vision training revisited. *Journal of Learning Disabilities, 18*, 2228–2236.

Kershner, J., & Hawke, W. (1979). Megavitamins and learning disorders: A controlled double-blind experiment. *Journal of Nutrition, 109*, 819–826.

Kruesi, M.J.P., Rapoport, J.L., Cummings, M., Berg, C.J., Ismond, D.R., Flament, M., Yarrow, M., & Zahn-Waxler, C. (1987). Effects of sugar and aspartame on aggression and activity in children. *American Journal of Psychiatry, 144*, 1487–1490.

Lennerstrand G., & Ygge, J. (1992). Dyslexia: Ophthalmological aspects 1991. *Acta Ophthalmologica, 70*, 3–13.

Levinson, H.N. (1989a). Abnormal optokinetic and perceptual span parameters in cerebellar-vestibular dysfunction and learning disabilities or dyslexia. *Perceptual Motor Skills, 68*, 35–54.

Levinson, H.N. (1989b). A cerebellar-vestibular explanation for fears/phobias: Hypothesis and study. *Perceptual Motor Skills, 68*, 67–84.

Levinson, H.N. (1989c). The cerebellar-vestibular predisposition to anxiety disorders. *Perceptual Motor Skills, 68*, 323–338.

Levinson, H.N. (1990). The diagnostic value of cerebellar-vestibular tests in detecting learning disabilities, dyslexia, and attention deficit disorder. *Perceptual Motor Skills, 71*, 67–82.

Lightstone, A., & Evans, B.J.W. (1995). A new protocol for the optometric management of patients with reading difficulties. *Ophthalmologic Physiology & Optometrics, 15*, 507–512.

Linscheer, W.G., & Vergroesen, J. (1994). Lipids. In M.E. Shils, J.A. Olson, & M. Shike (Eds.), *Modern nutrition in health and disease* (8th ed., pp. 47–88). Philadelphia: Lea & Febiger.

Liskov, T.P., Kerstetter, J., Baltimore, R.S., & Carpenter, T. (1997). Facts and myths about vitamins and minerals. In W.V. Tamborlane (Ed.), *The Yale guide to children's nutrition* (pp. 229–239). New Haven, CT: Yale University Press.

Lubar, J.F. (1989). Electroencephalographic biofeedback and neurological applications. In J.V. Basmajian (Ed.), *Biofeedback: Principles and practice for clinicians* (pp. 67–90). Baltimore: Williams & Wilkins.

Lubar, J.F. (1991). Discourse on the development of EEG diagnostics and biofeedback for attention-deficit/hyperactivity disorders. *Biofeedback & Self-Regulation, 16*, 201–225.

Lubar, J.O., & Lubar, J.F. (1984). Electroencephalographic biofeedback of SMR and beta for treatment of attention deficit disorders in a clinical setting. *Biofeedback & Self-Regulation, 9*, 1–23.

McCaleb, R. (1992). *Ginkgo biloba: Review.* Boulder, CO: Herb Research Foundation.

McLoughlin, J., Nall, M., Isaacs, B., Petrosko, J., Karibo, J., & Lindsey, B. (1983). The relationship of allergies and allergy treatment to school performance and student behavior. *Annals of Allergy, 51*, 506–510.

McNicol, J. (1992). *Your child's food allergies: Detecting and treating hyperactivity, congestion, irritability and other symptoms caused by common food allergies.* New York: John Wiley & Sons.

Menacker, S.J., Breton, M.E., Breton, M.L., Radcliffe, J., & Gole, G.A. (1993). Do tinted lenses improve reading performance of dyslexic children: A cohort study. *Archives of Ophthalmology, 111*, 213–218.

Middleton, E. (1988). Some biological properties of plant flavonoids. *Annals of Allergy, 61*, 53–57.

Mitchell, E.A., Aman, M.G., Turbott, S.H., & Manku, M. (1987). Clinical characteristics and serum essential fatty acid levels in hyperactive children. *Clinical Pediatrics, 26*, 406–411.

Muir, J.L. (1997). Acetylcholine, aging, and Alzheimer's disease. *Pharmacology, Biochemistry, and Behavior, 56*, 687–696.

Murray, M.T. (1995). Ginkgo biloba. In *The healing power of herbs: The enlightened person's guide to the wonders of medicinal plants* (2nd ed., pp. 143–161). Carmel, IN: Prima Publishing.

National Institutes of Health. (1982). Defined diets and childhood hyperactivity: A consensus conference. *Journal of the American Medical Association, 248*, 290–292.

Nemzer, E.D., Arnold, L.E., Votolano, N.A., & McConnell, H. (1986). Amino acid supplementation as treatment for attention deficit and hyperactivity. *Journal of the American Academy of Child and Adolescent Psychiatry, 25,* 509–513.

Polatajko, H.J. (1985). A critical look at vestibular dysfunction in learning-disabled children. *Developmental Medicine and Child Neurology, 27,* 283–292.

Pollitt, E., Saco-Pollitt, C., Leibel, R.L., & Viteri, F.E. (1986). Iron deficiency and behavioral development in infants and preschool children. *The American Journal of Clinical Nutrition, 43,* 555–565.

Rapp, D. (1991). *Is this your child? Discovering and treating unrecognized allergies in children and adults.* New York: William Morrow & Co.

Reichenberg-Ullman, J., & Ullman, R. (1996). *Ritalin-free kids: Safe and effective homeopathic medicine for ADD and other behavioral and learning problems.* Rocklin, CA: Prima Publications.

Rowe, K.S., & Rowe, K.J. (1994). Synthetic food coloring and behavior: A dose response effect in a double-blind, placebo-controlled, repeated measures study. *Journal of Pediatrics, 125,* 691–698.

Rydell, A.-M., & Sundeln, M.D.C. (1995). Characteristics of school children who are choosy eaters. *The Journal of Genetic Psychology, 156,* 217–229.

Sampson, H.A. (1997). Food allergy. *Journal of the American Medical Association, 278,* 1888–1894.

Sandstead, H.H. (1986). A brief history of the influence of trace elements on brain function. *American Journal of Clinical Nutrition, 43,* 293–241.

Saravis, S., Schachar, R., Zlotkin, S., Leiter, L.A., & Anderson, G.H. (1990). Aspartame: Effects on learning, behavior, and mood. *Pediatrics, 86,* 75–83.

Shaywitz, B.A., Sullivan, C.M., Anderson, G.M., Gillespie, S.M., Sullivan, B., & Shaywitz, S.E. (1994). Aspartame, behavior, and cognitive function in children with attention deficit disorder. *Pediatrics, 93,* 70–75.

Silver, L.B. (1991). Nonstandard therapy of learning disabilities. *Seminars in Neurology, 11,* 57–63.

Stevens, L.J., Zentall, S.S., Abate, M.L., Kuczek, T., & Burgess, J.R. (1996). Omega-3 fatty acids in boys with behavior, learning, and health problems. *Physiology & Behavior, 59,* 915–920.

Stevens, L.J., Zentall, S.S., Deck, J.L., Abate, M.L., Watkins, B.A., Lipp, S.R., & Burgess, J.R. (1995). Essential fatty acid metabolism in boys with attention-deficit hyperactivity disorder. *American Journal of Clinical Nutrition, 622,* 761–768.

Toren, P., Eldar, S., Sela, B.-A., Wolmer, L., Weitz, R., Inbar, D., Koren, S., Reiss, A., Weizman, R., & Laor, N. (1996). Zinc deficiency in attention-deficit hyperactivity disorder. *Biological Psychiatry, 40,* 1308–1310.

Tryphonas, H., & Trites, R. (1979). Food allergy in children with hyperactivity, learning disabilities, and/or minimal brain dysfunction. *Annals of Allergy, 42,* 22–27.

Walton, R.G., Hudak, R., & Green-White, R.J. (1993). Adverse reactions to aspartame: Double-blind challenge in patients from a vulnerable population. *Biological Psychiatry, 34,* 13–17.

Wender, E.H., & Solanto, M.V. (1991). Effects of sugar on aggressive and inattentive behavior in children with attention deficit disorder with hyperactivity and normal children. *Pediatrics, 88,* 960–966.

Williams, J.I., Cram, D.M., Tausig, F.T., & Webster, E. (1978). Relative effects of drugs and diet on hyperactive behaviors: An experimental study. *Pediatrics, 61,* 811–817.

Wolraich, M.L., Lindgren, S.D., Stumbo, P.J., Stegink, L.D., Appelbaum, M.I., & Kiritsy, M.C. (1994). Effects of diets high in sucrose or aspartame on the behavior and cognitive performance of children. *New England Journal of Medicine, 330,* 301–307.

Wolraich, M.L., Wilson, D.B., & White, J.W. (1995). The effect of sugar on behavior or cognition in children: A meta-analysis. *Journal of the American Medical Association, 274,* 1617–1621.

Wood, D.R., Reimherr, F.W., & Wender, P.H. (1985). Treatment of attention deficit disorder with DL-phenylalanine. *Psychiatric Research, 16,* 21–26.

Ygge, J., Lennerstrand, G., Axelsson, I., & Rydberg, A. (1993). Visual functions in a Swedish population of dyslexic and normally reading children. *Acta Ophthalmologica, 71,* 1–9.

Zametkin, A.J., Karoum, F., & Rapoport, J.L. (1987). Treatment of hyperactive children with D-phenylalanine. *American Journal of Psychiatry, 144,* 792–794.

BOOKS AND REVIEWS

Braly, J. (1992). *Dr. Braly's food allergy and nutrition revolution.* New Canaan, CT: Keats Publishing. (To order, call [800] 858-7014.)

Conners, C.K. (1989). *Feeding the brain: How foods affect children.* New York: Plenum. (To order, call [800] 221-9369.)

Crook, W.G. (1986). *The yeast connection: A medical breakthrough.* New York: Random House. (To order, call [800] 733-3000.)

Feingold, B.F. (1974). *Why your child is hyperactive.* New York: Random House. (To order, call [800] 733-3000.)

Ferguson, A. (1992). Definitions and diagnosis of food intolerance and food allergy: Consensus and controversy. *Journal of Pediatrics, 121,* S7–S11.

Herbert, V., & Subak-Sharpe, G.J. (1995). *Total nutrition.* New York: St. Martin's Press. (To order, call [212] 614-5151.)

Hersey, J. (1996). *Why can't my child behave?* Alexandria, VA: Pear Tree Press. (To order, call [703] 768-0070.)

Hunter, D. (1995). *The Ritalin-free child: Managing hyperactivity and attention deficits without drugs.* Ft. Lauderdale, FL: Consumer Press. (To order, call [305] 370-9153.)

Ingersoll, B.D., & Goldstein, S. (1993). *Attention deficit disorder and learning disabilities: Realities, myths and controversial treatments.* New York: Doubleday. (To order, call [800] 223-6834.)

Levinson, H.N. (1990). *Total concentration: How to understand attention deficit disorders with treatment guidelines for you and your doctor.* New York: M. Evans & Co. (To order, call [800] 879-4214.)

McNicol, J. (1992). *Your child's food allergies: Detecting and treating hyperactivity, congestion, irritability and other symptoms caused by common food allergies.* New York: John Wiley & Sons. (To order, call [800] 225-5945.)

Rapp, D. (1991). *Is this your child? Discovering and treating unrecognized allergies in children and adults.* New York: William Morrow & Co. (To order, call [800] 843-9389.)

Reichenberg-Ullman, J., & Ullman, R. (1996). *Ritalin-free kids: Safe and effective homeopathic medicine for ADD and other behavioral and learning problems.* Rocklin, CA: Prima Publications. (To order, call [800] 632-8676.)

Tamborlane, W.V. (Ed.). (1997). *The Yale guide to children's nutrition.* New Haven, CT: Yale University Press. (To order, call [203] 432-0940.)

Weintraub, S. (1997). *Natural treatments for ADD and hyperactivity.* Pleasant Grove, UT: Woodland Publishing. (To order, call [800] 777-2665.)

OTHER RESOURCES

The Feingold Association of the United States
Post Office Box 6550
Alexandria, VA 22306
(516) 369-9340

Herb Research Foundation
1007 Pearl Street
Suite 200
Boulder, CO 80302

National Center for Homeopathy
801 N. Fairfax Street
Suite 306
Alexandria, VA 22314
(703) 548-7790

11

Follow-Up and Coordination of Care

Attention-deficit/hyperactivity disorder (ADHD) is an ongoing disorder. Like any on-going disorder, there are periods when there are acute problems that need intensive intervention and other periods when the clinician's primary function is to monitor the child's symptoms to detect and manage small problems before they become larger problems. Previous chapters have covered the options for managing a variety of acute problems and the medical follow-up that is needed for the monitoring of specific medications used to treat ADHD. In this chapter, the clinician's role in the ongoing monitoring of ADHD symptoms and coordination of care for the child with ADHD is discussed. Frequently, the primary care physician is responsible for monitoring and coordinating care for children with ADHD, although, in some cases, a community mental health professional, a school psychologist or counselor, or a subspecialty physician is responsible.

The previous chapters of this book have provided much of the information that clinicians need to effectively monitor a child with ADHD. As the professional doing the monitoring, the clinician must have a broad knowledge of ADHD because he or she will have to assess the multiple areas in which ADHD can affect functioning and will have to either implement or direct the family to appropriate interventions. Clinicians must resist the tendency to consider only the interventions that are specific to their area of training, as in some cases the child's and family's needs will be best served by a professional in another field. For example, a psychologist who is monitoring a child with ADHD needs to know enough about medication to know when it would be appropriate to refer a child to consider starting or changing the child's medication, and a physician needs to know when it is important to consider the possibility that educational or behavioral interventions may be a better alternative than changes in medication. This chapter begins with a discussion of the areas of functioning that should be monitored at follow-up visits. Possible roles of different professionals in the follow-up care of children with ADHD are discussed as a guide for clinicians who are coordinating the care of children with ADHD.

FOLLOW-UP CARE

The initial assessment of children with ADHD will have identified current behavior and/or academic performance problems in school, behavior problems at home, and difficulties with peers. Initially, the child may require frequent visits to ensure that the problems are responding to the interventions, but once the problems have started to improve, less frequent follow-up will be needed. Eventually, most children with ADHD can be seen every 3–6 months to monitor progress with the identified problems and to detect new problems or provide anticipatory guidance regarding potential areas of difficulty. This usually requires obtaining information about the child's ADHD symptoms, other identified behavior problems, academic performance in school, and social functioning. Furthermore, the clinician needs to be aware of the new challenges that are likely to occur in these areas as the child with ADHD gets older. A follow-up evaluation form to help guide clinicians is provided in Appendix A.

MONITORING CHILD FUNCTIONING AT SCHOOL

Parents will provide clinicians with their impression of how the child is doing in school. Clinicians should assess the information on which this impression is based and encourage parents to take a proactive approach to obtaining information from teachers. A school–home note (see Chapter 6), regular meetings, or other consistent forms of communication between parents and teachers will help identify problems early and should facilitate a cooperative approach to their management. Parents who take a "no news is good news" approach to obtaining information from the school may not be aware of academic or behavior difficulties until they are reflected in a poor report card or a major problem in school. At this point, accumulated skill deficits and/or both the child's and the teacher's frustration may make intervention more difficult.

When parents consult a clinician about a behavior disturbance or poor performance on a test, the clinician must determine whether the event reflects a pattern of increasing problems in school or an isolated response to a series of unfortunate environmental events. For example, behavior problems in school may be an indication of an increase in ADHD symptoms. Alternatively, they could be related to a poor match between student and teacher or a pattern of teasing and scapegoating by other students on the playground. Similarly, a child may fail a test because a persistent problem with ADHD symptoms or a coexisting learning problem has left him or her deficient in the skills that are needed to keep up with classmates, or a child may fail because a trip, game, or other distraction prevented him or her from preparing. For clinicians to distinguish these possibilities, it usually is necessary for them to obtain some information directly from the school.

Monitoring ADHD symptoms in school often is done most efficiently by having teachers complete a brief behavior rating scale that focuses on ADHD symptoms. Such rating scales are reviewed in Chapter 2 and include the ADHD Rating Scale-IV and the Conners Teacher Rating Scale. When these rating scales are completed regularly, they allow one to compare how a child is doing at the current time with how they have done in the past. Furthermore, if the child has more than one teacher, then each teacher can complete a scale, which allows the clinician to distinguish a child who is having problems in one class from a child who is having problems in multiple settings. A recent report card may provide another means of monitoring a child's attention, activity level, and impulsivity. Often, report cards used in elementary schools require teachers to assess attention span and activity level, but for older children these areas may not be specifically assessed.

Report cards also provide an assessment of the child's academic performance; however, report cards may not help catch academic problems early as they are completed only three or four times per year. Clinicians should encourage parents to obtain information from teachers about their child's academic performance prior to visits or may want to ask teachers to complete the Brief Academic Screening Questionnaire (Appendix B) when they have them complete the rating scale. If the child is doing well on the report card or screening questionnaire and the parents do not have concerns about school performance, then no further assessment of academic performance is needed. A cover letter to help obtain this type of information from schools is included in Appendix C.

If the clinician determines that there is a pattern of increasing school problems, then he or she must try to determine whether the problem is related to the ADHD symptoms; learning problems; or other behavior, emotional, medical, or psychosocial problems. If both parents and teachers are reporting increased problems with attention and activity level in educational as well as social settings, then it is likely that ADHD symptoms are contributing to the worsening performance. Likewise, if parents or teachers report that the child can do the work (or homework) independently when they monitor the child carefully to keep him or her on task but will not complete work when not being monitored, then it is likely that ADHD symptoms need to be managed better. In contrast, if parents or teachers report that the child needs frequent help with the instructions, concepts, or skills, then a learning problem may be more likely. If parent and teacher reports are consistent in suggesting a worsening in ADHD symptoms, then a clinician may change the medical or behavioral interventions to better manage the ADHD symptoms. Clinicians should remember that the response to the change in the management plan is part of the ongoing assessment and that alternative explanations for the change in symptoms would again need to be considered if the academic performance did not improve.

If the reports of parents and teachers are not consistent in suggesting a worsening of the ADHD symptoms as the cause for the problems or if changes in the plan to manage the ADHD symptoms does not improve the child's academic performance, then an assessment of academic skills should be completed by a psychologist. Learning disabilities may be difficult to detect in early elementary school, so a psychoeducational assessment may need to be repeated if the child was young at the initial assessment or it has been more than a few years since the last assessment. Because many children with ADHD have coexisting learning problems, it is possible that both the ADHD and the learning problems are contributing to a worsening in a child's academic performance. In this situation, the clinician or clinicians involved in the child's care and the child's parents will need to work together with the child's teacher, special educator, or school psychologist to provide coordinated behavioral, educational, and pharmacological interventions.

It also is helpful for the clinician who is monitoring a child with ADHD to be aware of changes in school expectations that are likely to be difficult for the child with ADHD. As a child advances through each grade, there are increased demands on attention. Common manifestations of these increased demands are longer homework assignments (see Table 1) and more seat work. Although Table 1 suggests a gradual increase in the length of homework assignments, individual teachers can have varying expectations that may create difficulties for a child with ADHD during one school year but not another.

Transitions from elementary school to middle school and from middle school to high school are likely to be particularly difficult for children with ADHD. During elementary school, students are expected to have developed basic organizational skills that will allow them to keep track of books and assignments despite frequently changing classes and using a locker to store materials. These factors, along with increased academic demands, make the transition to middle school very difficult for many children[1] and are especially likely to cause difficulties for children with ADHD.[2] Furthermore, elementary school teachers are likely to view teaching organizational and study skills as one of their goals; thus, they usually are willing to provide accommodations or participate in interventions to teach these skills. Middle school teachers are more likely to assume that children have these skills and may be less familiar with or may have less time to devote to participation in interventions that target organizational or study skills. Coordinating interventions across different teachers also becomes more difficult. Although students may not articulate that they are overwhelmed with their school work, these problems may contribute to work avoidance or refusal, oppositionality, irritability, anxiety, and depression. Table 2 lists some suggestions for parents on preparing students for this transition.

The transition to high school may create similar difficulties for the adolescent with ADHD. Usually, there are even more teachers involved in the student's instruction. Furthermore, there are greater expectations for self-directed study skills and more long-term assignments. Adolescents with ADHD often have difficulties with planning these projects and at least initially are likely to need very close supervision to successfully complete them. Management often is complicated by the adolescent's desire for independence from his or her parents. This may lead to conflicts about the need for supervision in school as well as in other aspects of the adolescent's life (see Chapter 13).

MONITORING CHILD FUNCTIONING WITHIN THE FAMILY

During the follow-up visit for a child with ADHD, it is important to determine how the child is functioning within the family. Problems addressed at previous visits should be inquired about to determine whether the difficulties have been resolved and whether interventions are continuing to be used. The parents' attitude toward the child and the types of tasks and responsibilities that the child assumes within the home will provide

Table 1. Recommended duration of homework assignments

Grades 1–3	10–45 minutes/day
Grades 4–6	45–90 minutes/day
Grades 7–9	1–2 hours/day
Grades 10–12	1.5–2.5 hours/day

Source: Keith & DeGraff (1997).

Table 2. Preparing a student with ADHD for the transition to middle school or high school

1. Meet with the school principal or guidance counselor to identify recommended classes or teachers and to simplify the schedule as much as possible.

2. With the student, make an organized notebook, color coded by class, that includes a place for writing down homework assignments and a pocket in which to place completed assignments. Attatch the child's schedule to the inside front cover.

3. Familiarize the student with the building, schedule, and teachers before the first day of school.

4. If the child has been receiving special education services, then meet with the special education team or director of the middle or high school to determine the services to be provided in the new school. Develop a system for regular communication between you and all of the student's teachers. Delineate in writing the accommodations that will be made for your child in school. Accommodations to consider include test-taking modifications, use of tape recorders or computer aids, provision of a second set of books for home, and so forth.

5. Meet with teachers to develop a mechanism for ensuring that you are aware of assignments, especially tests and long-term assignments so that you can help the child with study skills and breaking down and organizing long-term assignments. Ask the school to assign one person to coordinate the efforts of teachers and serve as your contact person.

valuable information about how the family is functioning. It also will be important to identify situations or events within the family that may be sources of stress because they may directly affect the child's symptoms and also the amount of time or energy that parents have to manage ADHD symptoms.

The parents' attitude toward the child is a key indicator of the level of parent–child conflict. If parents are proud of their child's achievements, can describe many positive characteristics of their child, and can take a supportive approach to the difficulties that the child may be having, then the child and the family most likely are functioning well. Thus, it is as important for clinicians to ask about the child's accomplishments and fun things that parents and children do together as it is to ask about the problems. Clinicians who ask only about problems may hear about only the parents' difficulties or frustrations; however, if clinicians probe for positive aspects of the parent–child relationship but the parents can describe only difficulties and frustrations, then there is strong indication of a need for more intensive intervention.

Often, it is helpful to assess the types of tasks and responsibilities that the child is given at home. This will give clinicians an impression of parents' expectations for the child and the child's ability to meet these expectations. A significant discrepancy between parents' expectations and the child's performance suggests a need for intervention, especially when it is resulting in conflict within the family. As children get older, it is important for the parents and the child to discuss the relationship between demonstrating the ability to make responsible decisions at home (and school) and acquiring the additional privileges that the child desires. Frequently, parents need to make certain privileges or fun activities contingent on the child's completing specific tasks or responsibilities at home.

Clinicians may identify some families that have overcompensated for the child's ADHD. In these instances, the parents may have very low expectations for the child and may provide fun activities or privileges regardless of the child's behavior. Many families will express confusion about what to expect from the child because of the ADHD, and the disorder may become an excuse for failing to meet certain expectations. In these instances, clinicians can help guide the families toward developing reasonable expectations for the child with ADHD. Accommodation for the child's ADHD symptoms should be made as the parents and the clinician are developing the expectations that they believe the child can accomplish. Once the expectations are agreed on, ADHD should not be an excuse for failing to meet the expectations.

When behavior problems are present at follow-up, clinicians should consider the multiple factors that may be contributing to the problem. Often, the problems relate to the child's ADHD symptoms or the severe oppositional behaviors that may coexist with ADHD in 65% or more of cases[3]; however, one must consider other possibilities. As discussed previously, many children with ADHD develop coexisting internalizing disorders such as depression or anxiety. When behavior problems are associated with an increased level of irritability or moodiness, the child should be assessed for other signs of depression (see Chapters 2 and 3). Anxiety may manifest itself as an inability to complete tasks due to a perfectionistic concern about performing certain aspects of the task. Other psychiatric disorders, such as mania and obsessive-compulsive disorder, may be difficult to distinguish from ADHD at an initial evaluation. The clinician should remain open to the possibility that monitoring the child's symptoms over time will change one's impression of the primary problem. Cycles of elevated and depressed mood, suggestive of bipolar disorder, may become apparent. It may be necessary to develop a trusting relationship before a child will be willing to reveal important experiences or what they view as unusual symptoms such as obsessive thoughts or compulsive behaviors.

The child with ADHD exists within a family in which there are reciprocal interactions between the functioning of the child and the functioning of other family members. Because the functioning of other family members influences the child's functioning, it is imperative that the clinician who is caring for the child investigate the functioning of other family members. It is well documented that parents and siblings of children with ADHD are at increased risk not only for ADHD but also for other disorders such as depression, antisocial disorders, and substance dependence.[4] The presence of any of these problems in parents increases the risk of behavior problems in their children. Parental depression is a frequently missed risk factor that is important to detect because it may both decrease the parent's energy for managing a child's behavior and change the parent's perception of the child's behavior such that negative aspects of the behavior are emphasized.[5] If parental behavior or emotional disorders are present, then a supportive but frank discussion with them about the importance of getting help for themselves will be necessary. Clearly, stressors that may be influencing the child extend beyond psychiatric disorders. Medical illnesses in the child or other family members, birth of a sibling, relocation of the family, loss of a job, marital discord or divorce, and domestic violence are but a few of the many potential stressors that may lead to changes in the child's symptoms. In some cases, a clinician will be able to help families manage these situations or identify community resources to help the family. In addition, clinicians should not underestimate the value of a professional's interest, support, and encouragement during difficult times.

Finally, when problems exist, the clinician should determine what is being done to manage the problem. Often, parents and children engage enthusiastically in behavioral interventions at the beginning of treatment, which yields significant improvements in the child's behavior; however, behavioral interventions usually require a great deal of effort on the part of parents, and, once the novelty of the intervention wears off, children may show less interest in the interventions. Thus, there is a tendency not to sustain these interventions over time. Follow-up visits can be used to help parents modify the interventions to maintain their efficacy (see Chapter 5) and to recognize the efforts and skills of parents who have successfully modified the interventions themselves.

MONITORING THE CHILD'S RELATIONSHIPS WITH PEERS

How a child with ADHD is getting along with his or her peers is another important indicator of how well the child is functioning. The factors that contribute to the social problems of children with ADHD are discussed in Chapter 7. Some children may have many friends, whereas others may have only a few friends. Both of these situations can be consistent with good social adjustment; however, children without friends are at very high risk for behavior and emotional problems. If ADHD symptoms are interfering with a child's peer relationships, then they will be an important target for treatment.

Changes in functioning with peers can be helpful in assessing the factors that may be contributing to changes in functioning in other settings. For example, if a child with ADHD no longer has an interest in interacting with peers or participating in other previously enjoyed activities, then the possibility that depression is contributing to problems in other settings needs to be considered. Similarly, if a child whose ADHD symptoms previously have been well managed begins to have problems with attention, hyperactivity, and impulsivity with the peer group as well as in the school or family, then it supports the need to change the management of the ADHD symptoms.

A subgroup of adolescents with ADHD engage in high-risk behaviors such as substance use, school truancy, aggression, and stealing.[6] Adolescents may be hesitant to discuss whether they are involved in these activities but may more honestly discuss the high-risk behaviors of their friends or other adolescents in general. Discussing these activities with the adolescent may make it easier for the adolescent to discuss the high-risk behaviors in which he or she participates. Even if the adolescent continues to deny participation in these activities, clinicians should be aware that adolescents whose friends engage frequently in these activities are at increased risk for engaging in these behaviors themselves.

CHANGING THE TREATMENT PLAN

One of the most difficult decisions that clinicians must make when following children with ADHD is when and how to change the treatment plan. Does the child who is having difficulties in school need more academic assistance or accommodations, the addition or change in a behavioral intervention, or the addition of medication or change in the dosage of medication? Are behavioral interventions or changes in medication the best way to manage conflicts at home? Clearly, there are no absolute answers to these types of questions, and what happens in any individual case will depend on the opinions and experiences of the parents, child, other family members, clinicians, teachers, or other community members that the parents consult, along with resources available in the family, school, and community. The following thoughts are offered for clinicians to consider when recommending changes in the treatment plan, realizing that in individual cases there will be a wide variety of factors that influence the actual changes that are made to the treatment plan.

Perhaps most important is for the clinician to approach any change as part of an ongoing assessment process. Obtaining the clearest information possible about the child's response to the change in the intervention may confirm the clinician's impression or reveal that additional or alternative problems are present. For example, it may not be clear to the clinician whether a child has developed poor self-esteem and a sense of hopelessness related to repeated failure as a result of ADHD or has an underlying mood disorder. A clinician may elect to treat the ADHD symptoms while monitoring both the changes in the ADHD symptoms and the changes in the child's mood. Over time, it is likely to become clear whether the mood symptoms are related to the ADHD or additional treatment of the mood symptoms is needed.

The preceding discussion implies that it is best to make one change at a time and monitor the child's response to that change before making additional changes. Although this clearly is the best way to determine whether an intervention is having its desire effect, it requires that interventions be used sequentially, which may not be possible in some cases. In the previous example, the mood problems and the ADHD symptoms may be severe enough that the clinician elects to treat both simultaneously. For some children, ADHD symptoms may be causing such severe dysfunction that pharmacological, behavioral, and educational interventions need to be implemented at approximately the same time. In this situation, the clinician may need to wait until the situation has stabilized for a period of time and then consider withdrawing the most restrictive interventions one at a time to determine which interventions are critical to sustain the change.

It should be emphasized that this approach is especially important for pharmacological interventions. Increasingly, children with severe ADHD or ADHD with coexisting disorders are being treated with multiple medications. Over time, it can become unclear which medications actually are helping the child or even whether some of the symptoms that are being treated with medication are side effects of other medications that the child is taking. It can be difficult to convince parents or teachers of the importance of trial periods in which pharmacological interventions are withdrawn, but the information obtained usually is very valuable in the long-term management of the child's symptoms.

When parents come to clinicians with concerns about the behavior of a child with ADHD, the clinician needs to decide between recommending changes in behavioral or pharmacological interventions. Behavioral interventions are most effective at targeting specific problem behaviors or specific periods of the day that are a problem for a parent or a teacher. In contrast, medication will affect the child's behavior across a variety of settings and caregivers for the duration of action of the medication; thus, if the behavior problem is relatively isolated to a specific time period or specific behavior, then changes in behavioral treatments should be attempted before changes in medications are made. A child who is having difficulties with completing homework may do best with a behavioral intervention that targets homework completion. If getting ready for school in the morning is the major problem, then a behavioral intervention that focuses on the morning routine may remedy the situation. Conversely, if multiple teachers and/or caregivers are having significant problems with a wide variety of behaviors related to attention, hyperactivity, or impulsivity, then pharmacological interventions may more rapidly effect change in the behaviors. Clearly, the severity of the problems also needs to be considered. If the problems are widespread but mild, then sequential implementation of a series of behavioral interventions may improve the problems. If the problems are severe, then medications are more likely to be needed.

COORDINATION OF CARE

Multiple individuals are involved in the care of a child with ADHD. In most cases, it involves some combination of parents, school personnel, primary care physicians, community-based mental health professionals, and/or subspecialists. The role that a particular professional plays in the care of the child with ADHD varies with the clinician's training and interests as well as the other professionals involved. For clinicians from multiple professions to work well together, it is helpful to appreciate the roles that other professionals are well suited to serve and the factors that may limit or interfere with another professional's ability to manage certain aspects of a child's care. The following descriptions of the roles of different professionals are not meant to be exhaustive or to limit the role that a particular clinician may play; rather, they are provided to help clinicians appreciate the possible ways in which another professional may help them evaluate or treat a child with ADHD and the constraints that may interfere with the clinician's ability to manage certain aspects of the disorder.

Roles of the Primary Care Physician

The growth of managed care has emphasized the role of the primary care physician in managing and coordinating the care of children with chronic illnesses. ADHD is a chronic disorder that primary care providers often are in a good position to manage. The high prevalence of ADHD means that it is a disorder that primary care physicians see frequently. These physicians' ongoing relationships with children and families over a period of years provides a unique developmental perspective on the child's symptoms. Also, their relationship with the family is likely to provide them information about environmental or family stressors that may be influencing the situation. Families that have developed a trusting relationship with a physician over the years may be more willing to accept the physician's recommendations than those of other professionals.

Routine health supervision visits or medication checks provide an excellent opportunity to monitor the child's functioning at school, with family, and with peers. Anticipatory guidance about issues such as transitions in school, potential difficulties with long-term assignments, responsibilities in the home, risk-taking behaviors, driving, and college selection can help parents develop plans to manage these issues. When problems arise, primary care providers may provide recommendations to help the family or refer the family to other professionals.

Primary care providers play a vital role in helping families obtain help when it is needed. They can direct the family to appropriate mental health professionals or subspecialty physicians and may well be the gatekeeper for children to receive these services. They may be aware of community resources that are available to help the family and can assist families in advocating for their child with ADHD. Knowledge of education law (Chapter 8) can help physicians guide families to develop appropriate expectations for assistance from the school. Increasingly, managed care networks place the primary care physician in the position of advocating for needed medical and mental health referrals for individual children. As a group, primary care physicians can have a very important role in emphasizing to managed care providers the importance of appropriate mental health services for children with ADHD.

Managing ADHD in a primary care setting does create some difficulties for physicians. The time required to manage ADHD is the most frequently identified problem. Most visits in these settings are scheduled for 10–15 minutes, which may be enough time to monitor for medication effects and side effects; however, it is not enough time to perform the type of initial evaluation that is described in this book. If significant problems are identified during follow-up monitoring, then it may be necessary to schedule additional appointments to develop a management plan. One solution is for the physician to refer to other professionals for the diagnosis and monitoring of ADHD and to restrict one's role to the prescription and monitoring of medication; however, many primary care providers are not happy with this limited role. For instance, in one survey, more than half of pediatricians reported that they set aside special time to care for children with ADHD. More than half spend 1 hour or more on the initial evaluation, and few reported spending less than 30 minutes on the evaluation.[7] When extra time or extra appointments are needed, managed care insurance programs typically do not provide extra reimbursement for this time; thus, it is not surprising that the vast majority of physicians believe that they are not adequately reimbursed for the care of children with ADHD.[8]

The importance of communication with schools has been emphasized throughout this book; however, when written reports or rating scales are not sufficient, the schedules of schools and physicians often make communication difficult. Many primary care physicians set aside time early in the morning before they start seeing patients or at the end of the day to make telephone calls, but teachers or other school personnel often are not at the school during these times. Calls in the middle of the day may interrupt teachers during classes or physicians who are scheduled to see four or more patients per hour, providing little time for discussion. Perhaps e-mail or other modes of communication will facilitate communication between physicians and teachers in the near future.

Roles of the Community-Based Mental Health Professional

Families may seek or be referred for consultation with a mental health provider for the diagnosis or treatment of ADHD, or both. A mental health provider may see a child because of concerns about other problems and in the course of evaluation or treatment may believe that the child has ADHD. The mental health professional who is involved in assessment of ADHD should be able to coordinate his or her assessment with medical and educational information in order to identify ADHD and any coexisting disorders. The mental health professional may have more time to sort out problems and may be more familiar with the assessment of coexisting emotional or behavior disorders, learning disabilities, intrafamilial conflict, or other family stressors than the primary care physician; thus, if one suspects that significant coexisting disorders are present, then evaluation by a mental health provider should be considered. When coexisting disorders are present, periodic follow-up consultations with the mental health professional often are needed.

Although many primary care providers can offer parents basic recommendations on behavior management strategies, when the problems seem severe or when the recommendations do not result in improvement in the child's behavior, the child and family may need to be referred to a mental health professional. The mental health professional may assist the family in designing behavioral interventions for the home, provide consultation to the school, and help the family with locating community resources. A treatment plan for coexisting disorders and family conflicts or stressors should be developed. Most behavioral interventions have built-in mechanisms for monitoring the child's behavior. If adding medication or changing a medication dosage is recommended, then the mental health professional who is working with the child's physician may be able to use the monitoring systems developed for the behavioral intervention to help to determine whether the change in medication is improving the child's behavior.

Although community mental health professionals are well situated to assess and manage individual and family issues related to ADHD, managing the child's difficulties in school presents a significant challenge. Many of the issues are similar to those already discussed for the primary care physician. There is limited time for communication with teachers or other school personnel, and rarely do consultants work directly with the student in the school.[9] Problem-solving efforts that are not collaborative may have limited feasibility or acceptability. Meetings between the community professionals and school personnel may decrease this problem but are time consuming and expensive for families. Often, insurance companies do not cover these services.

Roles of the School Psychologist

The traditional role of school psychologists primarily has been to perform psychoeducational testing to identify children who have learning disabilities or other developmental disabilities that require special education services. A variety of factors contribute to a growing consensus that it is important for school psychologists to expand the services that they provide to children with ADHD. School often is the setting in which children with ADHD have serious problems; education law mandates the provision of services related to ADHD if the disorder is interfering with the child's adjustment to school (see Chapter 8). School psychologists are in an excellent position not only to obtain information about the child's cognitive functioning but also to obtain information and even observe the child's behavior in task situations and with peers. Furthermore, they can consult more easily with teachers and have better knowledge of school-based resources than community-based psychologists or physicians. They also can collect information on the efficacy of behavioral interventions or medications in the school.[10] Although in some communities school psychologists may be prepared to take on these additional roles, in many areas school psychologists still perform primarily a testing role. (For more information about the management of ADHD in a school setting, see DuPaul & Stoner, 1994.)

The potential of school psychologists to play a vital role in the assessment and treatment of ADHD is clear. The feasibility of this expanded role is limited both by variable training for this new role and by varying levels of support for this role among school administrators; however, there also are other issues. ADHD should not be diagnosed based on school information alone. Medical evaluation and information on the functioning of the child in the home is needed. Parents may be more willing to provide this information to their primary care physician or a community mental health professional whom they have consulted than to school personnel; thus, in most cases, the diagnosis will need to be made in collaboration with the physician and/or the community mental health provider.

Working in the school provides a major advantage for developing treatment plans for problems in the school; however, school psychologists may be limited in how strongly they can advocate for interventions that require significant increases in the allocation of resources to help a child. Even when this is not the case, parents may perceive that the school psychologists are trying to ration school resources. Furthermore, it usually is not appropriate for school psychologists to be involved in family interventions that often are needed for children with ADHD, and final decisions about the use of medications must be left to the child's parents and physician.

Roles of Subspecialists

A variety of subspecialists may be involved in the diagnosis and treatment of ADHD. These include child and adolescent psychiatrists, pediatric neurologists, and developmental and behavioral pediatricians. The most common reasons for the involvement of subspecialists is the presence of diagnostic or therapeutic dilemmas. For example, one should consider referral when considering the new diagnosis of ADHD in an adolescent or in a very young child, or when a child has a significant coexisting medical disorder such as poorly controlled seizures or **Tourette syndrome,** a severe coexisting emotional or behavior disturbance such as **major depressive disorder** or **conduct disorder,** a coexisting developmental disability or sensory impairment, or high levels of family stressors or conflicts. Children who do not improve while taking the medications that the primary care physician is experienced in using may be referred to a subspecialist. At some referral centers, multidisciplinary teams composed of some combination of psychologists, social workers, educators, and subspecialty physicians may be available to provide a well-coordinated evaluation and treatment for the most complicated or difficult-to-treat cases.

Subspecialty care often is time consuming and expensive. Families may need to travel quite a distance to see a subspecialist, which makes follow-up care difficult. In these situations, the subspecialist may not be aware of community or school resources to help the family. Prior to the evaluation for ADHD, subspecialists usually are not familiar with any aspect of a child's medical, behavioral, educational, developmental, or family history. Obtaining all of this information increases the time required for the evaluation and, thus, the expense of the evaluation. Although subspecialty care is needed for a subset of children with ADHD, there are many children with ADHD who do not need the services of a subspecialist.

CONCLUSION

Although the initial diagnosis and treatment plan for a child with ADHD is important, it is the management of the disorder over the long term that may have the greatest impact on outcome. Because ADHD affects children's performance in multiple settings, follow-up evaluations must monitor the child's functioning in the family and the community, in school, and with peers. The professionals who may be most helpful to the child and the family will vary depending on the setting in which dysfunction occurs and the coexisting conditions that are present. Given both the impact of managed care and the fact that families see their primary care physician for regular health supervision visits, it often is the primary care physician who is responsible for monitoring the child and coordinating care for the child with ADHD. In some instances, however, these functions may be performed more effectively by a community mental health professional, school psychologist, or subspecialty physician.

ENDNOTES

1. Eccles et al. (1996).
2. Shapiro, DuPaul, Bradley, & Bailey (1996).
3. Barkley (1998).
4. Hechtman (1996).
5. Fergusson, Lynskey, & Horwood (1993).
6. Faigel, Sznajderman, Tishby, Turel, & Pinus (1995).
7. Kwasman, Tinsley, & Lepper (1995).
8. Ibid.
9. Power, Atkins, Osborne, & Blum (1994).
10. Ibid.

REFERENCES

Barkley, R.A. (1998). *Attention-deficit hyperactivity disorder: A handbook for diagnosis and treatment.* (2nd ed.). New York: Guilford Press.

DuPaul, G.J., & Stoner, G. (1994). *ADHD in the schools: Assessment and intervention strategies.* New York: Guilford Press.

Eccles, J.S., Flanagan, C., Lord, S., Midgley, C., Roeser, R., & Yee, D. (1996). Schools, families, and early adolescents: What are we doing wrong and what can we do instead? *Journal of Developmental and Behavioral Pediatrics, 17,* 267–276.

Faigel, H.C., Sznajderman, S., Tishby, O., Turel, M., & Pinus, U. (1995). Attention deficit disorder during adolescence: A review. *Journal of Adolescent Health, 16,* 174–184.

Fergusson, D.M., Lynskey, M.T., & Horwood, L.J. (1993). The effect of maternal depression on maternal ratings of child behavior. *Journal of Abnormal Child Psychology, 21,* 245–269.

Hechtman, L. (1996). Families of children with attention deficit hyperactivity disorder: A review. *Canadian Journal of Psychiatry, 41,* 350–360.

Keith, T.Z., & DeGraff, M. (1997). Homework. In G.G. Bear, K.M. Minke, & A. Thomas (Eds.), *Children's needs: II. Development, problems and alternatives* (pp. 477–487). Bethesda, MD: National Association of School Psychologists.

Kwasman, A., Tinsley, B.J., & Lepper, H.S. (1995). Pediatricians' knowledge and attitudes concerning diagnosis and treatment of attention deficit and hyperactivity disorders: A national survey approach. *Archives of Pediatric and Adolescent Medicine, 149,* 1211–1216.

Power, T.J., Atkins, M.S., Osborne, M.L., & Blum, N.J. (1994). The school psychologist as manager of programming for ADHD. *School Psychology Review, 23,* 279–291.

Shapiro, E.S., DuPaul, G.J., Bradley, K.L., & Bailey, L.T. (1996). A school-based consultation program for service delivery to middle school students with attention-deficit/hyperactivity disorder. *Journal of Emotional and Behavioral Disorders, 4,* 73–81.

ADHD Follow-Up Evaluation

ADHD FOLLOW-UP EVALUATION

Child's name _____   Date of birth _____

Date of visit _____   Age _____

Chief concerns _____

_____

_____

Current medications   Efficacy of medications   Side effects of medications

Interim Educational History

School _____   Grade _____

Academic performance _____

    Work completion _____

    Work accuracy _____

    Assistance in classroom/special education placement _____

Behavior _____

_____

    Teacher ratings _____

    Behavioral interventions _____

    _____

Homework _____

    Length of time to complete _____

    Assistance needed _____

Interim Family Functioning

Behavior _____

    Responsibilities at home _____

    Oppositional behaviors _____

    Moodiness/irritability _____

    Child interests _____

    Sleep _____

    Appetite _____

    Behavioral interventions _____

Family stressors _____

    Changes in household members _____

    Changes in jobs/housing _____

    Conflict versus support from other caregivers _____

The Clinician's Practical Guide to Attention-Deficit/Hyperactivity Disorder
by Marianne Mercugliano, Thomas J. Power, and Nathan J. Blum   ©1999 by Paul H. Brookes Publishing Co.

Peer Relationships

Number of friends _____

Organized activities with peers _____ Problems _____

Unstructured activities with peers _____ Problems _____

Peer risk-taking behaviors _____

Interim Medical History

Allergies _____

Additional medications _____

Chronic illnesses/new diagnoses _____

Illnesses/hospitalizations _____

Symptoms: Headaches _____

                Stomachaches _____

                Changes in appetite _____

                Tics _____

                Staring spells _____

Physical Exam

Height _____   Percentile _____

Weight _____   Percentile _____

Pulse _____

BP _____

Other positive findings:_____

_____

_____

_____

Assessment and Plan

_____

_____

_____

_____

_____

_____

_____

_____

_____

_____

_____

The Clinician's Practical Guide to Attention-Deficit/Hyperactivity Disorder
by Marianne Mercugliano, Thomas J. Power, and Nathan J. Blum ©1999 by Paul H. Brookes Publishing Co.

Brief Academic Screening

BRIEF ACADEMIC SCREENING

Student _____ Date _____

Grade _____

Is this student receiving any additional educational assistance? If yes, then please describe:

_____

_____

Compared with other students in your class, rate this child's skills in the following subjects:

	Much below	Somewhat below	Average	Somewhat above	Much above
Reading	A	B	C	D	E
Math	A	B	C	D	E
Writing	A	B	C	D	E
_____	A	B	C	D	E
_____	A	B	C	D	E

How much assistance does this child need to complete work?

5 = Completes work independently

4 = Completes work, needs assistance similar to classmates

3 = Completes work, needs more assistance than classmates

2 = Completes most work, needs much more assistance than classmates

1 = Completes little work, even with a lot of assistance

How much difficulty does this child have with following instructions for academic assignments?

5 = No significant difficulties

4 = Occasionally does not follow the instructions for academic assignments

3 = Has some difficulties with following instructions, especially in large-group situations, but responds when directed

2 = Often does not follow instructions in large- or small-group situations and may not respond when directed

1 = Rarely follows instructions and usually does not respond to the teacher's efforts to redirect

Does the child turn in homework assignments? Almost always Usually Sometimes Rarely

Is homework completed correctly? Almost always Usually Sometimes Rarely

Please provide about this student's academic performance any comments that you think may be helpful: _____

_____

_____

_____

The Clinician's Practical Guide to Attention-Deficit/Hyperactivity Disorder
by Marianne Mercugliano, Thomas J. Power, and Nathan J. Blum   ©1999 by Paul H. Brookes Publishing Co.

Cover Letter

Date _____

Dear _____ :

Your student, _____ , is being seen for follow-up assessment and ongoing management of _____ . Your input regarding academic progress, social interactions, emotional functioning, and behavior in the school setting would be extremely valuable in assessing and modifying the current treatment plan. Please complete the enclosed brief academic screening questionnaire and behavior rating scale. Also, enclose a copy of the most recent report card and any interim student support team progress reports, psychoeducational testing results, or standardized achievement test scores (since _____). The parent/legal guardian has given permission (below) to release these records. Please make any additional comments that you believe are relevant at the bottom of either of the enclosed forms. Thank you in advance for your time.

Sincerely,

_____

_____

_____

Telephone _____

Fax _____

I agree with the above request and grant permission to personnel at _____ to release the requested documents and information to _____ at the above address/fax.

Legal guardian signature_____ Date _____

Attention-Deficit/ Hyperactivity Disorder Across the Life Span and Related Topics

The chapters in this section describe important components of the diagnosis and treatment of attention-deficit/hyperactivity disorder (ADHD) in specific age groups. Although much less research has been conducted in individuals who are younger or older than school-age children, several consistent concepts are emerging, some of which indicate commonalities across the life span and others that indiciate unique features by age group. These major concepts are reviewed here and are followed by a brief discussion of two other topics that are relevant to the fact that ADHD occurs in all age groups: long-term outcome and genetic transmission.

Many parents of preschool-age children are concerned about their children's activity levels, emotional lability, temper tantrums, and oppositional behavior; a short attention span is less of a concern at this age. A high activity level and emotional reactivity at this age may reflect enduring characteristics that are part of a constellation of symptoms that ultimately are diagnosed as ADHD. Alternatively, they may be transient, part of a temperamental style that can be minimized with proper management, or symptomatic of a different primary physical or developmental process. The differentiation of "normal" versus "pervasive and functionally impairing" degrees of these symptoms is one distinction that the clinician needs to make. In addition, the course of symptoms during the preschool years may be improvement or persistence. Children whose symptoms persist after 3 years of age may be more likely to have symptoms that progress to a problematic degree into the school years and will be more likely ultimately to be diagnosed with ADHD. Finally, the relatively high prevalence of coexisting or other developmental disorders in preschool-age children who are undergoing evaluation for ADHD (including language disorders, pervasive developmental disorders, and mental retardation) necessitates careful attention to these possibilities during the evaluation.

These children will be eligible for intervention through the public school system to address their learning and behavioral needs. During the preschool years, the clinician may be more likely to follow the child and the family over a period of time, assisting with further assessment and behavioral and other indicated interventions, before making a diagnosis of ADHD. As with older children, stimulant medication can be effective, but the incidence of side effects may be somewhat higher. More studies are needed to assess medication effects in preschool-age children, especially over time.

Clinicians who work with children and families with ADHD know that adolescence can be a particularly trying time for the individual with ADHD and his or her family. Although the assessment for ADHD in adolescents is not substantially different from that for school-age children (with the exception of the need for age-appropriate tests and rating scales), the specific issues addressed in treatment often are quite different. The demand for a greater volume of independent and abstract work in school; a more complex school and social schedule; and more complex relationships with peers, parents, and authority figures outside the home in the face of an increasing need for independence are particularly relevant treatment issues in this age group. Although stimulants continue to be effective in this age group, the higher incidence of affective and conduct disorders during adolescence increases the likelihood that nonstimulant or combination medication strategies will be needed.

Finally, there is a growing body of knowledge about the assessment and treatment of ADHD in adults, but it is still a field in relative "infancy." The final chapter focuses on information that is relevant for the clinician who is caring for a family in which ADHD symptoms are present in a parent and a child. A parent often begins to consider the possibility of this diagnosis for him- or herself after his or her child comes to the attention of a clinician as possibly having ADHD, although the explosion of information about ADHD aimed at the general public has resulted in more adults' seeking evaluations independent of their children. Certainly, more adults who were diagnosed as children will be thinking about whether their own children have ADHD. Given the genetic propensity for this disorder and the research that is aimed at identifying specific genes that are involved (discussed in the section "Genetics"), it is expected that the focus of parental, clinical, and research interest will shift to prevention, perhaps through a combination of modified early experience, more directed medical treatment, and gene therapy. It is hoped that this will provide an improved outlook for the impact of ADHD on the individual and on society.

OUTCOME

Outcome studies of ADHD have been affected by the use of different methodologies, each with different biases as well as the difficulties with performing long-term, prospective analyses. Nonetheless, certain patterns have emerged with some consistency. Overall, there appear to be three different patterns of adult outcome: resolution of symptoms in young adulthood (about 30%); persistence of some functionally impairing symptoms but overall adequate functioning (about 40%); and severe dysfunction associated with persistent symptoms, substance abuse, and antisocial behaviors (about 30%).[1] Adolescents may have a particularly difficult time before developing more constructive coping strategies in young adulthood.[2] Nonetheless, adults with a childhood diagnosis of ADHD complete fewer years of schooling and have lower-ranking occupations than adults without ADHD.[3] Outcome does not appear to differ substantially between males and females.[4] The strongest predictor of poor outcome is the diagnosis of **conduct disorder** (CD) in childhood, usually preceded by early-onset aggressive behavior and **oppositional defiant disorder**.[5] The presence of CD appears to explain the high rates of substance abuse and antisocial behaviors in adolescents with ADHD. In adulthood, the diagnosis of **antisocial personality disorder** rather than CD usually is made.

Predictors of positive outcome are less clear and not individually robust but as a group include high IQ score and socioeconomic status, parents' emotional stability and competence, early multimodal treatment, and positive peer relationships.[6] The relative lack of support for positive treatment effects in ADHD is disconcerting for clinicians but may in part be due to the fact that in the past, many study participants received short-term, selective rather than long-term, comprehensive treatments. A multicenter, multimodal treatment study of ADHD funded by the National Institutes of Health is nearing completion. One of the goals of this study is to assess the effects of various treatments on the 2-year follow-up status of children with ADHD with and without various coexisting diagnoses.[7]

GENETICS

Clinicians who work with children with ADHD are well aware that ADHD runs in families. Twin, adoption, and family epidemiological studies indicate that the familial clustering largely is genetic rather than "learned," yet there does not appear to be a simple **Mendelian inheritance pattern.** It is likely that if ADHD is caused primarily by a single gene, then additional factors influence its expression. Alternatively, it may be a polygenic disorder, or there may be several different genetic etiologies, perhaps related to clinically identifiable heterogeneous subgroups. The frequent presence of coexisting disorders adds to the genetic complexity.[8] Children with ADHD who do not have a positive family history have a higher incidence of prenatal and perinatal complications, suggesting that there may be multiple etiologies.[9]

Research that uses molecular genetic technology in combination with pedigree analysis has begun to provide information about candidate genes that may contribute to ADHD symptoms. Technology allows the detection of minute differences in genetic sequences between individuals in identifiable regions of specific chromosomes. Associations with ADHD or related symptoms have been found between specific forms of the **dopamine transporter**[10] and the **dopamine type 4 receptor**.[11]

Biederman and colleagues have performed extensive genetic-epidemiological studies in an attempt to improve our better understanding of the relationships between ADHD and coexisting disorders within families by comparing the frequency of combined disorders in the first- and second-degree relatives of **probands** with and without the coexisting disorder. Their results suggest that individuals with ADHD and their relatives are at greater risk for having **affective** and **antisocial disorders;** however, the nature of the association of these different types of coexisting disorders differs. **Major depressive disorder** (MDD) may share common familial vulnerabilities with ADHD in that it is present more frequently in the relatives of probands with either ADHD + MDD or ADHD alone. **Anxiety disorders** (AD) (see the list in Table 2 in Chapter 1) appear to be transmitted independently because there is an increased risk for AD in the relatives of probands with ADHD + AD, but not in those with ADHD alone. ADHD and AD are not necessarily transmitted together. ADD + CD appears to be a distinct subtype because there is an increased incidence of CD in the relatives of probands with ADHD + CD, not ADHD alone, and the two are consistently are transmitted together in relatives.[12]

ENDNOTES

1. Reviewed in Cantwell (1996a).
2. Klein & Mannuzza (1991).
3. Mannuzza, Klein, Bessler, Malloy, & Hynes (1997).
4. Klein & Mannuzza (1991).
5. Hechtman (1992), Wilson & Marcotte (1996).
6. Cantwell (1996b), Fischer, Barkley, Fletcher, & Smallish (1993), Hechtman (1992), Klein & Mannuzza (1991).
7. Arnold et al. (1997), Richters et al. (1995).
8. Reviewed in Faraone & Biederman (1994), Lombroso, Pauls, & Leckman (1994).
9. Sprich-Buckminster, Biederman, Milberger, Faraone, & Lehman (1993).
10. Cook et al. (1995).
11. Comings et al. (1996), LaHoste et al. (1996).
12. Biederman et al. (1992), Biederman, Faraone, Keenan, & Tsuang (1991).

REFERENCES

Arnold, L.E., Abikoff, H.B., Cantwell, D.P., Conners, C.K., Elliott, G., Greenhill, L.L., Hechtman, L., Hinshaw, S.P., Hoza, B., Jensen, P.S., Kraemer, H.C., March, J.S., Newcorn, J.H., Pelham, W.E., Richters, J.E., Schiller, E., Severe, J.B., Swanson, J.M., Vereen, D., & Wells, K.C. (1997). National Institute of Mental Health collaborative multimodal treatment study of children with ADHD (the MTA): Design challenges and choices. *Archives of General Psychiatry, 54,* 865–870.

Biederman, J., Faraone, S.V., Keenan, K., Benjamin, J., Krifcher, B., Moore, C., Sprich-Buckminster, S., Ugaglia, K., Jellinek, M.S., Steingard, R., Spencer, T., Norman, D., Kolodny, R., Kraus, I., Perrin, J., Keller, M.B., & Tsuang, M.T. (1992). Further evidence for family-genetic risk factors in attention deficit hyperactivity disorder. *Archives of General Psychiatry, 49,* 728–738.

Biederman, J., Faraone, S.V., Keenan, K., & Tsuang, M.T. (1991). Evidence of familial association between attention deficit disorder and major affective disorders. *Archives of General Psychiatry, 48,* 633–642.

Cantwell, D.P. (1996a). Attention deficit disorder: A review of the past 10 years. *Journal of the American Academy of Child and Adolescent Psychiatry, 35,* 978–987.

Cantwell, D.P. (1996b). Outcome and prognosis of attention deficit disorder and related disorders. *International Pediatrics, 11,* 304–306.

Comings, D.E., Wu, S., Chiu, C., Ring, R.H., Gade, R., Ahn, C., MacMurray, J.P., Dietz, G., & Muhleman, D. (1996). Polygenic inheritance of Tourette syndrome, stuttering, attention deficit hyperactivity, conduct, and oppositional defiant disorder: The additive and subtractive effect of the three dopaminergic genes—DRD2, D beta H, and DAT1. *American Journal of Medical Genetics, 67,* 264–288.

Cook, E.H., Stein, M.A., Krasowski, M.D., Cox, N.J., Olkon, D.M., Kieffer, J.E., & Leventhal, B.L. (1995). Association of attention-deficit disorder and the dopamine transporter gene. *American Journal of Human Genetics, 56,* 993–998.

Faraone, S.V., & Biederman, J. (1994). Genetics of ADHD. *Child and Adolescent Psychiatric Clinics of North America, 3,* 284–301.

Fischer, M., Barkley, R.A., Fletcher, K.E., & Smallish, L. (1993). The adolescent outcome of hyperactive children: Predictors of psychiatric, academic, social, and emotional adjustment. *Journal of the American Academy of Child and Adolescent Psychiatry, 32,* 324–332.

Hechtman, L. (1992). Long-term outcome in attention-deficit hyperactivity disorder [Monograph]. In G. Weiss (Ed.), Attention-deficit hyperactivity disorder, *Child and Adolescent Clinics of North America, 1,* 553–565.

Klein, R.G., & Mannuzza, S. (1991). Long-term outcome of hyperactive children: A review. *Journal of the American Academy of Child and Adolescent Psychiatry, 30,* 383–387.

LaHoste, G.J., Swanson, J.M., Wigal, S.B., Glabe, C., Wigal, T., King, N., & Kennedy, J.L. (1996). Dopamine D4 receptor gene polymorphism is associated with attention deficit hyperactivity disorder. *Molecular Psychiatry, 1,* 121–124.

Lombroso, P.J., Pauls, D.L., & Leckman, J.F. (1994). Genetic mechanisms in childhood psychiatric disorders. *Journal of the American Academy of Child and Adolescent Psychiatry, 33,* 921–938.

Mannuzza, S., Klein, R.G., Bessler, A., Malloy, P., & Hynes, M.E. (1997). Educational and occupational outcome of hyperactive boys grown up. *Journal of the American Academy of Child and Adolescent Psychiatry, 36,* 1222–1227.

Richters, J.E., Arnold, L.E., Jensen, P.S., Abikoff, H., Conners, C.K., Greenhill, L.L., Hechtman, L., Hinshaw, S.P., Pelham, W.E., & Swanson, J.M. (1995). NIMH collaborative multisite multimodal treatment study of children with ADHD: I. Background and rationale. *Journal of the American Academy of Child and Adolescent Psychiatry, 34,* 987–1000.

Sprich-Buckminster, S., Biederman, J., Milberger, S., Faraone, S.V., & Lehman, B.F. (1993). Are perinatal complications relevant to the manifestations of ADD? Issues of comorbidity and familiality. *Journal of the American Academy of Child and Adolescent Psychiatry, 32,* 1032–1037.

Wilson, J.M., & Marcotte, A.C. (1996). Psychosocial adjustment and educational outcome in adolescents with a childhood diagnosis of attention deficit disorder. *Journal of the American Academy of Child and Adolescent Psychiatry, 35,* 579–587.

Attention-Deficit/
Hyperactivity Disorder
in Preschool-Age Children

with Winifred Lloyds Lender

Preschool-age children may exhibit a variety of behaviors that concern parents, other family members, or preschool teachers. Most common, these behaviors include having tantrums, demanding too much attention, overactivity, low frustration tolerance, aggression, sleeping problems, toilet-training problems, food selectivity, and fears or worries. The reputation of 2-year-olds for being difficult to manage is recognized widely, but both the severity and the frequency of management problems seems to peak in 3-year-old children.[1] It often is around this time that a child's overactivity, low frustration tolerance, demands for attention, and oppositional behaviors lead parents or teachers to question whether a child has attention-deficit/hyperactivity disorder (ADHD). This chapter provides information that will help clinicians assess and manage concerns about ADHD in preschool-age children. The chapter begins by describing how ADHD manifests itself during the preschool period, then examines alternative explanations for these symptoms that need to be considered during the assessment. Recommendations about assessment procedures and behavioral and pharmacological treatment in this age group are provided.

INATTENTION, HYPERACTIVITY, AND IMPULSIVITY IN PRESCHOOL-AGE CHILDREN

Several studies of older children with ADHD have shown that their parents first report problems with overactivity, impulsivity, and difficulties with persistence on tasks in the preschool period.[2] Although the behavior of many preschool-age children is characterized by inattention, high activity levels, and impulsivity, parental concerns about these behaviors have been shown to identify children who change activities more during play, engage in activities for shorter periods of time, and get out of their seat more frequently during structured tasks than children who are not viewed as hyperactive by their parents.[3] Often, the symptoms of hyperactivity and impulsivity become apparent before the symptoms of inattention[4]; thus, the Predominantly Hyperactive-Impulsive Type of ADHD is most common during the preschool period,[5] but the majority of these children will have symptoms of inattention as they get older.

Although it is clear that preschool-age children with symptoms that resemble those of ADHD can be identified, it is important to understand the developmental course of these symptoms before concluding that they are related to ADHD symptoms at school age. Longitudinal research suggests that 45%–75% of preschool-age children with ADHD symptoms will continue to have these symptoms at school age and even in adolescence.[6] Although the stability of these behavioral symptoms over long periods of time is remarkable, there remains a significant group of children with symptoms during the preschool period who will not have problems at school age. Research suggests that the severity and the duration of symptoms may help clinicians distinguish the children who are likely to have continuing difficulties. Campbell (1987) found that children who continued to have problems at age 6 years were likely to have been rated as more restless, more inattentive, more disobedient, and more destructive at age 3 than the children who improved. Furthermore, those without persistent symptoms at age 6 showed a significant decrease in symptoms between ages 3 and 4 years, with further decreases in symptoms from ages 4 to 6 years. Those with persistent symptoms showed little decrease in symptoms from ages 3 to 4 years or from ages 4 to 6 years.

Other aspects of the child's **temperament** (see Chapter 5) are important to consider. Children who are not adaptable, who tend to have a negative mood, and who are very intense are more likely to have ongoing problems. This is especially true when these characteristics are combined with high levels of family life stressors, a disorganized home environment, and/or maternal depression.[7] Thus, when clinicians are assessing a preschool-age child and assessing the likelihood of ongoing symptoms, they should consider the severity of the child's current symptoms, duration of the symptoms, characteristics of the child's temperament, the presence of life stressors, and the family environment.

ASSESSMENT OF THE PRESCHOOL-AGE CHILD: DIFFERENTIAL DIAGNOSIS

The diagnosis of ADHD in the preschool-age child, like the diagnosis of ADHD in the older child, relies on the assessment of ADHD symptoms as well as the exclusion of other disorders. Although this process is similar to that used with the older child, the assessment of the younger child requires greater emphasis on the identification of developmental disorders that may first be detectable in the preschool period.

The assessment should include medical history; family history; physical examination; and, occasionally, laboratory studies to detect sensory impairments, seizures, hypo- or hyperthyroidism, and genetic or neurodegenerative disorders. This is described in Chapter 1.

Developmental disorders that may be present in children who are being evaluated for ADHD symptoms include language disorders, **mental retardation** (often termed *developmental delay* in the preschool years), and **pervasive developmental disorder**

(PDD). Children with significant delays in receptive and/or expressive language but nonverbal skills in the normal range are diagnosed with language disorders. Preschool-age children with language disorders are at increased risk for behavior problems including ADHD.[8] In addition to inattention, hyperactivity, and impulsivity, difficulties with verbal communication may contribute to their behavior problems. These children may find that defiant or disruptive behaviors are more effective for communicating their needs. Distinguishing whether disruptive behaviors are related to communication problems, to ADHD, or to both can be difficult. In most cases, if one suspects that communication problems are related to the disruptive behaviors, then the diagnosis of ADHD should be deferred until a speech-language pathologist or a psychologist helps the family to assess and manage the communication problems. The importance of eliciting extra help for these children and families is emphasized by studies that have demonstrated that the behavior problems of preschool-age children with language impairments tend to increase from the preschool- to school-age years, whereas the behavior problems of children without language impairments are more stable.[9] Finally, these children need to be monitored closely when they enter school as they are at increased risk for having **learning disabilities.**

A child with undiagnosed developmental delay or mental retardation may be less proficient in regulating his or her attention span and activity level than peers of the same chronological age and may be identified by parents or teachers as showing signs of ADHD. Children with mental retardation requiring extensive supports are detected easily in the preschool period, but many children with mental retardation requiring intermittent supports are not detected until they enter school. If the activity level and the attention span are appropriate for the child's **developmental age,** then the difficulties with attention span and activity level can be attributed to the mental retardation and not to a separate disorder of ADHD; thus, clinicians who assess preschool children for ADHD should be knowledgeable of the use of developmental screening tests that are helpful in detecting language disorders and mental retardation (see Gilbride, 1995, for a review of developmental screening tools). Children with mental retardation also can have ADHD; therefore, if the child's difficulties with activity level and attention span are significantly above what would be expected for a child of a similar developmental age, then a coexisting diagnosis of ADHD would be appropriate.

Children with PDD are characterized by severe impairments in reciprocal social interactions, impairments in communication and language skills, and repetitive or stereotypical behaviors. Parents may be concerned about delayed language development, the child's lack of interest in activities that interest peers, and the child's failure to look at or even acknowledge adults or children who are speaking to or attempting to interact with them (sometimes they are thought to be deaf). Many children with PDD engage in high levels of activity that may lead to concerns about ADHD. Although the symptoms of PDD can appear similar to ADHD, a careful history and observation of the child will reveal severe deficits in interpersonal skills, communication, and repetitive or other unusual behaviors that typically are not found in individuals with ADHD. The high activity level in children with PDD is so common that it is believed to be part of the underlying disorder; thus, an additional diagnosis of ADHD is not given. The high activity level, nevertheless, can be noted as a target for intervention.

In addition to developmental disorders, other psychiatric or psychological disorders can produce symptoms similar to ADHD. For example, children with oppositional defiant disorder (ODD) routinely fail to follow adults' instructions and, thus, may appear inattentive, hyperactive, or impulsive. In fact, 30%–60% of preschool-age children with ADHD, particularly males, are actively defiant or oppositional in the home and/or at school.[10] Other child characteristics, especially poor adaptability, and family factors such as poor parenting skills, a disorganized home environment, and high levels of life stressors, also may contribute to oppositional behaviors. Other psychiatric disorders such as depression, anxiety (except separation anxiety), and **obsessive-compulsive disorder** are less common in preschool-age children than in older children. When these disorders do occur in preschool-age children, symptoms such as irritability and inattention may cause parents or teachers to suspect that the child has ADHD. The history obtained should focus on all of the difficult or unusual behaviors in which the child engages, not just those thought to be indicative of ADHD (see the history format in Chapter 1 for a guide). Behavior rating scales, discussed later in this chapter, also may be helpful in screening for other behavior or emotional disorders. In addition, questions about life stressors, sources of support for the family, conflict within the family, and daily routines will reveal other factors that contribute to the child's behavior difficulties.

ASSESSMENT OF THE PRESCHOOL-AGE CHILD: ADHD SYMPTOMS

The diagnosis of ADHD in a preschool-age child is complicated by the fact that development occurs at a rapid pace during the preschool years, which results in many transient changes in behavior[11]; thus, it is very important to consider the duration of the symptoms when making a diagnosis of ADHD. Although the *Diagnostic and Statistical Manual of Mental Disorders, Fourth Edition* (DSM-IV)[12] recommends a duration of symptoms of at least 6 months to make the diagnosis of ADHD, a duration of symptoms of at least 12 months is recommended for the preschool-age child.[13] In some cases, especially with the younger preschool-age children, use of this criterion will mean that a diagnosis may not be established at the time of initial evaluation. Deferring the use of a diagnostic label should not prevent the initiation of behavioral counseling if the symptoms are causing significant distress.

The symptoms of ADHD as described in the DSM-IV (see the Introduction) are common in preschool-age children. This is especially true of the hyperactive-impulsive symptoms; thus, it is very important that clinicians assess not only the number of symptoms but also their severity. This should be assessed during the parent interview (see Appendix A for a screening questionnaire) as well as on a standardized rating scale with adequate norms for preschool-age children (described in the next section). The history should focus on detailed descriptions of behaviors that are believed to demonstrate hyperactivity, inattention, or impulsivity and how frequently these behaviors occur. In this manner, the clinician can judge independently whether the described behaviors seem out of the range of normal. For example, parents who complain that a 3-year-old child does not sit through dinner may be describing a child who does not sit through hour-long family dinners, or they may be describing a child who will not stay in his or her seat for longer than 5 minutes to eat. In this example, the initial concern is the same and suggests the possibility that the child is overactive, but only a detailed description of the event will allow the clinician to distinguish these two different situations. If the child is in preschool or child care, then a discussion with the caregiver in that setting allows the clinician to obtain an assessment of the child's activity level, attention span, and impulsivity across situations.

Rating scales also are helpful in the assessment of the severity of symptoms and provide an efficient way to obtain information from other care providers. If the child is in a preschool setting, then rating scales should be completed by the parents and the teacher. If scores on both parent and teacher rating scales are above the 93rd percentile (1.5 standard deviations above the mean) for children of the same age and gender, then it is very likely that the child's symptoms are severe. If a score above the 93rd percentile is obtained from only one of the two raters, then this may indicate that the demands on the child are different across settings, that the adults in each setting are employing different behavior management strategies, or that the adults have different perceptions about which behaviors are normal versus problematic. Behavioral interventions (described in the next section and in Chapter 6) should be implemented to help the child in the setting where he or she is having difficulties. Clinicians should continue to monitor the child carefully as additional symptoms that are indicative of ADHD may arise over time.

If the child does not attend a preschool, then it can be more difficult to determine the pervasiveness of the symptoms. At a minimum, information from each parent should be obtained. An experienced nanny or other caregiver may provide useful information. It will be crucial to assess the parents' skills in managing their child's behavior. If the clinician has concerns about these skills, then it is best to defer the diagnosis until after behavioral counseling or parent training has occurred.

ASSESSMENT OF THE PRESCHOOL-AGE CHILD: BEHAVIOR RATING SCALES

The use of parent and teacher behavior rating scales is an important component of any assessment battery. A discussion of the advantages and disadvantages of using rating scales to assess behavior can be found in Chapter 2. As is true of rating scales for school-age children, some scales for preschool-age children assess a wide range of behavioral and emotional issues, and others are more specific to ADHD. In most cases, it will make sense to use a wide-range scale for the initial assessment to screen for a range of behavior or emotional problems. Narrow-range scales that are specific to ADHD can be used for follow-up assessments or to assess the effects of interventions. There are fewer well-normed scales that are designed for use with preschool-age children than for school-age children. Information on some of the scales that do have norms for preschool-age children is provided next. (Ordering information for these scales is available at the end of this chapter.)

Rating Scales that Assess a Wide Range of Behaviors

1. The Behavior Assessment System for Children (BASC)[14] has parent and teacher scales for children ages 4–18 years, with a form that is specific to children ages 4–5 years. Both the parent and the teacher preschool forms yield scores for the child in the area of **internalizing problems,** with subscales for anxiety, depression, and withdrawal, and in the area of **externalizing problems,** with subscales for hyperactivity, aggression, and conduct problems. Other domains assessed include inattention, somatization, and atypical behaviors.
2. The Devereux Early Childhood Assessment[15] is appropriate for use with children ages 2–5 years. It can be completed by parents and teachers. The rating scale yields two general Problem Behavior scale scores, Internalizing Behaviors and Externalizing Behaviors, and two Protective Factors scale scores, Adaptability and Self-Efficacy.

3. The Child Behavior Checklist (CBCL)[16] has norms for children as young as age 2 years for parent report and age 5 years for teacher report. There is a scale for children ages 2–3 years that yields the following scores: Internalizing problems (subscales: Anxious/Depressed, Withdrawn), Externalizing problems (subscales: Aggressive Behavior, Destructive Behavior), and Other Behaviors (subscales: Sleep Problems, Somatic Problems). The scale for children ages 4–18 years is reviewed in Chapter 2.

4. The Behavioral Style Questionnaire (BSQ)[17] provides ratings of the nine temperament characteristics identified by Thomas, Chess, Birch, Hertzig, and Korn (1963): activity level, rhythmicity (regularity of physiological functions), approach-withdrawal to new stimuli, adaptability, intensity, mood, persistence/attention span, distractibility, and sensory threshold (amount of stimulation required to evoke responses). This questionnaire is designed for use with children between 3 and 7 years of age. It differs from the previous questionnaires in that it is not specifically designed to detect psychopathology; rather, it is helpful in identifying those aspects of a child's temperament (including but not limited to activity and attention span) that may make the child difficult for his or her parents to manage.

Rating Scales that Assess a Narrow Range of Behaviors

1. The ADHD Symptom Checklist-4,[18] which is appropriate for use with children ages 3–18 years, can be completed by both parents and teachers and provides the following scores: ADHD Inattentive Type, ADHD Hyperactive-Impulsive Type, ADHD Combined Type, and Oppositional Defiant Disorder. The items on each scale come directly from the DSM-IV description of symptoms for each of the disorders, and the scale contains specific information about how to resolve differences in parent and teacher ratings of the child's behavior.

2. The Conners' Rating Scale, Revised–Short Form[19] allows for parent and teacher rating of children ages 3–17 years. The rating scale yields a Hyperactivity score, an Oppositional score, Cognitive Problems, and an ADHD Index score. The ADHD Index is designed to screen for ADHD and contains the 12 items that were found to be most predictive of a diagnosis of ADHD using DSM-IV criteria.

ASSESSMENT OF THE PRESCHOOL-AGE CHILD: DIRECT OBSERVATION

Direct observation of the child during structured and unstructured tasks will provide valuable information about the child's development and behavior that may assist in the differential diagnosis. Although the child's behavior during the visit to the clinician's office may not be representative of the child's typical behavior (often, children are more attentive and compliant because of the novelty of the situation and the one-to-one attention that they receive), it can supply important information about the child's developmental capabilities, interaction patterns with parents, and temperament. The use of a structured activity with the child, such as a brief developmental inventory, provides information about the child's compliance, response style, attention to tasks, and level of skill development.

When assessing a preschool-age child, it is necessary to make accommodations based on the child's age. First, preschool-age children may resist being separated from their parents to go with the clinician into an unfamiliar room. To ameliorate any of the child's distress that is related to separation from the parents, it is recommended that the parents be present with the child during the evaluation. In addition, the clinician should remember that preschool-age children, particularly those suspected of having attention and activity problems, have a limited attention span and are able to remain seated for only brief periods of time. To prolong the child's attention span during the assessment, the clinician should have age-appropriate toys available for the child to play with when the parent is interviewed or should ask the parent to bring the child's favorite toys to the office. Reinforcers such as stickers can be offered for complying with office rules or for paying attention to tasks. Because the preschool-age child's behavior during an office visit may be different from his or her behavior in the home and at school, the clinician should ask the parents about the representativeness of the child's behavior during the session.

TREATMENT OF ADHD IN PRESCHOOL-AGE CHILDREN: FAMILY AND BEHAVIORAL COUNSELING

Parents of preschool-age children with ADHD report experiencing higher levels of stress that is related to their daily parental role than do parents of preschool-age children without ADHD and parents of older children with ADHD.[20] Not surprising, the interactions of mothers with their preschool-age children with ADHD are characterized by more commands, directives, criticism, supervision, and punishment than the interactions of mothers with their preschool-age children without ADHD.[21] In some cases, the majority of parent–child interactions are coercive.[22] In this situation, the child uses primarily aversive behaviors such as whining, tantrums, or aggression to get parental attention, to get access to desired tangible items such as candy or toys, and/or to escape parental task demands such as cleaning one's room. The more frequently that aversive behaviors are successful in gaining access to reinforcers or avoiding undesired situations, the more likely these behaviors are to occur in the future. Parents may respond to these behaviors by frequently threatening or punishing the child. The threats and punishments may stop the aversive behavior, at least briefly, and, thus, make it more likely that parents will use threats and punishments in the future. The majority of interactions, therefore, may involve whining, tantrums, and aggression on the part of the child and threats and punishments on the part of the parents.[23] Parents may feel frustrated and angry. Offhand advice from a family friend or others on child rearing may lead parents to feel incompetent and may contribute to poor self-esteem and feelings of hopelessness. Whenever a preschool-age child's behavior is eliciting these types of interactions between parents and child or these types of feelings in parents, counseling should be recommended, regardless of the diagnosis.

Counseling should incorporate both support for the parents and teaching of behavior management strategies as described in Chapter 6. The behavior management techniques that are used with preschool-age children are similar to those that are used with school-age children. The subsequent discussion emphasizes modifications that should be considered when these procedures are used with preschool-age children. With these children, it is especially important that the interventions focus on the use of reinforcers and consequences as opposed to verbal explanations and reasoning. Because a preschool-age child's reasoning skills are limited, providing the child with verbal explanations to decrease inappropriate behavior is not likely to be effective.[24] Moreover, if prolonged verbal interactions with the parent occur after inappropriate behavior, then the attention that the child is receiving during this interaction may reinforce the inappropriate behavior.

Reinforcement of Appropriate Behavior

As with older children, behavior management strategies for preschool-age children should focus on reinforcing appropriate behavior. For preschool-age children with ADHD, it is especially important that the reinforcer be immediate, clear, meaningful, and varied. The immediacy of a reinforcer is essential because the child must connect the behavior with the reinforcer; thus, providing the child with verbal praise and a sticker for sitting during circle time immediately after circle time will be more effective than providing the sticker at the end of the day. The immediacy of the reinforcer not only helps the preschool-age child connect clearly which behavior led to the reinforcer but also provides the child with a reminder about which behaviors are being encouraged and that good behavior "pays off."

Reinforcement should be clear. Telling a preschool-age child, "I liked your behavior during circle time," does not identify clearly which particular behavior is being rewarded. Instead, telling the child, "I like the way you sat still and kept your hands to yourself during circle time," identifies clearly to the child which specific behaviors are being reinforced. Similarly, when a tangible reinforcer is provided, it should be accompanied by a clear, understandable, and concise explanation.

In addition, a reinforcer must be meaningful to the child; it should be something that the child wants to earn. For preschool-age children, verbal praise, stickers, candy, visits to places that they enjoy, special playtime with parents, renting a video, extra time watching television, and toys typically are reinforcing; however, each child has his or her own individual preference for reinforcers. Although preschool-age children may be somewhat limited in their ability to identify and verbalize reinforcers that are most meaningful, the parent often is able to identify what their children really like. For a reinforcer to be meaningful, it also must be something to which the children do not have access all of the time. Providing the child with ice cream for sitting through dinner will not be meaningful if the child can have ice cream whenever he or she wants it throughout the day.

Finally, reinforcers are most effective when they are varied. One way to ensure variety is to use a grab bag system whereby the child picks from a bag filled with slips of paper, each naming a reinforcer that had been identified as being meaningful to the child. Varying reinforcers will prevent the child from satiating on any one reinforcer and will maintain interest in the behavior modification program.

Punishment

When inappropriate but nondangerous behaviors occur, it often is best to ignore them. For example, if a teacher ignores children who frequently call out during circle time and instead calls on children who raise their hands, then over time the children who call out are likely to learn to raise their hands when they want to speak. This process is referred to as **extinction.** As discussed in Chapter 6, the initial response to extinction may be an increase in inappropriate behavior; thus, ignoring is not a good strategy for aggressive or destructive behavior.

When destructive or aggressive behavior occurs, it is likely that a punishment procedure will be needed. Loss of privileges or **time-out** are punishment procedures that can be effective with preschool-age children. Privileges that preschool-age children may lose include use of a toy and television, videotape, or storytime. Other punishments include having to come inside the house early and having to go to bed early. For preschool-age children, the consequences will be most effective when they occur immediately after the problem behavior. For instance, if two children are fighting over a toy, then loss of the toy will be much more effective than losing television time later in the day.

Time-out is described in Chapter 5. When used with preschool-age children, the time-out procedure should be explained in clear and simple language. Often, it is useful to practice the time-out procedure before implementing it so that the child knows what to do. The preschool-age child should be placed in time-out for a briefer period than older children with a maximum of about 1 minute for each year of age. If the child is still screaming or having a tantrum at the end of this time period, however, then the time-out should be prolonged until the child has begun to calm down.

Whichever punishment procedure one uses, it is important to remember that punishment alone may decrease negative behavior but will not teach appropriate behaviors; thus, a behavior management plan that utilizes a punishment procedure must be coupled with a plan for the positive reinforcement of appropriate behavior.

TREATMENT OF ADHD IN PRESCHOOL-AGE CHILDREN: EDUCATIONAL CONSIDERATIONS

Preschool-age children with ADHD are noted to be extremely difficult to manage in the preschool classroom, and many are dismissed from preschool programs.[25] The preschool experience can be very frustrating to the child with ADHD and to his or her parents and preschool teacher. Often, all parties feel as though preschool has been a failure for the child and feel hopeless about the child's future schooling.

Certain preschool settings are more supportive for the child with ADHD. Specifically, a preschool program with a small student-to-teacher ratio, a consistent and predictable daily schedule, the option of a half-day program, and clear behavioral expectations is preferable for a child with ADHD. This program should provide the external structure that the child needs without being rigid about activities or routines. Preschool teachers should appreciate that all children learn and behave differently and should make accommodations to support the learning and behavior of the individual children. For example, the teacher should not adhere rigidly to certain behavioral expectations that the child with ADHD cannot meet (e.g., all children must sit quietly in circle time for 20 minutes) but should be willing to support accommodations to increase the child's ability to be successful in the class environment (e.g., after a child sits in circle time for 10 minutes, he or she may leave the circle and play quietly).

Behavioral interventions can be used effectively in preschool classrooms.[26] Procedures that involve children's earning tokens for following rules or losing tokens when breaking rules have been found to decrease disruptive behaviors. If the child earns the required number of tokens, then he or she can exchange them for a larger reward at the end of the day.[27]

TREATMENT OF ADHD IN PRESCHOOL-AGE CHILDREN: PHARMACOLOGICAL INTERVENTION

In many cases, the behavioral difficulties of preschool-age children with ADHD can be managed through parent counseling and education about ADHD along with behavior management strategies and identification of a supportive preschool program. There are some children, however, who, despite these interventions, continue to have hyperactivity, impulsivity, and inattention that cause persistent problems in the parent–child relationship, the preschool experience, and/or the child's ability to engage in developmentally appropriate peer relationships. For these preschool-age children, pharmacological treatment of the ADHD should be considered.

Stimulant medications such as methylphenidate (Ritalin) and dextroamphetamine (Dexedrine) have been shown to decrease hyperactivity, improve on-task behavior, and improve compliance with parental instructions in preschool-age children.[28] These improvements may result in fewer parental negative and controlling responses to the child's behavior. In combination with behavioral counseling, these medication effects could be very significant in interrupting a cycle of negative or coercive parent–child interactions; however, despite these effects, studies have demonstrated that from 33% to more than 67% of the parents of preschool-age children elect not to continue their children on stimulant medications after the study is over.[29]

The reasons that such a high percentage of parents elect not to continue stimulant medications in preschool-age children are not well studied, but it is likely that multiple factors contribute. Often, the effects of these medications are most dramatic in situations that place demands on the child for high levels of attention or low levels of activity and impulsivity. The effects may not even be observable in free-play situations. Preschool-age children are likely to spend a significant portion of their day in free-play situations in which the medications may not be as beneficial. Even in demand situations, there may be a lower response rate to stimulants in preschool-age compared with school-age children. Side effects also may be important. One study found that preschool-age children tended to develop a negative mood or become socially withdrawn while taking stimulant medication,[30] but others have not reported a high incidence of side effects.[31] Finally, treatment of behavior with medications may not be as acceptable to parents of preschool-age children as it is to parents of school-age children.

When methylphenidate is used in preschool-age children, it is usually is used at dosages of between 0.15 milligrams (mg)/kilogram (kg)/dose and 0.5 mg/kg/dose. Dextroamphetamine usually is used at dosages of between 0.15 mg/kg/dose and 0.3 mg/kg/dose. Generally, dosages toward the upper end of these ranges are more effective than lower dosages,[32] but because higher dosages may be associated with more side effects, the child should be started on a low dosage that can be increased if the child is not responding. Schleifer and colleagues (1975) reported the use of dosages above the range described here but also reported problems with negative mood and social withdrawal, suggesting that these may be dosage-related side effects. Similar to older children, the effects on appetite and growth are usually are mild, at least over the short run. There are not studies of children who began a long course of stimulant treatment during the preschool period.

In summary, stimulants may be an important component of a treatment package for preschool-age children. Clinicians and parents should agree ahead of time on which behaviors they expect the medication to change and then monitor the child's response. Side effects usually are mild and similar to those seen in school-age children, although, especially at high dosages, young children may be more susceptible to stimulants' negative effects on mood and social interactions.

The other medications that are used to treat ADHD in older children and adolescents have not been studied for preschool-age children. Anecdotal experience suggests that clonidine (Catapres) or guanfacine (Tenex) will decrease hyperactivity and impulsivity in some preschool-age children. Although parents often report an initial beneficial effect from these medications, in many cases the effect seems to decrease over time.

Dosage ranges for these medications in preschool-age children are not described, so one should start at a low dosage (0.05 mg/dose for clonidine and 0.5 mg/dose for guanfacine) at bedtime and titrate the dosage based on effects and side effects. Further information about these medications is available in Chapter 9. Tricyclic antidepressants generally are not recommended for the treatment of ADHD in preschool-age children, as no data exist to support their efficacy and younger children seem to be at increased risk for the cardiac side effects of these medications.[33]

CONCLUSION

Children who are inattentive, hyperactive, and impulsive can be identified during the preschool period and often will cause significant distress to their parents and preschool teachers. When this occurs, behavioral counseling should be provided either by the clinician or through referral to a mental health provider who has expertise in the management of preschool behavior problems. For a portion of these children, the problems with inattention, hyperactivity, and impulsivity will persist for more than 1 year. These children are likely to have ongoing problems at school age, and a diagnosis of ADHD will be appropriate for many of them. Stimulant medication may be an important part of a treatment plan that includes counseling and educational interventions, but stimulants may not be as effective an intervention for preschool-age children as they are for school-age children.

ENDNOTES

1. Crowther, Bond, & Rolf (1981), Lavigne et al. (1996).
2. Barkley, Fischer, Edelbrock, & Smallish (1990), McGee, Williams, & Feehan (1992).
3. Alessandri (1992), Campbell, Szumowski, Ewing, Gluck, & Breaux (1982).
4. Green, Loeber, & Lahey (1991).
5. Lahey et al. (1994).
6. Beitchman, Wekerle, & Hood (1978), McGee, Partridge, Williams, & Silva (1991).
7. Egeland, Kalkoske, Gottesman, & Erickson (1990), Sanson, Smart, Prior, & Oberklaid (1993).
8. Love & Thompson (1988).
9. Benasich, Curtiss, & Tallal (1993).
10. Barkley (1998).
11. Shelton & Barkley (1990).
12. American Psychiatric Association (1994).
13. Barkley (1990).
14. Reynolds & Kamphaus (1992).
15. LeBuffe & Naglieri (1998).
16. Achenbach (1986).
17. McDevitt & Carey (1978).
18. Gadow & Sprafkin (1997).
19. Conners (1997).
20. Mash & Johnson (1982, 1983).
21. Barkley (1988), Campbell (1990).
22. Patterson (1982).
23. Ibid.
24. Blum, Williams, Friman, & Christophersen (1995).
25. Barkley (1998).
26. McCain & Kelley (1993).
27. McGoey, DuPaul, & Power (1998).
28. Alessandri & Schramm (1991), Barkley (1988), Conners (1975).
29. Barkley (1988), Cohen, Sullivan, Minde, Novak, & Helwig (1981), Schleifer et al. (1975).
30. Schleifer et al. (1975).

31. Barkley (1988), Conners (1975).
32. Barkley (1988).
33. Green (1995).

REFERENCES

Achenbach, T.M. (1986). *Child Behavior Checklist for Ages 2–3*. Burlington: University of Vermont.

Alessandri, S.M. (1992). Attention, play, and social behavior in ADHD preschoolers. *Journal of Abnormal Child Psychology, 20*, 289–302.

Alessandri, S.M., & Schramm, K. (1991). Effects of dextroamphetamine on the cognitive and social play of a preschooler with ADHD. *Journal of the American Academy of Child and Adolescent Psychiatry, 30*, 768–772.

American Psychiatric Association. (1994). *Diagnostic and statistical manual of mental disorders* (4th ed.). Washington, DC: Author.

Barkley, R.A. (1988). The effects of methylphenidate on the interactions of preschool ADHD children with their mothers. *Journal of the American Academy of Child and Adolescent Psychiatry, 27*, 336–341.

Barkley, R.A. (1998). *Attention-deficit hyperactivity disorder: A handbook for diagnosis and treatment* (2nd ed.). New York: Guilford Press.

Barkley, R.A., Fischer, M., Edelbrock, C.S., & Smallish, L. (1990). The adolescent outcome of hyperactive children diagnosed by research criteria: I. An 8 year prospective follow-up study. *Journal of the American Academy of Child and Adolescent Psychiatry, 29*, 546–557.

Beitchman, J., Wekerle, C., & Hood, J. (1978). Diagnostic continuity from preschool to middle childhood. *Journal of the American Academy of Child and Adolescent Psychiatry, 26*, 694–699.

Benasich, A.A., Curtiss, S., & Tallal, P. (1993). Language, learning, and behavioral disturbances in childhood: A longitudinal perspective. *Journal of the American Academy of Child and Adolescent Psychiatry, 32*, 585–594.

Blum, N.J., Williams, G.E., Friman, P.C., & Christophersen, E.R. (1995). Disciplining young children: The role of verbal instructions and reasoning. *Pediatrics, 96*, 336–341.

Campbell, S.B. (1987). Parent referred problem three-year-olds: Developmental changes in symptoms. *Journal of Child Psychology and Psychiatry, 28*, 835–845.

Campbell, S.B. (1990). *Behavior problems in preschool children: Clinical and developmental issues*. New York: Guilford Press.

Campbell, S.B., Szumowski, E.K., Ewing, L.J., Gluck, D.S., & Breaux, A.M. (1982). A multidimensional assessment of parent-identified behavior problems in toddlers. *Journal of Abnormal Child Psychology, 10*, 569–592.

Cohen, N.J., Sullivan, J., Minde, K., Novak, C., & Helwig, C. (1981). Evaluation of the relative effectiveness of methylphenidate and cognitive behavior modification in the treatment of kindergarten-aged hyperactive children. *Journal of Abnormal Child Psychology, 9*, 43–54.

Conners, C.K. (1975). Controlled trial of methylphenidate in preschool children with minimal brain dysfunction. *International Journal of Mental Health, 4*, 61–74.

Conners, C.K. (1997). *Conners' Rating Scale Revised–Short Form: Technical manual*. North Tonawanda, NY: Multi-Health Systems.

Crowther, J.H., Bond, L.A., & Rolf, J.E. (1981). The incidence, prevalence, and severity of behavior disorders among preschool children in day care. *Journal of Abnormal Child Psychology, 9*, 23–42.

Egeland, B., Kalkoske, M., Gottesman, N., & Erickson, M.F. (1990). Preschool behavior problems: Stability and factors accounting for change. *Journal of Child Psychology and Psychiatry, 31*, 891–909.

Gadow, K.D., & Sprafkin, J. (1997). *ADHD Symptom Checklist-4*. Stony Brook, NY: Checkmate Plus.

Gilbride, K.E. (1995). Developmental testing. *Pediatrics in Review, 16*, 338–345.

Green, S.M., Loeber, R., & Lahey, B.B. (1991). Stability of mothers' recall of the age of onset of their child's attention and hyperactivity problems. *Journal of the American Academy of Child and Adolescent Psychiatry, 30*, 135–137.

Green, W.H. (1995). The treatment of attention-deficit hyperactivity disorder with nonstimulant medications. *Child and Adolescent Psychiatric Clinics of North America, 4*, 169–195.

Lahey, B.B., Applegate, B., McBurnett, K., Biederman, J., Greenhill, L., Hynd, G.W., Barkley, R.A., Newcorn, J., Jensen, P., Richters, J., Garfinkel, B., Kerdyk, L., Frick, P.J., Ollendick, T., Perez, D., Hart, E.L., Waldman, I., & Shaffer, D. (1994). DSM-IV field trials for attention deficit hyperactivity disorder in children and adolescents. *American Journal of Psychiatry, 151,* 1673–1685.

Lavigne, J.V., Gibbons, R.D., Christoffel, K.K., Arend, R., Rosenbaum, D., Binns, H., Dawson, N., Sobel, H., & Isaacs, C. (1996). Prevalence rates and correlates of psychiatric disorders among preschool children. *Journal of the American Academy of Child and Adolescent Psychiatry, 35,* 204–214.

LeBuffe, P., & Naglieri, J. (1998). *Devereux Early Childhood Assessment.* Villanova, PA: The Devereux Foundation.

Love, A.J., & Thompson, M.G. (1988). Language disorders and attention deficit disorders in young children referred for psychiatric services. *American Journal of Orthopsychiatry, 58,* 52–64.

Mash, E.J., & Johnson, C. (1982). A comparison of the mother–child interactions of younger and older hyperactive and normal children. *Child Development, 53,* 1371–1381.

Mash, E.J., & Johnson, C. (1983). Parental perceptions of child behavior problems, parenting self-esteem, and mother's reported stress in younger and older hyperative and normal children. *Journal of Consulting and Clinical Psychology, 51,* 68–99.

McCain, A.P., & Kelley, M.L. (1993). Managing the classroom behavior of an ADHD preschooler: The efficacy of a school–home note intervention. *Child and Family Behavior Therapy, 15,* 33–44.

McDevitt, S.C., & Carey, W.B. (1978). The measurement of temperament in 3–7 year old children. *Journal of Child Psychology and Psychiatry, 19,* 245–253.

McGee, R., Partridge, F., Williams, S., & Silva, P. (1991). A twelve year follow-up of preschool hyperactive children. *Journal of the American Academy of Child and Adolescent Psychiatry, 30,* 224–232.

McGee, R., Williams, S., & Feehan, M. (1992). Attention deficit disorder and age of onset of problem behaviors. *Journal of Abnormal Child Psychology, 20,* 487–502.

McGoey, K.E., DuPaul, G.J., & Power, T.J. (1998, April). *Response cost and positive reinforcement interventions: Reducing the disruptive behavior of preschool children at-risk for ADHD.* Paper presented at the annual conference of the National Association of School Psychologists, Orlando, FL.

Patterson, G.R. (1982). *Coercive family process.* Eugene, OR: Castalia.

Reynolds, C.R., & Kamphaus, R.W. (1992). *The Behavior Assessment System for Children.* Circle Pines, MN: American Guidance Service.

Sanson, A., Smart, D., Prior, M., & Oberklaid, F. (1993). Precursors of hyperactivity and aggression. *Journal of the American Academy of Child and Adolescent Psychiatry, 32,* 1207–1216.

Schleifer, M., Weiss, G., Cohen, N., Elman, M., Cvejic, H., & Kruger, E. (1975). Hyperactivity in preschoolers and the effect of methylphenidate. *American Journal of Orthopsychiatry, 45,* 38–50.

Shelton, T.L., & Barkley, R.A. (1990). Clinical developmental and biopsychosocial considerations. In R.A. Barkley (Ed.), *Attention deficit hyperactivity disorder: A handbook for diagnosis and treatment* (pp. 209–231). New York: Guilford Press.

Thomas, A., Chess, S., Birch, H.G., Hertzig, M.E., & Korn, S. (1963). *Behavioral individuality in early childhood.* New York: New York University Press.

RESOURCES FOR PARENTS

Carey, W.B. (1997). *Understanding your child's temperament.* New York: Macmillan.

Christophersen, E.R. (1988). *Little people.* Kansas City, MO: Westport Publishers.

Flick, G.L. (1996). *Power parenting for children with ADD/ADHD: A practical parent's guide for managing difficult behaviors.* West Nyack, NY: The Center for Applied Research in Education.

Greenspan, S.I., & Salmon, J. (1995). *The challenging child: Understanding, raising, and enjoying the five "difficult" types of children.* Reading, MA: Addison Wesley Longman.

Kurcinka, M.S. (1991). *Raising your spirited child: A guide for parents whose child is more intense, sensitive, perceptive, persistent, energetic.* New York: HarperCollins.

Nelson, J., Erwin, C., & Duffy, R. (1995). *Positive discipline for preschoolers.* Rocklin, CA: Prima Publishing Co. (To order, call [800] 632-8676)

Phelan, T.W. (1990). *1-2-3 Magic: Training your children to do what you want.* Glen Ellyn, IL: Child Management.

Turccki, S. (1985). *The difficult child.* New York: Bantam Books.

ORDERING INFORMATION FOR RATING SCALES

ADHD Symptom Checklist-4 (Parent and teacher scale)
Gadow & Sprafkin (1997)
Checkmate Plus
Post Office Box 696
Stony Brook, NY 11790-0696
(800) 779-4292

Behavior Assessment for Children (Parent and Teacher Rating Scales)
Reynolds & Kamphaus (1992)
American Guidance Service, Inc.
4201 Woodland Road
Circle Pines, MN 55014-1796
(800) 328-2560

Behavioral Style Questionnaire (Temperament scale for parents)
McDevitt & Carey (1978)
Behavioral-Developmental Initiatives East
1316 West Chester Pike
Suite 131
West Chester, PA 19382-6425
(800) 234-8303

Child Behavior Checklist (Preschool form for parents)
Achenbach (1986)
University Medical Education Associates
One South Prospect Street
Burlington, VT 05401-3456
(802) 656-8313

Conners' Rating Scale Revised–Short Form (Parent and teacher rating scales)
Conners (1997)
Multi-Health Systems Inc.
908 Niagara Falls Boulevard
North Tonawanda, NY 14120-2060
(800) 456-3003

Devereux Early Childhood Assessment (One form for parents and teachers)
LeBuffe & Naglieri (1998)
The Devereux Foundation
444 Devereux Drive
Post Office Box 638
Villanova, PA 19085
(610) 520-3000

A

Parent Behavior Screening
Questionnaire for Preschool-Age Children

PARENT BEHAVIOR SCREENING QUESTIONNAIRE FOR PRESCHOOL CHILDREN

Child's name _____ Date questionnaire completed _____

Date of birth _____

Which behaviors are of concern to you? _____

_____

For how long have you had concerns about these behaviors? _____

_____

Did the problematic behaviors start around the time of a transition in your child's life (e.g., when he or she entered child care, when a sibling was born, when a parent left the home)? If yes, then please explain: _____

_____

Has your child's behavior become more or less problematic over time? _____

For how long will your child sit during mealtimes? If it varies, then please give the range:

_____

Are problem behaviors more or less likely to occur during routines such as getting dressed in the morning or getting ready for bed? _____

How often do you have to repeat instructions or commands several times before your child responds? _____

For how long will your child engage in one activity other than watching TV? _____

Does your child display any problematic behaviors when interacting with his or her peers? If yes, then please explain: _____

_____

Which activities does your child enjoy? _____

_____

Which activities do you enjoy doing with your child, and how often do you do them?

_____

_____

Are there concerns about your child's behavior in any other setting besides the home (e.g., preschool, child care, sports groups, play groups)? If yes, then please describe: _____

_____

_____

Is your child's behavior more problematic with some adults than with others? If yes, then please explain: _____

_____

What have you found helpful in managing your child's behavior? _____

_____

The Clinician's Practical Guide to Attention-Deficit/Hyperactivity Disorder
by Marianne Mercugliano, Thomas J. Power, and Nathan J. Blum   ©1999 by Paul H. Brookes Publishing Co.

Peer Relationships

Number of friends _____

Organized activities with peers _____ Problems _____

Unstructured activities with peers _____ Problems _____

Peer risk-taking behaviors _____

Interim Medical History

Allergies _____

Additional medications _____

Chronic illnesses/new diagnoses _____

Ilnesses/hospitalizations _____

Symptoms: Headaches _____

                          Stomachaches _____

                          Changes in appetite _____

                          Tics _____

                          Staring spells _____

Physical Exam

Height _____   Percentile _____

Weight _____   Percentile _____

Pulse _____

BP _____

Other positive findings:_____

_____

_____

_____

Assessment and Plan

_____

_____

_____

_____

_____

_____

_____

_____

The Clinician's Practical Guide to Attention-Deficit/Hyperactivity Disorder
by Marianne Mercugliano, Thomas J. Power, and Nathan J. Blum   ©1999 by Paul H. Brookes Publishing Co.

13

Attention-Deficit/ Hyperactivity Disorder in Adolescents

with Edward Moss

There are special issues in the care of adolescents with attention-deficit/hyperactivity disorder (ADHD), regardless of whether they are presenting for an initial evaluation or have been diagnosed in childhood and have persistent symptoms. The criteria that are listed in the *Diagnostic and Statistical Manual of Mental Disorders, Fourth Edition* (DSM-IV)[1] are not different for adolescents; however, adolescents may be "restless" rather than excessively active, and they may have fewer symptoms.[2] The diagnosis of ADHD in adolescence may be hindered by the age of onset criterion, which first was introduced in the *Diagnostic and Statistical Manual of Mental Disorders, Third Edition* (DSM-III).[3] To establish chronicity, inattentive or hyperactive/impulsive symptoms must be present prior to age 7. The validity of this empirical age requirement is questionable and may discriminate arbitrarily against older adolescents who truly have ADHD. Some researchers have argued for a broader age cutoff, perhaps extending through childhood.[4]

The student who is diagnosed with ADHD in middle school, high school, or college commonly has the Predominantly Inattentive Type of ADHD, an above-average IQ score, and parents and teachers who have provided structure and support throughout the school years. Adolescents who previously were diagnosed with ADHD are likely to have a persistence of symptoms, including continued academic and social difficulties and intensified parent–child conflicts. In addition, coexisting **mood disorders** frequently become apparent in early adolescence. Specific concerns in the adolescent with ADHD include inability or lack of motivation to complete school work, disorganization, procrastination, declining grades, school failure, truancy, dropping out, the appearance of coexisting disorders (e.g., **depression, anxiety disorders** [AD], **conduct**

disorder [CD]), noncompliance with parental and school rules, difficulties with initiating or maintaining friendships, and friendships with undesirable companions.

ASSESSMENT OF ADHD AND COEXISTING DIAGNOSES IN ADOLESCENTS

Despite clear evidence that ADHD symptoms persist into adolescence and adulthood,[5] until the late 1980s and early 1990s there was a paucity of research into the assessment and treatment of ADHD beyond the childhood years. In a position paper distilling the clinical and scientific literature, the American Academy of Child and Adolescent Psychiatry outlined practice parameters for the assessment and treatment of children, adolescents, and adults with ADHD.[6] The approach to assessment offered is similar to the process described in this volume: clinical interviews with the child/adolescent and his or her parents, the collection of standardized rating scale data from parents and teachers, and review of medical and school records. Naturalistic observations in the classroom and in a less structured setting are recommended, although this often is impractical. Psychoeducational testing is recommended when there is any question of learning disabilities (LD) that may be exacerbating symptoms of ADHD, and more extensive neuropsychological testing is considered helpful but not essential to the diagnosis.

Among adolescents, ADHD may be mistaken for or co-occur with a number of cognitive and psychiatric disorders. Fundamental language and information-processing disorders are known to correlate with various behavior and psychiatric disorders including ADHD. For example, in a sample of 30 students identified as having central auditory processing disorders, Riccio, Hynd, Cohen, Hall, and Molt (1994) found that 50% also met strict diagnostic criteria for ADHD. Published rates of the coexistence of ADHD and specific LD (reading, mathematics, or written language) range from 10% to 92%, largely because of methodological differences in defining "learning disability." Teasing apart the LD and ADHD symptoms can present practical challenges but ultimately aids in more specific intervention.[7] Several psychometric and neuropsychological studies have demonstrated that students with reading disorders tend to display impairments on phonological and language-related tasks, whereas students with ADHD display more deficiencies on tests that assess executive functioning and working memory.[8]

For adolescents, the most common coexisting behavioral and psychiatric diagnoses are aggressive, **externalizing disorders,** such as **oppositional defiant disorder** (ODD) and CD, and affective, **internalizing disorders,** including **major depressive disorder** (MDD), **dysthymia,** generalized AD, and **obsessive-compulsive disorder.**[9] Attention has focused on the overlap between ADHD and pediatric **bipolar disorder.**[10] Diagnostic studies have indicated that ADHD can present with internalizing disorders (specifically, MDD, AD, and bipolar disorder) and is not simply a diagnostic artifact of these disorders.[11]

Adolescents with ADHD often experience problems with developing age-appropriate social relationships for a number of reasons. Their impulsive and/or inattentive behaviors may stigmatize them, and they are at high risk for experiencing other coexisting internalizing or externalizing disorders that further alienate them from their peers. There also is another group of students with ADHD who appear to display marked social impairment. These students are referred to as having a "social disability" or a nonverbal LD and typically display much lower Performance than Verbal IQ scores, serious impairment in visuospatial skills, weak mathematical abilities, and fine motor deficits.[12] For these adolescents, it is important to rule out **Asperger's syndrome** and **high-functioning autism.**

NONPHARMACOLOGICAL INTERVENTIONS FOR ADOLESCENTS

Adolescence is a particularly difficult time for students with ADHD for a variety of reasons. It is a time when, in addition to facing the usual challenges of adolescence, the student with ADHD (and the family that guides him or her) may face extra difficulties with school transitions, an increased volume and complexity of school work, learning to drive, managing social issues including sexuality, avoiding substance use and abuse, holding a part-time job, using good judgment in increasingly independent decision making, and establishing a healthy lifestyle including a positive self-identity. Counseling and educational interventions can make these challenges less daunting.

Counseling Interventions

Adolescence often begins around 10 years of age, especially in terms of an increase in defiance and parent–child problems. The desire for increasing independence and ambivalence about the consequences of that independence can be particularly intense for children with ADHD, who often have been, out of necessity, "micromanaged" by adults, especially parents, for as long as they can remember. Tension often develops because adolescents with ADHD frequently continue to manifest a need for close parental supervision and involvement, yet their needs do not diminish their desire for independence. Disrespectful behavior is a common chief concern at home in preadolescents with ADHD. The behavior management systems that may have worked well previously for home issues may not be effective. This is a time when families may need to begin or resume counseling with a mental health professional who has expertise with ADHD and adolescents to address the following issues:

- Defining roles for both parents in day-to-day management
- Assisting parents in being supportive of each other and consistent in enforcing rules
- Altering behavior management systems to reflect the child's increasing maturity and need for independence
- Involving the child to a greater degree in the development of the behavior management system through contracting and other methods
- Increasing individual work with the child to begin training in self-management strategies

Many of the counseling approaches that are described in Chapter 6 also are relevant to adolescents. Tailoring behavior management systems to the adolescent can be done by including the adolescent in the planning phase (e.g., agreement with choice of target behaviors and reinforcements), using privileges to reinforce responsible behavior (e.g., greater independence in the use of the family car for dates), and teaching the adolescent self-management strategies. Self-management strategies might include developing an organized approach to completing homework assignments and other tasks, problem solving in social and other kinds of problematic situations (e.g., responding to authority figures, resisting the temptations offered by undesirable peers), and strategies for anger or anxiety control. These approaches sometimes are referred to as *cognitive therapy* because they include modifying the way that the individual thinks about and interprets a situation as part of the basis for changing the way in which he or she responds.

Sessions of individual therapy, in addition to family behavioral counseling, are more commonly appropriate for adolescents than for younger children. Adolescents generally have been carrying an emotional burden longer and may need emotional support and treatment strategies for anxiety and/or depression in addition to treatment for ADHD if they are to make meaningful progress. (A discussion of the types of counseling strategies that are used to treat individuals with mood disorder or AD is beyond the scope of this chapter but can be found in Kendall et al., 1992, and Rehm & Sharp, 1995.) Finally, the typical parent–child conflict that occurs during the adolescent years usually is magnified in families with a child with ADHD, resulting in the need for a family counseling approach to lay the foundation for successful individual and behavior management approaches.[13]

Educational Interventions

Students with ADHD often experience increased difficulties in middle and high school. This is due to schedule factors (e.g., a more complex schedule, different classes and frequent room and schedule changes), teaching factors (e.g., more teachers with different styles and expectations, less time for individualized attention, increased note taking and learning from lectures), and academic factors (e.g., demands for reading speed and comprehension, longer writing assignments, more long-term assignments and requirements for research and organization of assignments). Unfortunately, it is not uncommon, especially for the student with coexisting reading or writing disabilities, to become overwhelmed and to avoid or refuse to do assignments. Parents should be on guard for academic problems before the situation deteriorates to this stage because, at this point, rekindling the student's motivation and compliance is a difficult process. Providing to parents anticipatory guidance about specific ways to reduce the impact of the schedule, teaching, and academic factors before the transition to middle school occurs can be helpful. Table 1 includes a variety of ways to help adolescents with ADHD with the academic transition to middle and high school.

Middle and high school students are eligible for and may be helped by the types of interventions in school that are discussed in Chapters 6 and 8; however, some modifications may be necessary or helpful because of the different structure of school and the different types of required work. Chapter 6 includes a section that is specific to educational interventions for adolescents.

A significant component of educational intervention for the middle and high school student should include the teaching of organizational and study skills. Help with study skills may be part of an individualized education program (IEP) or Section 504 plan, may be available at school in a more informal way, or may be obtained privately through a tutor. Frequently, commercial "learning center" chains offer this service. Organizational skills that are related to school work include the development of systems to keep track of the necessary materials but also include methods to organize the approach to assignments and note taking. For example, a student needs to learn how to set appropriate goals, break down a longer assignment into manageable parts, construct a written assignment, take notes from a lecture or a chapter, and study for tests.

MEDICATIONS FOR ADHD IN ADOLESCENTS

Stimulant medication use has increased during the 1990s, especially among adolescents. Approximately 4% of middle school students and 1% of high school students were taking methylphenidate (Ritalin) in 1995.[14] Most studies of medication effects and side effects over the years have included young adolescents and school-age children without analyzing outcomes separately by age. Among studies that are restricted to

Table 1. Interventions to assist with the transition to middle/secondary school

1. Meet with the principal/guidance counselor/head of special education in advance to simplify the schedule and between-class travel and to identify recommended teachers.

2. Familiarize the student with the building, schedule, itinerary, and personnel as much as possible in advance.

3. With the student, make an organized notebook, color-coded by class.

4. Identify a mentor at school (a homeroom teacher, guidance counselor, or some other adult, preferably with whom the student does not have a direct student–teacher relationship) who can help solve small problems before they become insurmountable. The mentor's role is to meet with the student and communicate with his or her teachers regularly to identify issues at early stages, to help develop interventions, and to disseminate them to all teachers to maximize consistency and follow-through.

5. Identify a peer in the same class for each of the major subjects who is a good student and with whom the student with ADHD feels comfortable communicating. The peer can be helpful if a homwork assignment is miscopied or not understood or if lecture notes need supplementation.

6. Get help with study skills. Some schools provide an organizational or study skills class or a period at the end of the day in which students can receive assistance with organization of assignments or getting started with homework. It may be more effective for students to learn study skills in the context of their own assignments, either through such a "homework class" or through private tutoring, which focuses on study skills using the student's assignments. "Study skills" for the adolescent with ADHD includes strategies for time management, note taking, studying, test taking, "chunking" projects into small parts, and staying alert while working.

7. Allow the adolescent with ADHD to assist a younger student or a peer with a different type of difficulty can be a powerful self-esteem enhancer and motivator.

adolescents, the positive response rate to stimulants appears to be similar to but perhaps somewhat less than that in younger children.[15] There is some difficulty with making direct comparisons because the criteria for positive response and degree of positive response vary between studies. In any case, stimulants should be considered the first-line medication for the adolescent with uncomplicated ADHD. Although the rate of metabolism of methylphenidate decreases with age,[16] some adolescents need dosages of 80–120 milligrams per day for successful treatment. The pattern of effects and side effects should be used to guide dosing. Magnesium pemoline, although effective and tolerated well by adolescents,[17] has been associated with acute liver failure resulting in death or the need for transplant in a small number of children, adolescents, and adults. It is likely to be used less frequently until the risk factors for this adverse effect are identified.

Tricyclic antidepressants (TCAs) (desipramine, imipramine, nortriptyline, amitriptyline) have been shown to have substantial positive effects in studies that included adolescents. Direct comparison of the effectiveness of a stimulant and a TCA has been done in several studies of children, some of which included adolescents but none of which specifically targeted adolescents. Results differ among studies, but the majority report that the stimulant is more effective.[18] Cardiovascular effects including increased pulse rate, blood pressure, and electrocardiographic changes can occur during use of TCAs (see Chapter 9) and must be monitored but do not seem to be more frequent or problematic in adolescents than in younger children.[19] Suicide by overdose of TCAs always is a concern.

Studies of other drugs found to be at least somewhat effective for ADHD (monoamine oxidase inhibitors [MAOIs], bupropion, clonidine, guanfacine) included adolescents but did not evaluate them separately.[20] The selective serotonin reuptake inhibitors (SSRIs) may be helpful for coexisting conditions; and the mood stabilizers (lithium, valproic acid, carbamazepine) may be helpful for juvenile mania, aggression, and **episodic dyscontrol.** Venlafaxine (Effexor) may be useful for depression, but as of 1998 has not been studied widely in children or adolescents.

SPECIAL CONCERNS FOR ADOLESCENTS WITH ADHD

Health and Safety

Studies indicate that individuals with ADHD are at greater risk of receiving speeding tickets and license suspensions and for being involved in auto accidents, including those resulting in personal injury.[21] In simulated driving experiments, they have both poor driving skills (e.g., observing traffic signals) and decreased steering control (e.g., erratic steering); however, they do not have less knowledge about driving rules and skills.[22] Adolescents (and young adults) with ADHD and ODD or CD are at even greater risk of poor driving outcomes than those with ADHD alone.[23] Parents should spend time in the car with their adolescent to understand their driving habits. Behavior management programs that stress both behavior while driving and responsible use of the car may be important. Some parents may choose to limit the use of the car initially, allowing increased use in response to the demonstration of responsible behavior. Parents also may make rules to maximize alertness and decrease distractibility. For example, having music on may be helpful or harmful for a particular child, but switching radio stations or using a car phone while driving are likely to be dangerous distractions for all adolescents with ADHD. Likewise, parents may need to limit the number of passengers and help their adolescent learn to tell passengers what they may and may not do in order to limit distractions. An additional way for parents to encourage responsible driving is to have a "no punishment policy" regardless of other circumstances if their child calls home when they find themselves a passenger with someone who is driving irresponsibly.

ADHD, especially in association with coexisting CD, depressive disorder, and AD, is a predictor of early-onset cigarette smoking. In a study by Milberger, Biederman, Faraone, Chen, and Jones (1997), 19% of children and adolescents with ADHD smoked, in contrast to 10% of children and adolescents without ADHD. Clinicians should provide anticipatory guidance about smoking when a child with ADHD is 12–13 years of age because 25% of the smokers in the study started before they were 15 years of age. Cigarette smoking during pregnancy has been shown to increase the risk for ADHD, even when maternal ADHD is controlled for[24]; therefore, women with ADHD who smoke during pregnancy may have an even greater risk of having a child with ADHD than their genetic risk would predict.

Sexual activity is another area in which adolescents with ADHD seem to fare worse. A long-term follow-up study still in progress indicates that adolescents with ADHD have more sexual partners, are more likely to contract a sexually transmitted disease, and have more unplanned pregnancies than a control group.[25]

ADHD often has been reported to be a risk factor for substance abuse, but it appears that during adolescence, coexisting CD and bipolar disorder are the mediating factors.[26] In adults, ADHD itself is a risk factor, suggesting that an increase in the rate of substance abuse occurs in late adolescence and early adulthood.[27] There is virtually no research about mixing prescribed stimulants and recreational drugs. Marijuana is the most common drug of abuse among adolescents with ADHD.[28] Its active ingredient, tetrahydrocannabinol, binds to neuronal receptors with high density in several parts of the brain including the **mesolimbic dopamine system,** which also is an important site for the activity of stimulants and antidepressants. Thus, there is a neurobiological basis for the interaction of these substances even though this has not been extensively studied or documented. Case reports suggest that individuals who smoke marijuana while taking TCAs may be at risk for rapid or greater intoxication, mental status changes, and tachycardia.[29] Similar reports of an increased sense of intoxication, to the point of having **hallucinations** and **delusions,** have been reported by adolescents who combined marijuana and stimulants (M. Mercugliano, unpublished observation). Likewise, adolescents should be informed that possible physical and mental untoward additive effects may occur when two stimulants are combined (e.g., either amphetamine or cocaine with a prescribed stimulant or antidepressant) or that the combination of a stimulant with a sedating agent (e.g., alcohol, barbiturate) may cause unpredictable physical or mental effects.

The subject of the improper use of prescribed stimulants commonly is discussed and reported in the lay press to be a significant problem. It is not clear how prevalent the problem actually is, although it is enough of a concern that many clinicians have tended to prescribe magnesium pemoline for their adolescent and young adult patients because of its lower abuse potential. Clinicians who are involved with adolescents who are taking stimulants for ADHD generally do not believe that these students are abusing medication. It is reasonable to ask adolescents about their experience with this issue. It may be brought up in the context of the larger issue of the social acceptability of their medication: "Do you have any concerns about taking medication at school? How have your friends and other students reacted to this? Has anyone asked you for some of your medication?" This is another area in which parents and clinicians should provide some anticipatory guidance, perhaps in the form of role playing, about appropriate responses if someone asks to try or to buy some of the adolescent's medication. Although some states have laws that require complete record keeping for controlled substances, all prescribing clinicians should keep prescription records in such a way that they can see at a glance how frequently prescriptions are being requested. Any prescription request that occurs prior to expected need should result in an inquiry. Occasionally, a parent is self-medicating or medicating a sibling, or there is a problem with medication not being properly accounted for at school. Although prescriptions can be lost in the mail, recurrent problems to the same address should be investigated.

Juvenile Justice System

Contact with the juvenile justice system may occur in two ways. The first is through being a status offender, including offenses such as truancy, curfew breaking, and running away. The second is by breaking a law.[30] Parents may need guidance in three areas: 1) preventing or minimizing involvement, 2) understanding what will occur if their child is arrested, and 3) knowing how to provide information to the court about their child's disability.

Minimizing involvement in a broad sense means reducing the likelihood that a youth will develop antisocial behaviors. A significant number of adolescents with ADHD will have some involvement with the juvenile justice system, usually for a relatively minor offense, but will not have long-term or pervasive antisocial behaviors.[31] A smaller number will have CD, sometimes diagnosed as **antisocial personality disorder** in adulthood. These individuals generally have pervasive signs of antisocial behavior, most commonly premeditated aggression before the age of 10 (not the responsive, reactive, or impulsive aggression that is common in ADHD). (A discussion of the contributing factors and prevention strategies for CD is beyond the scope of this chapter but is reviewed in McBurnett, 1996.) Briefly, interventions include careful supervision, especially in regard to peer involvement; consistent discipline; self-esteem, social, and other skill-building activities; and the treatment of associated disabilities.

Adolescents with ADHD need anticipatory guidance, perhaps with role playing, about what to say when they find themselves in risky situations. This is critical because they may not have the skills or the self-confidence to know how to respond most effectively in a new or highly stressful situation. "I'm not going to do this, so I'm leaving," or something similar should be practiced. When confronted by a police officer, the adolescent with ADHD is at risk of getting into more trouble because of his or her impulsivity. Regardless of what the adolescent has or has not done, running away, mouthing off, or lying about the situation may be his or her response under stress. Role playing this situation can be practiced. This is a difficult situation because the adolescent should be compliant and respectful, yet, ideally, a minor should not answer questions until his or her parents arrive. Once present, the parents may decide that the adolescent should not answer questions until an attorney arrives. In minor (nonviolent) offenses, a juvenile usually is released to his or her parents. If the adolescent refuses to answer questions until an attorney arrives, then he or she will be detained during that time. If the investigation results in a decision to charge, then an arraignment hearing (the formal act of charging) will be scheduled. If the adolescent has been defiant or uncooperative or if the offense involves violence, then he or she may be held in a detention center until arraignment. At the arraignment, a decision will be made to release or detain pending the trial. It is critical that the parents provide to their attorney information about their child's disability, its treatment, and any special educational interventions that are in place, not as an excuse for leniency, but so that the attorney can inform the court about its relationship to the actions under investigation and subsequent decisions about detention, restitution, and the maintenance of ongoing needed services. In the interim, a probation officer will be assigned to collect information. It is in the child's best interest to attend school regularly during this time if he or she has not been detained and that the parents cooperate with the probation officer and comply with any recommendations made between hearings. If the adolescent is found to be delinquent at the trial, then a disposition hearing will be scheduled. Possible dispositions include probation or incarceration. Incarceration may occur at a treatment facility or a correctional facility. Arguments against incarceration for individuals with disabilities include vulnerability to victimization and inability to receive services deemed necessary in their IEPs.[32]

Clearly, parents and clinicians have an important role to play in advocating for appropriate treatment and meaningful restitution when an adolescent with ADHD becomes involved with the juvenile justice system. When an adolescent escapes in-depth involvement in the juvenile justice system, parents may be so relieved that they just want to put the incident behind them. If the child has been guilty of breaking family or community rules, however, then it is critical that the parents impose an appropriate restitution. Otherwise, they risk undermining their own authority and sending the message that it is all right to break rules as long as you do not get caught.

ADHD and College

Postsecondary education is an issue for many families with a child with ADHD. One question is whether a child should go to college. Many factors should enter into this decision, but the fact that the child has ADHD should not, in and of itself, be a deciding factor. The desire to study further, sufficient mastery of prerequisite skills, and recognition of the need and desire for increased self-management are requirements for a successful college experience. Many students with ADHD feel that they need a "break" from school or do not have clear goals for the future, even though they want to attend college eventually. They may work, attend a technical school or a community college, or pursue an interest in more depth as a way of exploring career options. Clinicians may need to help parents see that, in some cases, delaying college ultimately may allow it to be a more successful experience.

More than 100,000 students with documented LD graduate from high school annually, and up to 300,000 are attending college.[33] Exact estimates are lacking for the number of high school and college students diagnosed with ADHD, but Barkley[34] estimated that 1%–3% of college students meet criteria for this diagnosis. These facts, coupled with the existence of specific legislation that protects the rights of students with learning and attention disorders (see Chapter 8), have led to an explosion of college programs and services for students with LD and/or ADHD. Fortunately, there are multiple resources to assist students and their families, including specific guides to colleges.[35] Crucial considerations when selecting colleges include the size of the college, the distance from home, the general student–teacher ratios, and the availability of individualized learning accommodations. Parents and students should be strongly encouraged to explore the academic and social supports that are available for students with ADHD and/or LD. Several colleges and universities have specific programs, usually involving extra academic/organizational supervision and study skills assistance, that can be tremendously helpful to the student with ADHD who may have a harder time than the average student with adjusting to the less-structured academic schedule of postsecondary education. In addition, counseling, mentoring, and informal help with personal decision making from dormitory resident advisors can be helpful in making a successful personal and social adjustment.

Among college administrators, there is growing consensus regarding the documentation that students must provide when they are claiming to have a learning or attention disorder and are requesting special learning accommodations (e.g., tutors, note takers, extended time for tests, alternative test formats, separate rooms for testing). Many colleges employ LD specialists or have a committee of faculty, staff, and counselors to set policies for the institution. These specialists or committees determine the minimum acceptable criteria for the presence of a learning or attention disorder. A "doctor's note" often will not suffice; a data-based report identifying specific symptoms may be required. The evaluation and resulting report must be recent (usually within the past 12–24 months), or an updated reevaluation may be requested; however, the quality of an assessment is considered more important than its timing. Efforts then will be made to match available accommodations to a student's particular weaknesses rather than simply offer an array of possible adaptations.

Unfortunately, it is extremely common for college students not to disclose their learning or attention problems, fearing that they will not be accepted into the college or that they will be denied financial aid or other opportunities. When a crisis occurs, such as failing an exam or a class, students and/or their parents then may produce documentation of their disorder and request immediate services. This places an unexpected and unfair burden on faculty and staff. For this reason, many colleges now require students to disclose their learning or attention disorders upon admission or prior to taking a potentially challenging course in order to receive available accommodations. The publication of a set of guidelines for the documentation of LD in adolescents and adults[36] should help to standardize procedures for students, parents, and colleges.

TALKING TO ADOLESCENTS ABOUT ADHD

It is critical to actively involve the adolescent in the process of assessment, decision making, and treatment in order to achieve effective treatment outcomes. Part of normal adolescence involves the increasing understanding of one's physical and mental health and the acceptance of responsibility for one's health and behavior. This process may be particularly difficult for adolescents with ADHD, in part because of the core symptoms of ADHD and in part because they are likely to have been "micromanaged" by parents and teachers throughout childhood, out of necessity. The prospect of independent adulthood is likely to be both desirable and frightening to the adolescent who has grown up having his or her clothes laid out, bookbag organized, schedule regimented, and required activities listed on a star chart on the refrigerator. This, as well as often persistent difficulties with social judgment, risk-taking behavior, and poor insight into one's own behavior and role in adverse outcomes, can lead to particularly conflictive parent–adolescent relationships.

The primary care clinician ideally will be a trusted and respected objective adult who has established rapport with the adolescent through a long history of respecting and addressing his or her concerns. Taking a few minutes to speak privately about the preadolescent's or adolescent's perceptions of how things are going at school; how things are going with teachers, parents, peers, and siblings; and about moods, behavior, and medication helps immensely to establish rapport and sometimes may provide important information not provided or not known by parents. This should be done both during initial assessments and at follow-up visits. At some point, at the discretion of the clinician and based on the individual circumstances, as with all adolescents, issues of sexual activity, smoking, and alcohol and other drug use should be discussed with the goal of providing information to assist the adolescent in making health-promoting choices. In certain situations, parents may want to have some private time with the clinician. When information is provided separately, situations will arise in which the clinician will need to facilitate the sharing of this information between parent and adolescent to begin to adequately resolve a concern.

Discussion about medication effectiveness and side effects generally are conducted most efficiently with parent and adolescent together as this rarely is an area in which the adolescent has information that he or she wants to keep private and often is an area of disagreement. Most often, a parent sees the effectiveness of the medication and the adolescent does not. Sometimes the adolescent wants to discontinue medication because of side effects that the parent does not perceive or does not perceive to be significant enough to outweigh its benefits. **Dysphoria,** social withdrawal, a lack of spontaneity (both socially and occasionally in athletic endeavors), and a lack of humor are likely to be real effects when they are reported. It may be difficult, especially for the child who is not verbally skillful, to describe these effects. They often are of grave concern to the adolescent yet not witnessed by the parent and, thus, may be at the root of parent–child conflicts about medication compliance. Likewise, for adolescents as well as for younger children, the stigma that is attached to going to the nurse's office to take medication for ADHD is real. Aside from making suggestions to school personnel about how to handle this situation in a sensitive manner, alternative medications or regimens may need to be considered. When disagreements about effectiveness rather than side effects are the issue, it often is helpful to make a contract with the adolescent to participate in an objective reevaluation of medication effectiveness with an agreement by both parents and adolescent to abide by the results of the trial. Such a trial may need to be set up differently from the original trial that was conducted to assess medication effectiveness for a variety of reasons. Brief teacher questionnaires about classroom behavior and performance may not address adequately the target symptoms for an adolescent. Sometimes, a more individualized assessment by one or a few key teachers, a coach, and/or a mentor over the course of several weeks on and then off medication is more helpful. The adolescent can participate by helping to choose the outcome measures (e.g., teacher rating scales, grades on assignments and tests) or the teachers or other adults who will be asked to provide input. When medication-related disagreements cannot be resolved by a semi-objective assessment such as this, family counseling may be needed to address the issue in the context of other parent–child issues.

CONCLUSION

Although the teenage years can be difficult for an individual with ADHD and his or her family, it also can be a time of great progress. Increased maturity, a sense of responsibility, the development of hobbies and strong friendships based on shared interests, a sense of empathy, and interest in social concerns often begin to appear during this time. These traits provide parents with positive reinforcement for their continued efforts on behalf of their child and provide the adolescent with a positive self-image. The clinician can support both parents and adolescents by highlighting these positive attributes.

ENDNOTES

1. American Psychiatric Association (1994).
2. American Psychiatric Association (1994), reviewed in Cantwell (1996).
3. American Psychiatric Association (1980).
4. Applegate et al. (1997), Barkley & Biederman (1997).
5. Reviewed in Goldstein (1997).
6. Dulcan & Benson (1997).
7. Reviewed in Jensen, Martin, & Cantwell (1997), Rostain (1997).
8. Purvis & Tannock (1997), Seidman, Biederman, Faraone, Weber, & Ouellette (1997), Pennington & Ozonoff (1996).
9. Reviewed in Jensen et al. (1997), Butler, Arredondo, & McCloskey (1995).
10. Reviewed in Geller & Luby (1997).
11. Milberger, Biederman, Faraone, Murphy, & Tsuang (1995).
12. Denckla (1993), Greene, Biederman, Faraone, Sienna, & Garcia-Jetton (1997).
13. Robin & Foster (1989).
14. Safer, Zito, & Fine (1996).
15. Reviewed in Faigel, Sznajderman, Tishby, Turel, & Pinus (1995), Spencer et al. (1996).
16. Clein & Riddle (1995).
17. Riggs, Thompson, Mikulich, Whitmore, & Crowley (1996).
18. Reviewed in Spencer et al. (1996).
19. Wilens et al. (1996).
20. Spencer et al. (1996).
21. Barkley, Guevremont, Anastopoulos, DuPaul, & Shelton (1993), Barkley, Murphy, & Kwasnik (1996), Nada-Raja et al. (1997).
22. Barkley et al. (1996).
23. Barkley et al. (1993), Nada-Raja et al. (1997).
24. Milberger, Biederman, Faraone, Chen, & Jones (1996).
25. Barkley (1996).
26. Biederman et al. (1997), Boyle et al. (1992).
27. Biederman et al. (1995).
28. Reviewed in Wilens, Biederman, & Spencer (1997).

29. Wilens et al. (1997).
30. Reviewed in Rouse (1997).
31. Reviewed in McBurnett (1996).
32. Drizin & Eligator (1997).
33. Figures from the American Council on Education, reviewed in Richard (1997).
34. Reviewed in Richard (1997).
35. E.g., Kravets & Wax (1997), Mangrum & Strichart (1997).
36. Association on Higher Education and Disability (1997).

REFERENCES

American Psychiatric Association. (1980). *Diagnostic and statistical manual of mental disorders* (3rd ed.). Washington, DC: Author.

American Psychiatric Association. (1994). *Diagnostic and statistical manual of mental disorders* (4th ed.). Washington, DC: Author.

Applegate, B., Lahey, B.B., Hart, E.L., Biederman, J., Hynd, G.W., Barkley, R.A., Ollendick, T., Frick, P.J., Greenhill, L., McBurnett, K., Newcorn, J.H., Kerdyk, L., Garfinkel, B., Waldman, I., & Shaffeer, D. (1997). Validity of the age-of-onset criterion for ADHD: A report from the DSM-IV field trials. *Journal of the American Academy of Child and Adolescent Psychiatry, 36,* 1211–1221.

Association on Higher Education and Disability (AHEAD). (1997). *Guidelines for documentation of a learning disability in adolescents and adults.* Columbus, OH: Author.

Barkley, R.A. (1996). Research: A discussion with Russell A. Barkley, Ph.D. In *ADD and adolescence: Strategies for success from CH.A.D.D.* (pp. 131–132). Plantation, FL: Children and Adults with Attention Deficit Disorders.

Barkley, R.A., & Biederman, J. (1997). Toward a broader definition of the age-of-onset criterion for attention-deficit hyperactivity disorder. *Journal of the American Academy of Child and Adolescent Psychiatry, 36,* 1204–1210.

Barkley, R.A., Guevremont, D.C., Anastopoulos, A.D., DuPaul, G.J., & Shelton, T.L. (1993). Driving-related risks and outcomes of attention deficit hyperactivity disorder in adolescents and young adults: A 3- to 5-year follow-up survey. *Pediatrics, 92,* 212–218.

Barkley, R.A., Murphy, K.R., & Kwasnik, D. (1996). Motor vehicle driving competencies and risks in teens and young adults with attention deficit hyperactivity disorder. *Pediatrics, 98,* 1089–1095.

Biederman, J., Wilens, T., Mick, E., Faraone, S.V., Weber, W., Curtis, S., Thornell, A., Pfister, K., Jetton, J.G., & Soriano, J. (1997). Is ADHD a risk factor for psychoactive substance abuse disorders? Findings from a four-year prospective follow-up study. *Journal of the American Academy of Child and Adolescent Psychiatry, 36,* 21–29.

Biederman, J., Wilens, T., Mick, E., Milberger, S., Spencer, T.J., & Faraone, S.V. (1995). Psychoactive substance abuse disorders in adults with attention deficit hyperactivity disorders (ADHD): Effects of ADHD and psychiatric comorbidity. *American Journal of Psychiatry, 152,* 1652–1658.

Boyle, M.H., Offord, D.R., Racine, Y.A., Szatmari, P., Fleming, J.E., & Link, P.S. (1992). Predicting substance abuse in late adolescence: Results from the Ontario child health study follow-up. *American Journal of Psychiatry, 149,* 761–767.

Butler, S.F., Arredondo, D.E., & McCloskey, V. (1995). Affective comorbidity in children and adolescents with ADHD. *Annals of Clinical Psychiatry, 7,* 51–55.

Cantwell, D.P. (1996). Attention deficit disorder: A review of the past 10 years. *Journal of the American Academy of Child and Adolescent Psychiatry, 35,* 978–987.

Clein, P.D., & Riddle, M.A. (1995). Pharmacokinetics in children and adolescents. *Child and Adolescent Psychiatric Clinics of North America, 4,* 59–75.

Denckla, M.B. (1993). The child with developmental disabilities grown up: Adult residual of childhood disorders. *Neurology Clinics, 11,* 105–125.

Drizin, S.A., & Eligator, L.J.M. (1997, Winter). A parent's guide to the juvenile justice system. *Attention!,* 31–36.

Dulcan, M.K., & Benson, R.S. (1997). American Academy of Child and Adolescent Psychiatry: Official action. Summary of the practice parameters for the assessment and treatment of children, adolescents, and adults with ADHD. *Journal of the American Academy of Child Adolescent Psychiatry, 36,* 1311–1317.

Faigel, H.C., Sznajderman, S., Tishby, O., Turel, M., & Pinus, U. (1995). Attention deficit disorder during adolescence: A review. *Journal of Adolescent Health, 16,* 174–184.

Geller, B., & Luby, J. (1997). Child and adolescent bipolar disorder: A review of the past 10 years. *Journal of the American Academy of Child and Adolescent Psychiatry, 36,* 1168–1176.

Goldstein, S. (1997). *Managing attention and learning disorders in late adolescence and adulthood: A guide for practitioners.* New York: John Wiley & Sons.

Greene, R.W., Biederman, J., Faraone, S.V., Sienna, M., & Garcia-Jetton, J. (1997). Adolescent outcome of boys with attention-deficit/hyperactivity disorder and social disability: Results from a 4-year longitudinal follow-up study. *Journal of Consulting and Clinical Psychology, 65,* 758–767.

Jensen, P.S., Martin, D., & Cantwell, D.P. (1997). Comorbidity in ADHD: Implications for research, practice, and DSM-IV. *Journal of the American Academy of Child and Adolescent Psychiatry, 36,* 1065–1079.

Kendall, P.C., Chansky, T.E., Kane, M.T., Kim, R.S., Kortlander, E., Ronan, K., Sessa, F.M., & Siqueland, L. (1992). *Anxiety disorders in youth: Cognitive-behavioral interventions.* Needham Heights, MA: Allyn & Bacon.

Kravets, M., & Wax, I.F. (1997). *The K & W guide to colleges for the learning disabled: A resource book for students, parents, and professionals.* New York: Random House.

Mangrum, C.T., & Strichart, S.S. (1997). *Peterson's guide to colleges with programs for students with learning disabilities and or attention deficit disorders* (5th ed.). Princeton, NJ: Peterson's Guides.

McBurnett, K. (1996, Winter). ADD and delinquency. *Attention!,* 20–26.

Milberger, S., Biederman, J., Faraone, S.V., Chen, L., & Jones, J. (1996). Is maternal smoking during pregnancy a risk factor for attention deficit hyperactivity disorder in children? *American Journal of Psychiatry, 153,* 1138–1142.

Milberger, S., Biederman, J., Faraone, S.V., Chen, L., & Jones, J. (1997). ADHD is associated with early initiation of cigarette smoking in children and adolescents. *Journal of the American Academy of Child and Adolescent Psychiatry, 36,* 37–44.

Milberger, S., Biederman, J., Faraone, S.V., Murphy, J., & Tsuang, M.T. (1995). ADHD and comorbid disorders: Issues of overlapping symptoms. *American Journal of Psychiatry, 152,* 1793–1799.

Nada-Raja, S., Langley, J.D., McGee, R., Williams, S.M., Begg, D.J., & Reeder, A.I. (1997). Inattentive and hyperactive behaviors and driving offenses in adolescence. *Journal of the American Academy of Child and Adolescent Psychiatry, 36,* 515–522.

Pennington, B.F., & Ozonoff, S. (1996). Executive functions and developmental psychopathology. *Journal of Child Psychology and Psychiatry, 37,* 51–87.

Purvis, K.L., & Tannock, R. (1997). Language abilities in children with attention deficit hyperactivity disorder, reading disability, and normal controls. *Journal of Abnormal Child Psychology, 25,* 133–144.

Rehm, L.P., & Sharp, R.N. (1995). Strategies for childhood depression. In M. Reinecke, F.M. Dattilo, & A. Freeman (Eds.), *Cognitive therapy with children and adolescents* (pp. 103–123). New York: Guilford Press.

Riccio, C.A., Hynd, G.W., Cohen, M.J., Hall, J., & Molt, L. (1994). Comorbidity of central auditory processing disorder and attention-deficit hyperactivity disorder. *Journal of the American Academy of Child and Adolescent Psychiatry, 33,* 849–857.

Richard, M.M. (1997). College programs and services. In S. Goldstein (Ed.), *Managing attention and learning disorders in late adolescence and adulthood: A guide for practitioners* (pp. 266–286). New York: John Wiley & Sons.

Riggs, P.D., Thompson, L.L., Mikulich, S.K., Whitmore, E.A., & Crowley, T.J. (1996). An open trial of pemoline in drug-dependent delinquents with attention-deficit hyperactivity disorder. *Journal of the American Academy of Child and Adolescent Psychiatry, 35,* 1018–1024.

Robin, A.L., & Foster, S.L. (1989). *Negotiating parent adolescent conflict: A behavioral-family systems approach.* New York: Guilford Press.

Rostain, A.L. (1997). Assessing and managing adolescents with school problems. *Adolescent Medicine: State of the Art Reviews, 8,* 57–76.

Rouse, G.E. (1997, Winter). ADD and the juvenile justice system. *Attention!,* 27–30.

Safer, D.J., Zito, J.M., & Fine, E.M. (1996). Increased methylphenidate usage for attention deficit disorder in the 1990s. *Pediatrics, 98,* 1084–1088.

Seidman, L.J., Biederman, J., Faraone, S.V., Weber, W., & Oullette, C. (1997). Toward defining a neuropsychology of attention deficit hyperactivity disorder: Performance of children and adolescents from a large clinically referred sample. *Journal of Consulting and Clinical Psychology, 65,* 150–160.

Spencer, T., Biederman, J., Wilens, T., Harding, M., O'Donnell, D., & Griffin, S. (1996). Pharmacotherapy of attention-deficit hyperactivity disorder across the life cycle. *Journal of the American Academy of Child and Adolescent Psychiatry, 35,* 409–432.

Wilens, T.E., Biederman, J., Baldessarini, R.J., Geller, B., Schleifer, D., Spencer, T.J., Birmaher, B., & Goldblatt, A. (1996). Cardiovascular effects of therapeutic doses of tricyclic antidepressants in children and adolescents. *Journal of the American Academy of Child and Adolescent Psychiatry, 35,* 1491–1501.

Wilens, T.E., Biederman, J., & Spencer, T.J. (1997). Case study: Adverse effects of smoking marijuana while receiving tricyclic antidepressants. *Journal of the American Academy of Child and Adolescent Psychiatry, 36,* 45–48.

RESOURCES FOR PARENTS AND ADOLESCENTS

Alexander-Roberts, C. (1995). *ADHD & teens: A parent's guide for making it through the tough years.* Dallas, TX: Taylor Publishing. (To order, call [214] 637-2800.)

Amen, D.G. (1996). *A teenager's guide to A.D.D.* Fairfield, CA: MindWorks Press. (To order, call [800] 626-2720 x400.)

Association on Higher Education and Disability (AHEAD). (1997). *Guidelines for documentation of a learning disability in adolescents and adults.* Columbus, OH: Author. (Available: http://www.ahead.org; [614] 488-4972)

Bramer, J. (1996). *Succeeding in college with attention deficit disorders: Issues and strategies for students, counselors, and educators.* Plantation, FL: Specialty Press. (To order, call [800] 233-9273.)

Dendy, C.A.Z. (1995). *Teenagers with ADD: A parent's guide.* Bethesda, MD: Woodbine House. (To order, call [800] 843-7323.)

Dinkmeyer, D., & McKay, G.D. (1990). *Parenting teenagers: Systematic training for effective parenting (STEP).* New York: Random House. (To order, call [800] 733-3000.)

Kravets, M., & Wax, I.F. (1997). *The K & W guide to colleges for the learning disabled: A resource book for students, parents, and professionals.* New York: Random House. (To order, call [800] 726-0600.)

Mangrum, C.T., & Strichart, S.S. (1997). *Peterson's guide to colleges with programs for students with learning disabilities or attention deficit disorders* (5th ed.). Princeton, NJ: Peterson's Guide. (To order, call [800] 225-0261.)

Nadeau, K.G., & Biggs, S.H. (1995). *School strategies for ADD teens.* New York: Magination Press. (To order, call A.D.D. Warehouse [800] 233-9273.)

Nadeau, K.G. (1994). *Survival guide for college students with ADD or LD.* New York: Magination Press. (To order, call [800] 374-2721.)

Phelan, T.W. (1993). *Surviving your adolescents.* Glen Ellyn, IL: Child Management. (To order, call [800] 442-4453.)

Quinn, P.O. (1995). *Adolescents and ADD: Gaining the advantage.* New York: Magination Press. (To order, call [800] 374-2721.)

Quinn, P.O. (Ed.). (1994). *ADD and the college student: A guide for high school and college students with attention deficit disorder.* New York: Magination Press. (To order, call [800] 374-2721.)

Attention-Deficit/ Hyperactivity Disorder in Adults

with Edward Moss

The subject of attention-deficit/hyperactivity disorder (ADHD) in adults is relevant for this book because, although it is presumed that the readers primarily are involved in the care of children, the strong heritability of ADHD means that they are, in fact, involved in the care of *families* with ADHD. Parents with ADHD often first question the possibility of the diagnosis for themselves when their children are diagnosed and may seek from their child's clinician information about evaluations and treatment for themselves. In addition, the potential adverse effects of parental ADHD on parenting and marital accord must be identified and treated as these factors may have a substantial effect on the child's symptoms and the success of the child's treatment.

Approximately 60% of children with ADHD have symptoms that will persist into adulthood. Although thorough epidemiological studies of adults are lacking, based on the prevalence in childhood, it has been estimated that between 1% and 3% of adults may have ADHD.[1] Studies at the level of an individual family indicate a significantly increased risk of ADHD in the parents and siblings of children with ADHD and in the siblings and children of adults with ADHD.[2] There also appears to be an increased risk for other disorders in the parents of children with ADHD, including **antisocial disorders,** substance abuse disorders, **anxiety disorders,** and **manic depressive disorder.**[3]

PRESENTATION AND CLINICAL CHARACTERISTICS OF ADHD IN ADULTS

The increased visibility of adult ADHD in the popular literature has contributed to growing numbers of adults who are requesting an evaluation for ADHD. Compared with childhood, a higher percentage of individuals who present for an initial evaluation in adulthood are female.[4] Specific chief complaints in adults include chronic job or relationship difficulties, poor organization or memory, difficulties with thinking clearly or confusion, and mood or self-esteem problems.[5]

The core features of ADHD in adults are not different from those in children, although they may be expressed differently, and it has been suggested that fewer symptoms may be present in adults who nonetheless experience significant functional impairment.[6] Commonly described characteristics of adults with ADHD are listed in Table 1.[7] These characteristics result in a number of outcomes or epidemiological findings in adults with ADHD, which are listed in Table 2.[8] It should be noted that most studies have compared individuals who have ADHD with normal rather than psychiatric controls, so it cannot be assumed that these findings are specific to ADHD. Also, the increased prevalence of antisocial behavior in adulthood is not uniform but, as in adolescence, is highly correlated with the previous diagnosis of **conduct disorder**.[9]

THE DIAGNOSIS OF ADHD AND COEXISTING DISORDERS IN ADULTS

Researchers and clinicians alike continue to ponder the best way to assess adults for ADHD and its common coexisting disorders. It is widely accepted that for an adult to be diagnosed with ADHD, he or she must have had symptoms in childhood that would have met diagnostic criteria for ADHD; the symptoms must have persisted in some form to the present (i.e., there must be continuity/stability of symptoms); and the current symptoms must be present to a degree that causes functional impairment.

It is not yet clear whether interview of the adult alone will lead to sufficient diagnostic reliability; therefore, whenever possible, it is important to verify and elaborate presenting symptoms by interviewing other informants, such as the patient's spouse or partner, parents, siblings, or close friends.[10] In particular, parents and siblings can provide important information regarding the presence of symptoms in childhood; however, some patients may prefer not to disclose their symptoms to family, friends, or co-workers. Others may not have good relationships with family members, perhaps as a result of their symptoms of ADHD. Reviewing previous school records, including report cards and standardized test scores, such as the Iowa Tests of Basic Skills, Metropolitan Achievement Tests (MAT), and Scholastic Aptitude Test (SAT), also is recommended.[11] Review of academic records can be particularly helpful for detecting the presence of comorbid learning disabilities. A thorough review of scholastic records can

Table 1.   Characteristics of adults with ADHD

---
 1. Difficulties with concentrating; easy mental fatigue, especially late in the day; distractibility
 2. Shifting from one uncompleted activity to another, not following through on tasks or projects
 3. Disorganization, forgetfulness
 4. Procrastination, stubbornness
 5. Stress intolerance, low frustration tolerance, impulsivity (primarily verbal)
 6. Fluctuating low mood, low self-esteem, intermittent explosiveness
 7. Some degree of "obliviousness" visually, auditorily, and socially
 8. Easily bored, easily dissatisfied
 9. Difficulties with establishing or maintaining a routine
10. Restless, fidgety, difficulties with remaining still through quiet activities, difficulties with settling to sleep

---

Table 2. Findings in adults with ADHD

1. Chronic conflicts with peers, spouses, authority
2. Higher rates of separation, divorce
3. Academic and occupational "underachievement"
4. Frequent job changes
5. Poorer driving records
6. Increased substance abuse, court appearances, antisocial personality disorder
7. Increased mood/anxiety disorders, more suicide attempts (probably in females, still controversial in males)
8. High rates of cigarette smoking with early onset and difficulties with quitting

be critical for discriminating erratic academic performance (which may be more indicative of symptoms of ADHD) from a specific learning disability such as a persistent reading disability. Comments from teachers often are especially revealing and can be particularly useful for discerning the hyperactive-impulsive symptoms of childhood that usually diminish over time. On occasion, information from previous educational, psychological, neurological, or psychiatric evaluations may exist. This also can assist in establishing the chronicity of the presenting symptoms. In some cases, access to previous records may not be possible because of the age of the adult or his or her geographical locale.

The diagnosis of ADHD specific to adults is not discussed in the *Diagnostic and Statistical Manual of Mental Disorders, Fourth Edition* (DSM-IV),[12] but there is interest in knowing whether the criteria should be different from those applied to children. Wender and colleagues have made significant contributions to the assessment of ADHD in adults with development of the Utah Criteria[13] and the Wender-Utah (self-report) Rating Scale and Parent Rating Scale.[14] Factor analysis of the Wender-Utah Rating Scales indicates that five factors exist for males and females with ADHD, although they are somewhat different by gender. For males, they include conduct problems, learning problems, stress intolerance, attention problems, and poor social skills. For females, they include **dysphoria,** impulsive/conduct problems, learning problems, attention/organizational problems, and unpopularity.[15]

Murphy and Barkley (1996a, 1996b) established normative values for the occurrence of ADHD symptoms for adults of different age ranges using the DSM-IV criteria in a rating scale format (0 = never or rarely, 1 = sometimes, 2 = often, 3 = very often). It is analogous to the ADHD-IV rating scale (see Chapter 2). Norms are available for the inattentive and hyperactive subscales, as well as total score. Scales for current symptoms as well as retrospective recall from childhood exist. It is suggested that scores that are greater than 1.5 standard deviations above the mean be considered clinically significant.

The Brown Attention-Deficit Disorder Scales[16] were designed specifically to assess the presence and the severity of symptoms that are associated with ADHD. They also can be useful for monitoring treatment response. There are two versions of this brief symptom inventory, for adolescents (ages 12–18) and for adults. They are designed to be completed by the patient and a close relative (parent or spouse). In addition to overall threshold scores that indicate the presence or absence of ADHD, there are five subscales that provide insight into specific problems with organization and procrastination, sustained attention, recall and working memory skills, sustained energy and effort, and mood and irritability.

These rating scales can assist the clinician with obtaining information about symptoms of ADHD, which, in combination with historical and other interview information, can help to support or refute a diagnosis of ADHD. In addition, however, diagnostic criteria for other disorders that may be present instead of or in addition to ADHD must be sought. These include learning disorders, **affective disorders, personality disorders,** and substance abuse. When historical data suggest an onset of symptoms in adulthood, it also is important to exclude neurological conditions that can affect higher cognitive functions.

The widely known Minnesota Multiphasic Personality Inventory (MMPI)[17] is a lengthy and comprehensive self-report measure that assesses acute and chronic symptoms of a variety of psychiatric disorders and personality disorders. This test has been renormed (MMPI-2[18]). Although these inventories were not developed specifically to assess symptoms associated with ADHD, they offer a broad overview of personality traits. This can be very useful for providing insight into an individual's patterns of mood and behavior and aids in discriminating between ADHD and other types of psychopathology.[19] Compared with healthy control subjects, adults with ADHD exhibit elevations on multiple clinical scales on the MMPI, indicating a mild to moderate level of general psychological distress. Analysis of the MMPI subscales indicates that adults with ADHD mainly endorsed feelings of depression and anxiety.[20] To explore these symptoms and assess their severity, it is helpful to employ brief self-rating scales such as the Spielberger State-Trait Anxiety Inventory[21] and the Beck Depression Inventory.[22]

PSYCHOMETRIC TESTING

As with the assessment of children and adolescents, clinical interviews and behavioral rating scales are the primary tools that are used to determine the presence or absence of ADHD. Although direct information from teachers about school functioning is an important part of the diagnostic process when working with children, this rarely is available for adults or older adolescents. The ongoing feedback about progress and intervention effectiveness that is available from a student's teacher also is unavailable for adults. Psychoeducational or neuropsychological testing, therefore, may play a more central role in obtaining information about an individual's cognitive, academic, and adaptive functioning.

Numerous studies of children, adolescents, and adults with ADHD have documented deficiencies in neuropsychological variables such as attention and concentration, executive functioning, and memory and learning.[23] A comprehensive neuropsychological evaluation, performed by a neuropsychologist who is skilled in the assessment of learning and attention disorders, can provide valuable information regarding an individual's unique pattern of cognitive and academic strengths and weaknesses. The data acquired through this type of extensive testing also can provide detailed information that can be applied directly to vocational planning.[24] Neuropsychological evaluations are very costly, however, and typically are not reimbursed by insurance companies unless there is a prior history of a medical disorder that is thought to affect cognitive functioning (e.g., brain injury, seizure disorder, significant drug or alcohol use). Neuropsychologists also are somewhat rare outside urban areas. For these reasons, a shorter screening assessment (about 2 hours) that utilizes abbreviated measures of cognitive functioning, brief and sustained attention and concentration, cognitive speed and flexibility, verbal memory, reading and math skills, and mood and personality (see Table 3) may be more cost-effective. If specific areas of weakness are detected, then they can be probed with immediate or delayed follow-up testing.

Table 3. Brief psychometric test battery

Behavior and Mood

Brown ADD Scales (Brown, 1996)

Minnesota Multiphasic Personality Inventory, Second Edition (MMPI-2) (Hathaway & McKinley, 1989)

Beck Depression Inventory (Beck, Steer, & Brown, 1996)

State-Trait Anxiety Inventory (Spielberger, Gorsuch, & Lushene, 1970)

Intellectual Functioning

Kaufman Brief Intelligence Test (K-BIT) (Kaufman & Kaufman, 1990)

Wechsler Adult Intelligence Scale-Revised (WAIS-R) (Wechsler, 1981)

Memory

California Verbal Learning Test (CVLT) (Delis, Kramer, Kaplan, Ober, & Fridlund, 1983)

CVLT-A (through age 16), (Delis, Kramer, Kaplan, & Ober, 1993)

Attention/Concentration

Trail-Making Test (Reitan, 1979)

Consonant Trigrams (Peterson & Peterson, 1959)

Paced Auditory Serial-Addition Task (PASAT) (Gronwall, 1977)

Continuous Performance Tests (CPT)

Conners' CPT (Conners, 1990)

Gordon Diagnostic System (GDS) (Gordon, 1983)

Tests of Variables of Attention (TOVA) (Greenberg, 1988)

Cognitive Flexibility

Wisconsin Card Sorting Test (Heaton, 1981)

Halstead Category Test (Reitan, 1979)

Scholastic Abilities

Woodcock-Johnson Tests of Achievement–Revised (Woodcock & Johnson, 1990)

MEMORY PROBLEMS

Complaints of deficient memory skills and forgetfulness often are among the first symptoms that are presented by adults who seek assessment for ADHD. Verbal and nonverbal learning and memory problems also have been reported for young males with ADHD.[25] On formal testing using the California Verbal Learning Test,[26] adults with ADHD exhibit much weaker verbal learning skills than those of control subjects and below expectations based on their normal cognitive functioning.[27] The crux of this problem appears to be an inability to organize and mentally manipulate efficiently incoming information. This deficiency in "working memory" or "effortful processing" has been reported in adults with ADHD across a number of tasks requiring rapid and automatic responding, including digit span, continuous performance tests, and the Trail-Making Test[28].[29]

CONTINUOUS PERFORMANCE TESTS

The most commonly used continuous performance tests (CPTs) include the Conners' Continuous Performance Test,[30] The Gordon Diagnostic System,[31] and the Tests of Variables of Attention.[32] The value and limitations of office-based measures of attention and concentration are more thoroughly discussed in Chapter 3.

CPTs assess multiple variables of attention, including reaction time, sustained attention, and the ability to inhibit incorrect responding. Some are relatively lengthy, requiring the subject to focus attention for more than 20 minutes. Although the length of the task is thought to increase the likelihood of inducing boredom and errors, many adolescents and adults with ADHD can focus their attention sufficiently to achieve normal scores on these CPT tasks. Nonetheless, there are reports that adults with ADHD perform poorly on these measures.[33] Qualitatively, a CPT may be extremely difficult for individuals with a low tolerance for frustration; they may attain normal scores but become quite agitated by these tasks.

ADHD FRAUD

Infrequently, "healthy" patients seek a diagnosis of ADHD to achieve a secondary gain, such as acquiring a medical disability and associated Supplemental Security Income (SSI) benefits.[34] Others may seek to forestall the loss of a job by claiming to have a medical disability. Finally, there have been several reports in the lay press suggesting that some students and their parents may be pressuring clinicians to provide a diagnosis of ADHD or learning disability to gain a competitive edge by circumventing foreign language requirements, timed tests, and full course loads. Although there are no published figures for these types of misrepresentation, they appear to be rare occurrences. The large majority of adults who seek ADHD evaluations are experiencing bona fide symptoms of ADHD or some other disorder.

ISSUES FOR COUPLES

A number of factors contribute to relationship difficulties when a partner has ADHD. Adults (either the affected or unaffected partner) may not recognize ADHD or know much about it. If they are aware of it, then they may not have insight into the specific effects that it has on a variety of behaviors. Even when they are aware of all of these issues, managing the complexity of day-to-day life with home, family, and job can be overwhelming with the additional challenge of ADHD. The issues may be somewhat different for parents and childless couples. When a child's diagnosis triggers the consideration of ADHD in a parent, the parents may be so overburdened with the task of supporting their child that they do not have the time, energy, or financial resources to give their own relationship the attention that it requires. Although this sentiment is expressed by many parents, the core organizational deficits of ADHD make it especially difficult for adults with ADHD to manage multiple roles and responsibilities. They may experience feelings of guilt, blame, or denial to a degree that impairs their ability to meet their child's needs or function well as a couple. With increased public awareness of ADHD and its strong genetic component, increasing numbers of adults become a couple with the knowledge that one has ADHD. Some are aware of their risk of having a child with ADHD and may seek anticipatory knowledge/guidance about this. These individuals may start with less knowledge/experience but may have the opportunity to learn to manage ADHD as a couple before adding the demanding task of parenting.

The scenarios just described highlight the importance of education about ADHD as the first, critical component of treatment. Fortunately, there are several good resources for adults who want to address the impact of ADHD on their relationship with their partner (see the "Resources" section at the end of this chapter). When reading and discussing together are not sufficient or are not possible because of significant preexisting conflicts in the relationship, marital counseling with a counselor who is familiar with ADHD in adults should be recommended. Certain therapists who are listed as family therapists have sufficient expertise in ADHD to be able to assist families with both the child-oriented aspects of counseling (e.g., parent training in behavior management strategies, social skills training, school consultation) and the marital aspects, but this often is not the case.

Wender (1996) described in many adults with ADHD an interpersonal "obtuseness" that may be the adult equivalent of the misreading of social cues that often is described among children with ADHD. Such behavior may easily be interpreted as a lack of caring, concern, or respect by a partner who does not understand its origins. The resulting negative feedback may exacerbate the symptoms of depression or explosiveness in the partner with ADHD who does not understand the origins of these accusations. Specific issues that commonly are addressed in marital counseling are

- The development of insight into the effects of ADHD on each partner
- Time, stress, and "life" management
- The development of a plan to share day-to-day responsibilities that takes into account both partners' needs, strengths, and weaknesses
- Learning to communicate about all of the above issues in an ongoing effective and supportive manner

PARENTING ISSUES

Optimum parenting of a child with ADHD requires certain characteristics and skills. Helpful characteristics include patience, flexibility, consistency, and a high tolerance threshold for minor annoyances. Helpful skills include the ability to listen to and play with the child, address small problems before they become big ones, maintain a routine, good organizational skills, and excellent diplomacy and advocacy skills. The child with ADHD has an increased need for day-to-day supervision, consistency, support, and direct assistance, which may tax the organizational abilities of a parent with ADHD. In addition, the noise, activity, noncompliance, and periodic general chaos that can be part of the household milieu can be difficult for a parent with low stress/frustration tolerance to manage calmly. Conversely, the parent with ADHD may view tasks that are difficult for the child with ADHD to master as not particularly important, thereby reducing certain potential areas of conflict. The parent may have a strong sense of identification with the child, which, if channeled in positive ways, can be an asset to the child's developing sense of self and self-esteem.

Implementing on a consistent basis behavior management and other effective parenting skills may be more difficult for the parent with ADHD. Having ADHD accentuates the need for parents to work together, support and coach each other, identify each other's strengths and weaknesses, and alternate taking breaks from the ongoing intense levels of involvement that a child with ADHD requires. A parent with ADHD may need more direct assistance with developing and maintaining the use of behavior management strategies, which may result in a need for greater use of counseling services and less "doing it by the book." Direct counseling may help the parent with ADHD better identify how his or her own symptoms might affect parenting skills and how to channel this knowledge into more effective parenting.

ISSUES IN THE WORKPLACE

The **Americans with Disabilities Act (ADA)** of 1990 (PL 101-336) prohibits discrimination in employment against individuals with disabilities and requires employers to make reasonable accommodations for people with disabilities to meet job requirements. This may have relevance for adults with ADHD and adolescents who are working during school vacations. The ADA applies to all employers who have more than 15 employees and is enforced by the U.S. Equal Employment Opportunity Commission. The **Rehabilitation Act of 1973** (PL 93-112) includes similar provisions and applies to employers who receive federal dollars (e.g., government agencies, public/private schools). Under the ADA, protection is afforded in all areas of employment, including recruitment, hiring, salary and benefits, advancement, and firing. For an individual with ADHD, workplace issues usually relate to a request for accommodations or concern about discrimination in advancement. The first of these issues is discussed further because a clinician can provide guidance in this area. In some cases, advice from an attorney who has expertise in disability advocacy may be required. Concerns about discrimination require advice from an attorney.

For the purposes of these laws, a *disability* is defined as a condition that substantially limits a major life activity such as learning or working. "Reasonable" accommodations include those that do not impose an undue hardship, either financial or otherwise, on the employer. Examples of workplace accommodations for ADHD include modifying the work environment to minimize distractions; writing instructions; providing frequent feedback, technological aids, specialized training, and extra time to complete tasks; and breaking down tasks into manageable units. Occasionally, job restructuring or reassignment may need to be requested.

In preparation for requesting accommodations, the adult with ADHD should

1. Provide the employer with information about ADHD
2. Provide the employer with a statement about specific symptoms and their functional impact on the major life activities of relevance (in this case, work)
3. Obtain a supporting statement from the clinician about the diagnosis and its functional impact
4. Develop an intervention plan with emphasis on strategies that the employee can use without the employer's direct intervention to minimize functional impairment (e.g., organize the work environment; use a calculator, Dictaphone, spell checker, electronic reminder, daily planner)
5. Describe the requested accommodations and how they would help with minimizing symptoms and accomplishment of work-related goals
6. Refine the intervention after a trial period, and put it in writing

The clinician may be of assistance in providing information for the employer, writing a supportive letter, and providing ideas for accommodations based on the individual target symptoms. In general, the courts have been supportive of employers who have made good-faith attempts to make accommodations. Issues at this level highlight the importance of good career counseling for individuals with ADHD, beginning in adolescence. Choosing a career that accentuates the strengths and minimizes the weaknesses of individuals with ADHD (and the specific individual under discussion) is a critical first step to minimizing performance issues in the workplace.[35]

NONPHARMACOLOGICAL TREATMENT

A variety of approaches to nonpharmacological treatment are available, although this is a relatively new area of research and clinical endeavor. In addition to couples therapy, which focuses on the marital relationship and parenting issues, nonpharmacological treatment for the adult may include education, individual psychotherapy, cognitive retraining, coaching, career counseling, tutoring, speech therapy, and participation in support groups. Also, the treatment of any coexisting disorders (including substance use) is a critical component of therapy.

Psychotherapy can be used to address several of the problems associated with ADHD, including controlling emotions (e.g., anger, depression) and managing maladaptive behaviors (e.g., social withdrawal, addiction). A "cognitive therapy" approach frequently is used, which involves reframing the way that the client thinks about and interprets conditions that lead to unwanted responses. Developing the ability for self-advocacy also is an important goal of therapy. Cognitive "retraining" refers to learning and using compensatory strategies to manage the task requirements of work and daily life. It most commonly involves learning organizational, time management, and social skills as well as self-monitoring/self-regulatory techniques.

Coaching is a unique treatment in which an individual with ADHD works closely with a mentor or "coach" in person or by telephone for assistance, guidance, and encouragement in the setting in which the assistance is needed.[36] For example, if an individual with ADHD is having difficulties with meeting the demands of his or her job because of ADHD (as opposed to lack of the basic skills required to perform the job), then the coach might spend a day with the client at the office to help organize the desk, daily planner, and approach to tasks and follow this with daily telephone calls for a period of time to provide reminders, assistance, and support until the new routines are internalized. Coaching often includes cognitive retraining.

PHARMACOLOGICAL TREATMENT

Medications that have been used to treat ADHD in particular in adults include stimulants, tricyclic antidepressants (TCAs) (desipramine and nortriptyline), bupropion, monoamine oxidase inhibitors (MAOIs) (pargyline and deprenyl), and venlafaxine. There are far fewer studies of adults than there are of children, and little information is available about the relationship between medication response and gender or patterns of comorbidity.

Studies of stimulant effects on adults with ADHD are most common, yet there are only a small number of controlled studies, most of methylphenidate. The positive response rate varies across studies from 25% to 78%, noting that different inclusion and positive response criteria were used. Spencer and colleagues[37] showed the highest response rate and reported that this may have been due to careful documentation of childhood onset, assessment of comorbidity, and the use of a dosage of 0.3 mg/kg three times daily. This resulted in some subjects' receiving more than 20 mg of methylphenidate per dose, which generally has not been used in previous studies. There was a linear dose response, but a positive response was noticeable even at the lowest dosage of 0.16–0.17 mg/kg three times daily. Five of the 23 subjects in this study did not tolerate the highest dosage, the most common side effects of which were decreased appetite, insomnia, and increased anxiety. Spencer et al. (1995) noted that medication effectiveness was not affected by gender or the presence of mild to moderate comorbid depression or anxiety, although the number of subjects may have been too small to detect a difference. Outcome measures that have been shown to improve in adults who are taking stimulants include self-reports of concentration, distractibility including during reading, mental fatigue, refocusing after an interruption, memory,[38] some neuropsychological measures (although the ones that improve differ between studies),[39] and marital and occupational functioning.[40]

Three studies of TCAs indicated effectiveness without undue side effects. Approximately 68% of subjects showed "much improvement" while taking 160 mg/day of desipramine, and 42% were much improved while taking 80 mg/day of nortriptyline.[41] Some individuals in these reports were followed with ongoing positive effects for up to 12 months, whereas other medication studies of adults have been short term. The aminoketone antidepressant bupropion has shown moderate to marked improvement in 74% of subjects with few side effects in an open study,[42] whereas both the MAOIs[43] and venlafaxine[44] have resulted in moderate improvement but a significant rate of intolerable side effects. The side effects of these medications are similar to those discussed in Chapter 9. Confirmatory, controlled studies of the TCAs and bupropion are needed to establish their effectiveness, relative effectiveness compared with stimulants, and side effects with respect to comorbid disorders in adults with ADHD.

Case reports indicate that combinations of stimulants with other medications including beta-blockers, selective serotonin reuptake inhibitors, buspirone, TCAs, benzodiazepines, and mood stabilizers may be effective in certain circumstances, but efficacy and safety have not been documented in controlled studies. Ratey, Greenberg, and Lindem (1991) reported that three adult subjects had further improvement of methylphenidate effects from the addition of nadolol. Methylphenidate reportedly helped focusing, distractibility, and impulsivity; adding nadolol reduced tenseness, anxiety, and temper.

Success in the treatment of adult ADHD frequently requires concomitant or initial treatment of a coexisting disorder. When depression or substance abuse is present, it can be safer and more effective to address these diagnoses first. The use of stimulants in the context of substance abuse or the potential for substance abuse is an important issue for clinicians who treat adults. In general, the addiction should be treated and followed by a drug-free period and reassessment of the ADHD symptoms before instituting stimulant treatment. Nonpharmacological strategies should be employed during this period to assist with ADHD-related issues to reduce the risk of self-medicating. Short-acting dexedrine has been reported to have euphoric effects that may increase the risk for addiction.[45] In addition, when stimulants are used in combination with other medications that may increase their effects (e.g., sympathomimetics, TCAs), the clinician should ask about feelings of euphoria (and subsequent dysphoria). Regimens that produce these effects (whether as a result of the medication itself, medication combination, or individual susceptibility) should be discontinued, especially in the patient who is at risk for substance abuse. Finally, the combination of therapeutic agents for ADHD, such as stimulants or TCAs, with recreational drugs has not been investigated sufficiently. Wilens, Biederman, and Spencer (1997) reported a case series of adolescents who experienced central nervous system and cardiovascular toxicity after smoking marijuana while they were taking TCAs.

When the parent of a child with ADHD also is taking medication for ADHD, the parent may be able to provide unique and useful information to the child's prescribing clinician. Positive and negative effects in a parent may help to guide the clinician's choice of an alternative medication for the child. In addition, when both are taking the same medication, troublesome but "invisible" side effects (e.g., dysphoria, social withdrawal) may be experienced by the child but better articulated by the parent. Likewise, effective strategies for certain manageable problems may come to light through the parent (e.g., decreasing stomach upset by taking medication with a full glass of liquid). Finally, the parent has a unique opportunity to model the responsible use of medication.

CONCLUSION

The assessment and management of ADHD in adults is a more recent but rapidly expanding field of endeavor. Assessing and addressing the impact of ADHD in a parent often is an important aspect of effective treatment for the child. The clinician should be aware of the possibility of parental ADHD or associated disorders from the family history taken during the child's initial evaluation. As the clinician develops rapport with the family in the context of providing care for the child with ADHD, he or she may be able to help them assess the impact of adult ADHD on the family and the need for specific treatment.

ENDNOTES

1. Reviewed in Cantwell, (1996), Shaffer (1994), Wilens, Biederman, et al. (1995).
2. Biederman, Faraone, et al. (1995), Faraone & Biederman (1994).
3. Ibid.
4. Cantwell (1996).
5. Silver (1992).
6. Cantwell (1996).
7. Cantwell (1996), Silver (1992).
8. Barkley, Murphy, & Kwasnik (1996a), Biederman, Wilens, et al. (1995), Cantwell (1996), Coger, Moe, & Serafetinides (1996), Mannuzza, Klein, Bessler, Malloy, & Hynes (1997), Mannuzza et al. (1991), McDermott, Spencer, & Wilens (1995), Milberger, Biederman, Faraone, Chen, & Jones (1997), Rey, Morris-Yates, Singh, Andrews, & Stewart (1995).
9. Klein & Mannuzza (1991).
10. Weiss & Hechtman (1993), Wender (1995).
11. Murphy & LeVert (1995).
12. American Psychiatric Association (1994).
13. Wender (1995).
14. Ward, Wender, & Reimherr (1993).
15. Stein et al. (1995).
16. Brown (1996).
17. Lachar (1974).
18. Hathaway & McKinley (1989).
19. Goldstein (1997), Holdnack, Moberg, Arnold, Gur, & Gur (1994).
20. Holdnack et al. (1994).
21. Spielberger, Gorsuch, & Lushene (1970).
22. Beck, Steer, & Brown (1996).
23. E.g., Downey, Stelson, Pomerleau, & Giordani (1997), Holdnack, Moberg, Arnold, Gur, & Gur (1995).
24. Nadeau (1997).
25. Mealer, Morgan, & Luscomb (1996).
26. Delis, Kramer, Kaplan, Ober, & Fridlund (1983).
27. Holdnack et al. (1995).
28. Ibid.
29. Barkley, Murphy, & Kwasnik (1996b), Downey et al. (1997).
30. Conners (1990).
31. Gordon (1983).
32. Greenberg (1988).
33. Barkley et al. (1996b).
34. Gordon, Barkley, & Murphy (1997).
35. Latham & Latham (1995).
36. Hallowell (1995).
37. Spencer et al. (1996), Spencer et al. (1995).
38. Nadeau (1996).
39. Denckla (1991).
40. Nadeau (1996), Wender (1995).

41. Wilens et al. (1996), Wilens, Biederman, et al. (1995).
42. Wender & Reimherr (1990).
43. Reviewed in Wender (1995), Wilens, Biederman, Spencer, & Prince (1995).
44. Adler, Resnick, Kunz, & Devinsky (1995).
45. Wilens, Spencer, & Biederman (1995).

REFERENCES

Adler, L.A., Resnick, S., Kunz, M., & Devinsky, O. (1995). Open-label trial of venlafaxine in adults with attention deficit disorder. *Psychopharmacology Bulletin, 31,* 785–788.

American Psychiatric Association. (1994). *Diagnostic and statistical manual of mental disorders* (4th ed.). Washington, DC: Author

Americans with Disabilities Act (ADA) of 1990, PL 101-336, 42 U.S.C. §§ 12101 *et seq.*

Barkley, R.A., Murphy, K.R., & Kwasnik, D. (1996a). Motor vehicle driving competencies and risks in teens and young adults with attention deficit hyperactivity disorder. *Pediatrics, 98,* 1089–1095.

Barkley, R.A., Murphy, K.R., & Kwasnik, D. (1996b). Psychological adjustment and adaptive impairments in young adults with ADHD. *Journal of Attention Disorders, 1,* 41–54.

Beck, A.T., Steer, R.A., & Brown, G.K. (1996). *Manual for the Beck Depression Inventory* (2nd ed.). San Antonio, TX: The Psychological Corporation.

Biederman, J., Faraone, S.V., Mick, E., Spencer, T., Wilens, T., Kiely, K., Guite, J., Ablon, J.S., Reed, E., & Warburton, R. (1995). High risk for attention deficit hyperactivity disorder among children of parents with childhood onset of the disorder: A pilot study. *American Journal of Psychiatry, 152,* 431–435.

Biederman, J., Wilens, T., Mick, E., Milberger, S., Spencer, T.J., & Faraone, S.V. (1995). Psychoactive substance use disorders in adults with attention deficit hyperactivity disorder (ADHD): Effects of ADHD and psychiatric comorbidity. *American Journal of Psychiatry, 152,* 1652–1658.

Brown, T.E. (1996). *Brown Attention-Deficit Disorder Scales manual.* San Antonio, TX: The Psychological Corporation.

Cantwell, D.P. (1996). Attention deficit disorder: A review of the past 10 years. *Journal of the American Academy of Child and Adolescent Psychiatry, 35,* 978–987.

Coger, R.W., Moe, K.L., & Serafetinides, E.A. (1996). Attention deficit disorder in adults and nicotine dependence: Psychological factors in resistence to recovery? *Journal of Psychoactive Drugs, 28,* 229–240.

Conners, C.K. (1990). *Conners' Continuous Performance Test.* North Tonawanda, NY: Multi-Health Systems.

Delis, D.C., Kramer, J.H., Kaplan, E., & Ober, B.A. (1993). *Manual for the California Verbal Learning Test: Children's Version.* San Antonio, TX: The Psychological Corporation.

Delis, D.C., Kramer, J., Kaplan, E., Ober, B.A., & Fridlund, A. (1983). *California Verbal Learning Test, Research Edition (CVLT) manual.* San Antonio, TX: The Psychological Corporation.

Denckla, M.B. (1991). Attention deficit hyperactivity disorder: Residual type. *Journal of Child Neurology, 6S,* S42–S48.

Downey, K.K., Stelson, F.W., Pomerleau, O.F., & Giordani, B. (1997). Adult attention deficit hyperactivity disorder: Psychological test profiles in a clinical population. *Journal of Nervous and Mental Disease, 185,* 32–38.

Faraone, S.V., & Biederman, J. (1994). Genetics of ADHD. *Child and Adolescent Psychiatric Clinics of North America, 3,* 284–301.

Goldstein, S. (1997). Evaluating adults. In S. Goldstein (Ed.), *Managing attention and learning disorders in late adolescence and adulthood: A guide for practitioners* (pp. 87–177). New York: John Wiley & Sons.

Gordon, M. (1983). *The Gordon Diagnostic System.* DeWitt, NY: Gordon Systems.

Gordon, M., Barkley, R.A., & Murphy, K.R. (1997). ADHD on trial. *The ADHD Report, 5,* 1–4.

Greenberg, L. (1988). *Tests of Variables of Attention.* Los Alamitos, CA: Universal Attention Disorders.

Gronwall, D.M.A. (1977). Paced Auditory Serial-Addition Task: A measure of recovery from consussion. *Perceptual and Motor Skills, 44,* 367–373.

Hallowell, E.M. (1995). Coaching: An adjunct to the treatment of ADHD. *The ADHD Report, 3,* 7–9.

Hathaway, S.R., & McKinley, J.C. (1989). *Minnesota Multiphasic Personality Inventory* (2nd ed.). Circle Pines, MN: NCS Assessments.

Heaton, R.K. (1981). *A manual for the Wisconsin Card Sorting Test.* Odessa, FL: Psychological Assessment Resources.

Holdnack, J.A., Moberg, P.J., Arnold, S.E., Gur, R.E., & Gur, R.C. (1994). MMPI characteristics in adults diagnosed with ADD: A preliminary report. *International Journal of Neuroscience, 79,* 47–58.

Holdnack, J.A., Moberg, P.J., Arnold, S.E., Gur, R.C., & Gur, R.E. (1995). Speed of processing and verbal learning deficits in adults diagnosed with attention deficit disorder. *Journal of Neuropsychiatry, Neuropsychology and Behavioral Neurology, 8,* 282–292.

Kaufman, A.S., & Kaufman, N.L. (1990). *Kaufman Brief Intelligence Test.* Circle Pines, MN: American Guidance Service.

Klein, R.G., & Mannuzza, S. (1991). Long-term outcome of hyperactive children: A review. *Journal of the American Academy of Child and Adolescent Psychiatry, 30,* 383–387.

Lachar, D. (1974). *The MMPI: Clinical assessment and automated interpretation.* Los Angeles: Western Psychological Services.

Latham, P.H., & Latham, P.S. (1995, Spring). Succeeding in the workplace with ADHD. *Attention!,* 40–43.

Mannuzza, S., Klein, R.G., Bessler, A., Malloy, P., & Hynes, M.E. (1997). Educational and occupational outcome of hyperactive boys grown up. *Journal of the American Academy of Child and Adolescent Psychiatry, 36,* 1222–1227.

Mannuzza, S., Klein, R.G., Bonagura, N., Malloy, P., Giampino, T.L., & Addalli, K.A. (1991). Hyperactive boys almost grown up. *Archives of General Psychiatry, 48,* 77–83.

McDermott, S.P., Spencer, T., & Wilens, T.E. (1995, Fall). Commonsense about adult ADHD. *Attention!,* 36–41.

Mealer, C., Morgan, S., & Luscomb, R. (1996). Cognitive functioning of ADHD and non-ADHD boys on the WISC-III and WRAML: An analysis within a memory model. *Journal of Attention Disorders, 1,* 133–147.

Milberger, S., Biederman, J., Faraone, S.V., Chen, L., & Jones, J. (1997). ADHD is associated with early initiation of cigarette smoking in children and adolescents. *Journal of the American Academy of Child and Adolescent Psychiatry, 36,* 37–44.

Murphy, K., & Barkley, R.A. (1996a). Prevalence of DSM-IV symptoms of ADHD in adult licensed drivers: Implications for clinical diagnosis. *Journal of Attention Disorders, 1,* 147–161.

Murphy, K., & Barkley, R.A. (1996b). Updated adult norms for the ADHD Behavior Checklist for Adults. *ADHD Report, 4,* 12–16.

Murphy, K.R., & LeVert, S. (1995). *Out of the fog: Treatment options and coping strategies for adult attention deficit disorder.* New York: Hyperion-Skylight Press.

Nadeau, K.G. (1996). *Adventures in fast forward: Life, love, and work for the ADD adult.* New York: Brunner/Mazel.

Nadeau, K.G. (1997). *ADD in the workplace: Choices, changes, and challenges.* New York: Brunner/Mazel.

Peterson, L.R., & Peterson, M.J. (1959). Short-term retention of individual verbal items. *Journal of Experimental Psychology, 58,* 193–198.

Ratey, J.J., Greenberg, M.S., & Lindem, K.J. (1991). Combination of treatments for attention deficit disorder in adults. *Journal of Nervous and Mental Disease, 179,* 699–701.

Rehabilitation Act of 1973, PL 93-112, 29 U.S.C. §§ 701 *et seq.*

Reitan, R.R. (1979). *The manual for the administration of neuropsychological test batteries for children and adults.* Tucson, AZ: Neuropsychology Laboratory.

Rey, J.M., Morris-Yates, A., Singh, M., Andrews, G., & Stewart, G.W. (1995). Continuities between psychiatric disorders in adolescents and personality disorders in young adults. *American Journal of Psychiatry, 152,* 895–900.

Shaffer, D. (1994). Attention deficit hyperactivity disorder in adults. *American Journal of Psychiatry, 151,* 633–638.

Silver, L.B. (1992). Diagnosis of attention-deficit hyperactivity disorder in adult life. *Child Adolescent Psychiatric Clinics of North America, 1,* 325–334.

Spencer, T., Biederman, J., Wilens, T., Harding, M., O'Donnell, D., & Griffin, S. (1996). Pharmacotherapy of attention-deficit hyperactivity disorder across the life cycle. *Journal of the American Academy of Child and Adolescent Psychiatry, 35,* 409–432.

Spencer, T., Wilens, T., Biederman, J., Faraone, S.V., Ablon, S., & Lapey, K. (1995). A double-blind, crossover comparison of methylphenidate and placebo in adults with childhood-onset attention-deficit hyperactivity disorder. *Archieves of General Psychiatry, 52,* 434–443.

Spielberger, C.D., Gorsuch, R.L., & Lushene, R.E. (1970). *Manual for the State-Trait Anxiety Inventory for Children.* Palo Alto, CA: Consulting Psychologist Press.

Stein, M.A., Sandoval, R., Szumowski, E., Roizen, N., Reinecke, M.A., Blondis, T.A., & Klein, Z. (1995). Psychometric characteristics of the Wender Utah Rating Scale: Reliability and factor structure for men and women. *Psychopharmacology Bulletin, 31,* 425–433.

Ward, M.F., Wender, P.H., & Reimherr, F.W. (1993). The Wender Utah Rating Scale: An aid in the retrospective diagnosis of childhood attention deficit hyperactivity disorder. *American Journal of Psychiatry, 150,* 885–890.

Wechsler, D. (1981). *Wechsler Adult Intelligence Scale (Revised) manual.* San Antonio, TX: The Psychological Corporation.

Weiss, G., & Hechtman, L.K. (1993). *Hyperactive children grown up* (2nd ed.). New York: Guilford Press.

Wender, P.H. (1995). The treatment of ADHD in adults. In *Attention deficit hyperactivity disorder in adults* (pp. 144–197). New York: Oxford University Press.

Wender, P.H. (1996). Phenomenology of adult ADHD. *The ADHD Report, 4,* 11–12.

Wender, P.H., & Reimherr, F.W. (1990). Bupropion treatment of attention deficit hyperactivity disorder in adults. *American Journal of Psychiatry, 147,* 1018–1020.

Wilens, T.E., Biederman, J., Prince, J., Spencer, T.J., Faraone, S.V., Warburton, R., Schleifer, D., Harding, M., Linehan, C., & Geller, D. (1996). Six-week, double-blind, placebo-controlled study of desipramine for adult attention deficit hyperactivity disorder. *American Journal of Psychiatry, 153,* 1147–1153.

Wilens, T.E., Biederman, J., & Spencer, T.J. (1997). Case study: Adverse effects of smoking marijuana while receiving tricyclic antidepressants. *Journal of the American Academy of Child and Adolescent Psychiatry, 36,* 45–48.

Wilens, T.E., Biederman, J., Spencer, T.J., & Prince, J. (1995). Pharmacology of adult attention deficit/hyperactivity disorder: A review. *Journal of Clinical Psychopharmacology, 15,* 270–279.

Wilens, T.E., Spencer, T.J., & Biederman, J. (1995). Pharmacotherapy of adult ADHD. In K.G. Nadeau (Ed.), *A comprehensive guide to attention deficit disorders in adults* (pp. 168–188). New York: Brunner/Mazel.

Woodcock, R.W., & Johnson, M.B. (1990). *Manual for the Woodcock-Johnson Tests of Achievement.* Allen, TX: DLM Teaching Resources.

RESOURCES

The ADDed Line. A newsletter, most useful for adults, 3790 Loch Highland Parkway, Roswell, GA 30075; (800) 928-4028.

Attention! (CH.A.D.D.), Spring 1977, issue devoted to Adults and ADD. Children and Adults with ADHD (CH.A.D.D.), 499 NW 70th Avenue, Suite 101, Plantation, FL 33317; (954) 587–3700.

Goldstein, S. (1997). *Managing attention and learning disorders in late adolescence and adulthood: A guide for practitioners.* New York: John Wiley & Sons. (To order, call [800] 225-5945.)

Gordon, M., & McClure, F.D. (1996). *The down and dirty guide to adult ADD* (book or audiocassette). DeWitt, NY: GSI Publications Inc. (To order, call [800] 550-2343.)

Halowell, E.M., & Ratey, J.J. (1995). *Driven to distraction: Recognizing and coping with attention deficit disorder from childhood through adulthood.* New York: Touchstone Books. (To order, call [800] 223-2336.)

Hartmann, T. (1993). *Attention deficit disorder: A different perception.* Grass Valley, CA: Underwood Books. (To order, call [800] 788-3213.)

Hartmann, T. (1994). *Focus your energy: Succeeding in business with attention deficit disorder.* New York: Pocket Books. (To order, call [800] 223-2348.)

Hartmann, T. (1995). *ADD success stories: A guide to fulfillment for families with attention deficit disorder.* Grass Valley, CA: Underwood Books. (To order, call [800] 788-3213.)

Hartmann, T. (1996). *Beyond ADD: Hunting for reasons in the past and present.* Grass Valley, CA: Underwood Books. (To order, call [800] 788-3213.)

Kelly, K., & Ramundo, P. (1993). *You mean I'm not lazy, stupid, or crazy?!: A self-help book for adults with attention deficit disorder.* Cincinnati, OH: Tyrell & Jerem Press. (To order, call [513] 751-4352.)

Kelly, K., Ramundo, P., & Ledingham, D.S. (1997). *The ADDed dimension: Everyday advice for adults with ADD.* New York: Scribner. (To order, call [212] 632-4965.)

Kilcarr, P.J., & Quinn, P.O. (1997). *Voices from fatherhood: Fathers, sons, and ADHD.* New York: Brunner/Mazel. (To order, call [800] 825-3089.)

Latham, P.S., & Latham, P.H. (1994). *Succeeding in the workplace: Attention deficit disorder and learning disabilities in the workplace. A guide for success.* Washington, DC: JKL Communications. (To order, call [202] 223-5097.)

Murphy, K.R., & LeVert, S. (1995). *Out of the fog: Treatment options and coping strategies for adult attention deficit disorder.* New York: Hyperion-Skylight Press. (To order, call [212] 633-4400.)

Nadeau, K.G. (1995). *A comprehensive guide to attention deficit disorder in adults: Research, diagnosis, and treatment.* New York: Brunner/Mazel. (To order, call [800] 825-3089.)

Nadeau, K.G. (1996). *Adventures in fast forward: Life, love, and work for the ADD adult.* New York: Brunner/Mazel. (To order, call [800] 825-3089.)

Nadeau, K.G. (1997). *ADD in the workplace: Choices, changes, and challenges.* New York: Brunner/Mazel. (To order, call [800] 825-3089.)

The National Coaching Network, Post Office Box 353, Lafayette Hill, PA 19444.

Phelan T.W. (1994). *Adults with attention deficit disorder* [Video]. Glen Ellyn, IL: Child Management, Inc. (To order, call [800] 442-4453.)

Solden, S. (1995). *Women with attention deficit disorder: Embracing disorganization at home and in the workplace.* Grass Valley, CA: Underwood Books. (To order, call [916] 274-7997.)

Weiss, L. (1996). *ADD on the job: Making your ADD work for you.* Dallas, TX: Taylor Publishing. (To order, call [214] 677-2800.)

Weiss, L. (1996). *Attention deficit disorder in adults: Practical help for sufferers and their spouses* (Rev. ed.). Dallas, TX: Taylor Publishing. (To order, call [214] 637-2800; workbook also available)

Weiss, G., & Hechtman, L.T. (1993). *Hyperactive children grown up* (2nd ed.). New York: Guilford Press. (To order, call [800] 365-7006.)

Wender, P.H. (1995). *Attention deficit hyperactivity disorder in adults.* New York: Oxford University Press. (To order, call [800] 451-7556.)

Whiteman, T.A., Novotini, M., & Petersen, R. (1995). *Adult ADD: A reader friendly guide to identifying, understanding, and treating adult attention deficit disorder.* Colorado Springs, CO: Pinon Press. (To order, call [800] 366-7788.)

Glossary

achievement tests: tests that measure grade-level achievement of academic skills such as reading, mathematics, spelling, and writing

active engaged time: the amount of time that children spend actively attending to instruction

adrenoleukodystrophy: one of the leukodystrophies, a group of progressive neurological disorders that affect primarily white matter caused by peroxisomal enzyme defects; the childhood X-linked form is characterized by initial behavioral and academic deterioration with rapid progression to spastic paraparesis, swallowing difficulty, vision loss, impaired cortisol response, and seizures

affective disorders: general term including both mood and anxiety disorders

Americans with Disabilities Act (ADA) of 1990 (PL 101-336): a civil rights law passed in 1990 extending previous rights of individuals with disabilities related to equal access and reasonable accommodations in employment in both private and public settings

antioxidants: chemicals such as vitamin C, vitamin E, and pycnogenol that reduce the generation of free radicals from oxygen, which can lead to DNA damage

antisocial disorders: disorders that are characterized by infraction of laws and serious infringement on the rights of others, such as substance abuse, stealing, and aggression (e.g., conduct disorder, antisocial personality disorder)

antisocial personality disorder: a diagnosis in adults with an earlier diagnosis of conduct disorder characterized by a persistent pattern since the age of 15 years of the disregard for and violation of the rights of others, including at least three of the following: unlawful behavior, lying, impulsivity, irritability and aggressiveness, recklessness, irresponsibility, and lack of remorse

anxiety disorders: includes generalized anxiety disorder, obsessive-compulsive disorder, separation anxiety disorder, panic attacks, agoraphobia, social phobia and other phobias, and posttraumatic stress disorder

Asperger's syndrome: one of the pervasive developmental disorders characterized by relatively good cognitive functioning and verbal skills; relatively poor visual-perceptual skills; and an area of in-depth knowledge, usually in a mechanical or scientific domain

basal ganglia: A group of subcortical brain nuclei that function in the integration and coordination of information from higher (e.g., cortical) and lower (e.g., brainstem) brain regions; includes caudate/putamen (also called striatum) and globus pallidus

behavioral contracting: negotiating with a child rules of conduct as well as the consequences for following or not following the rules

bipolar disorder: (also called manic depressive disorder) a form of mental illness characterized by alternating depression and mania; in children, cycling is less common: a chronic course of irritability, tantrums, conduct problems, and depression is more typical

catecholamines: neurotransmitters with a similar chemical structure, including norepinephrine, epinephrine, and dopamine

categorical approach to assessment: diagnostic assessment to determine the presence or absence of a disorder following specific criteria

central auditory processing disorder: a disorder characterized by difficulties with the accurate detection of, processing of, and response to verbal information presented aurally; manifested as difficulties with attention, listening, "mis-hearing," and poor verbal recall

cerebral glucose metabolism: a measure of the metabolic activity in the brain or specific brain region based on the detection of the rate of glucose utilization with the injection of a radioactively labeled glucose analogue and positron emission tomography

classwide peer tutoring: pairing students in a classroom to provide tutoring to each other following a detailed script

collagen: the major fibrous structural proteins of the body that are prominent in skin, muscle, cartilage, and bone

compulsion: a repetitive behavior induced by a recurring unwanted thought (e.g., "I must step on every crack in the sidewalk or I will be hit by a car")

conduct disorder: one of the disruptive behavior disorders with childhood onset characterized by the persistent violation of the rights of others and societal norms, including at least three of the following: verbal or physical aggression, use of weapons, physical cruelty, forced sexual activity, stealing, fire setting, deliberate property destruction, lying, truancy, or running away from home

continuous performance tests: office-based tasks that assess a child's ability to sustain attention and refrain from impulsive responding

curriculum-based assessment: the assessment of students using materials that closely correspond to curriculum materials

delusion: a false belief that is firmly maintained despite incontrovertible evidence

depression: a general term that refers to a group of disorders characterized by low mood, tearfulness, lack of pleasure, psychomotor agitation or slowing, fatigue, feelings of worthlessness or low self-esteem, poor concentration, thoughts of death, and changes in sleep and appetite

developmental age: "cognitive" age (e.g., a child with a chronological age of 10 years and an IQ score of 50 could be estimated to have a developmental age of 5 years)

developmental coordination disorder: a motor disorder characterized by coordination and motor skill deficits not accounted for by cognitive impairments, cerebral palsy, or neuromuscular disease and most often characterized by clumsiness, poor performance in sports, and poor handwriting

developmental language disorder: slow development of receptive and expressive language skills compared with expectations based on IQ score for overall intelligence; primarily manifests as delayed development of language and social communication skills; by school age, single-word language skills may appear normal, but connected language, reading, reading comprehension, and/or writing may be impaired

dimensional approach to assessment: assessment of the severity of behavior and/or emotional problems by comparing an individual's functioning with that of peers of similar age and gender

disruptive behavior disorders: a category that includes ADHD, oppositional defiant disorder, and conduct disorder

dopamine transporter: the protein on the surface of dopamine neurons that takes up dopamine after it has been released into the synapse in order to terminate its effect

dopamine type 4 receptor: one of five subtypes of the receptor for dopamine

due process: the mandated series of steps in the process of resolving a disagreement between parents and the educational system related to the provision of special education services or accommodations

dysmorphic features: atypical physical characteristics, most often of the facial features, that may signal an abnormality in the developmental process; dysmorphic features of the head and face may relate to developmental abnormalities of the brain

dysphoria: disquiet, restlessness, malaise

dysthymia: a mood disorder characterized by symptoms of depression that are more chronic and less severe than those meeting criteria for major depressive disorder

Education for All Handicapped Children Act of 1975 (PL 94-142): an educational law passed in 1975 defining the rights of children with disabilities to a free appropriate public education in the least restrictive environment possible, outlining the process by which individualized education programs would be developed, and the due process by which conflicts would be resolved

emotional regulation: a child's ability to control his or her emotional responses in a social situation

eosinophilia: an excess of circulating eosinophils, white blood cells with unique staining properties, often associated with allergic reactions and parasitic infections

episodic dyscontrol: a psychiatric term not presently in use in the DSM-IV referring to episodic extremely disruptive or aggressive behavior

externalizing: a general term referring to disruptive symptoms including overactivity, impulsivity, oppositionality, aggression, and other antisocial behaviors

extinction: ceasing to provide positive reinforcement in response to a person's behavior

fetal alcohol syndrome: occurs after substantial alcohol exposure in utero and is characterized by poor growth, microcephaly, mental retardation, neuropsychiatric disorders, and characteristic facial dysmorphic features; *fetal alcohol effects* refers to the occurrence of some of these features without mental retardation

fragile X syndrome: an X-linked syndrome caused by a fragile site on the X chromosome, which is a region of nucleotide triplet repeat. Clinical features in males include mental retardation, hyperactivity, characteristic facial dysmorphic features, and large testicles (after puberty); some males have learning disabilities instead of mental retardation; carrier females show a range of effects, but many have learning disabilities and affective disorders

free radical scavenger: chemicals, such as pycnogenol and vitamin E, that inactivate free radicals, the molecular decomposition products of oxygen

generalized anxiety disorder: a disorder characterized by excessive anxiety and worry in many settings and about many subjects that causes functional impairment

generalization: transferring a skill learned in one setting (e.g., in a physician's office) to another situation (e.g., at school)

goal setting: negotiating with a person specific goals for performing a task

hallucination: a sensory perception in the absence of its existence in the real world

high-functioning autism: refers to an individual who meets criteria for a diagnosis of autism but has normal cognitive skills; differs from Asperger's syndrome in that individuals with Asperger's syndrome have relatively spared language function and a useful, in-depth knowledge base in a particular technical area

hostile attributional bias: the tendency to infer hostile intentions on the part of a peer provocateur when the cause of the provocation is ambiguous

Individuals with Disabilities Education Act (IDEA) of 1990 (PL 101-476): an education law passed in 1990 that updates and strengthens PL 94-142 and extends to infancy the right to early intervention services for children at risk

instructional match: the correspondence between the curriculum and the skill level of the student

Instructional Support Teams: school-based, interdisciplinary teams of professionals that design and implement interventions for children with academic and/or behavior problems

internalizing: a general term referring to symptoms of depression, anxiety, low self-esteem, withdrawal, and somatization

IQ–achievement discrepancy: a significant difference between standard scores on achievement tests and IQ measures calculated (usually) by a statistical regression method, widely used in the educational system as an indicator of learning disability

IQ tests: tests that propose to measure a child's ability to problem-solve in language and nonlanguage domains as opposed to his or her acquired academic skills

kinesthetic abilities: skills related to recognition of the position or movement of the body or body part in space

learning disability: a heterogeneous group of disorders manifested by significant difficulties in the acquisition and use of listening, speaking, reading, writing, reasoning, or mathematical abilities; intrinsic to the individual and are presumed to be due to a dysfunction of the central nervous system; may occur with but are not primarily due to sensory impairment, mental retardation, social/emotional disturbances, or culturally or environmentally based lack of exposure

Mainstream Assistance Teams: see **Instructional Support Teams**

major depressive disorder: one of the depressive disorders characterized by at least five specific symptoms that fall into the categories listed under depression, occurring as a change from previous status, and lasting for at least 2 weeks

mania: a state characterized by abnormally and persistently elevated, expansive, or irritable mood including some of the following symptoms: grandiosity, decreased need for sleep, talkativeness, flight of ideas, distractibility, increased goal-directed activity, or excessive involvement in pleasurable activities

manic depressive disorder: see **bipolar disorder**

Mendelian inheritance pattern: genetic inheritance characterized by an autosomal dominant, autosomal recessive, or X-linked pattern

mental retardation: significant global delay in achieving developmental milestones accompanied by delayed adaptive skills; further specified as a full-scale score of less than approximately 70 (specifics vary by test) on a standardized IQ test

mesolimbic dopamine system: the group of dopamine neurons in the ventral tegmental area of the midbrain that projects to the part of the basal ganglia and cortex involved in cognitive/emotional regulation and reward

modeling: behaviors demonstrated by a peer or adult to help the child learn adaptive social strategies

mood disorder not otherwise specified: a functionally impairing problem with mood that does not meet criteria for a specific disorder

mood disorders: a general term referring to all of the various depressive disorders

narrow-range rating scales: assess a specific cluster of behavior and/or emotional problems

neurocutaneous signs: skin findings characteristic of neurological disorders in which the development of the skin and brain both are abnormal (because they are derived from the same precursor cells)

neurofibromatosis I: an autosomal dominant neurocutaneous disorder characterized by café-au-lait spots on the skin; ocular and bone abnormalities; and optic gliomas, hamartomas, and other tumors of the brain; learning disabilities and ADHD are common

neutropenia: a paucity of circulating neutrophils, white blood cells with specific histologic and functional properties, related to defense against bacterial infections

nonverbal learning disorder/disability: a learning and behavior profile characterized by marked deficits in spatial reasoning, visual-motor functioning, math calculation, written expression, attention, organization, and social skills

norm-referenced measures: assessment instruments indicating how an individual is functioning in relation to peers with similar background characteristics, in particular, age

nystagmus: an involuntary, rapid, rhythmic movement of the eyeball that may be horizontal, vertical, rotatory, or mixed

obsession: a recurrent, persistent thought, impulse, or image that is unwanted and distressing

obsessive-compulsive disorder: characterized by functionally impairing obsessions and compulsions; obsessions are recognized as unreasonable, and the individual has attempted to suppress them; compulsions are designed to reduce the distress of the obsessions but recognized to have little real connection with them

obsessive-compulsive features: a description applied to individuals with some characteristics of obsessive-compulsive disorder but not to a sufficiently significant degree to warrant the diagnosis

oppositional defiant disorder: one of the disruptive behavior disorders characterized by at least four symptoms such as having a bad temper; blaming others; arguing; annoying others and being easily annoyed; actively defying; and frequently being angry, spiteful, or vindictive

oscillopsia: a visual condition in which objects that are still appear to move

panic disorder: characterized by recurrent discrete periods of intense fear or discomfort manifested by physical and psychological symptoms for no appropriate reason

personality disorders: a group of disorders characterized by core features of unusual cognitive interpretations of events, inappropriate affectivity, and disordered impulse control and interpersonal functioning; types of personality disorders with further specified characteristics include paranoid, schizoid, schizotypal, borderline, antisocial, histrionic, and narcissistic

pervasive developmental disorder: a group of disorders characterized by impairments in language, communicative and social functioning, associated with a restricted repertoire of activities; includes autism, pervasive developmental disorder not otherwise specified, childhood disintegrative disorder, **Asperger's syndrome,** Rett's syndrome, and Landau-Kleffner syndrome

pervasive developmental disorder not otherwise specified: the diagnosis used when the qualitative but not quantitative degree of impairment is similar to autism; there is clinical overlap with high-functioning autism and **Asperger's syndrome**

phenylketonuria: an autosomal-recessive inborn error of metabolism tested for as part of newborn screening programs in which phenylalanine cannot be converted to tyrosine; lack of treatment (elimination of phenylalanine from the diet) causes mental retardation

phobia: a persistent, intense, irrational fear of a specific object, place, or situation

phonological (articulation) disorder: a developmental disorder limited to the pronunciation of words

positive reinforcement: providing a consequence that increases the probability that a behavior will occur

posttraumatic stress disorder: persistent reexperience of a horrific experience in the form of overarousal, distressing recollections, and physical and psychological symptoms

proband: a patient who is the initial member of a family to come under study

punishment: consequence that decreases the probability that a response will occur in the future

pyridoxine-responsive seizures: a seizure disorder, usually apparent in infancy, that responds to high dosages of pyridoxine (vitamin B_6)

radioallergosorbent test: a method for testing for an allergic response to a specific protein that involves radioactive tagging of the protein-antiserum complex

RAST test: see **radioallergosorbent test**

Rehabilitation Act of 1973 (PL 93-112): a civil rights law that protects individuals with disabilities from discrimination by any organization receiving federal funds; Section 504 is the most relevant part of the law for ADHD/school issues and relates to access, accommodations, and due process

reinforcer: consequence that increases the probability that a response will occur in the future

response cost: removal of a reinforcement when the child performs an inappropriate behavior

role play: practicing the use of adaptive behaviors in hypothetical situations under the close supervision of a counselor, teacher, or parent

Romberg test: a neurological examination procedure indicative of cerebellar balance function in which the subject is asked to remain still with the feet together, arms outstretched, palms facing up, and eyes closed; a variant is used to test labyrinthine function

salicylates: a category of chemical compounds (the least known of which is acetylsalicylic acid [aspirin]) that are variations on a core structure of acetic or benzoic acid

separation anxiety disorder: unique to children and characterized by developmentally inappropriate and excessive anxiety about separation from home or from primary caregivers

school–home note: a daily or weekly report of student performance in school that is sent home to the parents for review and reinforcement

Section 504 of the Rehabilitation Act of 1973: see **Rehabilitation Act of 1973**

self-evaluation: a determination by an individual as to how well he or she has performed a task using a recording sheet

self-monitoring: self-observation to determine whether a specific behavior has occurred

social knowledge: knowing how one should act in a social situation

social performance: the way that a person actually behaves in a social situation

social problem solving: five steps to solving social problems: problem identification, generation of alternative solutions, consideration of consequences of each alternative, selection and use of a specific strategy, and evaluation of the efficacy of specific strategy

strabismus: deviation of the position of one or both eyes such that the visual axes of the eyes are not parallel

structured interviews: a highly systematic format for conducting clinical interviews that facilitates diagnostic decision making using classification systems such as the DSM-IV

Student Support Teams: see **Instructional Support Teams**

temperament: the characteristic way in which an individual experiences and reacts to the environment; characteristics described as part of the temperamental profile include intensity, adaptability, rhythmicity, mood, activity level, distractibility, sensory threshold, persistence, and approachability

thyrotoxicosis: the manifestations of overactivity of the thyroid gland, including difficulties with gaining weight, increased pulse, heat intolerance, and nervousness

tics (motor/vocal): brief, staccato, repetitive, semi-involuntary movements or sounds

time-out: systematic removal of a child from the opportunity to acquire positive reinforcement

token reinforcement: reinforcing behavior with tokens or points that can be exchanged for backup reinforcements such as privileges or toys

Tourette syndrome: the most complex tic disorder, characterized by multiple motor tics and at least one vocal tic that wax and wane over time, with onset before age 21 and in the absence of a specific known neurological lesion; symptoms must be present for at least 1 year to make the diagnosis; often associated with obsessive-compulsive disorder, ADHD, and problems with mood regulation

tuberous sclerosis: an autosomal dominant neurocutaneous syndrome characterized by seizures, mental deficiency, adenoma sebaceum and ash-leaf depigmented lesions of the skin and sclerotic "tubers" in the brain

Turner's syndrome: a sex chromosome abnormality in females (XO) in which one X chromosome is missing, characterized by short stature; broad chest; short, webbed neck; lymphedema; and learning disability (predominantly visual-perceptual)

vestibular-cerebellar system: includes the middle ear, the vestibular nerve, the vestibular nerve's nuclei in the brainstem, and the connections of all of these parts to the cerebellum

wide-range rating scales: assess many dimensions of behavioral and/or emotional functioning

Williams syndrome: result of a microdeletion in the elastin gene characterized by hypercalcemia in infancy, mental retardation, characteristic facies, joint and feeding problems, and a neurobehavioral profile characterized by (among other things) relatively spared speech abilities and an active, outgoing personality in childhood

XYY: a chromosomal abnormality in males, consisting of an extra Y chromosome, that may be associated with tall stature, learning disabilities, and externalizing behavior

Index